D1309690

Life in the Balance

Life in the Balance
Procedural Safeguards in Capital Cases

Welsh S. White

Foreword by Hugo Adam Bedau

Ann Arbor
The University of Michigan Press

This book is dedicated to my wife Linda.

1987 1986 1985 1984   4 3 2 1

Library of Congress Cataloging in Publication Data

White, Welsh S., 1940–
   Life in the balance.

   1. Capital punishment—United States—Addresses,
essays, lectures. 2. Criminal procedure—United States—
Addresses, essays, lectures. I. Title.
KF9227.C2W45   1984   345.73′077   84-7346
ISBN 0-472-10052-1   347.30577

Foreword

Viewing the death penalty today in the appropriate perspective is not as easy to do as it might seem. A few years ago, in the aftermath of the Supreme Court's refusal to declare the death penalty to be an unconstitutionally "cruel and unusual punishment," it was remarked that "the significance of the availability or non-availability of the death penalty as a sanction could hardly be *under*estimated." Coming as this did from Norval Morris and Gordon Hawkins, in their *Letter to the President on Crime Control*, it was a sobering thought for both proponents and opponents of executions. What is more, it was probably correct. As these lines are being written there are well over a thousand persons under sentence of death in three dozen states—the greatest number in the nation's history and a total unmatched in this century in any country within what *Time-Life-Fortune* used to call "the free world." Even so, the ultimate fate of these hundreds will have little or no impact on the crime rate or on public attitudes toward violence and security. The fraction of all convicted offenders sentenced to death each year and then executed is so tiny that it effectively destroys any possible deterrent and retributive benefits the defenders of capital punishment might point to, just as it reduces to relative insignificance the likelihood of executing the innocent. For the tens of thousands of other offenders who are arrested and convicted each year, punishment will typically be imprisonment and eventual release. The death penalty will be entirely irrelevant to them and to the day-to-day workings of the criminal justice system.

The impact on our legal system produced by the desire to preserve capital punishment at any cost, however, is another story. If we shift our attention away from the current scene to its historical origins, we can hardly *over*estimate the importance of the death penalty. From the earliest years on these shores, the enactment of statutes threatening death for the commission not only of murder or rape but of many other offenses, capital trials and subsequent conviction and execution of capital felons have constituted a familiar and conspicuous pattern. For two centuries, the challenges to this practice mounted by moralists and other reformers have left permanent marks on our criminal justice system. The invention of degrees of murder (with the death penalty confined to persons convicted of "first-degree" murder only), the construction of prisons suitable for long-term incarceration (thereby providing a tolerably effective alternative to hanging or exile), the authority of trial courts to exercise sentencing discretion (thus increasing the frequency with which capital felons were sentenced not to death but to a "life" term in prison), the provision of defense counsel in capital cases from the time of the accused's arraignment (thereby preventing the worst violations of due process), the obligation of appellate courts to review all capital sentences in their jurisdiction (to reduce the likelihood of arbitrary and grossly inequitable death sentences)—these are among the most conspicuous features of the present death penalty system. Each arose out of the struggle over abolishing lethal penalties. Anyone interested in the future of the criminal justice system and its treatment of the most dangerous convicts could do worse than give careful attention to how the death penalty is currently regulated and administered, since that attention will be rewarded by discovery of the cracks in the system that are vulnerable to pressure and change.

It is in this light that we can best appreciate the contributions of Welsh S. White in the pages that follow. Among the several volumes recently devoted to examining the death penalty in contemporary America, White's is unique because of his single-minded scrutiny of what it is that makes capital executions *lawful*. He asks us to consider carefully whether penalties of death are currently being meted out in conformity with the requirements of the Constitution and the rule of law, as these are interpreted not only by the appellate courts but by sensitive and informed intelligence. At the risk of oversimplification, the major theme running through the chapters of this book may be stated in the following challenge: We must give up our present system of administering the death penalty as an exercise in lawful punishment, and either introduce changes in procedure that legislatures and appellate courts seem unwilling to adopt and enforce, or abolish the death penalty altogether, something they are even more reluctant to do. There is, to be sure, the other alternative: We can confess that our commitment to justice under law, due process, equal protection, and procedural fairness in trying, sentencing, and punishing the worst criminals is halfhearted and inconsistent, not to say downright hypocritical.

After a reading of the results of White's investigations, it will be impossible for anyone to dodge this dilemma on grounds of ignorance or disbelief. The author does not try to advance his argument by presenting the reader with firsthand accounts of what actually happens in the capital trial courtrooms of America (though, of course, he often cites such events), any more than he tries to provide sociological or criminological evidence to bolster his case. His preoccupation is more general and theoretical, as well as jurisprudential; hence narratives or case studies or statistically oriented investigations cannot suffice for his purposes. Thus, his critique of "death-qualified juries" in capital cases and of the damning testimony from expert psychiatric witnesses who attest to the "future dangerousness" of convicted murderers awaiting sentencing, to cite but two of the practices he evaluates, shows that the general assumptions on which public prosecutors, legislatures, appellate courts, and the general public presumably defend them cannot be rationally and morally supported. Rather, as he argues, in the best of circumstances such juries and such testimony impose costs that no decent and self-respecting society should be willing to pay.

Not surprisingly, perhaps, the current state of the law on capital punishment, as it emerges from White's investigations, is little more than an uneasy compromise among those who firmly refuse to give up the death penalty altogether, others who would destroy executions root and branch once and for all, and still others whose strongest commitment is tangential to the central controversy because it is governed by the desire to preserve federalism and state sovereignty and to curb an "activist" and "noninterpretivist" federal judiciary. In our impatience to see these compromises resolved, we may forget just how recent it is that the judiciary and the legal profession in this country have been willing to confront the morally objectionable aspects of the death penalty in terms of constitutional law. As White explains in his introduction and in the opening chapter, the very first hints from the Supreme Court that the death penalty might be an unconstitutionally "cruel and unusual punishment" were heard a mere two decades ago. In the ensuing (and continuing) struggle over the constitutional limits to be placed on the death penalty, the Supreme Court itself has contributed at least as much obscurity as clarity to the basic moral and constitutional issues involved. Since 1976, when *Gregg v. Georgia* and its companion cases were decided, the Court has settled that although the death penalty as such may not be unconstitutional, its mandatory or arbitrary imposition is; and in any case it must be used to punish only those crimes, like murder, for which its severity is not "disproportionate." However, if Professor White's analysis and evaluation are correct—as I believe they are—the death sentence for murder is still being imposed and carried out by procedures that cannot survive the closest scrutiny; they are jerry-built, with awkward and unstable features. Their product, in the apt phrase of Professor Charles L. Black, Jr., is still "caprice and mistake."

Not long ago, in a survey of the national death penalty scene, *Time* magazine quoted with approval the words of a young attorney engaged full-time in anti–death penalty litigation. Reflecting on his work, he lamented, "We've become technicians. The great moral issues have been removed from the legal arena." And so they have, at least for the time being and if their current manner of deployment is measured against the style in which they were presented to legislatures in the 1950s and the appellate courts in the 1960s. Nevertheless, the detailed studies gathered in this book are proof, if proof be needed, that these great moral issues can still be brought to bear in shaping the legal technicalities of current and future criticism of capital punishment. Or at least they can be when they are in the hands of an able and resourceful scholar, such as we have in the author of this book. With these essays Welsh S. White establishes himself as one of the nation's leading thinkers on the litigational, jurisprudential, and constitutional aspects of our current death penalty system. That system is in a condition of acute crisis, no matter from what direction it is surveyed. It deserves to be, as this book convincingly shows.

Hugo Adam Bedau
Tufts University

Acknowledgments

Grateful acknowledgment is made to the following publishers for permission to reprint the author's previously published articles:

Columbia Law Review for the review of Michael Meltsner's book. Copyright © 1983 by the Directors for the Columbia Law Review Association, Inc. All rights reserved. This article, "A Book Review—*Cruel and Unusual: The Supreme Court and Capital Punishment*," originally appeared at 74 COLUM. L. REV. 319 (1974). Reprinted by permission. Rewritten *infra* as "A Comment on *Furman v. Georgia*."

Northwestern University School of Law for "Waiver and the Death Penalty: The Implications of *Estelle v. Smith*." Reprinted by special permission of *The Journal of Criminal Law & Criminology*, © 1981 by Northwestern University School of Law, vol. 72, no. 4. "The Psychiatric Examination and the Fifth Amendment Privilege in Capital Cases." Reprinted by special permission of *The Journal of Criminal Law & Criminology*, © 1984 by Northwestern University School of Law, vol. 74, no. 3.

University of Cincinnati College of Law for "*Witherspoon* Revisited: Exploring the Tension between *Witherspoon* and *Furman*." Reprinted from 45 U. CIN. L. REV. 19 (1976).

University of Pennsylvania Law Review for "Police Trickery in Inducing Confessions." Reprinted from 127 W. PA. L. REV. 3 (1979). Copyright 1979 by the University of Pennsylvania.

University of Pittsburgh Law Review for "Death-Qualified Juries: The 'Prosecution-Proneness' Argument Reexamined." Reprinted from 41 U. PITT. L. REV. 353 (1980). "Disproportionality and the Death Penalty: Death as a Punishment for Rape." Reprinted from 38 U. PITT. L. REV. 145 (1976).

Contents

Introduction

In large part, these essays developed as a result of my exposure to capital punishment litigation. When I attended law school in the early sixties, I was privileged to have Anthony G. Amsterdam as my criminal law teacher. Although Amsterdam is a superb law professor, he is probably best known today as a litigator who has argued brilliantly and indefatigably on behalf of those opposed to the death penalty. Because of my admiration for him, I became interested in the issue of capital punishment, and in 1971 I became involved in writing briefs on behalf of capital defendants. Since then, I have participated in a number of death penalty cases that have presented a wide variety of issues, ranging from the constitutionality of state death penalty statutes to the permissibility of particular questions asked to prospective jurors on voir dire. This exposure has greatly broadened my understanding of our system of capital punishment and it has directed me to some of the specific issues that are addressed in these essays. I should emphasize, however, that I view myself as a scholar, not a litigator. In writing these essays, I have attempted to be as objective as possible and to present both sides of the issues. Whether I have succeeded, only the reader can judge.

The issues covered here are varied. One essay concerns the admissibility of confessions obtained by police trickery; another, the constitutional problems raised by the practice of death-qualifying juries in capital cases; and still another, the admissibility of government psychiatric testimony in capital and noncapital cases. But there is a single underlying theme. All of the essays relate in one way or another to the procedural safeguards to be employed in capital cases. The admissibility of a defendant's confession will often be a hotly disputed issue in a capital case; a capital defendant's chances will obviously be affected by the composition of the body that determines his guilt and punishment; and psychiatric testimony will often be of critical importance both because the insanity defense is unusually likely to be raised in capital cases and because, once the defendant has been convicted of a capital crime, psychiatric testimony may be extremely influential in shaping the penalty decision.

To place these essays in context, some overview of relevant United States Supreme Court decisions is helpful. The Court's watershed decision relating to capital punishment is *Furman v. Georgia*.[1] After *Furman* invalidated the then-existing form of capital punishment in 1972, the death penalty was left in a kind of constitutional limbo. This interval, which lasted four years, may be labeled the post-*Furman* era of capital punishment. In 1976, in *Gregg v. Georgia*,[2] the Court ushered in a new era, which may be labeled the post-*Gregg* era, by holding that the death penalty as such is not unconstitutional. In the first section of this introduction I will address issues that were particularly relevant to the post-*Furman* era. In the next section I will focus on the post-*Gregg* era. Finally, I will take a brief look at the future, commenting on some of the issues related to capital punishment that are likely to be resolved in the next decade.

The Post-*Furman* Era

Furman v. Georgia

Prior to 1972, almost every state provided that once a defendant was convicted of a capital offense, the jury should have absolute discretion to determine whether a sentence of death or life imprisonment should be imposed. In *Furman v. Georgia*, however, the United States Supreme Court decided that death penalties imposed pursuant to that system of capital punishment are in violation of the cruel and unusual punishment clause of the Eighth Amendment. The thread that appeared to unite the five separate opinions written in support of this result was a perception that that system had produced results that were too arbitrary and capricious to be constitutionally tolerable. According to the majority, there was no proper basis for distinguishing between the comparatively small number of capital defendants sentenced to death and the much larger group of defendants convicted of equally heinous capital crimes. Accordingly, as one justice put it, the death penalties before the Court were "[c]ruel and unusual in the same way that being struck by lightning is cruel and unusual. . . . [Those sentenced] . . . are among a capriciously selected random handful upon whom the sentence of death has in fact been imposed."[3]

Furman's ruling had the immediate effect of invalidating nearly all then-existing death penalty statutes. The majority did not decide, however, whether capital punishment as such was unconstitutional. Nor did it provide any clear guidance as to what type of capital punishment would be most likely to pass constitutional muster.

In the wake of *Furman*, thirty-five state legislatures passed new capital punishment statutes. These new statutes sought to meet the constitutional concerns articulated by the *Furman* majority by providing either that a mandatory sentence of death should be imposed upon conviction for a capital offense, or that once a defendant was convicted of a capital offense the capital sentencing decision should be based on a weighing of statutorily specified aggravating and mitigating circumstances. Although these statutes resulted in many new death sentences, the constitutional legitimacy of capital punishment remained undetermined for four years. In the light of the opinions in *Furman*, the constitutionality of these statutes seemed to depend particularly on the answers to two questions. First, could a reallocation of the sentencing authority in capital cases cause a change from the pattern of arbitrary and capricious capital sentencing condemned by *Furman*? And second, assuming the alteration in sentencing discretion would have this effect, would this new system of capital punishment be constitutional?

The first two essays in this collection deal separately with these two questions. In the essay entitled "A Comment on *Furman v. Georgia*" I argue that in light of the predictable practical operation of our criminal justice system, the change to a mandatory or guided-discretionary system of capital punishment may shift the capital sentencing discretion exercised by the jury to other parts of the system, but it will neither alter the fundamentally discretionary character of capital sentencing nor change the pattern of rare, arbitrary, and freakish death penalties condemned by *Furman*. This argument was considered and rejected by the Court in *Gregg v. Georgia*.[4] Nevertheless, as I shall indicate,[5] the Court may have to reconsider this argument in a different context at some future time.

In the second essay, entitled "Witherspoon Revisited: Exploring the Tension between *Witherspoon* and *Furman*," I take a different tack. Assuming that the shift to a different system of capital sentencing will render the sentencing decision less discretionary, I explore the question whether the resulting system of capital punishment will be unconstitutional because it does not provide the individualized sentencing judgment demanded by the Eighth Amendment. The essay focuses especially on the Court's decision in *Witherspoon v. Illinois*,[6] a 1968 ruling that precludes the prosecution from excluding for cause all jurors who have conscientious scruples against the death penalty. *Witherspoon*'s underlying premise appears to be that, for reasons drawn from the Eighth Amendment, "[a] jury can do little more—and must do nothing less—than express the conscience of the community on the ultimate question of life or death."[7] As the essay explains, it follows from this premise that individualized sentencing is constitutionally required, and, therefore, that mandatory capital punishment is unconstitutional.

Moreover, if *Witherspoon* requires individualized sentencing, then the tension between *Witherspoon* and *Furman* becomes obvious. How can the Court reconcile the need to allow the sentencing authority to consider every aspect of the capital defendant so as to arrive at a properly individualized sentence with *Furman*'s requirement that capital sentencing discretion be channelled so as to avoid an arbitrary and capricious pattern of death sentences? Although the essay's conclusions are tentative, I suggest that the task may be impossible, in which event the only appropriate solution is the abolition of capital punishment.

Witherspoon v. Illinois

The "*Witherspoon* Revisited" essay is not exclusively concerned with the constitutionality of the new statutes. In it I also analyze the procedural safeguards provided by *Witherspoon* and explore the extent to which those safeguards will be available to defendants prosecuted under the new statutes. This portion of the essay's analysis remains relevant. Despite the fact that *Witherspoon* was decided in the pre-*Furman* era, the case remains an important part of our constitutional fabric, and its holding is of vital significance in current capital punishment litigation.

Witherspoon is a fascinating but perplexing decision. Its constitutional underpinnings have always been unclear, lower courts have had enormous difficulty in administering it,[8] and commentators have criticized it as going either too far or not far enough.[9] The Court holds that a death sentence cannot be carried out if it is imposed by a jury from which veniremen were excluded for cause simply because they expressed general objections or conscientious or religious scruples against the death penalty.[10] At the same time, the Court indicates that *Witherspoon*'s holding will not apply if the only veniremen excluded for cause are those who make it unmistakably clear that they will automatically vote against the imposition of capital punishment, regardless of the evidence presented at trial.[11] The line that separates these two groups of veniremen is not very clear. A prospective juror may be absolutely opposed to capital punishment but still feel that there *might* be some case in which she would at least want to consider the evidence before deciding whether to vote against the death penalty. In this type of situation, the distinction between opposing the death penalty and automatically voting against it may be too subtle for ordinary minds to grasp. Whether a particular individual fits into one category as opposed to another may indicate more about her approach to language than it does about her real feelings about capital punishment. No wonder the courts have so much difficulty in administering the test. Making the distinctions required by *Witherspoon* is difficult enough under the best of circumstances. Making them on the basis of answers given in the voir dire is almost impossible.

The Court asserts that the imposition of the death penalty by the death-qualified jury in the *Witherspoon* case was unconstitutional because the government had "stacked the deck against the [defendant]."[12] Yet, by permitting the disqualification of veniremen who say they would automatically vote against the death penalty, the Court seems to indicate that the government is permitted to stack the deck against the defendant as long as it doesn't stack it too much. After all, if the prosecution is permitted to exclude the not insignificant segment of the population that will absolutely refuse to impose the death penalty under any circumstances, the jury will be chosen from a population that is more favorable to the death penalty than the population at large. As I shall attempt to explain below, this point is far more significant today than it was when *Witherspoon* was decided.

The Post-*Gregg* Era

The post-*Gregg* era of capital punishment bears scant resemblance to the pre-*Furman* era, during which a state's system of capital punishment was subjected to little or no constitutional scrutiny. The Court's recognition that death is a uniquely harsh form of punishment has led it to erect a system under which a death penalty cannot be constitutionally imposed unless it survives a variety of forms of scrutiny. To simplify slightly,[13] the required scrutiny may be divided into two parts. First, the use of capital punishment is subject to basic substantive limitations; and second, capital defendants must be afforded particular procedural safeguards.

Substantive Limitations

The substantive limitations imposed on capital punishment may be stated succinctly. Since the Eighth Amendment prohibits excessive punishments,[14] death as a penalty for a particular crime will not be constitutional unless the punishment is penologically justified and is not disproportionate to the offense for which it is imposed.[15] These two principles are analytically severable. A punishment may be penologically justified in the sense that it serves a valid penological end such as deterrence, yet be disproportionate to the offense because it inflicts more pain than the offender deserves.[16] In *Gregg v. Georgia*, the Court adopted a standard of scrutiny that affords considerable deference to a legislature's judgment concerning capital punishment's penological justification,[17] suggesting that the proportionality test might emerge as the more important substantive limitation. In a subsequent case,[18] however, the Court tended to merge the two principles, suggesting that the substantive judgment must be ultimately based on an assessment of both penological justification and proportionality.

The last five essays included in this volume were written during the post-*Gregg* era. Of these five, four relate to procedural safeguards. Only one, entitled "Disproportionality and the Death Penalty: Death as a Punishment for Rape," is concerned with substantive limitations. In a sense, this essay is more dated than any of the others. In it I argue that death is a disproportionate punishment for the crime of rape. About six months after the essay was published, the Court essentially adopted this position, holding that death is a constitutionally disproportionate punishment for the crime of raping an adult woman.[19] Nevertheless, the essay may be of current interest for two reasons. First, it seeks to identify the criteria to be used in making a disproportionality assessment. Identifying these criteria may be important because, as the update to this essay explains, the Court's recent decision in *Enmund v. Florida*[20] suggests that the disproportionality limitation may become increasingly significant.

Moreover, the essay may be of interest because it deals with the issue of race—an issue the Court's Eighth Amendment decisions have largely avoided despite the fact that it looms large in the administration of capital punishment. Drawing upon well-documented studies, the essay concludes that death as a punishment for rape was imposed disproportionately often upon black men convicted of raping white women and that this disparity could be explained only as one that occurred as a result of racial discrimination. The question that these figures raise, of course, is whether racial discrimination plays a significant part in the current administration of capital punishment.

In comparison to the pre-*Furman* data relating to the imposition of capital punishment for the crime of rape, the current figures pertaining to the composition of death row do not appear to present a stark picture of discrimination. As of June 20, 1983, there were 1,202 inmates on death row; 623, or 51.83 percent, of these inmates were white.[21] Given the differing crime rates of whites and nonwhites, these figures are not inconsistent with a conclusion that the death penalty is being even-handedly applied.

Nevertheless, a closer look at the administration of the death penalty reveals some interesting phenomena. Recent studies of selected locations in southern states indicate that the historical pattern of imposing the death penalty more readily upon the black killer of a white victim is still present.[22] The most exacting of these studies[23] focused exclusively on death row inmates convicted of felony-murder in Florida between 1972 and 1977. Using the race of the defendant and the race of the victim as variables, Professor Hans Zeisel found that a person arrested for the felony-murder of a white victim was more than thirty times as likely to be sentenced to death as a person arrested for the felony-murder of a black victim.[24] In addition, a black defendant arrested for the felony-murder of a white victim was almost twice as likely to be sentenced to death as a white defendant arrested for the felony-murder of a white victim.[25]

These figures certainly indicate that race continues to influence the administration of capital punishment. Moreover, Zeisel's account of the sequel to the presentation of this data is illuminating. During the three-year period after the Fifth Circuit dismissed the data as constituting no more than an allegation of racial discrimination,[26] the percentage of defendants sentenced to death for the felony-murder of a black victim approximately tripled.[27] In seeking to explain this change, Zeisel recounts two specific instances in which Florida prosecutors argued fervently and successfully for the death penalty in cases in which the defendant was white and the victim black.[28]

Zeisel's claim that the sequel amounts to a prosecutorial admission of social discrimination[29] seems dubious. Just as a person's effort to take greater care does not ordinarily amount to an admission of prior negligence,[30] a prosecutor's effort to guard against racial discrimination does not necessarily constitute an admission that such discrimination existed in the past. Nevertheless, the sequel provides a striking illustration of the prosecutor's ability to manipulate the system. In the specific cases recounted by Zeisel, the prosecutor's emphasis on the need to avoid racial discrimination may have led the jury to condemn a defendant who would otherwise have been spared. If the prosecutor can so easily manipulate the administration of capital punishment, the question arises whether the procedural safeguards developed by the Court in the post-*Gregg* era can ever be sufficient in themselves to attain the Court's goal of establishing a just and rational system of capital punishment.

The Procedural Safeguards

The post-*Gregg* decisions have placed greatest emphasis on providing procedural safeguards for capital defendants.[31] *Gregg* itself established the framework within which such safeguards must be evaluated by suggesting that a capital defendant's rights could best be protected by a bifurcated trial in which the issues of guilt and penalty would be determined in separate proceedings.[32] In subsequent cases, the Court has emphasized that in light of the post-1972 awareness of the magnitude of the interest involved when a defendant's life is at stake, a heightened concern has emerged for maintaining procedures that appear to and in fact do afford rationality and fairness to capital defendants.[33] Accordingly, during the post-*Gregg* era, the Court's capital punishment decisions have been primarily concerned with scrutinizing the fairness of procedures applied at both the guilt and penalty stages of the capital trial.[34]

Of the myriad procedural issues that may arise, some that are of particular significance may be divided into four categories. The risk of a capital defendant's execution is likely to be importantly affected by

1. the composition of the jury that determines guilt;
2. the composition of the sentencing authority;
3. the rules governing admissibility of evidence at the guilt trial;
4. the rules governing admissibility of evidence at the penalty trial.

The final four essays in this volume deal with aspects of each of these problems.

In the essay entitled "Death-Qualified Juries: The 'Prosecution-Proneness' Argument Reexamined" I return to the subject of *Witherspoon* and examine some of the legal issues that arise because of the prosecution's right to select a death-qualified jury in capital cases. In capital cases in most jurisdictions, the prosecution is allowed to exclude from the jury all those who would absolutely refuse to vote for a sentence of death. The essay touches briefly upon death-qualification's effect on the sentencing jury. It raises the question whether a sentencing jury that was selected by excluding the substantial segment of the community who are absolutely opposed to capital punishment can "maintain [the] link between contemporary community values and the penal system," which has become an essential ingredient of the Eighth Amendment. This question, which is examined in much greater depth by Professor Stephen Gillers,[35] has never been considered by the Supreme Court.

The "Death-Qualified Juries" essay is primarily concerned with the appropriate composition of the jury that determines guilt. In view of the Court's concern for establishing special procedural safeguards for capital defendants, it is ironic that the practice of death-qualification probably operates to place the capital defendant at a critical disadvantage during the guilt stage of the proceedings. The reason that death-qualification causes this disadvantage was set forth in a seminal article written by Professor Walter Oberer[36] more than twenty years ago. The image projected by Professor Oberer was of a capital defendant's guilt being decided by a group of Madame DeFarges.[37] Put less starkly, the prosecution-proneness thesis is that as compared to the jury used in noncapital cases, the death-qualified jury is more likely to favor the prosecutor on the issue of guilt.

The essay evaluates the legal validity of the prosecution-proneness claim. It considers recent empirical data indicating that death-qualified juries will be more favorably disposed to the prosecution than non-death-qualified ones, and it assesses this data in light of the Supreme

Court decisions pertaining to both the legal relevance of empirical data and the appropriate standard that must be met to establish the unconstitutionality of a jury that is tilted in favor of the prosecution on the issue of guilt. An examination of the empirical data reveals that although there are methodological problems with nearly all of the studies, the data taken as a whole convincingly supports the prosecution-proneness thesis. Analysis of the leading Supreme Court cases, especially the recent decision of *Ballew v. Georgia*,[38] then leads to the conclusion that the form of death-qualification presently employed in capital cases constitutes a violation of a capital defendant's rights under the Sixth and Fourteenth Amendments.

In the post-*Gregg* era of capital punishment, the death-qualified jury presently in use may be analogized to a structurally flawed bridge that is no longer stable enough to be safe but yet remains in use because it seems too expensive to repair or replace it. As the update to the "Death-Qualified Juries" essay indicates, the basis for challenging the constitutionality of the death-qualified jury is even stronger today than it was when the original essay was written. Yet to date no court has definitively held that the death-qualified jury is unconstitutional.[39] Obviously, from a court's perspective the issue is an agonizing one. If the prosecution-proneness argument is accepted, then not only the death sentences but also the convictions of nearly every inmate now on death row will be thrown into question. In addition, the convictions of many prisoners not sentenced to death will also be subject to attack because the essence of the prosecution-proneness claim is that the defendant is placed at an unfair disadvantage with respect to the determination of guilt. If the Supreme Court were to invalidate every conviction returned by a death-qualified jury, the impact of *Furman v. Georgia*,[40] which vacated some 600 death penalties, would appear small by comparison. This is not to say that the Court is incapable of formulating an approach to this problem that would minimize the impact on the administration of justice, but clearly the problem of the death-qualified jury represents a formidable jurisprudential challenge. How the courts, and particularly the Supreme Court, will deal with this challenge is one of those imponderable questions that await future resolution.

In the next essay, entitled "Police Trickery in Inducing Confessions," I deal with the law relating to the admissibility of a criminal defendant's confession. During the thirty-year period between 1936 and 1966, two-thirds of the confession cases reviewed by the Supreme Court were those in which the defendant received the death penalty.[41] As these and subsequent Supreme Court cases[42] indicate, the government is particularly likely to try to introduce a confession in very serious cases, especially murder cases in which the defendant's life may be at stake.

Moreover, a defendant's confession will generally be extremely impressive evidence to the jury. Thus, in death penalty cases, whether the defendant lives or dies may turn upon whether the jury is permitted to hear the defendant's confession. In discussing this subject I have drawn heavily on the work of Professor Yale Kamisar,[43] and some familiarity with his work would be helpful to a full understanding of the issues presented in the essay.

The essay focuses especially on situations in which the police induce incriminating statements by using subtle interrogation techniques rather than by overtly overbearing the defendant's will. Although a variety of issues are considered in the essay, perhaps the most interesting discussion relates to the ways in which police trickery may undermine the constitutional safeguards guaranteed to defendants by cases such as *Miranda v. Arizona*.[44] For example, one thesis is that when a defendant is deceived as to whether an interrogation is taking place, the effect of the applicable Fifth and Sixth Amendment rights is negated. After explaining and elaborating on this principle, I discuss whether other types of police deception may result in a similar undermining of the applicable safeguards.

This discussion sets the stage for the next essay, which concerns the admissibility of defendants' incriminating statements in capital cases. In *Estelle v. Smith*[45] the Court vacated defendant's death sentence on the ground that the introduction of government psychiatric testimony at the penalty trial resulted in a violation of defendant's Fifth and Sixth Amendment rights. The essay "Waiver and the Death Penalty: The Implications of *Estelle v. Smith*" deals with the implications of *Smith*'s Fifth and Sixth Amendment analysis. After explaining the immediate impact of the Court's twin holdings, I focus on the standard of waiver that should be applied when a capital defendant's Fifth and Sixth Amendment rights are at issue. Although *Smith* does not deal systematically with this question, a close reading of the Court's opinion discloses an embryonic awareness of the need for stricter standards in capital cases. The essay explores these aspects of the Court's opinion, and, drawing also on insights contained in earlier decisions, suggests that ultimately, capital defendants should be afforded an opportunity to consult an attorney before being allowed to waive their Fifth and Sixth Amendment rights. If this reading of *Smith* is accepted, it will obviously have a profound impact on the admissibility of evidence at capital trials.

In the final essay, "The Psychiatric Examination and the Fifth Amendment Privilege in Capital Cases," I deal with the problem of determining the circumstances under which government psychiatric testimony will be admissible at a capital trial. *Smith* provokes an examination of this issue because it is the first case to hold that the Fifth

Amendment privilege applies to a government psychiatric examination. In limiting its holding, *Smith* reserved decision of the question whether a defendant who presents his own expert psychiatric testimony at some stage of the proceedings may thereby forfeit the right to raise Fifth Amendment objections to evidence of an examination by a government psychiatrist. In dealing with the various aspects of this question, I found it necessary to come to terms with a variety of issues, including the general problem of defining the circumstances under which a defendant may be forced to choose between his Fifth Amendment privilege and some other constitutional right. From my perspective, this final essay is the most interesting of the group, because it deals with issues that are the most complex and challenging of those considered in this volume.

The issues discussed in the "Psychiatric Examination" essay may also be of considerable practical importance. Ultimately, their resolution will have a profound impact on the nature and quality of expert psychiatric testimony presented in capital cases. And in certain capital cases, the value of such testimony probably cannot be overestimated. Often a capital defendant's commission of a heinous offense is virtually undisputed. Thus, in deciding whether the defendant should be sentenced to death, the jury will be particularly concerned with obtaining some information that will enable them to understand why the defendant acted as he did. For this purpose, psychiatric testimony offered on behalf of either the government or the defendant may be absolutely critical. Accordingly, the rules governing the admissibility of such evidence may determine whether a defendant will live or die.

The Future

More on Procedural Safeguards

If the recent past is an accurate guide, then in the immediate future the Court is likely to be most concerned with examining the procedural safeguards afforded to capital defendants. For example, the Court may examine the scope of some recent procedural decisions, such as *Lockett v. Ohio*[46] and *Gardner v. Florida*;[47] *Lockett* holds that the sentencer may not be precluded from considering as a mitigating factor any relevant evidence that the defendant chooses to offer as a basis for imposing a sentence of less than death. In some future case, the Court may need to consider the validity of state statutes that place the burden of proving mitigating circumstances on the defendant,[48] require that the sentencing jury impose the death penalty if it finds that the aggravating circumstances outweigh the mitigating circumstances,[49] or require that the jury impose a death sentence if it finds at least one statutorily defined aggravating circumstance and no statutorily defined mitigating circumstances.[50] The Court may need to decide whether such statutes are contrary to *Lockett* because they do not permit the sentencer to exercise its independent judgment as to whether mitigating evidence presented by the defendant should be a basis for refusing to impose the death penalty.

Lockett is also significant in that it is one of a series of cases that constitutionalizes the rules of evidence to be applied at the penalty stage of a capital trial.[51] Because of the Court's special concern for ensuring reliability in the capital sentencing procedure, any rule of evidence applied by a state at the penalty stage will be subjected to constitutional scrutiny.[52] To take one illustration, *Lockett* guarantees a capital defendant the right to present relevant evidence concerning the circumstances of the offense and the character of the offender.[53] In this context, the Court will eventually need to establish a constitutional definition of relevance. For example, should the defendant be permitted to present expert testimony that the death penalty will not be an effective deterrent? Or that it will have no deterrent effect when imposed for the particular type of crime of which the defendant has been convicted? In clarifying the appropriate evidentiary rules on these and other issues, the Court may also become involved with defining the appropriate limits on argument by counsel. For example, will defense counsel be permitted to argue about the mental and physical cruelty involved in execution? And will *Furman*'s concern with avoiding the irrational or arbitrary infliction of capital punishment lead the Court to restrict the prosecutor from presenting inflammatory arguments at either the guilt or penalty stage?

Gardner v. Florida[54] was one of the first post-*Gregg* cases to emphasize the need for especially reliable procedures when a defendant's life is at stake. *Gardner*'s holding prohibits a sentencing judge from imposing a capital sentence on the basis of evidence not disclosed to defense counsel. In clarifying the scope of *Gardner*'s holding, the Court may have to delineate the type of evidence that may properly be relied on by a judge who is making a capital sentencing determination. Beyond that, however, the Court may also eventually have to reconsider whether the capital sentencing decision may properly be vested in a judge instead of a jury.[55]

The latter question is of particular significance. Although the judge has final capital sentencing authority in only eight states, two of those states—Alabama and Florida—have accounted for a significant proportion of the present death row population. Professor Gillers's incisive analysis of this issue[56] suggests the nature of the constitutional issues to be decided. One argument raised by Gillers is that jury sentencing is needed to measure the community's "evolving standards of decency" with respect to either the death penalty or to its application in a particular category of cases.[57] The Court's analysis in *Enmund v. Florida*[58] appears to lend strength to this argument. In *Enmund* the Court indicated that, although a third of the states authorize death as a penalty for an accomplice to a felony-murder, juries' disinclination to impose the death penalty for this type of offense is a strong indicator of society's view that capital punishment in this situation is excessive.[59] The Court's reasoning suggests that analysis of jury sentencing may be the best means of gauging the community's acceptance of death as a penalty for a particular category of offense. If so, then given the empirical evidence that suggests the wide difference between judges and juries in terms of both their ability to represent the community[60] and their performance on capital sentencing,[61] it seems questionable whether a judge may adequately substitute for a jury in fulfilling this function. Thus, the Court will have to determine whether judicial sentencing can maintain the link between contemporary community standards and the death penalty that has been found to be an essential ingredient of the Eighth Amendment.

Of the many other issues relating to procedural safeguards that might be considered by the Court, one in particular deserves mention. Under our present system of constitutional law, a defendant's constitutional rights ordinarily must be asserted by counsel in order to be preserved. Thus, the procedural safeguards now available to a capital defendant will be valueless unless counsel asserts them. Accordingly, to make sure that the procedural safeguards established during the post-*Gregg* era will be meaningful, the Court must define the standard of effective representation in a capital case.

Professor Gary Goodpaster's analysis of this issue[62] is especially illuminating. Drawing on substantial empirical data relating to litigation at the penalty stage of a capital trial, he emphasizes that defense counsel's function at the penalty phase is quite different from her function at the guilt phase. Rather than defending her client against evidence offered by the prosecution, she must assume the role of presenting an affirmative case for life.[63] In particular, counsel must take advantage of defendant's right to present mitigating evidence. In most cases, two types of evidence will be especially valuable: first, testimony that will point to some redeeming characteristics in the defendant so that the jury may be enabled to identify with him as a human being; and second, evidence that will provide the jury with some understanding of why the defendant acted as he did. Goodpaster argues that a defense attorney who fails to present any evidence of this type at the penalty trial is not providing a capital defendant with the effective assistance of counsel that is mandated by the Sixth Amendment.[64]

In addition to formulating his view of the appropriate Sixth Amendment standard, Goodpaster compares results between cases in which counsel presented appropriate evidence at the penalty trial and those in which her performance was clearly deficient. He merely confirms the view of most knowledgeable observers when he finds that effective representation does make a difference. Although not discussed by Goodpaster, the case of John Spinkellink[65] presents a striking example of how defense counsel's failure to present mitigating evidence may have been the decisive factor in causing defendant's death sentence and eventual execution. Spinkellink was not guilty of a particularly heinous capital crime. In fact, even the assistant attorney general who represented the prosecution admitted that "he was probably the least obnoxious individual on death row in terms of the crime he committed."[66] In addition, substantial mitigating evidence could have been presented at the penalty trial. Spinkellink had a troubled childhood because his father, who had been a hero in the Second World War, committed suicide. Prison psychiatrists concluded that his criminal behavior was in large part due to his father's suicide and that he was amenable to treatment. Inexplicably, none of this evidence was presented, and Spinkellink was sentenced to death and executed. On the other hand, Goodpaster recounts cases[67] in which perpetrators of atrociously brutal crimes have been spared the death sentence after defense counsel presented persuasive mitigating evidence at the penalty stage.

In addition to emphasizing the importance of the effective assistance of counsel, these results raise fundamental questions about the efficacy of the procedural safeguards established by the Court during the post-*Gregg* era. The purpose of the safeguards is to secure the evenhanded application of capital punishment. But just as the prosecutor's ability to manipulate the system affects its operation,[68] the capital defendant's chances of avoiding execution in many cases largely depends on the quality of his counsel's representation. Can this imperfection in the system be changed? As Professor Charles Black has said, to effect a real change, "every capital defendant [would have to] be furnished by the state, at every stage, with the best counsel money can buy, and with completely adequate funds for investigation, for expert witnesses, and for everything else that you or I would hock our souls to get if we had anyone dear to us standing accused of a capital offense."[69] Since this change is not likely to occur, the objective of securing the evenhanded application of capital punishment is likely to remain an illusory goal.

The Ultimate Question: Determining the Constitutionality
of Capital Punishment

In *Furman* the Court held essentially that capital punishment as administered by the system then in effect was unconstitutional. In upholding the death penalty statute before it in *Gregg*, the Court held that the death penalty as such is not an unconstitutional punishment for murder. Although the *Gregg* plurality also indicated that the safeguards provided by the Georgia statute would be sufficient to distinguish the post-*Gregg* system of capital punishment from the system condemned in *Furman*, the Court was obviously not in a position to decide whether capital punishment as administered pursuant to the post-*Gregg* system would be unconstitutional. To decide that question it would have to evaluate the pattern of results actually produced by the new system.

At some point in the future, the Court will undoubtedly be required to pass on the constitutionality of the death penalty as administered by the post-*Gregg* system of capital punishment. In deciding this question, the Court could adopt *Furman*'s approach of assessing the extent to which the death penalty is evenhandedly applied by comparing those defendants who happen to be on death row with the larger population of defendants who were convicted of capital crimes but not sentenced to death. This approach, however, would fail to take account of the changes in the system wrought by the post-*Gregg* era. The strict scrutiny that is now mandated in capital cases has had a significant impact on the operation of the system. Under the pre-*Furman* system, a majority of those sentenced to death were actually executed. Under the post-*Gregg* system, however, the reverse is true. In fact, as Jack Greenberg has pointed out, "virtually all capital sentences . . . that have been litigated to conclusion have been reversed."[70]

In the next decade, this pattern may change to some degree, but barring a significant change in our system it is not likely to change drastically. Capital sentences are not reversed so frequently merely because states are engaging in a few erroneous practices that may be easily corrected. Rather, as Greenberg documents,[71] capital convictions and sentences have been reversed on a wide variety of legal grounds. Although it is difficult to pinpoint the reason for these multifarious reversals, it seems clear that they cannot be attributed simply to the state's lack of familiarity with the rules to be applied in the post-*Gregg* era. To some degree, errors may proliferate because a capital trial is a sensational event in which emotions run high and the special procedures involved magnify the chances of error. But more importantly, the number of reversals is large because appellate courts scrutinize capital cases more closely.[72] The Court has committed us to a system of capital punishment that will minimize the risk of error, and as a general rule our system is not able to meet the requisite standard of reliability. Thus, the number of people sentenced to death may continue to be large but the number actually executed will remain small. In operation then, the death penalty will be applied far more "freakishly" under this system of capital punishment than it was under the system condemned by the Supreme Court in *Furman*.

In passing on the constitutionality of this system of capital punishment, the Court should examine whether the death penalty as administered serves a valid penological end. Under *Enmund v. Florida*[73] the only appropriate penological justifications for the death penalty appear to be deterrence and retribution.[74] Thus, the proper question to ask is whether a death penalty imposed pursuant to our present system of capital punishment can make a measurable contribution to either of these goals.

Deterrence, of course, is an issue that is surrounded by controversy. Abolitionists contend that there is no evidence that the death penalty is a more effective deterrent than life imprisonment under any circumstances. Proponents of capital punishment contend the contrary. It is generally undisputed, however, that a punishment is most likely to serve as an effective deterrent if the individual potentially subject to it believes that it will be swiftly and certainly imposed. Thus, if a defendant is contemplating the commission of a capital offense, such as the murder of a police officer, capital punishment will be most likely to serve as a deterrent if it will cause him to think along the following lines: "I want to kill that officer; but I must also consider that if I am caught and convicted of this offense, I will be executed." In the post-*Gregg* era, however, no defendant would hold this opinion unless he were seriously misinformed about the administration of the death penalty. In fact, an informed defendant would know that even if he were to be sentenced to death for a capital offense, his chances of being executed for that offense would be relatively slight. Under these circumstances, it seems clear that the threat of capital punishment does not serve as a more effective deterrent than the threat of life imprisonment.

The issue of retribution is a more difficult one. Although the Court has discussed this theory in various contexts, in *Enmund* it appeared to equate retribution with limiting an offender's punishment to his just deserts. Under this view, a proponent of capital punishment might argue that the few capital defendants who are actually executed certainly receive no more than their just deserts. The safeguards provided by the Court are designed to ensure not only that the facts pertinent to a death sentence are reliably determined but also that capital punishment is reserved only for those few heinous offenders who are most deserving of death. In the process of protecting the defendant's constitutional rights, the system may winnow out many other offenders who are scarcely distinguishable, but if the system works at all, it should follow that the few people who are executed are at least among those who deserve to die.

Therefore, so the argument goes, these few executions may be justified on the ground that they serve the penological goal of retribution.

In response to this argument, two related points may be made. First, retribution cannot be considered in a vacuum. What an offender's "just deserts" actually are depends heavily on the contemporary scale of values. In mid-eighteenth-century England, highwaymen (robbers) were clearly viewed as deserving of death.[75] In the early nineteenth century, Americans thought all murderers deserved to die.[76] Today, the formal pronouncements of our system of justice seem to express a judgment that the most heinous murderers deserve to die, but the actual operation of our system belies it. Out of the eligible category of murderers, only a handful are actually executed. This may indicate a de facto change in our scale of values. Cannot the fact that we do not generally execute even our most heinous murderers be viewed as an implicit judgment that even that category of offenders is no longer deserving of the punishment of death?

Moreover, in the context of our present system there is another dimension to the issue of retribution. A defendant who is executed against his will does not merely suffer the penalty of death. Recent empirical evidence[77] lends credence to Camus's statement that "[a]s a general rule, a man is undone by waiting for capital punishment well before he dies. Two deaths are inflicted on him, the first being worse than second, whereas he killed but once."[78] A defendant who is executed against his will suffers that penalty after lingering on death row for years, enduring the physical restraints and psychological debilitation that pertain to that type of confinement,[79] the mounting anguish of uncertainty about whether his death sentence will be carried out,[80] and, finally, the terrible realization that he is one of the unlucky few who will actually be executed. In time, our commitment to maintaining a just and humane system of criminal justice should lead us to the conclusion that this type of punishment is not the just desert of any human being.

NOTES

1. 408 U.S. 238 (1972).
2. 428 U.S. 153 (1976).
3. 408 U.S. at 309–10 (Stewart, J., concurring).
4. 428 U.S. at 195.
5. *See infra* text following note 63.
6. 391 U.S. 510 (1968).

7. *Id*. at 519 n.15.

8. *See generally* Comment, *Jury Selection and the Death Penalty: Witherspoon in the Lower Courts*, 37 U. CHI. L. REV. 759 (1970).

9. *See, e.g*., A. BICKEL, THE SUPREME COURT AND THE IDEA OF PROGRESS 74 (1970) (criticizing *Witherspoon* on ground that it fails to meet the argument made by Justice White in dissent); Gillers, *Deciding Who Dies*, 129 U. PA. L. REV. 1, 84 (1980) (arguing for extension of *Witherspoon*).

10. 391 U.S. at 522.

11. *Id*. at 522 n.21.

12. *Id*. at 523.

13. For a much more detailed and sophisticated exposition of the Eighth Amendment limitations promulgated by *Gregg v. Georgia*, see Liebman & Shepard, *Guiding Capital Sentence Discretion Beyond the "Boiler Plate": Mental Disorder as a Mitigating Factor* 66 GEO. L.J. 757 (1978).

14. *See* Gregg v. Georgia, 428 U.S. 153, 173 (1976).

15. *Id*.

16. To take an extreme example, it might be concluded that imposing a jail sentence on all jaywalkers would be the most effective means of deterring this offense. Nevertheless, the punishment would be disproportionate to the offense because nobody would assert that a jaywalker is deserving of such harsh treatment.

17. *See* 428 U.S. at 174–76.

18. Enmund v. Florida, 102 S. Ct. 3368 (1982).

19. *See* Coker v. Georgia, 433 U.S. 584 (1977).

20. 102 S. Ct. 3368.

21. *See Death Row*, U.S.A., June 20, 1983, at 1.

22. *See* Zeisel, *Race Bias in the Administration of the Death Penalty: The Florida Experience*, 95 HARV. L. REV. 456 (1981); Bowers & Pierce, *Arbitrariness and Discrimination Under Post-Furman Capital Statutes*, 26 CRIME & DELINQ. 563 (1980).

23. *See* Zeisel, *supra* note 22.

24. Zeisel, *supra* note 22, at 460.

25. *Id*. at 461.

26. *See* Spinkellink v. Wainwright, 578 F.2d 582, 613 (5th Cir. 1978).

27. Zeisel, *supra* note 22, at 465.

28. *Id*. at 465–66.

29. Zeisel, *supra* note 22, at 464.

30. *See generally* 2 J. WIGMORE, EVIDENCE § 283 (3d ed. 1940).

31. In the recent decision of California v. Ramos, 103 S. Ct. 3446 (1983) the Court articulated its basic approach:

> In ensuring that the death penalty is not meted out arbitrarily or capriciously, the Court's principle concern has been more with the *procedure* by which the State imposes the death penalty than with the substantive factors the State lays before the jury as a basis for imposing death, once it has been determined that the defendant fits within the category of persons eligible for the death penalty.

Id. at 3451 (emphasis in original).

32. 428 U.S. at 195.

33. *See, e.g.*, Gardner v. Florida, 430 U.S. 349, 358 (1977).

34. In *Gregg* the Court also emphasized that the Georgia statute before it provided for special appellate review of death sentences. Under the statute, the Georgia Supreme Court is required to review every death sentence to determine whether it is supported by the evidence and whether it was imposed under the influence of passion, prejudice, or any other arbitrary factor. *Gregg*'s pivotal plurality opinion stated that this "provision . . . serves as a check against the random or arbitrary imposition of the death penalty." 428 U.S. at 206 (plurality opinion of Stewart, J.). Neither *Gregg* nor any subsequent case has decided whether this type of provision is constitutionally required.

35. *See* Gillers, *supra* note 9.

36. *See* Oberer, *Does Disqualification of Jurors for Scruples Against Capital Punishment Constitute Denial of Fair Trial on Issue of Guilt?*, 39 Tex. L. Rev. 545 (1961).

37. *See* Oberer, *supra* note 36, at 552.

38. 435 U.S. 223 (1978).

39. *But see* Grigsby v. Mabry, 569 F. Supp. 1273 (1983), discussed in the update to the "Death-Qualified Juries" essay.

40. 408 U.S. 232 (1972).

41. *See* Y. Kamisar, Police Interrogation and Confessions 75 (1980).

42. *See, e.g.*, Estelle v. Smith, 451 U.S. 454 (1981) (death sentence); Brewer v. Williams, 430 U.S. 387 (1977) (sentence of life imprisonment).

43. *See* Y. Kamisar, *supra* note 41.

44. 384 U.S. 436 (1966).

45. 451 U.S. 454 (1981).

46. 438 U.S. 586 (1978).

47. 430 U.S. 349 (1977).

48. *See, e.g.*, 42 Pa. Cons. Stat. Ann. § 9711(c)(iii) (1978).

49. *See, e.g.*, 42 Pa. Cons. Stat. Ann. § 9711(c)(iv) (1978).

50. *See, e.g.*, 42 Pa. Cons. Stat. Ann. § 9711(c)(iv) (1978).

51. In addition to *Lockett, see, e.g.*, Green v. Georgia, 442 U.S. 95 (1979), and Gardner v. Florida, 430 U.S. 349 (1977).

52. *See, e.g.*, Green v. Georgia, 442 U.S. 95 (1979) (holding that state's application of hearsay rule to exclude particular mitigating evidence offered by defendant was unconstitutional).

53. *See* 438 U.S. at 604 n.12.

54. 430 U.S. 349 (1977).

55. In upholding Florida's statute, the Court in Profitt v. Florida, 428 U.S. 242 (1976), specifically held that vesting the final capital sentencing decision in the judge rather than the jury is not unconstitutional. *See* 428 U.S. at 252.

56. *See* Gillers, *supra* note 9, at 39–74.

57. *See* Gillers, *supra* note 9, at 69–74.

58. 102 S. Ct. 3368 (1982).

59. *See* 102 S. Ct. at 3375–76.

60. *See* Gillers, *supra* note 9, at 63–66.

61. *See* H. Kalven & H. Zeisel, The American Jury 436 (1966).

62. *See* Goodpaster, *The Trial For Life: Effective Assistance of Counsel in Death Penalty Cases*, 58 N.Y.U. L. REV. 299 (1983).

63. *See* Goodpaster, *supra* note 62, at 338.

64. *See* Goodpaster, *supra* note 62, at 335–36.

65. *See* Clark, *Spinkellink's Last Appeal*, NATION, Oct. 1979, at 385, 404–14, *reprinted in* H. BEDAU, THE DEATH PENALTY IN AMERICA 224–33 (3d ed. 1982).

66. *See* Greenberg, *Capital Punishment as a System*, 91 YALE L.J. 908, 926 (1982).

67. *See* Goodpaster, *supra* note 62, at 360–63.

68. *See supra* text following note 30.

69. Black, *Death Sentences and Our Criminal Justice System*, in H. BEDAU, *supra* note 65, at 360–61.

70. Greenberg, *supra* note 66, at 919.

71. *See* Greenberg, *supra* note 66, at 919–22.

72. This close standard of review may be constitutionally mandated. *See supra* note 34.

73. 102 S. Ct. 3368 (1982).

74. In *Enmund*, the Court considered only these two penological justifications while holding that the death penalty is unconstitutional when applied to a defendant who neither took, attempted to take, nor intended to take the life of another.

75. *See generally* Langbein, *Shaping the Eighteenth-Century Criminal Trial: A View From the Ryder Sources*, 50 U. CHI. L. REV. 1 (1983).

76. *See* Woodson v. North Carolina, 428 U.S. 280, 289 (1976).

77. *See* Johnson, *Warehousing for Death: Observations on the Human Environment of Death Row*, 26 CRIME & DELINQ. 545 (1980).

78. A. Camus, *Reflections on the Guillotine*, in RESISTANCE, REBELLION AND DEATH 205 (A. Camus ed. 1969).

79. *See* Johnson, *supra* note 77, at 558–62.

80. Of course, prisoners sentenced to death but not executed also have to endure the hardships associated with being confined on death row. When, as is generally the case, these prisoners are spared because it is determined that their death sentences were erroneous, the suffering imposed on them obviously cannot be justified by any viable theory of retribution.

A Comment on *Furman v. Georgia*

On June 29, 1972, the Supreme Court in a per curiam decision reversed death penalties imposed pursuant to four state statutes, holding that each of the penalties was imposed in violation of the cruel and unusual punishment clause of the Eighth Amendment.[1] In reaching this result, the Court did not agree on a common rationale. Indeed, each member of the five-justice majority wrote a separate opinion in support of the result.[2] Nevertheless, the breadth of the Court's rationale clearly extends far enough to invalidate the jury-discretionary form of capital punishment that presently exists in this country. The common thread that brings together the various members of the majority was perhaps expressed most vividly by Justice Stewart.

These death sentences are cruel and unusual in the same way that being struck by lightning is cruel and unusual. For all the people convicted of rapes and murders in 1967 and 1968, many just as reprehensible as these, the petitioners are among a capriciously selected random handful upon whom the sentence of death has in fact been imposed.[3]

The other members of the majority shared Justice Stewart's perception that our present system of capital punishment permits results that are too arbitrary and capricious to be constitutionally tolerable.

The *Furman* decision was spectacular not only in its immediate impact (sparing the lives of more than 600 prisoners on death row and invalidating capital punishment legislation in more than forty states), but also because the litigators who argued in favor of abolition engineered their triumph despite the fact that precedent, the composition of the Court, and the climate of the country all seemed to be heavily stacked against them. When the Legal Defense Fund began its legal attack on the death penalty in 1963, there was scant reason to believe that the Supreme Court would be disposed toward effecting a humanitarian reform in that area. In that year three justices could not find a fourth to grant certiorari on the question whether imposing the death penalty for rape was a cruel and unusual punishment.[4] And just five years before, Chief Justice Warren and three other members of the Court's liberal bloc dismissed the possibility of invalidating the death penalty "in a day when it is still widely accepted."[5]

Eight years later, when *Furman* was argued, the federal government imposed capital punishment for twenty-three crimes (thirteen civilian and ten military) and capital legislation was still on the books in forty-one states and the District of Columbia. Moreover, in the preceding term, the Court had apparently signaled its reluctance to interfere with capital punishment by decisively rejecting a well-formulated constitutional attack on two of the procedures used in capital cases.[6] And finally, increasing fears of urban crime and campus disorder were reflected by the election of a law and order administration and the appointment of four strict constructionists to the Supreme Court. In this atmosphere, the prospects for victory appeared remote. Indeed, in his account of the *Furman* litigation,[7] Professor Michael Meltsner is merely summarizing the view held by most informed observers when he says that prior to the Court's decision it appeared that "a victory for abolition would rank among the greatest surprises in American legal history."[8]

How was the Legal Defense Fund able to effect this startling upset? In part its success can be attributed to the dedication of the lawyers associated with the project and to the guiding genius of Anthony Amsterdam, a man whom Meltsner aptly describes as "the most versatile and talented lawyer of [his] generation."[9] With Amsterdam mapping the strategy, the Fund developed a battery of constitutional arguments and raised them in every case in which the execution of a defendant was imminent. This strategy had two important results.

First, by establishing a moratorium on capital punishment, the Fund was able to change the legal issue raised: the court was confronted with the question not whether capital punishment should be abolished, but whether it should be resumed. By the time *Furman* was decided, the five-year moratorium had caused a pileup of more than 600 people on death row. An awareness that these lives hung in the balance played a significant though imponderable part in shaping the Court's decision. Although in a legal sense the Supreme Court invalidated the existing practice of capital punishment, on a more practical level the Court averted the spectacle of the bloodbath that would have marked the resumption of legalized killing.

Second, and even more significant, the constitutional arguments developed by the Fund resulted in a series of test cases that even when not immediately successful had the effect of educating the Court about various aspects of capital punishment. For example, in arguing to the Eighth Circuit in *Maxwell v. Bishop*,[10] the Fund introduced a statistical survey on the imposition of capital punishment for rape cases in fourteen southern states that showed that the death penalty was being applied discriminatorily against black men convicted of raping white women.[11] When *Maxwell* reached the Supreme Court, the Court's grant of certiorari limited the issue to the constitutionality of vesting standardless discretion in the jury to impose the death sentence.[12] Yet Amsterdam's argument to the Court brilliantly exposed the interrelationship between a standardless system and the possibility of discrimination.

I think that this Court would not, for example, sustain an Arkansas sentencing procedure which provided that every man convicted of rape should roll the dice and if it came up 7 or 11 he would die; any other number, he would live.

Actually, what Arkansas has done is worse. It is worse because I assume that the dice would not decide on the grounds of race, and it is worse because the 2 out of 12 chances are at least identical.[13]

Although the Court ultimately refused to accept either of the arguments made in *Maxwell*,[14] the effect of Amsterdam's arguments is seen in nearly all of the concurring opinions in *Furman*. A recognition that the jury-discretionary system of capital punishment results in an arbitrary and capricious, if not a discriminatory, selection of victims infused the Court's analysis and was obviously the critical factor for most if not all of the justices comprising the majority.[15]

Despite the educative effect of earlier arguments, from a legal perspective the issue presented in *Furman* created extraordinary problems for the litigators arguing in favor of abolition. Since the issue before the Court concerned the constitutionality of capital punishment under the cruel and unusual punishment clause of the Eighth Amendment, the Legal Defense Fund was faced with the initial problem of showing that a punishment was cruel and unusual despite the fact that it was widely practiced when the Eighth Amendment was adopted. Although this difficulty could be met by relying on cases holding that in applying the Eighth Amendment in changing times, the courts are to be guided by "the evolving standards of decency that mark the progress of a maturing society,"[16] the Fund was still confronted with the problem of convincing the Court that a penalty that was on the books in forty-one states and that continued to be imposed by juries was nevertheless contrary to our "evolving standards of decency." If capital punishment were really contrary to contemporary values, would not the legislature have abolished it? The fact was that the legislature had not done so; how could the Court justify itself as better able to judge our prevailing standards of decency? Amsterdam's brilliantly conceived answers to these questions formed the core of the Fund's argument:

The American people, Amsterdam argued, accept the death penalty *only* on the statute books—in theory, that is, but not in practice. The evidence demonstrates that Americans will not in fact tolerate its general, even-handed application. Our society accepts the death penalty, he contended, solely because it is applied "sparsely, and spottily to unhappy minorities." The numbers selected are so few, their plight so invisible, and their background so unappealing, that "society can readily bear to see them suffer torments which would not for a moment be accepted as penalties of general application to the populace."[17]

In short, contemporary society's rejection of capital punishment is seen in its unwillingness to allow the death penalty to be evenhandedly applied. The intolerable discrepancy between the law as stated and applied shows that the death penalty is contrary to our evolving standards of decency.

The Court's decision in *Furman* represents a historic triumph for the litigators who labored on behalf of the defendants involved in that case. Unfortunately, however, *Furman* is not the final chapter in the struggle to abolish capital punishment. Although the Court's decision apparently invalidated all death sentences imposed pursuant to a system in which the sentencing authority is vested with complete discretion as to whether a sentence of death shall be imposed,[18] three of the five justices comprising the majority reserved decision on the constitutionality of statutes imposing a mandatory sentence of death upon conviction.[19] In the wake of *Furman*, more than twenty states have reinstituted capital punishment, generally attempting to avert the impact of *Furman* by providing for some form of mandatory capital punishment.[20] In some of these states, death sentences are now being imposed much more frequently than they were under the pre-*Furman* system. In North Carolina, for example, the first half year of the new system[21] has resulted in the imposition of death sentences approximately eight times more frequently than under the jury-discretionary system formerly in effect.[22]

In the near future, the Court will have to consider the constitutionality of statutes imposing mandatory capital punishment. If those statutes are upheld, then, ironically, the decision in *Furman* may have the ultimate effect of reducing a capital defendant's chances of avoiding execution. As Justice Blackmun stated in dissent, mandatory capital punishment is "regressive . . . for it eliminates the element of mercy in the imposition of punishment."[23]

Whether mandatory capital punishment will eventually be upheld will depend in part on the way the case introducing the issue is presented and the composition of the Court at the time it is decided. Nonetheless, a proper analysis of the problem must begin by considering the rationale of the *Furman* case. Although extracting a consistent theory from the separate concurring opinions is difficult, a close reading of the five opinions yields at least two principles against which the constitutionality of mandatory capital punishment must be tested.

First, the Court's focus on the results produced by jury-discretionary capital punishment[24] indicates that *Furman* is premised on the view that such a system produces a constitutionally intolerable pattern of death sentences. Although the Court limited its holding to invalidating capital sentences imposed pursuant to the jury-discretionary system, the rationale of the concurring justices is broad enough to invalidate any system of capital punishment that allows a discretionary judgment to produce a rare, arbitrary, freakish, and discriminatory application of the death penalty.[25]

Obviously, administration of the new mandatory statutes will involve significant discretionary judgments because the statutes function in a system that is honeycombed with discretion. The prosecutor's wide discretion—both in determining what charges to bring and in accepting pleas of guilty to lesser-included charges—is particularly likely to be exercised in capital cases. An experienced trial judge explains the reason:

Since time immemorial [prosecutors] will prefer to get a definite conviction, without the tremendous expense that goes with a murder trial, the taking of a chance that a jury may not convict, or that some technical error will be made in the heat of trial which will result in a reversal by an Appellate Court.[26]

Not surprisingly, therefore, the available empirical evidence indicates that a substantial majority of defendants charged with capital offenses plead guilty to a lesser-included noncapital offense.[27]

The prosecutor is not the only possessor of discretion in our criminal justice system. The executive, through his virtually unlimited power to grant clemency, has always played a substantial role in the administration of capital punishment.[28] In addition, the jury has significant discretion—even under a mandatory system—due to its power to convict a defendant of a lesser-included noncapital offense.[29] And both trial and appellate judges have at their disposal various discretionary techniques that may cause a capital sentence to be avoided.[30]

Thus, since changing to a mandatory system will have the effect of shifting some of the discretion exercised by the jury to others (particularly the prosecutor and the executive), and thereby obscuring the visibility of the discretionary judgments, it can only increase the potential for arbitrary and discriminatory application of the death penalty. In light of this predictable practical effect, one must conclude that the mandatory statutes will exhibit all of the vices that *Furman* found antithetical to the values of the Eighth Amendment.

On a more fundamental level, since *Furman* was based on the Eighth Amendment, the Court's holding was necessarily premised upon a finding that contemporary society's de facto rejection of jury-discretionary capital sentencing indicates that capital punishment is contrary to our current standards of decency. Under this analysis, *Furman* was concerned with rarity and freakishness in the application of the death penalty less as independent constitutional concerns than as indicators of society's repudiation of capital punishment. Accepting Amsterdam's claim that the death penalty must be judged on the basis of what society does with it,[31] the Court found that under the jury-discretionary system capital punishment was imposed too arbitrarily and infrequently to withstand constitutional scrutiny.[32] Thus, the jury-discretionary form of the death penalty was merely the historical matrix within which the indicia of societal repudiation of the death penalty appeared. Accordingly, the enactment of mandatory statutes will be constitutionally relevant only if it evidences a new willingness to tolerate death as a criminal penalty when applied evenhandedly to all members of the population. But the context within which the statutes have been established makes it impossible for a court to attribute this significance to their enactment.

Although the new statutes vary in that some provide a mandatory death sentence upon conviction for first-degree murder[33] while others apply only upon conviction of more narrowly specified categories of homicide,[34] they are alike in that they neither prohibit the jury from returning a verdict for a lesser-included offense[35] nor limit the exercise of prosecutorial discretion or executive clemency. Because of the discretionary framework within which the statutes operate, legislators (and their constituents) must obviously be aware that the first-degree murder statutes will be applied in much the same way as the old jury-discretionary statutes; thus, we can confidently predict that the death penalty will continue to be imposed arbitrarily and infrequently.

In systems of capital punishment that impose the death penalty upon conviction for more narrowly defined crimes, the constitutionally relevant indicia of repudiation will be even more apparent. The narrowness of the categories will necessarily cause the death penalty to be imposed very seldom, and the arbitrary selection of victims will stem not only from the exercise of discretion by the agencies involved in the administration of justice but also and primarily from the arbitrary categories selected by the legislature in what Justice Harlan once labeled their fruitless effort "[t]o identify before the fact those characteristics of criminal homicides and their perpetrators which call for the death penalty . . . ."[36] If our "evolving standards of decency" with respect to capital punishment are measured by the extent to which we will allow the death penalty to be imposed, the enactment of statutes that allow it to be imposed only for narrowly drawn categories of homicide that cannot be meaningfully distinguished from other forms of homicide[37] provides decisive evidence of societal repudiation.

Despite the strength of the constitutional arguments in favor of abolition, the ultimate effect of the Court's decision in *Furman* remains problematic. There is a risk that the Court will uphold the constitutionality of the post-*Furman* capital legislation and thus allow the resumption of legalized killing under a system that by eliminating the jury's power to dispense mercy provides less protection to capital defendants than the system invalidated by *Furman*. Against this risk, however, must be weighed the possibility that *Furman v. Georgia* will signal not only the end of the death penalty but the beginning of an era in which a new respect for the sanctity of human life will infuse our efforts to develop a civilized and responsible system of justice.

NOTES

1. Furman v. Georgia, 408 U.S. 238 (1972).
2. The five justices comprising the majority were Brennan, Marshall, Douglas, Stewart, and White. The four justices appointed by President Nixon each wrote a dissenting opinion.
3. 408 U.S. at 309–10 (Stewart, J., concurring).
4. Rudolph v. Alabama, 375 U.S. 889 (1963).
5. Trop v. Dulles, 356 U.S. 86, 99 (1958) (plurality opinion of Warren, C.J.).
6. McGautha v. California, 402 U.S. 183 (1971) (upholding the constitutionality of procedures that vested standardless capital sentencing discretion in the jury and required the jury to determine the issue of guilt and capital punishment in a unitary procedure).
7. M. MELTSNER, CRUEL AND UNUSUAL: THE SUPREME COURT AND CAPITAL PUNISHMENT (1973).
8. M. MELTSNER, *supra* note 7, at 287.
9. *Id.* at 72.
10. 398 F.2d 138 (8th Cir. 1968), *rev'd on other grounds*, 398 U.S. 262 (1970).
11. M. MELTSNER, *supra* note 7, at 100.
12. 393 U.S. 997 (1968).
13. M. MELTSNER, *supra* note 7, at 161.
14. The Court never passed on the equal protection claim presented to the Eighth Circuit in *Maxwell*. In *McGautha* the Court rejected the claim that vesting standardless capital sentencing discretion in the jury violates due process. *See supra* note 5.
15. *See supra* note 3 and accompanying text.
16. Trop v. Dulles, 356 U.S. 86, 101 (1958) (plurality opinion of Warren, C.J.). *See* Robinson v. California, 370 U.S. 660, 666 (1962); Weems v. United States, 217 U.S. 349, 378 (1910).
17. M. MELTSNER, *supra* note 7, at 182.
18. The scope of the *Furman* rule is plain not only because the death penalties invalidated in the cases before the Court were imposed by juries with discretionary capital sentencing power, but also because in Moore v. Illinois, 408 U.S. 786 (1972), while dealing with a sentence of death imposed pursuant to a similar statute, Justice Blackmun wrote for an unanimous Court that "the Court today has ruled that the imposition of the death penalty under statutes such as those of Illinois is violative of the Eighth and Fourteenth Amendments, *Furman v. Geor-*

gia . . . . The sentence of death . . . may not now be imposed." 408 U.S. at 800. And if *Moore* could leave any doubt, the Court, at the time of *Furman* and on its authority, vacated the death sentence in some 117 other capital cases involving innumerable discretionary sentencing statutes from twenty-six states. *See* Stewart v. Massachusetts, 408 U.S. 845 (1972), and companion cases. These holdings, as well as the *Furman* majority's analysis, appear to establish that death sentences imposed pursuant to any kind of discretionary sentencing system are unconstitutional. *But see* State v. Dixon, 283 So. 2d 1 (Fla. 1973) (upholding the constitutionality of death sentences imposed by a judge upon recommendation of a jury whose discretion was guided by standards).

19. 408 U.S. at 257 (Douglas, J., concurring); *id*. at 307–09 (Stewart, J., concurring); *id*. at 310–11 (White, J., concurring).

20. *See, e.g.*, State v. Waddell, 282 N.C. 431, 444–45, 194 S.E.2d 19, 28 (1973); State v. Dickerson, 298 A.2d 761 (Del. 1972); 1973 N.M. Laws, ch. 109, § 2, *amending* N.M. STAT. ANN. § 40A-29-2 (Supp. 1973).

21. In North Carolina, as in Delaware, the new system was established when the state supreme court held that in first-degree murder cases *Furman*'s invalidation of jury-discretionary capital punishment had the effect of transforming statutes that vested the jury with capital sentencing discretion into ones that mandated a death sentence upon conviction. *See supra* note 13.

22. Between mid-June (when the post-*Waddell* system began to be applied) and the end of 1973, twenty-one persons were sentenced to death. Under the jury-discretionary system, seven persons were condemned in 1969 and three in 1970. *See* U.S. DEP'T OF JUSTICE, BUR. OF PRISONS, NATIONAL PRISONER STATISTICS, CAPITAL PUNISHMENT 1930–1970, at 21, 23 (Aug. 1971).

23. 408 U.S. at 413 (dissenting opinion of Blackmun, J.).

24. *See supra* text accompanying note 2.

25. *See, e.g.*, Justice Stewart's language quoted at note 9 *supra*.

26. State v. Faison, No. S-550-57 (Bergen County Ct. Nov. 21, 1958), *quoted in* Bedau, *Death Sentences in New Jersey*, 19 RUTGERS L. REV. 1, 30 (1964).

27. *See, e.g.*, Alschuler, *The Prosecutor's Role in Plea Bargaining*, 36 U. CHI. L. REV. 50, 53 (1968); Carney & Fuller, *A Study of Plea Bargaining in Murder Cases in Massachusetts*, 3 SUFFOLK U.L. REV. 292 (1969); Specter, Book Review, 76 YALE L.J. 604, 608 (1967). Empirical evidence also suggests that plea bargaining is even more likely to take place where a mandatory sentence is involved. *See* D. NEWMAN, CONVICTION: THE DETERMINATION OF GUILT OR INNOCENCE WITHOUT TRIAL 113–30, 178–80 (1966).

28. *See generally* Note, *Executive Clemency in Capital Cases*, 39 N.Y.U. L. REV. 136 (1964).

29. In most jurisdictions, conviction of a lesser-included noncapital offense will be sustained even if the evidence presented to the jury shows that the defendant was either guilty of the capital offense or guilty of nothing. *See, e.g.*, Taylor v. Commonwealth, 186 Va. 587, 591, 43 S.E.2d 906, 908 (1947).

30. *See, e.g.*, Stein v. New York, 346 U.S. 156, 196 (1953) (dictum):

When the penalty is death, we, like state court judges, are tempted to strain the evidence and even, in close cases, the law in order to give a doubtfully condemned man another chance.

For an analysis of a state supreme court's utilization of special standards of review in capital cases, see McDonald, *Capital Punishment in South Carolina: The End of an Era*, 24 S. CAR. L. REV. 762 (1972).

31. *See supra* text accompanying note 8.

32. Justice White comes close to explicitly articulating this analysis:

The short of it is that the policy of vesting sentencing authority primarily in juries—a decision largely motivated by the desire to mitigate the harshness of the law and to bring community judgment to bear on the sentence as well as guilt or innocence—has so effectively achieved its aims that capital punishment within the confines of the statutes now before us has for all practical purposes run its course.

408 U.S. at 313 (White, J., concurring).

33. *See, e.g.*, State v. Waddell, 282 N.C. 431, 194 S.E.2d 19 (1973).

34. *See, e.g.*, VA. CODE § 53-291 (1950) (pre-*Furman* statute imposing mandatory capital sentence upon prisoner convicted of killing a prison guard or other noninmate in the prison).

35. After analyzing the jury's traditional role in capital cases, the *Furman* dissent concluded that:

Real change [from the results produced by the discretionary system could only] be brought about if legislatures provided mandatory death sentences in such a way as to deny juries the opportunity to bring in a verdict on a lesser charge; under such a system, the death sentence could only be avoided by a verdict of acquittal.

408 U.S. at 401 (Burger, C.J., dissenting).

36. McGautha v. California, 402 U.S. 183, 204 (1971).

37. The narrowly drawn statutes generally attempt to define capital homicide according to the victim's occupational status (*e.g.*, as a police officer or prison guard). A system of capital punishment founded on this kind of distinction flies in the face of studies that show that when compared to life imprisonment, the death penalty does not deter homicidal assaults on police officers or prison guards. *See* Campin, *Does the Death Penalty Protect State Police?*, in THE DEATH PENALTY IN AMERICA 301 (H. Bedau ed., rev. ed. 1967) [hereinafter cited as H. Bedau]; Sellin, *Does the Death Penalty Protect Municipal Police?*, in H. Bedau, *supra* at 284; Sellin & Thorsten, *Homicides and Serious Assaults in American Prisons*, 14 ARISTOTEHAN UNIVERSITY OF THESSALONIKI, ANNUAL OF THE SCHOOL OF LAW AND ECONOMICS 139 (1966). Moreover, this victim-oriented system is clearly contrary to the well-accepted view that "individual culpability is not always measured by the category or the crime committed." 408 U.S. at 402 (Burger, C.J., dissenting).

A Comment on *Furman*: Update

In *Gregg v. Georgia*[1] the Court emphatically rejected the argument that the discretionary aspects of our criminal justice system render the post-*Furman* death penalty statutes unconstitutional.[2] Instead, the Court held that a jury-discretionary system of capital punishment will be valid under *Furman* so long as the legislature "ensures that the sentencing authority is given adequate information and guidance."[3] In particular, the Court emphasized the importance of providing a bifurcated procedure for apprising the sentencing body of all relevant evidence and standards so that its sentencing discretion could be appropriately channeled.[4]

Following *Furman*, the Court in *Gregg* expressed a continuing concern with avoiding the arbitrary imposition of capital punishment.[5] At the same time, in *Woodson v. North Carolina*,[6] decided on the same day as *Gregg*, the Court held mandatory capital punishment unconstitutional. One ground for the Court's decision was that mandatory capital punishment does not allow the sentencer to make an individualized judgment about whether the offender should be sentenced to die.[7] Since *Gregg* and *Woodson*, the Court has placed much greater emphasis on the need to maintain individualized sentencing than on the need to curb the sentencer's discretion in order to avoid arbitrary results. In fact, in its most recent interpretation of *Furman*, the Court held that the aggravating circumstances specified in a state death penalty statute may serve the function of merely "narrowing the category of persons convicted of murder who are eligible for the death penalty."[8] Thus, once the sentencing authority finds that a single aggravating circumstance is present, it may exercise virtually unbridled discretion in determining whether a death penalty shall be imposed.

In terms of curbing the sentencer's discretion, the difference between this system of capital punishment and the one condemned in *Furman* is very slight. In theory, of course, there is a difference. As Professor Stephen Gillers says, requiring the sentencer to find an aggravating circumstance before considering the imposition of the death penalty "potentially reduces the number of persons subject to arbitrary action simply by reducing the pool of capital defendants."[9] Under most statutes, however, the aggravating circumstances taken together are so broad that almost any traditional first-degree murder case could be found to include at least one of them.[10] Thus, although the new death penalty statutes do provide standards to guide the sentencer's exercise of discretion, the guidelines may be so broad and amorphous as to have the effect of vesting the capital sentencer with almost the same total discretion that the pre-*Furman* statutes vested in the sentencing jury.[11] Accordingly, if there is a significant difference between our present system of capital punishment and the one that existed before *Furman*, it does not lie in the restraints placed on the exercise of capital sentencing discretion.

NOTES

1. 428 U.S. 153 (1976).
2. *Id*. at 199 (plurality opinion of Stewart, J.).
3. *Id*. at 195 (plurality opinion of Stewart, J.).
4. *Id*.
5. *See* 428 U.S. at 198.
6. 428 U.S. 280 (1976).
7. 428 U.S. at 303–05.
8. Zant v. Stephens, 103 S. Ct. 2733, 2742 (1983).
9. Gillers, *Deciding Who Dies*, 129 U. PA. L. REV. 1, 27 (1980).
10. For example, the Georgia statute, which is the model most current death penalty statutes now follow, provides nine aggravating circumstances for the capital crime of murder. See GA. CODE § 27-2534.1(b) (1933) (Supp. 1982). Among them are most cases of felony-murder, including those involving the felony of aggravated battery, § 27-2534(b)(2), all cases in which the murder was committed for the purpose "of receiving money or any other thing of monetary value," § 27-2534.1(b)(4), all cases in which the murderer "has a substantial history of serious assaultive criminal convictions," § 27-2534.1(b)(1), and all cases in which the murderer either directed another or was directed by another to commit the crime, § 27-2534.1(b)(6). It is pretty difficult to identify any type of murder that could not properly be found to fall within one of these categories.
11. For an elaboration of this point, see Ledewitz, *The Requirement of Death: Mandatory Language in the Pennsylvania Death Penalty Statute*, 21 DUQ. L. REV. 103, 121 n.90 (1982).

Witherspoon Revisited: Exploring the Tension between Witherspoon and Furman

Witherspoon v. Illinois[1] marked the Supreme Court's first solid entry into the capital punishment thicket. Although the presence of a capital sentence undoubtedly had influenced the Court in many previous cases,[2] *Witherspoon* was the first case in which the Court actually invalidated a procedure that played an integral part in the administration of the death penalty.

In *Witherspoon* the defendant was tried pursuant to an Illinois statute that vested the jury with discretion as to whether a defendant convicted of first-degree murder should be sentenced to death or life imprisonment. At the time of the defendant's trial, another Illinois statute permitted a challenge for cause of any juror who stated that he had conscientious scruples against capital punishment or that he opposed it. The trial court excluded forty-seven veniremen because of their views on the death penalty, including thirty-nine who were not questioned as to whether their views would compel them to vote invariably against the death penalty. In reversing the death penalty imposed by this jury, the Supreme Court held that the death penalty can never be carried out

if the jury that imposed or recommended it was chosen by excluding veniremen for cause simply because they voiced general objections to the death penalty or expressed conscientious or religious scruples against its infliction. No defendant can constitutionally be put to death at the hands of a tribunal so selected.[3]

In a footnote, the Court amplified this holding by stating that veniremen

cannot be excluded for cause simply because they indicate that there are some kinds of cases in which they would refuse to recommend capital punishment. And a prospective juror cannot be expected to say in advance of trial whether he would in fact vote for the extreme penalty in the case before him. The most that can be demanded of a venireman in this regard is that he be willing to *consider* all of the penalties provided by state law, and that he not be irrevocably committed, before the trial has begun, to vote against the penalty of death regardless of the facts and circumstances that might emerge in the course of the proceedings. If the *voir dire* testimony in a given case indicates that veniremen were excluded on any broader basis than this, the death sentence cannot be carried out even if applicable statutory or case law in the relevant jurisdiction would appear to support only a narrower ground of exclusion.[4]

The Court clarified the intended scope of this language by adding that its decision has no bearing on a state's power to exclude veniremen who make it

> unmistakably clear (1) that they would *automatically* vote against the imposition of capital punishment without regard to any evidence that might be developed at the trial of the case before them, or (2) that their attitude toward the death penalty would prevent them from making an impartial decision as to the defendant's *guilt*.[5]

Thus, at a minimum, *Witherspoon* held that under a system of jury-discretionary capital punishment, a venireman may not be excluded for cause because of his views on the death penalty, unless (1) his views are unmistakably clear, *and* (2) his views would compel him to vote automatically against imposition of the death penalty *or* would prevent him from making the required impartial determination of guilt or innocence.

Witherspoon was significant not only because of its immediate impact—the Court's retroactive holding[6] resulted in the immediate vacation of about 150 capital sentences and provided ammunition for attacking nearly all of the remaining pre-*Witherspoon* death penalties[7]—but also because the constitutional evaluation of death-qualification committed the Court to scrutinizing other closely intertwined procedural aspects of capital punishment[8] and to considering the constitutionality of the pattern of death sentences produced by the total system of capital punishment.[9] Moreover, since *Witherspoon* vacated a large number of death sentences on procedural grounds, it highlighted the legal system's capacity for allowing a seemingly arbitrary infliction of the death penalty[10] and thereby may have hastened the *Furman*[11] decision, which invalidated all death sentences imposed pursuant to a system of jury-discretionary capital punishment because of the Court's perception that the prevailing system resulted in an arbitrary and uneven application of capital punishment.

Although *Furman* laid waste to almost all the then-existing capital punishment legislation,[12] the rapid enactment of new legislation renewed the capital punishment controversy while shifting the issues involved to a new legal terrain. Broadly speaking, the post-*Furman* statutes may be divided into two categories: "mandatory" statutes, which impose an automatic sentence of death upon conviction of a specifically defined crime,[13] and "guided discretionary" statutes, which provide the jury with a list of aggravating and mitigating circumstances and allow or require them to impose the death penalty for murder[14] (and in some cases rape),[15] if at least one aggravating circumstance and no mitigating circumstances are present. Particular death penalties imposed pursuant to these statutes may be attacked on procedural grounds. In addition, the system of capital punishment involved may be attacked broadly on the basis that the new legislation does not remedy the defects perceived by the majority in *Furman* or is otherwise invalid under the cruel and unusual punishment clause of the Eighth Amendment.[16]

In the post-*Furman* era, the implications of *Witherspoon* will be significant in several aspects. First, and most obviously, *Witherspoon*'s holding limiting the prosecutor's right to a death-qualified jury under jury-discretionary statutes may be extended to limit or eliminate the prosecutor's right to a death-qualified jury under either of the new statutes. If the extension is made, *Witherspoon* becomes relevant to the question whether the new systems of capital punishment have removed the constitutional defects perceived in *Furman*. Moreover, the rationale applied by the Court in *Witherspoon* may have Eighth Amendment implications relevant to the Court's ultimate decision on the constitutionality of capital punishment. The first part of this article deals with the limitations imposed by *Witherspoon* on the new systems' use of a death-qualified jury and with the possible constitutional implications of these limitations. The second part explores *Witherspoon*'s underlying rationale and its potential effect on the constitutionality of death penalties imposed by the new systems.

Witherspoon's Restrictions upon Death-Qualification Applied to the New Systems of Capital Punishment

Death-Qualification under Mandatory Systems of Capital Punishment

Witherspoon's Applicability

At least one state has held that since the *Witherspoon* case involved a jury-discretionary system of capital punishment, *Witherspoon*'s holding imposed no restrictions on a state's right to have a death-qualified jury administer a mandatory system of capital punishment.[17] Such a holding seems to take insufficient account of *Witherspoon*'s rationale. Central to *Witherspoon*'s result was a finding that with respect to the penalty determination "the jury fell woefully short of that impartiality to which the [defendant] was entitled under the Sixth and Fourteenth Amendments."[18] Thus, whenever a death penalty determination is involved, *Witherspoon* mandates that such a determination be made by an impartial jury.[19] The state might argue that under a mandatory system of capital punishment, the jury is making no penalty determination at all; it is simply adjudicating the guilt or innocence of the defendant. According to this argument, there is no need for a jury impartial as to penalty since under a mandatory statute the jury does not determine penalty. Therefore, the state should be free from *Witherspoon*'s restrictions on death-qualification. But the argument proves too much: if the jury is not imposing a penalty but is only adjudicating guilt, the state has no interest in the jurors' views on capital punishment. When the jury in a criminal case is confined to a determination of guilt or innocence, it is generally improper for either side to refer to punishment,[20] much less to make it a subject of inquiry in the preliminary voir dire.[21] Through the practice of death-qualification, the state gratuitously impresses upon the jury that they are dealing with a capital case, one in which they will be forced to make a death penalty determination. Given this context, the state should not be permitted to ignore reality and claim that the jury is not making a death penalty determination.[22]   From the defendant's viewpoint, there is no difference between a death sentence expressly imposed by the jury and one following directly upon a jury's conviction of guilt. To him, both are imposed by the jury. On the subject of death penalties imposed by the jury, *Witherspoon* was adamant:

Whatever else might be said of capital punishment, it is at least clear that its imposition by a hanging jury cannot be squared with the constitution. The State of Illinois has stacked the deck against the petitioner. To execute this death sentence would deprive him of his life without due process of law.[23]

This statement reflects a concern for ensuring that no capital sentence be imposed by a jury that does not represent accurately the community views on capital punishment. In view of the breadth of the principle articulated, it would appear unduly restrictive to apply *Witherspoon* to only one of the many systems used in making a penalty determination. Whether capital punishment is imposed pursuant to a discretionary sentencing decision or pursuant to an adjudication of guilt, its imposition by a "hanging jury" is prohibited. In order to ensure that the defendant has the "luck of the draw" in an "unstacked deck," *Witherspoon*'s prohibitions on death qualification must be observed.

If *Witherspoon* is applied to a system of mandatory capital punishment, its first exception to the prohibition against death-qualification presents no difficulty. The crucial issue concerns the applicability and scope of the second exception. *Witherspoon* states that its holding has no bearing on a state's power to exclude veniremen who make it "unmistakably clear . . . that their attitude toward the death penalty would prevent them from making an impartial decision as to the defendant's *guilt*."[24] A capacity to "make an impartial decision" certainly implies a state of mind conforming to the principle that the verdict be rendered upon the law and the evidence.[25] The state may argue that a venireman meets the test for exclusion whenever he unequivocally states that in *some* cases involving the type of crime with which the defendant is charged, his views on capital punishment would prevent him from rendering a verdict in accordance with the law and the evidence.

However, allowing exclusion for cause in this type of situation would clash with the underlying rationale and some of the language of *Witherspoon*. *Witherspoon* expressly stated that veniremen cannot be excluded because they "indicate that there are some kinds of cases in which they would refuse to [impose] capital punishment."[26] Excluding veniremen who indicate that there are some cases in which they could not vote for a verdict mandating capital punishment would have precisely this effect. Moreover, the basic premise of *Witherspoon* is that a capital defendant is entitled to an impartial penalty determination; the decision whether a man deserves to live or die must be made on scales which are not tipped deliberately toward death.[27] *Witherspoon*'s detailed holding attempts to delineate the precise type of death-qualification which will tip the scales towards death: "The state cross[es] the line of neutrality," whenever it goes beyond eliminating veniremen who "stat[e] in advance of trial that they would not even consider returning a verdict of death."[28] In a mandatory system, any exclusion beyond that authorized in the first exception clashes with the underlying rationale of the *Witherspoon* rule and unduly tips the scales towards death.

If this analysis appears to accord insufficient weight to *Witherspoon*'s second exception, it should be remembered that the second exception was articulated at a time when the prevailing system of capital punishment gave the jury two distinct functions: adjudicating guilt and making a capital penalty determination. Since a venireman opposed to capital punishment would be able to block the imposition of the death penalty without distorting his adjudication of guilt,[29] there would be scant reason for him to believe that his opposition capital punishment would render him incapable of rendering an impartial verdict.[30] In this context, therefore, there was no reason to perceive the second exception as clashing with the basic line of neutrality established in *Witherspoon*. Under a mandatory system, however, there is an obvious clash between *Witherspoon*'s basic rule of neutrality and the second exception to the stated rule. If the second exception is applied, the scales are tipped toward the death penalty. This violates *Witherspoon*'s principle of neutrality.

Based on the opinion itself, it would appear that *Witherspoon*'s line of neutrality should be preserved even if the second exception has to be eliminated. *Witherspoon*'s prohibition against allowing the selection of a jury that is tipped away from neutrality appears to be uncompromising:

[A] State *may not* entrust the determination of whether a man should live or die to a tribunal organized to return a verdict of death.[31]

. . . the decision whether a man deserves to live or die *must be made* on scales that are not deliberately tipped toward death.[32]

Whatever else might be said of capital punishment, it is at least clear that its imposition by a hanging jury *cannot be* squared with the constitution.[33]

In contrast, *Witherspoon* was quite explicit in stating that the two exceptions to the basic rule established were not part of the holding.[34] It emphasized that "nothing we say today bears upon the power of the state" to exclude veniremen in these situations.[35] The clear implication is that the exceptions to *Witherspoon*'s rule will be recognized only to the extent that they do not infringe upon the basic line of neutrality established by the Court. Where the exceptions do so infringe, adherence to *Witherspoon*'s basic rule of neutrality must prevail.

Analysis of the competing interests involved leads to the same conclusion. *Witherspoon*'s retroactive holding[36] reflects a judgment that the defendant's interest in having an impartial penalty determination is a fundamental one.[37] Such a judgment seems appropriate. As Justice Stewart, concurring in *Furman v. Georgia*,[38] recognized, "the penalty of death differs from all other punishments not in degree but in kind."[39] Because of the magnitude of the stakes involved, the defendant's interest in a constitutionally fair penalty determination should not be compromised.[40] In measuring the state's interest, it is important to weigh both the interest's legitimacy and the availability of alternative techniques for protecting the interest.[41] In the present situation, the state's ostensible interest is the legitimate one of protecting an impartial verdict. That interest can be protected by other means. When a defendant is charged with an offense carrying a mandatory death sentence, the state is not precluded from charging the defendant with lesser-included offenses carrying sentences up to life imprisonment. So long as the jury will render an impartial verdict on these charges, the state's interest in obtaining an impartial verdict is protected with respect to these offenses. With respect to the capital offense, the state has an additional interest in delegating the decision whether a death sentence will be imposed to a group of citizens who will not refuse to vote for a verdict resulting in a death penalty because of any conscientious scruples they may have. However, this is exactly the interest which *Witherspoon* held to be impermissible.[42] On balance, therefore, the defendant's interest should clearly prevail. Under a mandatory system, *Witherspoon* should absolutely prohibit exclusion of veniremen for opposition to capital punishment unless a venireman unequivocally states that he will refuse in all cases to vote for a verdict carrying a mandatory death penalty or that he will not be able to render an impartial verdict on charges against the defendant that do not carry an automatic sentence of death.

Death-Qualification under a Guided Discretionary System of Capital Punishment

With respect to the guided discretionary statutes, *Witherspoon*'s application is clearer. Patterned on the provisions outlined in section 201.6 of the Model Penal Code,[43] the guided discretionary statutes generally provide that the jury shall impose a sentence of death upon a finding of at least one aggravating circumstance and no mitigating circumstances.[44] Despite their increased complexity, these statutes are similar to the mandatory statutes in that upon the jury's finding of certain circumstances both require the imposition of a death sentence.[45] However, there are two distinctions between the two types of statutes, both of which indicate more clearly that *Witherspoon* applies. First, whereas under the mandatory statute a capital sentence is imposed by law, a jury administering a guided discretionary statute actually imposes the death sentence. This formal distinction makes *Witherspoon*'s language prohibiting the "imposition" of a death sentence by a "hanging jury"[46] more directly applicable to guided discretionary statutes.[47] Secondly, whereas under a mandatory statute, the jury considers only the question of guilt, a jury administering a guided discretionary statute makes separate determinations of guilt and sentence. Because of the jury's dual function the conflict that develops between the second exception and *Witherspoon*'s underlying rationale when the case is applied to mandatory statutes is not present here.[48] In the context of a guided discretionary statute, *Witherspoon* precludes exclusion of a venireman for opposition to capital punishment, unless the venireman unequivocally states that he will refuse in all cases to vote for a death penalty[49] or that he will be unable to render an impartial verdict.

Constitutional Implications of *Witherspoon*'s Limitations on Death-Qualification

The Mandatory Statutes

The potential reverberations of *Witherspoon*'s restrictions on death-qualification are most striking in the case of the mandatory statutes. In *Furman*, the two pivotal justices, White and Stewart,[50] reserved decision on the constitutionality of mandatory capital punishment and appeared to premise their judgment on the view that a system of capital punishment is unconstitutional when, by vesting discretion with the jury, it permits the arbitrary and infrequent application of capital punishment.[51] In view of these objections to the pre-*Furman* system of capital punishment, the mandatory statutes were enacted with the objective of completely eliminating the jury's capital sentencing discretion. However, in light of *Witherspoon*'s restrictions on death-qualification, the new statutes do not succeed in their objective.

Under *Witherspoon*, veniremen who state that they would not always be able to return capital verdicts in accordance with the evidence would have to be included on the jury.[52] Thus, if the capital crime were first-degree murder, jurors who would sometimes refuse to return capital verdicts despite their view that the evidence warranted a finding of first-degree murder would have to be included. In view of the substantial portion of the population fitting within this category,[53] there is a significant probability that any given jury would contain at least one juror who would refuse to vote for a capital verdict in some cases where the evidence warranted such a verdict.[54] A jury containing one or more such veniremen would in some cases be unwilling to vote for a capital verdict, even though every juror was convinced beyond a reasonable doubt that the evidence mandated a finding of first-degree murder. In such cases, the jury would be directly exercising its discretion to dispense mercy because it deemed the death penalty an inappropriate punishment.

Of course, this was exactly the function fulfilled by the juries administering the jury-discretionary statutes condemned by the Supreme Court in *Furman*. The only difference between the two types of juries is that whereas those administering the pre-*Furman* statutes were vested by the capital sentencing statutes with standardless capital sentencing discretion, those administering the post-*Furman* mandatory statutes are vested with this discretionary power not by the terms of the sentencing statute, but as a result of *Witherspoon*'s restrictions on death-qualification.

Arguably, this formal distinction, between a statute that expressly provides for jury discretion and one that allows it because of the implications of *Witherspoon*, could be used to support the constitutionality of the mandatory statutes. In condemning the jury-discretionary statutes in *Furman*, both Justices White and Stewart identified as a salient feature of the statutes that the "legislative will is not frustrated if the penalty is never imposed."[55] Justice White gave particular weight to this point, emphasizing that

legislative judgment with respect to the death penalty loses much of its force when viewed in the light of the recurring practice of delegating sentencing authority to the jury and the fact that a jury, in its own discretion and without violating its trust or any statutory policy, may refuse to impose the death penalty no matter what the circumstances of the crime.[56]

Clearly, the statutory policy is violated when the jurors exercise a sentencing discretion that is not explicitly granted by the terms of the statute. Since the fatal discretion is not inherent in the statute, and in fact contravenes the legislative will, it cannot be said that the statute itself violates *Furman*. Ultimately, however, the force of this argument is less than compelling. To Justices White and Stewart, the primary significance of the legislative grant of discretion to the jury under the pre-*Furman* death penalty statutes was that it "permit[ted] this unique penalty to be so wantonly and so freakishly applied."[57] If the jury in fact exercises unguided discretion, whether this discretion is directly or implicitly conferred would appear to make no difference. The same capacity for arbitrary and infrequent application of the death penalty exists. And, therefore, a strong argument emerges that because of the jury discretion created by *Witherspoon*, the mandatory statutes are unconstitutional under *Furman*.

The Guided Discretionary Statutes

With respect to the guided discretionary statutes, the analysis is basically similar. Although there is a strong argument that the delegation of any discretionary capital sentencing authority to the jury is unconstitutional under *Furman*,[58] it can be argued that by channeling the jury's exercise of discretion, these statutes provide sufficient safeguards against the arbitrary and infrequent application of capital punishment to distinguish them from the statutes condemned in *Furman*.[59] Under the Pennsylvania statute,[60] the jury is directed to impose the death penalty if they find that a first-degree murder was "committed by means of torture"[61] (or if one of several other aggravating circumstances is found) and if there is no finding of one of three mitigating circumstances (i.e., "the age, lack of maturity, or youth of the defendant at the time of killing").[62] Although juries may disagree as to the meaning of terms such as "torture" and "lack of maturity,"[63] these terms arguably provide it with directions that, while limiting the types of cases that will be subject to the death penalty, increase the probability that like cases will be treated alike. Thus, in cases where a defendant has committed first-degree murder through means any juror would characterize as "torture" and no mitigating circumstances are present, the death penalty will be imposed. Arguably, the possibility of arbitrary and infrequent application of the death penalty has been eliminated or at least reduced, because it will no longer be possible to point to any other similar cases (i.e., involving "torture" and no mitigating circumstances) where the jury declined to impose the death penalty.

However, as in the case of the mandatory statutes,[64] this argument is undercut by the effect of *Witherspoon*. A venireman who would refuse to impose the death penalty in some cases where he would find that first-degree murder was committed by "torture" and no statutorily defined mitigating circumstances were present could not be excluded.[65] Thus, in all cases where even one such venireman was present on the jury, the certainty that the death penalty would be imposed upon a finding of the statutorily defined circumstances would be dissipated. The effect of *Witherspoon* would be to create a further exercise of discretion that would in turn increase the potential for arbitrary and uneven application of the death penalty.

Moreover, the force of Justices White's and Stewart's dictum is less compelling in this situation than in one involving a system of mandatory capital punishment. The state could argue that in view of the defined "aggravating" and "mitigating" circumstances, a jury could not "refuse to impose the death penalty no matter what the circumstances of the crime" without "violating" a "statutory policy."[66] However, the defined circumstances are generally so amorphous and subject to individual definition that it would be difficult to say that the legislative policy really directs that a death penalty should be imposed in any give case.[67] Thus, the argument that the implications of *Witherspoon* render the guided discretionary statute unconstitutional under *Furman* is at least as strong as the claim that the mandatory statutes are unconstitutional.

Witherspoon's Effect on the Ultimate Question of the Constitutionality of Capital Punishment

The Conflict between *Witherspoon* and *Furman*

From the foregoing, it appears that there is considerable tension between *Witherspoon* and *Furman*. Whereas *Furman* places restrictions on the extent to which a state may use a jury-discretionary system in applying capital punishment, *Witherspoon* forces the state to vest a greater degree of discretion in juries administering the new systems of capital punishment. Thus, in administering a new death penalty statute, the state may be caught in a dilemma under which death penalties imposed in compliance with *Furman* are invalid under *Witherspoon* and death penalties imposed in compliance with *Witherspoon* are invalid under *Furman*.

Further analysis of *Witherspoon* reveals that this conflict is not accidental but stems directly from the underlying rationale of the two cases. *Witherspoon*'s central premise was that "a state may not entrust the determination of whether a man should live or die to a tribunal organized to return a verdict of death."[68] As Justice White points out in dissent, however, this premise is subject to challenge, because under prior decisions fixing the punishment for a given offense is a legislative, not a judicial, function "subject only to constitutional limitations, more particularly the eighth amendment."[69] Using this principle as his starting point, Justice White argues that:

The Court does not deny that the legislature can impose a particular penalty, including death, on all persons convicted of certain crimes. Why, then, should it be disabled from delegating the penalty decision to a group who will impose the death penalty more often than would a group differently chosen?[70]

The Court directly responds to this question in a footnote that begins by emphasizing that the Illinois statute did not by its terms make the death penalty mandatory or preferred but rather provided that it would be "an optional form of punishment which [the jury remains] free to select or reject as it [sees] fit."[71] The majority then asserts that "one of the most important functions any jury can perform in making such a selection is to maintain a link between contemporary community values and the penal system. . . ."[72] As Professor Bickel has pointed out, however, this portion of the Court's response does not adequately meet Justice White's objection because

on Mr. Justice White's view, which precisely fits the situation, Illinois had expressed a community value through its legislature. It had said that the death penalty was somewhat preferred and that the decision whether or not to impose it should be made by citizens who were unsqueamish about it.[73]

Since the construction of state law is the exclusive province of the state's highest court,[74] Illinois's delegation of capital sentencing responsibility to a group of citizens "who were unsqueamish about" imposing capital punishment could not be invalidated in the absence of a determination that this legislative policy was unconstitutional. The Court directly premised its finding of unconstitutionality on the due process clause.[75] However, in describing the "link between contemporary community values and the penal system" as one without which the determination of punishment could hardly reflect "the evolving standards of decency that mark the progress of a maturing society,"[76] the Court obliquely referred to the cruel and unusual punishment clause of the Eighth Amendment. The quoted language is taken from the plurality opinion of *Trop v. Dulles*[77] and represents one variation of the standard to be applied in measuring penal legislation against this clause.[78]

Thus, it can be argued that *Witherspoon* is based on a determination that for reasons drawn from the Eighth Amendment, the death penalty may be imposed only when a jury of citizens accurately reflecting the community's views on capital punishment makes an individualized judgment that this uniquely harsh penalty is appropriate. This determination leads to the conclusion that mandatory capital punishment is unconstitutional. If an individualized judgment in each particular case is required, and even a legislative delegation to those who are relatively unsqueamish is precluded, a wholesale legislative determination that the death penalty shall be imposed for certain crimes without any individualized consideration whatsoever is patently unconstitutional.

In light of *Witherspoon*'s underlying rationale, the basis for the tension between *Witherspoon* and *Furman* becomes apparent. Whereas *Witherspoon* requires an individualized discretionary death penalty determination by the jury, *Furman* condemns death penalties imposed pursuant to systems that vest the exercise of individualized discretion in the jury.[79] However, this does not mean that the two cases are inconsistent. While *Witherspoon* condemns mandatory capital punishment, *Furman* does not uphold its constitutionality. Although only two members of the *Furman* majority specifically condemned all forms of capital punishment,[80] the three justices who based their judgments on more limited grounds did not indicate a belief that mandatory capital punishment would be constitutionally valid; they simply reserved judgment on this question.[81] Moreover, without discussing the constitutionality as such of mandatory capital punishment, the four dissenting justices clearly expressed the view that when measured against "our evolving standards of decency," this system of capital punishment is less valid than the system condemned in *Furman*, because, as Justice Blackmun stated, the mandatory system "is regressive and of an antique mold, for it eliminates the element of mercy in the imposition of punishment. I thought we had passed beyond that point in our criminology long ago."[82]

Thus, *Furman* does not overrule *Witherspoon*. However, reconciliation of the two holdings may lead to the conclusion that no system of capital punishment can withstand constitutional scrutiny. By requiring an individualized determination as to whether capital punishment will be imposed, the implications of *Witherspoon* outlaw any system of mandatory capital punishment;[83] *Furman*, read literally, eliminates all other systems by invalidating death penalties imposed pursuant to systems vesting capital sentencing discretion in the jury.[84] *Furman* may be read more narrowly as eliminating only those systems of capital punishment that vest the jury with a sentencing discretion that creates the potential for arbitrary, infrequent, and discriminatory application of the death penalty.[85] Even under this construction, however, it is difficult to find that any death penalty will be constitutionally valid under both *Witherspoon* and *Furman*. By its determination that the death penalty can be imposed only on an individualized basis by juries accurately reflecting community values on capital punishment, *Witherspoon* necessarily permits wide divergence in the standards employed by the various juries called upon to make a capital sentencing determination.

In making an individualized judgment, representatives of some communities may be willing to impose the death penalty in most cases authorized by the legislature, whereas representatives of other communities may be much more selective about the imposition of capital punishment. Moreover, as an individualized determination implies, the unique features of any given case may have a great deal of bearing on any particular jury's judgment. In short, it is simply impossible to require individualized sentencing determinations that accurately reflect community values and at the same time expect these sentencing determinations to be made in accordance with anything close to uniform standards. In the words of Justice Stewart, we are again confronted with "legal systems that permit this unique penalty to be so wantonly and so freakishly imposed."[86] The only viable solution to this dilemma is to abolish all forms of capital punishment.

The Court is not required to read *Witherspoon* and *Furman* as abolishing all forms of capital punishment. *Witherspoon*, decided in 1968 by a divided Court, did not directly hold that mandatory capital punishment is unconstitutional or that an individualized sentencing determination by a jury accurately reflecting community values is a prerequisite to a constitutionally valid death sentence. *Furman*, a 5-4 per curiam decision with no majority opinion, decided only that death sentences imposed pursuant to the statutes then before the Court were unconstitutional. However, the implications of the two decisions provide a profound insight into capital punishment's inherent deficiencies. The insight was expressed by Professor Charles Black in the following general terms: "Though the justice of God may indeed ordain that some should die, the justice of man is altogether and always insufficient for saying who these may be."[87] Based on the perceptions of the Court expressed in *Witherspoon* and *Furman*, Professor Black's thought could be rephrased in specific legal terms as follows: Although capital punishment per se may be theoretically constitutional, there is no system for administering this uniquely harsh punishment that will ensure to defendants both the individualized discretionary consideration and the freedom from arbitrary and capricious results that "our evolving standards of decency" demand.

NOTES

The author would like to acknowledge his gratitude to his friend JoAnn Stone, who encouraged him to write this article, and his research assistant Frank England, who verified many of the footnotes.

1. 391 U.S. 510 (1968).

2. *Compare* Powell v. Alabama, 287 U.S. 45 (1932) (holding a defendant has an absolute right to counsel in a capital case) *with* Betts v. Brady, 316 U.S. 455 (1942) (deciding defendant's right to counsel in noncapital cases on a case-by-case basis). *See also* Reid v. Covert, 354 U.S. 1, 77 (1957) (Harlan, J., concurring); Stein v. New York, 346 U.S. 156, 196 (1953) ("When the penalty is death, we, like state court judges, are tempted to strain the evidence and even, in close cases, the law in order to give a doubtfully condemned man another chance.") (dictum).

3. 391 U.S. at 522–23.

4. *Id*. at 522 n.21 (emphasis in original).

5. *Id*. at 522–23 n.21 (emphasis in original).

6. *Id*. at 523 n.23.

7. In almost any case in which capital punishment is imposed by a jury, defense could argue later that the *Witherspoon* requirements were not complied with in the selection of the jury. At the time *Witherspoon* was decided, most states provided for death-qualified juries and either specifically allowed exclusion of scrupled veniremen on much wider grounds than those authorized in *Witherspoon* or in practice allowed challenges for cause of scrupled veniremen where the rigid *Witherspoon* requirements were not met. *See generally* Comment, *Jury Selection and the Death Penalty*: Witherspoon *in the Lower Courts*, 37 U. Chi. L. Rev. 759 (1970).

8. For example, the practice of death-qualification seemed closely connected to the then almost universal practice of giving the jury total discretion as to whether or not the death penalty should be imposed upon conviction of a capital crime. The Court upheld the constitutionality of this procedure in the face of a due process attack in McGautha v. California, 402 U.S. 183 (1971). *But see infra* note 9.

9. In Furman v. Georgia, 408 U.S. 238 (1972), the Court held that death sentences imposed pursuant to the jury-discretionary system considered in *McGautha* were unconstitutional under the cruel and unusual punishment clause of the Eighth Amendment.

10. For example, Richard Speck, the convicted killer of seven nurses, was able to have his death sentence vacated on *Witherspoon* grounds. See Speck v. Illinois, 41 Ill. 2d 177, 242 N.E.2d 208 (1968), *rev'd and remanded in part*, 403 U.S. 946 (1971). On the other hand, a perpetrator of a less heinous crime who was sentenced to death after pleading guilty or after a jury trial in which no *Witherspoon* violation occurred in the selection of the jury would not be entitled to this relief.

11. *See* Furman v. Georgia, 408 U.S. 238, 293 (1972) (Brennan, J., concur-

ring); *id*. at 249–52 (Douglas, J., concurring); *id*. at 309–10 (Stewart, J., concurring); *id*. at 313 (White, J., concurring); *id*. at 364–65 (Marshall, J., concurring).

12. *See id*. at 417 (Powell, J., dissenting):
The Court's judgment removes the death sentences previously imposed on some 600 persons awaiting punishment in state and federal prisons throughout the country. At least for the present, it also bars the States and the Federal Government from seeking sentences of death for defendants awaiting trial on charges for which capital punishment was heretofore a potential alternative.

13. IND. CODE § 35-13-4-1(1) (1973) (murder of any police officer, corrections employee, or fireman acting in the line of duty); N.C. GEN. STAT. § 14-17 (1973) (first-degree murder), § 14-21 (1974) (first-degree rape); VA. CODE § 18.2-31 (1975) (kidnapping with murder, murder for hire, murder of prison employee).

14. PA. STAT. ANN. tit. 18, § 1311 (Purdon 1974) (death sentence imposed if jury, in addition to convicting of first-degree murder, finds defendant guilty of at least one statutory aggravating circumstance in the absence of a statutory mitigating circumstance); FLA. STAT. ANN. § 921.141 (West 1974) (jury renders advisory sentence to court based upon statutory aggravating and mitigating circumstances; however, judge makes final determination as to whether or not capital sentence will be imposed).

15. GA. CODE ANN. § 26-2001 (1968).

16. For example, it could be argued that a particular death penalty statute was constitutionally excessive in the sense that it provided for imposition of penalties disproportionate to the gravity of the offense, see Weems v. United States, 217 U.S. 349 (1909), or that the death penalty per se is in violation of the cruel and unusual punishment clause. *Compare* People v. Anderson, 6 Cal. 3d 628, 493 P.2d 880, 100 Cal. Rptr. 152 (1972).

17. Justus v. State, 542 P.2d 598 (Okla. Crim. App. 1975).

18. 391 U.S. at 518.

19. The underlying rationale relied on by the Court to support this conclusion is that "a state may not entrust the determination of whether a man should live or die to a tribunal organized to return a verdict of death." 391 U.S. at 521. For an analysis of the implications of this rationale, see *infra* notes 73–83 and accompanying text.

20. *See, e.g.*, Chapman v. United States, 443 F.2d 917 (10th Cir. 1971) (failure to allow comment on mandatory minimum sentence for narcotics violation not error); Jackson v. State, 2 Ala. App. 226, 57 So. 110 (1911) (refusal to allow defense counsel to state the penalty for embezzlement held proper); State v. Harris, 258 La. 720, 247 So. 2d 847 (1971) (refusal to allow defense counsel to tell the jury the mandatory minimum sentence for robbery held proper); Toone v. State, 144 Tex. Crim. 98, 161 S.W.2d 90 (1942) (upholding refusal to allow defense counsel to tell the jury that conviction of forgery would result in a life sentence).

21. Although "[p]reservation of the opportunity to prove actual bias is a guarantee of a defendant's right to an impartial jury," Dennis v. United States, 339 U.S. 162, 171–72 (1950), numerous cases have held that where a venireman states that he can render an impartial verdict based solely on the evidence

presented at trial, in the absence of unusual circumstances, defense counsel is precluded from inquiring into particular matters that might affect the venireman's impartiality. *See, e.g.*, Connors v. United States, 158 U.S. 408 (1895) (upholding refusal to allow voir dire questioning about venireman's political beliefs in election fraud case).

The possibility that a particular venireman's awareness of the penalty will in fact render him unable to return an impartial verdict may be protected against by a general inquiry as to whether the venireman knows of any reason why he would be unable to render an impartial verdict. *See* 158 U.S. at 414–15 (dictum).

22. The North Carolina Supreme Court has held that the jury trying a first-degree murder case must be told that the penalty upon conviction is death. *See* State v. Britt, 285 N.C. 256, 204 S.E.2d 817 (1974). Such a requirement appears to have no other purpose than to impress upon the jury the fact that they will be required to make a death penalty determination.

23. 391 U.S. at 523.

24. *Id*. at 522–23 n.21 (emphasis in original).

25. *See* United States v. Woods, 299 U.S. 123, 145–46 (1936) (dictum).

26. 391 U.S. at 522 n.21.

27. *Id*. at 521–22 n.20.

28. *Id*. at 520.

29. At the time *Witherspoon* was decided most states provided that a death penalty could not be imposed unless the jury unanimously agreed that death was the appropriate punishment. *See, e.g.*, PA. STAT. ANN. tit. 18, § 4701 (Purdon 1959) (requiring judge to impose sentence of life where jury disagrees as to whether defendant should be sentenced to death or life imprisonment). *But see* FLA. STAT. ANN. § 794.011 (West 1974) (rape punished by death unless a majority of the jury recommends mercy).

30. Of course, where disagreement among the jurors on the issue of capital punishment would result in a new penalty proceeding (*e.g.*, CAL. PENAL CODE § 190.1 (West 1973)), a venireman conceivably might be concerned that his vote for a guilty verdict might result eventually in the imposition of a death sentence. However, this possibility seems quite remote.

31. 391 U.S. at 521 (emphasis added).

32. *Id*. at 521–22 n.20 (emphasis added).

33. *Id*. at 523 (emphasis added).

34. *Witherspoon*'s precise holding was delineated at *id*. at 522 and amplified at *id*. n.21.

35. *Id*. at 522 n.21.

36. *Id*. at 523 n.22.

37. In recent years, the Court has applied a three-part test to determine whether a newly announced constitutional decision should be given retroactive effect. *See* Stovall v. Denno, 388 U.S. 293, 297 (1967) (dictum). As *Witherspoon*'s footnote suggests, the most significant of the three prongs is the extent to which the new rule is designed to remove a defect in the fact-finding process. *See* 391 U.S. at 523 n.22. *See generally* Williams v. United States, 401 U.S. 646, 653 (1971).

38. 408 U.S. 238 (1972).

39. *Id.* at 306 (Stewart, J., concurring).

40. *Cf.* Marion v. Beto, 434 F.2d 29 (5th Cir. 1971) (holding that because of the magnitude of the stakes involved, the improper exclusion of even a single venireman must result in vacation of the death penalty).

41. *See* 391 U.S. at 520 n.18. *See generally* Sherbert v. Verner, 374 U.S. 398, 407 (1963).

42. 391 U.S. at 522–23.

43. MODEL PENAL CODE § 201.6 (Proposed Final Draft No. 1, 1961).

44. *See supra* text at notes 14–15.

45. *But see* FLA. STAT. ANN. § 921.141 (West 1974), discussed *supra* at note 14.

46. *See* 391 U.S. at 523.

47. *Compare supra* text at notes 22–23.

48. *Compare supra* text at notes 29–42.

49. Where the guided discretionary statutes require imposition of the death penalty upon certain findings by the jury, arguably the first exception to *Witherspoon* is met when a venireman states in unmistakable terms that he would absolutely refuse to impose capital punishment in *any case* where its imposition would be required by statute.

50. Chief Justice Burger's dissent recognizes the Stewart and White opinions as defining the "scope of the Court's ruling" in *Furman*. 408 U.S. at 397.

51. Justice Stewart's eloquent statement of this point was as follows:

These death sentences are cruel and unusual in the same way that being struck by lightning is cruel and unusual. For, of the people convicted of rapes and murders in 1967 and 1968, many just as reprehensible as these, the petitioners are among a capriciously selected random handful upon whom the sentence of death has in fact been imposed. . . . I simply conclude that the Eighth and Fourteenth Amendments cannot tolerate the infliction of a sentence of death under legal systems that permit this unique penalty to be so wantonly and so freakishly imposed.

Id. at 309–10 (Stewart, J., concurring). For Justice White's substantially similar analysis, *see id.* at 313.

52. *See supra* text at notes 31–42.

53. According to *Witherspoon*, a 1966 poll indicated that 42 percent of the population favored the death penalty and 47 percent opposed it. Moreover, a 1971 Harris poll indicated that a very substantial proportion of the population would be unable to vote for the death penalty in certain cases in which strict application of the new statutes would mandate its imposition. For example, 41 percent of the sample stated that they could not vote for the death penalty in a case in which a wife used poison to murder her husband, and 38 percent of the sample stated that they could not vote for the death penalty in a case where a convict serving a life sentence killed a prison guard while trying to escape. *See* LOUIS HARRIS & ASSOC., STUDY No. 2016, at 3e (1971) (on file at NAACP Legal Defense and Educational Fund, 10 Columbus Circle, Suite 2030, New York, N.Y. 10019).

54. For example, if 40 percent of the eligible veniremen would in some cases refuse to impose a capital verdict despite their evaluation of the evidence,

the chance that no such juror would serve on a jury of twelve randomly selected jurors is obtained by multiplying 0.60 (the probability of selecting a juror whose views on capital punishment would not impede his capacity to return a capital verdict) by itself 12 times. $(0.60)^{12} = 0.002$. Thus, the probability that at least one scrupled juror would serve on any jury is $1 - 0.002 = 99.8\%$.

55. 408 U.S. at 309 (Stewart, J., concurring); *id*. at 311 (White, J., concurring).

56. *Id*. at 314.

57. *Id*. at 310 (Stewart, J., concurring). Justice White also stressed that as a result of the delegation of discretion to the jury, the imposition of the death penalty had fallen into virtual desuetude. *See id*. at 313 (White, J., concurring).

58. By the terms of their opinions, each of the five concurring justices in *Furman* appeared to condemn any system of capital punishment that delegated sentencing discretion to the jury. Justice Brennan (*id*. at 257–306) and Justice Marshall (*id*. at 314–74) shared the view that the death penalty is unconstitutional per se regardless of the presence or absence of the sentencer's discretion. As Chief Justice Burger stated, those two justices "concluded that the Eighth Amendment prohibits capital punishment for all crimes and under all circumstances." *Id*. at 375. Justice Douglas (*id*. at 240–57) made clear that he would strike down any discretionary capital punishment provision, reserving only the question of the constitutionality of a mandatory capital punishment provision. "Whether a mandatory death penalty would otherwise if evenhandedly applied be constitutional is a question I do not reach." *Id*. at 257. Justice Stewart (*id*. at 306–10) specified those statutes that make "the death penalty the mandatory punishment" as the only ones that by his view could be outside the constitutional holding he supported. *Id*. at 307. His opinion covered legislative enactments which "have not provided that the death penalty shall be imposed upon all those who are found guilty . . . and not ordained that death shall be the automatic punishment . . . ." *Id*. at 308. Under these circumstances "death sentences are the product of a legal system that brings them . . . within the very core of the Eighth Amendment's guarantee . . . ." *Id*. at 309. Justice White (*id*. at 310–13) similarly reserved only the question of "[t]he facial constitutionality of statutes requiring the imposition of the death penalty." *Id*. at 310. His opinion directly spoke to "the constitutionality of capital punishment statutes under which . . . the legislature does not itself mandate the penalty in any particular class or kind of case . . . , but delegates to judges or juries the decisions as to those cases, if any, in which the penalty will be utilized." *Id*. at 311.

59. This argument has been accepted by several lower court decisions. *See, e.g.*, State v. Dixon, 283 So. 2d 1 (Fla. 1973), *cert. denied*, 416 U.S. 943 (1974); Coley v. State, 231 Ga. 829, 204 S.E.2d 612 (1974). *See generally* 87 HARV. L. REV. 1690, 1698–1712 (1974).

60. PA. STAT. ANN. tit. 18, § 1311 (Purdon 1974).

61. *Id*. § 1311(d)(1)(viii).

62. *Id*. § 1311(d)(2)(i).

63. For example, "torture," which connotes the intentional infliction of extreme pain, could reasonably be found to exist in almost any premeditated killing, or in none; "lack of maturity" could include physical immaturity, emotional

immaturity, educational or intellectual deficiency, or an undeveloped moral sense. Moreover, the statute nowhere provides any specification as to the degree of "immaturity" that will suffice to constitute a "mitigating circumstance."

64. *See supra* text at notes 50–57.

65. *See supra* text at note 52.

66. *Compare supra* text following note 56.

67. *See supra* note 63. Furthermore, some guided discretionary statutes do not mandate the imposition of the death penalty. *See, e.g.*, FLA. STAT. ANN. § 921.141 (West 1974).

68. 391 U.S. at 521.

69. Bell v. United States, 349 U.S. 81, 82–83 (1955).

70. 391 U.S. at 541 (White, J., dissenting).

71. *Id.* at 519 n.15.

72. *Id.*

73. A. BICKEL, THE SUPREME COURT AND THE IDEA OF PROGRESS 74 (1970).

74. Shuttlesworth v. Birmingham, 382 U.S. 87, 91 (1965); Speiser v. Randall, 357 U.S. 513, 519 (1958); Winters v. New York, 333 U.S. 507, 514 (1948).

75. 391 U.S. at 523.

76. *Id.* at 519 n.15.

77. 356 U.S. 86, 101 (1958) (plurality opinion of Warren, C.J.).

78. *See also* Robinson v. California, 370 U.S. 660 (1961) (the standard applied by the Court referred to "the light of contemporary human knowledge").

79. *See supra* text at notes 50–54.

80. *See* 408 U.S. at 257–306 (Brennan, J., concurring). *Id.* at 314–74 (Marshall, J., concurring).

81. *See supra* note 58.

82. 408 U.S. at 413 (Blackmun, J., dissenting). *See also id.* at 401 (Burger, C.J., dissenting).

83. *See supra* text at notes 50–54.

84. *See supra* note 59.

85. *See supra* text at note 58.

86. 408 U.S. at 310 (Stewart, J., concurring).

87. C. BLACK, CAPITAL PUNISHMENT: THE INEVITABILITY OF CAPRICE AND MISTAKE (1974).

Witherspoon Revisited: Update

Since the publication of this essay, the Supreme Court has provided one significant interpretation of *Witherspoon*. In *Adams v. Texas*[1] the Court considered the constitutionality of a Texas statute that provided that a prospective juror shall be disqualified from serving in a capital case "unless he states under oath that the mandatory penalty of death or imprisonment for life will not affect his deliberations on any issue of fact."[2] After holding that *Witherspoon* applies to the bifurcated procedure employed by Texas in capital cases,[3] the Court invalidated the Texas statute on the ground that the statute allowed veniremen opposed to capital punishment to be excluded on a broader basis than that permitted by *Witherspoon*.[4]

In holding that *Witherspoon* applies to the Texas system of capital punishment, *Adams* constitutes an important extension of *Witherspoon*. As Justice Rehnquist noted in dissent,[5] Texas's death penalty statute is significantly different from the pre-*Furman* Illinois statute that was before the Court in *Witherspoon*. Whereas the Illinois statute vested total capital sentencing discretion in the jury, the Texas statute requires imposition of the death penalty if, after finding defendant guilty of a capital crime, the jury at the penalty stage answers three questions in the affirmative.[6] As Justice Rehnquist says, the Texas statute does not appear to vest significant sentencing discretion in the jury.[7] Indeed, as the dissent intimates,[8] the Texas system of capital punishment comes perilously close to limiting the jury's discretion beyond the point that is constitutionally permissible.[9] Thus, in holding that *Witherspoon* applies to the Texas system of capital punishment, the Court essentially accepts one of the arguments made in the "*Witherspoon* Revisited" essay. It is now clear that *Witherspoon* applies to any constitutionally valid system of capital punishment. Thus, its limitations on the prosecutor's right to exclude jurors for cause constitute an integral part of the post-*Gregg* system of capital punishment.[10]

The "*Witherspoon* Revisited" essay also suggested that the only way to resolve the tension between *Witherspoon*'s insistence on individualized sentencing and *Furman*'s limitation on the amount of capital sentencing discretion that may be vested in the jury would be to abolish capital punishment. Obviously, the Court has not adopted this suggestion. Since holding in *Gregg v. Georgia*[11] and *Woodson v. North Carolina*[12] that guided discretionary capital punishment is constitutional but mandatory capital punishment is not, the Court has not systematically explored the tension between the requirement of individualized sentencing and *Gregg*'s mandate that the capital sentencing authority be guided by standards that will channel its exercise of discretion so as to avoid arbitrary results.[13]

As I have already indicated,[14] however, the post-*Gregg* cases have clearly placed more emphasis on the individualized sentencing requirement than on avoiding the potential for allowing an arbitrary and capricious pattern of death sentences. Thus, in *Lockett v. Ohio*[15] the Court held that except in the rarest kind of capital case,[16] the Constitution requires that the sentencer "not be precluded from considering *as a mitigating factor*, any aspect of defendant's character or record and any circumstances of the offense that the defendant proffers as a basis for a sentence less than death."[17] Clearly, this requirement reduces the extent to which the jury's discretion may be effectively channeled by guidelines. Since the jury must be allowed not only to consider almost any evidence that the defendant chooses to present but also to vote against the death penalty on the basis of this evidence, the jury's discretion with respect to the evaluation of mitigating evidence is certainly as untrammeled as it ever was.[18]

On the other hand, as a result of *Lockett*'s requirement, the post-*Gregg* system of capital punishment has made a very serious commitment to the principle of requiring individualized sentencing in capital cases. Now, more than ever before, a capital defendant has a right to have the death penalty determination made on the basis of a complete evaluation of his character and the circumstances of the offense. Thus, although the tension between *Witherspoon* and *Furman* still exists, the Court's post-*Gregg* decisions demonstrate a clear preference for *Witherspoon*'s commitment to individualized sentencing.

NOTES

1. 448 U.S. 38 (1980).
2. TEX. PENAL CODE ANN. § 12.31(b) (Vernon 1974), *quoted in* 448 U.S. at 42.
3. 448 U.S. at 45.
4. *Id*. at 49–51.
5. *Id*. at 54 (Rehnquist, J., dissenting).
6. The three questions to be answered are (1) whether defendant's conduct "was committed deliberately and with the reasonable expectation that the death of deceased or another would result"; (2) "whether there is a probability that the defendant would commit criminal acts of violence that would constitute a continuing threat to society"; and (3) "if raised by the evidence," whether defendant's

conduct "was unreasonable in response to the provocation, if any, by the deceased." *See id.* at 53 (Rehnquist, J., dissenting).

7. *Id.* at 54 (Rehnquist, J., dissenting).

8. *Id.*

9. For a discussion of this issue, see Hertz & Weisberg, *In Mitigation of the Penalty of Death:* Lockett v. Ohio *and the Capital Defendant's Right to Consideration of Mitigating Circumstances*, 69 CAL. L. REV. 317, 332–41 (1981); Gillers, *Deciding Who Dies*, 129 U. PA. L. REV. 1, 37–38 n.166 (1980).

10. While holding that *Witherspoon* applies to the new statutes, the Court did not fully delineate the scope of that application. The Court held that the Texas statute was unconstitutional because it would exclude prospective jurors who in stating that they would be affected by the possibility of the death penalty might mean "only that the potentially lethal consequences of their decision would invest their deliberations with greater seriousness and gravity or would involve them emotionally." 448 U.S. at 49–50. In dicta, the Court added that *Witherspoon* would not permit the exclusion of veniremen who stated that they would honestly find the facts required by the Texas death penalty statute but that the prospect of a death penalty might affect their "honest judgment of the facts" or "what they may deem to be a reasonable doubt." 448 U.S. at 50. The Court did not decide, however, whether a venireman could properly be excluded for cause if she stated that in some (but not all) cases her opposition to the death penalty would preclude her from answering the three statutory questions in the affirmative, despite her view of the evidence. Under a strict reading of *Witherspoon*, such a venireman would not be subject to exclusion because her voir dire statement does not make it unmistakably clear that she would automatically vote against the death penalty, regardless of the evidence presented.

11. 428 U.S. 153 (1976).

12. 428 U.S. 280 (1976).

13. For a detailed discussion of this problem, see Liebman & Shepard, *Guiding Capital Sentencing Discretion Beyond the "Boiler Plate": Mental Disorder as a Mitigating Factor*, 66 GEO. L.J. 757 (1978).

14. *See supra* "A Comment on *Furman*: Update'" at text accompanying notes 7–8.

15. 438 U.S. 586 (1978).

16. The pivotal plurality opinion reserved decision as to whether a mandatory death sentence might be constitutional when assigned to narrow categories of homicide—"as, for example, when a prisoner—or escapee—under a life sentence is found guilty of murder." 438 U.S. at 604 n.11 (plurality opinion of Burger, C.J.).

17. 438 U.S. at 604 (plurality opinion of Burger, C.J.).

18. For further discussion of the extent to which the sentencing jury's discretion remains unfettered, see *supra* "A Comment on *Furman*: Update" at text accompanying notes 9–11.

Disproportionality and the Death Penalty: Death as a Punishment for Rape

Introduction

The Legal Background

The Supreme Court's holding that under a properly drawn statute capital punishment is a permissible punishment for murder[1] appears to have brought the wheel in capital punishment litigation full circle. The full-blown attack on the legality of the death penalty was triggered by the Court's decision in *Rudolph v. Alabama* in 1963, when three justices dissenting from a denial of certiorari argued that the Court should "consider whether the Eighth and Fourteenth Amendments . . . permit the imposition of the death penalty on a convicted rapist who has neither taken nor endangered human life."[2] This somewhat meager encouragement produced massive litigation attacking first the procedures used in capital punishment cases and finally the death penalty itself.[3] The path charting the Court's response to these unprecedented challenges can only be described as tortuous and unpredictable. In 1968, the Court in *Witherspoon v. Illinois*[4] effected a significant procedural reform by holding that death penalties imposed by strictly death-qualified juries[5] are in violation of the due process clause. Three years later, in *McGautha v. California*,[6] the Court rejected due process attacks on two other procedures prevalent in capital cases, upholding the constitutionality of allowing a discretionary death penalty determination to be made by a jury authorized to exercise its discretion in the absence of any standards, and allowing this determination to be made in a unitary proceeding at which the defendant's guilt or innocence is also at stake.[7] Through its more recent decisions, however, the Court in effect has stood *McGautha* on its head. In *Furman v. Georgia*[8] the Court found that the pattern of death sentences imposed under the prevailing system of capital punishment established that imposition of the death penalty pursuant to that system was in violation of the cruel and unusual punishment clause; and in a series of cases decided on July 2, 1976, the Court made it clear that *Furman* should not be interpreted as holding that the death penalty itself was unconstitutional (the necessary evidence of societal rejection having been supplied by the pattern of death sentences imposed within the matrix of a standardless discretionary system) but rather that it was the delegation of standardless capital sentencing discretion to the jury—a procedure previously held valid in *McGautha*—that rendered death penalties imposed pursuant to that procedure constitutionally invalid.[9]

However, in holding that imposition of the death penalty for the crime of murder pursuant to a system that provides adequate procedural safeguards will not violate the Eighth and Fourteenth amendments, the Court narrowed the scope of its holding by emphasizing that

We are concerned here only with the imposition of capital punishment for the crime of murder, and when a life has been taken deliberately by the offender.[10]

In the same passage the Court specifically reserved decision on the

question whether the taking of the criminal's life is a proportionate sanction where no victim has been deprived of life—for example, when capital punishment is imposed for rape, kidnapping, or armed robbery that does not result in the death of any human being.[11]

In its first order list for the 1976–77 term, the Court accepted certiorari on the question whether capital punishment may be constitutionally imposed upon conviction for a rape not resulting in death.[12] Thus, it appears likely that the Court will soon be required to decide whether death as a punishment for rape is constitutionally excessive in some or all situations. In other words, the issue of disproportionality posed by Justice Goldberg in 1963 appears destined to be the focal point in the next round of capital punishment litigation.

The Theoretical Problem

Commenting on the *Rudolph* dissent in 1964, Professor Herbert Packer concluded that the doctrine of proportionality was not a legitimate device for limiting application of the death penalty.[13] Given the undeveloped state of the doctrine in 1964, this assessment may have been accurate. The contention of this essay, however, is that at present the doctrine may be usefully and appropriately used to hold that death is a constitutionally disproportionate punishment for all rapes not resulting in death. In developing this thesis, the section of the essay following the heading "Theoretical Underpinnings of the Doctrine" will examine the doctrinal basis for the concept of proportionality; the section following "Identifying the Relevant Criteria" will seek to identify the criteria to be utilized in determining whether a particular sentence is a constitutionally disproportionate punishment for a particular crime; and that following "Applying the Doctrine of Proportionality to Death as a Punishment for

Rape" will apply the relevant criteria to the situation where death is imposed as a punishment for rape.

Theoretical Underpinnings of the Doctrine

The concept of proportionality insofar as it is relevant to an interpretation of the Eighth Amendment has its historical roots in the writings of Beccaria, Montesquieu, and other figures of the Enlightenment.[14] *Beccaria*'s treatise *On Crimes and Punishment*,[15] which was published in Italy in 1764, developed the idea that punishments must be correlated to offenses.[16] As Justice Douglas observed, Beccaria's work had a profound influence on "American thought in the critical years following our revolution."[17] The principle that punishments must be "proportioned to the crime" was specifically articulated by Jefferson,[18] among others; and this concept was expressed either directly or indirectly in most of the early state constitutions or declarations of rights.[19] Thus, the doctrine of proportionality as a limitation on criminal punishment was well entrenched even before the constitutional prohibition on cruel and unusual punishments was enacted.

From the beginning, this doctrine had two interrelated but severable branches. Arguing from an essentially utilitarian posture, Beccaria reasoned that punishments should be no more severe than that "necessary to preserve the deposit of the public."[20] Thus, the state should exact no more punishment than is necessary to achieve a proper end of the criminal law such as deterrence. While application of this principle would not necessarily preclude stricter penalties for less serious offenses,[21] Beccaria was adamant in also insisting that the scale of punishments should be commensurate with the harm done to society by the offender.[22]

Later commentators have clarified the theoretical basis for the second branch of Beccaria's doctrine. The principle that the degree of punishment should be proportioned to the moral gravity or seriousness of the offense does not stem from a utilitarian premise but from an independent principle of justice. Thus, as H.L.A. Hart has argued, despite the vagaries of opinion on the ends of criminal punishment, this principle of proportionality should be a fundamental limiting principle:

There are many different ways in which we think it morally incumbent on us to *qualify* or *limit* the pursuit of the utilitarian goal by the methods of punishment. Some punishments are ruled out as too barbarous or horrible to be used whatever their social utility; we also limit punishments in order to maintain a scale for different offences which reflects, albeit very roughly, the distinction felt between the moral gravity of these offenses. Thus we make some approximation to the ideal of justice of treating morally like cases alike and morally different ones differently.[23]

Professor Hart's analysis provides the beginning of an answer to Professor Packer's criticism of the doctrine of proportionality sketched by Justice Goldberg in the *Rudolph* dissent. The second and third issues raised by Justice Goldberg as worthy of consideration were whether using death to "protect a value other than human life" is constitutionally excessive and whether "the permissible aims of punishment (e.g., deterrence, isolation, rehabilitation) [could] be achieved as effectively by punishing rape less severely than by death."[24] Reading these two issues in conjunction, Professor Packer concludes that it is "odd" to suggest that it is disproportionately severe to use death to protect a value other than human life because "Justice Goldberg apparently rules out retribution as a permissible end of punishment."[25] He goes on to assert that if the permissible ends of punishment are the utilitarian goals identified by Justice Goldberg, then death as a punishment for rape is at least as rational as it is as a punishment for murder.[26] However, in light of Professor Hart's analysis, the fallacy in this argument is in failing to separate the two issues raised by Justice Goldberg. Even if we assume that imposing the death penalty may be rationally thought to serve a utilitarian goal such as deterrence, this does not preclude a determination that the limits imposed by an independent principle of justice mandate a conclusion that death is a disproportionately severe punishment for rape in some or all situations. The point, as Professor Packer has elsewhere recognized,[27] is not that retribution must be an end of the criminal law but rather that retribution (or some concept closely related thereto) must play a part in limiting the degree of punishment that may be exacted under any utilitarian theory.

However, identifying the concept of proportionality as one that springs from immutable principles of justice does little to supply the concept with content. Moreover, commentators have not dealt with this problem in any depth. Professor Hart has suggested two rough yardsticks. While it is generally accepted that "the relative gravity of punishments is to reflect moral gravity of offences"[28] the concept of "moral gravity" is clouded by "the deeply entrenched notion that the measure should not be, or not only be, the subjective wickedness of the offender but the amount of harm done."[29] Using these indicators, Professor Hart is able to sketch what is admittedly only a very rough and ambiguous scale:

The guiding principle is that of a proportion within a system of penalties between those imposed for different offences where these have a distinct place in a commonsense scale of gravity. This scale itself no doubt consists of very broad judgments both of relative moral iniquity and harmfulness of different types of offense . . . .[30]

Professor Packer, too, while noting that the principle of proportionality should be a limitation on punishment, has not attempted any systematic definition of the criteria to be used in applying the doctrine either in general or in an Eighth Amendment context.[31] Thus, in order to identify the criteria relevant to an Eighth Amendment application of the doctrine, it is necessary to turn to the cases that have specifically dealt with this issue.

Identifying the Relevant Criteria

The *Weems* Case

In *Weems v. United States*[32] a disbursing officer for the Coast Guard in Manila was convicted in a Philippine court for falsely entering in his cash book outlays of 616 pesos. For this offense, the defendant was sentenced to *cadena temporal*, which provided for a minimum term of twelve years' imprisonment at hard and painful labor (defendant's actual term of imprisonment was fifteen years) with harsh accessory provisions, including one that required him to "always carry a chain at the ankle, hanging from the wrists,"[33] and another that subjected him to surveillance from the state during the remainder of his life.[34]

In condemning the law providing for these punishments as violative of the cruel and unusual punishment clause, the Court assessed society's acceptance of such provisions.[35] While expressing distaste for the harsh accessory provisions,[36] the Court's holding was fundamentally based on a conclusion that contemporary society viewed the law's rigid twelve-year minimum imprisonment to be a disproportionately harsh punishment for the offense:

Such penalties for such offenses amaze those who have formed their conception of the relation of a state to even its offending citizens from the practice of the American commonwealths, and believe that it is a precept of justice that punishment for crime should be graduated and proportioned to the offense.[37]

In order to support this conclusion, the Court went on to make some brief comparisons. Preliminarily, Justice McKenna noted that the legislation in question "has no fellow in American legislation."[38] Turning to a comparison between the Philippine law and federal laws, the Court found the punishment provided by the former to be greater than the federal penalties for clearly more serious crimes such as homicide, misprision of treason, and robbery;[39] moreover, it found that the federal embezzlement statute punished a substantially similar offense by a maximum that was one-sixth as long as the minimum prison term provided by the punishment of *cadena temporal*.[40] Finally, the Court turned to Philippine legislation and found that the similar (or possibly more serious) offense of forging or counterfeiting obligations or securities of the United States or of the Philippine islands was punishable by a maximum of fifteen years' imprisonment.[41] On the basis of these comparisons, the Court found that more was at stake "than different exercises of legislative judgment";[42] it concluded that invalidation of the provision was necessary to restrain the penal law within its constitutional limitations and prevent its use as an instrument of terror.[43]

Refinement of the *Weems* Doctrine: The Evolving Criteria in the Lower Courts

Following *Weems*, the doctrine of proportionality remained largely quiescent for several decades.[44] Recently, however, the doctrine's significant resurgence[45] has made it an integral part of both the state and federal interpretations of either the Eighth Amendment prohibition on cruel and unusual punishment or the substantially similar prohibition contained in most state constitutions.[46] In applying the doctrine, lower courts have attempted to refine *Weems*'s analysis while maintaining touch with the objective criteria applied by the Supreme Court. Such criteria may be divided into roughly three categories: (1) a judgment as to the relative seriousness (on some penological scale) of the offense being punished; (2) comparisons with penalties provided for similar offenses in other jurisdictions; (3) comparisons with penalties provided for more serious offenses in the same jurisdiction.

Judgments as to the Relative Seriousness of the Offense

A judgment as to the relative seriousness of the crime in question is, of course, a prerequisite to some of the comparisons required by the other criteria.[47] However, courts have not perceived the "nature of the offense" criteria as a mere adjunct to the other tests but as one having independent significance. Thus, there have been cases in which penalties that meet the objective criteria defined in the second and third categories have nevertheless been upheld because of the court's conclusion that the offenses in question are so severe that the harsh penalties imposed are not disproportionate to the offenses.[48]

In order to assess the seriousness of an offense, it is necessary to bear in mind the nature of the modern doctrine of proportionality. The doctrine's central role is to impose a requirement of some kind of equivalence between the punishment and the offense.[49] Equivalence, of course, is a murky concept; but it is clear that in seeking to make appropriate correlations between punishments and crimes, crimes should be graded on a scale of gravity, the focus being on shared notions of the justice in a moral sense of imposing severe punishments for particular crimes and not on the utilitarian benefits to be gained by imposing such punishments. Thus, the recent cases that purport to deal with this criterion by asking whether the legislature could rationally conclude that the sentence imposed serves a valid penological goal appear wide of the mark.[50] Difficult though it may be, an attempt to assess the seriousness of the offense in an absolute sense should be made.

In making this kind of assessment, courts have directly or indirectly sought to draw upon shared notions about the moral gravity of the offender or the harm a particular offense causes to society. Specifically, the courts have almost invariably asked whether the crime is violent or non-violent and attempted to assess the degree of danger the typical offender presents to society. Thus, in *In re Lynch*,[51] while holding that an indeterminate sentence of life imprisonment for a second offense of indecent exposure was excessive punishment in violation of California's prohibition against "Cruel or unusual punishments,"[52] the California Supreme Court emphasized that commission of the offense generally involves "no physical aggression or even contact"[53] and that the typical offender exhibits a "pattern of nonviolence."[54] In *Hart v. Coiner*,[55] while invalidating a life sentence imposed pursuant to West Virginia's recidivist statute following defendant's convictions for writing a check on insufficient funds, transporting forged checks across state lines, and perjury,[56] the Sixth Circuit stressed that the defendant's offenses were not against the person and did not involve any danger of violence to person or property.[57] Cases invalidating statutes imposing mandatory minimum sentences upon conviction for marijuana offenses have similarly stressed that lengthy prison sentences for these nonviolent offenses are so excessive as to shock the conscience.[58]

However, complete nonviolence is not a prerequisite to a finding of disproportionality. In *Ralph v. Warden*,[59] the Fourth Circuit dealt with a rape case in which defendant threatened the victim and her young son with death if she did not submit. While not denying that rape is a violent offense or that the specific rape before them was violent, the court emphasized that "there are rationale gradations of culpability that can be made on the basis of injury to the victim."[60] It held that death is a constitutionally excessive penalty for rape when the victim's life is neither taken nor endangered.[61] In another rape case, the Kentucky Court of Appeals held that the penalty of life imprisonment without benefit of parole was cruel and unusual punishment when applied to a juvenile offender.[62] While admitting that the law was legitimately designed to deal with dangerous offenders who would be a constant threat to society, the court found that the law was defective in that it allowed a sentence to be predicated on the improper premise that a youth "will remain incorrigible for the rest of his life."[63]

Comparisons with Penalties Provided for More Severe Offenses in the Same Jurisdiction

The relevance of a comparison between the penalty imposed for the offense in question and penalties imposed for more serious offenses in the same jurisdiction was clearly articulated by the California Supreme Court in *In re Lynch*:

> The underlying but unstated assumption appears to be that although isolated excessive penalties may occasionally be enacted, e.g., through "honest zeal" [quoting *Weems*] generated in response to transitory public emotion, the Legislature may be depended upon to act with due and deliberate regard for constitutional restraints in prescribing the vast majority of punishments set forth in our statutes. The latter may therefore be deemed illustrative of constitutionally permissible degrees of severity; and if among them are found more serious crimes punished less severely than the offense in question, the challenged penalty is to that extent suspect.[64]

Applying the more serious offense yardstick obviously requires a determination that certain crimes are more serious than the offense in question. This determination can most easily be made in a situation where the offense is a lesser-included offense: that is, where it is impossible to commit some greater offense without having first committed all the elements of the offense in question. Where it appears that the penalty imposed for the lesser-included offense exceeds the penalty provided for the greater offense, courts have routinely held such penalties to be in violation of the Eighth Amendment.[65]

However, this criterion has been applied even when the offense in question is not a lesser-included offense. In *Downey v. Perini*[66] the Sixth Circuit compared Ohio's twenty-year minimum sentence for sale of marijuana with the lesser penalties imposed for violent crimes: among them, kidnapping, armed robbery, and voluntary manslaughter.[67] Finding no rational basis for the discrepancy, the court held the Ohio statute to be constitutionally excessive.[68] In *Hart v. Coiner*[69] the Fourth Circuit analyzed the validity of a life sentence imposed pursuant to West Virginia's recidivist statute upon conviction for three nonviolent crimes[70] by comparing the "penalties provided for grave crimes of violence."[71] After noting that second-degree murder, arson, assault with intent to kill, and administering poison with intent to kill were all punished by lesser terms of imprisonment, the court concluded that the defendant was the victim of "irrationally disparate treatment"[72] and condemned his punishment as constitutionally excessive. Similarly, in invalidating a statute imposing an indeterminate sentence of six months to life upon a second conviction for indecent exposure, the California Supreme Court gave significant weight to their conclusion that the punishment provided was far more severe than that imposed upon a second conviction for other offenses which are "indisputably more serious."[73] Among the crimes identified by the court as fitting within this category were manslaughter, mayhem, arson, and burglary.[74] Thus, it appears that a challenged penalty will be at least constitutionally suspect when it appears that within the same jurisdiction crimes that are more violent and/or productive of more obvious harm to society are punished less severely.[75]

Comparisons with Penalties Provided for Similar Offenses in Other Jurisdictions

In considering the issue of disproportionality, courts have invariably compared the challenged penalty with punishments prescribed for the same or similar offenses in other jurisdictions. There are obvious justifications for using this criterion. If the vast majority of jurisdictions do not authorize a particular penalty for a particular crime, this constitutes strong evidence that "our evolving standards of decency" (as reflected by prevailing public opinion) have progressed to the point where the penalty in question is considered excessive.[76] Moreover, the element of arbitrariness that necessarily arises when a harsh penalty is imposed as a result of what appears to be a geographical accident is an additional sign of excessiveness. Unlike *Weems*, the courts that have recently applied this technique have attempted to make exhaustive comparisons between the penalty in question and that imposed for similar crimes in other jurisdictions. Thus, in *Hart v. Coiner*[77] the Fourth Circuit made a detailed comparison between West Virginia's recidivist statute and the recidivist statute in effect in all other jurisdictions. It concluded that "West Virginia's recidivist scheme is among the top four in the nation in terms of severity, and may be number one."[78] Similarly, in *Downey v. Perini*[79] the Sixth Circuit emphasized that the minimum penalties for the marijuana offenses before them in that case[80] were more severe than those applied by any other state.[81] Moreover, a federal case invalidating a twenty-year penalty imposed upon conviction for simple assault again applied this criterion, comparing the penalty imposed with that in effect for similar offenses in all other jurisdictions.[82]

And, finally, in assessing the proportionality of death as a penalty for rape, the Fourth Circuit made an extensive survey of penalties for rape imposed in jurisdictions throughout the world. Thus, the court observed that

Congressional action in recently repealing the death penalty for rape in the District of Columbia follows a worldwide trend. Presently the United States is one of only four nations in which rape is punishable by death, and in this country 34 states punish rape only by imprisonment. In none of the 16 remaining states is death mandatory, but it is retained as a sentencing alternative. It appears, therefore, that the overwhelming majority of the nations of the world, legislatures of more than two-thirds of the states of the Union, and Congress . . . now considered [sic] the death penalty to be an excessive punishment for the crime of rape.[83]

The court also gave weight to views expressed in model penal legislation, noting that repeal of the death penalty for rape has been recommended in both the proposed Federal Criminal Code of the National Commission on Reform of Federal Criminal Law and the Model Penal Code of the American Law Institute.[84] Thus, it appears that at least where a penalty as severe as death is at stake, penalties imposed for similar offenses in every possible jurisdiction will bear materially upon the issue of disproportionality.

The Impact of the 1976 Death Penalty Cases

In *Gregg v. Georgia*[85] the pivotal plurality opinion of the Court reaffirmed the doctrine of proportionality,[86] and applied the doctrine to hold that death is not "invariably" a disproportionate punishment for the crime of deliberate murder.[87] However, the plurality's analysis in support of this determination was not free from ambiguity. Justice Stewart's only explicit statement relating to the subject was the observation that death "is an extreme sanction, suitable to the most extreme of crimes."[88] If this statement indeed represented the sum total of the Court's analysis, it might be inferred that application of the doctrine of proportionality rests totally on ad hoc value judgments concerning the severity of the sanction and the severity of the crime.[89] However, the plurality earlier identified three indicators of societal acceptance and used them to determine whether the sentence of death for muder is in itself contrary to our evolving standards of decency.[90] Moreover, in *Woodson v. North Carolina*[91] the plurality used the same three indicators to conclude that imposing death as an automatic punishment for murder is contrary to our evolving standards of decency, and therefore in violation of the cruel and unusual punishment clause.[92] Clearly, the question whether society accepts the death penalty as a punishment for murder in some or all situations is closely if not inextricably related to the question whether society accepts the death penalty as a punishment that is not disproportionately severe for the crime of murder in some or all situations. Moreover, in view of the doctrine developed in *Weems*[93] and refined by the lower courts,[94] assessing the degree of societal acceptance for imposing a particular punishment upon conviction of a particular crime has at least significant bearing on the issue of disproportionality. Therefore, the Court's analysis of indicators of societal acceptance should be taken as identifying criteria that are relevant to the determination of disproportionality.

The indicia of societal acceptance that the plurality found particularly relevant to its judgment on the Eighth Amendment question were "history and traditional usage, legislative enactments, and jury determinations."[95] Justice Stewart's analysis of capital punishment's history led him to the conclusion that while "the imposition of the death penalty for the crime of murder has a long history of acceptance both in the United States and England,"[96] mandatory capital punishment has never been found to be an appropriate or satisfactory means of applying the death penalty.[97]

In supporting this conclusion, the plurality relied to some extent on statements of knowledgeable historians;[98] however, it relied most heavily on its analysis of the other two indicators. In upholding death as a penalty for murder, Justice Stewart particularly emphasized the significance of the "legislative response to *Furman*,"[99] pointing out that "at least 35 states have enacted new statutes that provide for the death penalty for at least some crimes that result in the death of another person."[100] On the other hand, in holding that mandatory capital punishment is unconstitutional, the plurality pointed to the fact that while legislation imposing mandatory capital punishment flourished until the beginning of the twentieth century, by 1963 legislatures in every jurisdiction abandoned it in favor of either a jury-discretionary sentencing scheme or complete abolition.[101] The Court went on to find that the post-*Furman* legislative adoption of a number of mandatory statutes did not evince a reversal of societal values but merely manifested attempts on the parts of these legislatures to avoid the impact of the *Furman* ruling.[102] Through this analysis, the Court refined *Weems*'s focus on a comparison between the challenged penalty and punishments for similar crimes in other jurisdictions. In order to gauge societal acceptance, it appears necessary not only to examine the actual number of relevant legislative enactments but also to analyze the legislative trend. If it seems that the prevailing legislative judgment points towards an abandonment of the punishment in question, this will be important evidence of societal repudiation.

The plurality also assessed evidence relating to jury determinations.

With respect to discretionary capital punishment as a penalty for murder, Justice Stewart found that the increasingly rare imposition of the death penalty did not necessarily evidence societal repudiation because it "may well reflect the humane feeling that this most irrevocable of sanctions should be reserved for a small number of extreme cases."[103] However, he also emphasized that under the post-*Furman* statutes, juries have in fact imposed a substantial number of death penalties.[104] With respect to mandatory capital punishment, on the other hand, the plurality found that "at least since the Revolution, American jurors have, with some regularity disregarded their oaths and refused to convict defendants where a death sentence was the automatic consequence of a guilty verdict."[105] In addition, Justice Stewart noted that in first-degree murder cases juries with sentencing discretion do not impose the death penalty with any great regularity.[106] Drawing on these observations, his opinion concluded that the actions of juries evidence a societal repudiation of death as a mandatory punishment for first-degree murder.[107] Based on the plurality's analysis, it appears that, as with the case of legislative enactments, an evaluation of jury determinations turns upon the quality as well as the quantity of such determinations. Where it appears that the jury's imposition of a sentence is not only rare in an absolute sense but irrational in the sense that the sentences imposed may not be distinguished on the basis of a legally recognized standard, this may be taken as decisive evidence of societal repudiation.

Under the plurality's analysis, then, it appears that additional criteria must be used in applying the doctrine of proportionality. First, if possible, some effort should be made to derive the punishment's historical roots. Where did the punishment come from? And what has been the history of its usage in a general sense? More specifically, the Court mandates an analysis of both the legislative trend and the extent to which the punishment is actually imposed by juries.

Summary of Relevant Criteria

In view of the Supreme Court's most recent contribution to the doctrine of proportionality, it appears that there are now essentially five categories of criteria which must be used in applying the doctrine to assess the validity of a particular punishment for a particular crime. They are: (1) judgments as to the seriousness of the crime in question; (2) comparisons with penalties imposed for more serious offenses; (3) evaluation of the punishment's history; (4) analysis of the legislative trend; and (5) assessment of the extent to which juries actually apply the punishment. Neither the Supreme Court nor any lower court has indicated the precise weight that should be afforded any of these factors or sought to devise a formula to be used in applying them. However, in light of the Court's interpretation of the Eighth Amendment, it seems obvious that in applying the various criteria the ultimate objective is to measure the degree of societal acceptance of the punishment in question.[108] If the indicators show that society views a punishment for an offense to be too harsh, then the punishment is constitutionally excessive when applied for that offense.

Applying the Doctrine of Proportionality to Death as a Punishment for Rape

Judgment as to the Relative Seriousness of the Offense

A glance at history reveals that rape has never been considered as serious a crime as murder. Perhaps the most striking evidence of this appears in the law of Moses. Although murder, adultery, disobedience by a child to his parents, blasphemy, and sodomy were all apparently capital offenses, according to a learned commentator, the offense of rape "was punishable not by death but by payment of damages and by an injunction to marry the victim."[109] The eighteenth-century view of the relative seriousness of rape in comparison to other crimes was reflected by Thomas Jefferson in 1776. Responding to a charge that he favored the abolition of punishments, Jefferson responded:

Punishments I know are necessary, and I would provide them, strict and inflexible, but proportioned to the crime. Death might be inflicted for murder and perhaps for treason. . . . Rape, burglary etc. punish by castration, all other crimes by working on high roads, rivers, gallies, etc. a certain time proportioned to the offense.[110]

Rape, then, was classified with other serious felonies such as burglary; clearly, however, it ranked as a distinctly lesser offense than the extreme crime of murder. If the death penalty were to be applied for rape, it would have to be applied for a number of other serious felonies as well.

If anything, the difference perceived in the seriousness of murder and rape is wider now than it was two hundred years ago. While it might have been once believed that a woman's chastity was as important as her life, no rational person would hold this view today. Rape is an offensive, violent crime, one which is clearly harmful to society; but as the Fourth Circuit said in *Ralph v. Warden*, "there are rational gradations of culpability that can be made on the basis of injury to the victim."[111] When compared to murder, the lesser injury to the rape victim is obvious, and even when compared to other serious felonies such as kidnapping, robbery, or aggravated assault and battery, it is not at all clear that rape would be perceived by most victims as causing the greatest injury. Contemporary acceptance of this view is reflected in the Model Penal Code's gradation of offenses. Whereas murder is set apart from all other crimes and made a capital offense when committed under aggravated circumstances,[112] rape, along with kidnapping[113] and robbery,[114] is categorized as a second-degree felony unless committed under aggravated circumstances.[115] When the specified aggravated circumstances are present, these crimes become first-degree felonies subject to a minimum term of imprisonment not to exceed ten years and a maximum of life imprisonment.[116] Thus, it appears that on any rational scale of seriousness, rape ranks as a distinctly lesser offense than murder and as no more serious than a number of other serious felonies.

Comparison with Penalties Provided for Murder

Legislation in seven states currently provides that capital punishment shall be imposed upon conviction of certain types of rape. Table 1 compares the penalties provided for rape in these states with the penalties provided for murder in the same jurisdictions. Each of the seven provides for capital punishment in some murder cases; and all but one of them provide that there will be some cases where the death penalty is applicable to a murder case but would not be applicable to a rape case where the circumstances are otherwise similar.[117] Somewhat strikingly, however, in five of the jurisdictions, there are situations in which the death penalty may or must be imposed when the offender rapes his victim but would not be applicable if the offender murdered his victim under precisely similar circumstances. For example, if a nineteen-year-old Mississippi defendant is convicted of raping an eleven-year-old female, he must be sentenced to death; had he murdered the eleven-year-old female instead of raping her, however, he would not be subject to the death penalty unless some extraordinary additional circumstances were present.[118] Similarly, the Louisiana statute provides that a rapist who uses force to overcome the victim's utmost resistance must be sentenced to death; but a Louisiana murderer who used force to overpower a victim's utmost resistance would not, under the Louisiana statute, be subject to capital punishment in the absence of a finding of additional aggravating circumstances.[119] These provisions show that in some situations rape as such is punished more severely than murder.

In Florida and Georgia, the circumstances that will justify a death sentence in rape cases will always also authorize the imposition of capital punishment in a murder case. However, under the applicable statutes in both states, it is apparent that there will be some noncapital murders that based on any rational criteria appear to be more serious than any conceivable form of rape. Thus, in both states it appears that murders committed in the following ways will not be subject to the death penalty: (1) a murderer carefully plots the death of his enemy and effects that death by means of a relatively painless poison; (2) acting upon a sudden passion not caused by reasonable provocation, a murderer beats a young child to death; (3) a man carrying on an adulterous affair threatens his paramour with death when she rejects him, and then several days later shoots her in cold blood while she is pleading for mercy.[120] If murder is really the most "extreme of crimes," it would seem that murders of this character, or even less atrocious ones, are more serious than any rape, or certainly more serious than many of the rapes that are subject to capital punishment under the two statutes.

Thus, in five jurisdictions the legislature directly provides that in some situations rape as such will be punished more severely than murder. And in all seven jurisdictions certain rapes are subject to the death penalty while murders that are at least as serious if not more serious than the prescribed rapes are subject to a lesser penalty. This anomaly suggests that in dealing with the crime of rape, the seven legislatures in question have responded irrationally. At best, their capital penalty provisions may be characterized as a product of " 'honest zeal,' generated in response to transitory public emotion";[121] as such, they are constitutionally suspect.

Analysis of the Legislative Trend

Table 2 shows that only seven jurisdictions currently have legislation that provides death as a penalty for rape. Further, three of these seven, Florida, Mississippi, and Tennessee, authorize the death penalty only when the victim is of tender years. Thus, with respect to the Georgia statute that allows the death penalty to be imposed for rape in a wide variety of situations, the language of the Fourth Circuit in *Hart v. Coiner* is apt: "[it] is among the top four in the nation in terms of severity, and may be number one."[122] Based on the analysis applied in *Hart* and other lower court cases, the death penalty provisions in effect in four states (and probably in all seven) are constitutionally suspect.[123] When more than four-fifths of the states reject death as a penalty for rape, this is substantial evidence that the imposition of death as a punishment for this offense is now contrary to our "evolving standards of decency."

But in the light of the plurality's analysis in *Gregg* and *Woodson*, a mere numbers count is insufficient. The trend of the legislation must also be examined. In his *Rudolph* dissent in 1963, Justice Goldberg referred to "the trend both in this country and throughout the world against punishing rape by death."[124] At that time, nineteen American jurisdictions authorized death as a discretionary penalty for rape in some or all situations.[125] When *Ralph v. Warden* was decided in 1970, only sixteen states and the federal government retained the death penalty for rape.[126] A better than 10 percent decrease in the space of seven years would appear to evidence a fairly significant trend toward abolition.[127]

Two years later the Court's decision in *Furman* provided a watershed for capital punishment legislation. As the Court indicated in *Gregg*, the invalidation of almost all then-existing capital punishment legislation provided legislatures with an opportunity to reflect their current views on the propriety of capital punishment.[128] But whereas at least thirty-five states enacted new statutes providing for imposition of the death penalty in certain murder cases,[129] only six enacted new legislation providing for death as a penalty in any case of rape.[130] Because of the other eleven jurisdictions' failure to enact new capital legislation for rape, the number of jurisdictions retaining the death penalty was cut by more than 50 percent in the space of just a few years. Clearly, the trend toward abolition is direct and proceeding apace. When the country is viewed as a whole, there is certainly room for argument that death as a punishment for rape has now "been rejected by the elected representatives of the people."[131]

The History of Death as a Punishment for Rape: Analysis
of the Georgia Legislation

The fact that relatively few jurisdictions retain death as a penalty for rape might not be decisive evidence of societal rejection of the punishment in the country as a whole if it appeared that there were some special justification for applying this unique penalty in those jurisdictions. Therefore, an inquiry into the historical roots of this penalty in one state is particularly instructive.

Prior to the Civil War, the Georgia penal code expressly provided that rape committed by a white man would be punished by a term of imprisonment;[132] in 1816 the maximum term of imprisonment was fixed at twenty years.[133] On the other hand, by separate legislation, it was provided first, that slaves or "free persons of color" could be given a discretionary death sentence for any crime;[134] and then, in 1816, that the punishment of slaves and "free persons of color" for the crime of rape or attempted rape of a free white female should be death.[135] One year after the abolition of slavery, a facially color-blind statute was enacted, giving juries discretion to sentence any man convicted of rape to either death or not more than twenty years' imprisonment.[136] In light of this history, it appears clear that at least in one southern state the sole original purpose of the legislation making rape a capital offense was to perpetuate a dual system of justice: one in which only black men convicted of raping white women would be subject to capital punishment. At the least, this history does not enhance a claim that there are legitimate justifications for death as a penalty for rape in a few isolated jurisdictions.

Jury Determinations

Finally, it is important to examine the extent to which juries actually impose the death penalty for rape. A review of the nationwide statistics supports Justice Stewart's conclusion that the death penalty's "imposition for rape is extraordinarily rare."[137] Table 3 shows that from 1963 to 1974 the number of death sentences imposed for rape has averaged less than ten per year and that in most regions of the country no death sentences for this crime have been imposed at all. Table 4 allows a comparison between the death sentences imposed for rape and both reported rapes and rape convictions. Based on these figures, it is obvious that in the recent past a convicted rapist's chances of receiving the death sentence have been miniscule and his chances of execution virtually nil.

Moreover, a breakdown on the race of those sentenced to death casts these figures in a yet more sinister light. Of the 455 men executed for rape since 1930, 89.5 percent have been nonwhite.[138] A study of the death sentences for rape imposed over a twenty-year period in eleven southern states shows that "among 1,265 cases in which the race of the defendant and the sentence are known, nearly seven times as many blacks were sentenced to death than were whites;"[139] and "black defendants whose victims were white were sentenced to death approximately 18 times more frequently than defendants in any other racial combination of defendant and victim."[140] Based on these figures, it appears that the reason death is rarely imposed for the crime of rape is that that sentence is reserved almost exclusively for cases in which southern black men are convicted of raping southern white women.[141]

In the wake of the post-*Furman* capital punishment legislation, imposition of death sentences has generally increased. Nevertheless, the number of rape cases in which a death sentence has been imposed has remained small in comparison to the total number of rape convictions.[142] And where death penalty determinations remain discretionary (and therefore constitutionally valid), analysis of the currently available data shows that the death penalty is actually imposed in only a small proportion of those cases in which defendants would be eligible for capital punishment under the applicable statute.[143] Moreover, the disparity between the number of death sentences imposed for murder and the number imposed for rape is striking. Justice Stewart noted in *Gregg* that by the close of 1974 at least 254 persons had been sentenced to death since *Furman*, and by the end of March 1976, more than 460 persons were subject to death sentences.[144] As Table 3 indicates, only about 10 percent of those sentenced to death from the time of *Furman* to the close of 1974 were sentenced for rape. Moreover, application of *Woodson*'s ban on mandatory capital punishment invalidated death sentences imposed pursuant to the Louisiana, Mississippi, North Carolina, and Tennessee statutes.[145] As a result the number of inmates sentenced to death for the crime of rape as of February 3, 1977 has been reduced to 5.[146]

Based on these figures, it appears that in our recent history death as a penalty for rape has been applied only in a few southern jurisdictions; and that within these jurisdictions, the penalty has not only been imposed with great infrequency but has been reserved primarily for the same type of offense (black rapist–white victim) that led to the institution of death as a penalty for rape in the first place.

Conclusion

Whether death is a constitutionally disproportionate punishment for rape ultimately turns on whether contemporary society views this punishment as appropriate for this offense. Death as a punishment for rape is on the statute books in only seven jurisdictions. This is some indication that the country as a whole rejects this punishment. Moreover, even within the seven minority jurisdictions, crimes that seem indisputably more serious than any rape are subject to a lesser punishment than death. This lends support to a claim that the legislation on the books in those jurisdictions results from some kind of aberration and does not truly reflect societal acceptance of death as a punishment for rape even in specific parts of the country.

Nevertheless, if such provisions appeared to be a legitimate legislative response to unique local problems, there might at least be a colorable claim that despite the evidence to the contrary, society does in fact accept death as an appropriate punishment for rape under certain circumstances. However, a glance at the history and the application of a representative statute reveals that no reasonable attempt can be made to justify the death penalty provisions on this basis. The legislative history of Georgia's rape statutes indicates that the sole original purpose for the death penalty provision was to allow for the imposition of the death penalty in a case where a black man raped a white woman. Examination of jury determinations in all rape–death penalty cases shows that the death penalty has always been imposed with disproportionate frequency in this type of situation. Indeed, a white rapist's chances of receiving the death penalty are virtually negligible. Thus, it appears that the only special justification for the rape–death penalty in the few jurisdictions retaining the penalty are racial considerations. The juries' virtually complete rejection of the death penalty in cases involving white rapists evidences that even within the minority jurisdictions, society accepts the death penalty for rape only as one to be reserved for a few isolated pariahs and refuses to accept it as one that will be regularly, fairly, and evenhandedly applied to offenders meeting the criteria identified by the statutes. In view of this overwhelming evidence of societal repudiation, it is appropriate for the Court to hold that death is a disproportionate punishment for the crime of rape.

TABLE 1. Disproportionality and Death Penalty

State	Rape	Murder
Florida	Death penalty may be imposed upon person 18 years of age or older who rapes a person 11 years of age or younger. FLA. STAT. ANN. §§ 794.11, 775.082, 921.141 (West 1976).	Death penalty may be imposed upon any defendant who murders another. FLA. STAT. ANN. §§ 782.041, 775.082, 921.141 (West 1976).
Georgia	Death penalty may be imposed upon defendant who commits rape provided at least one of the three following statutorily defined aggravating circumstances is found: (1) offender had a prior capital felony conviction; (2) the rape was committed while the offender was engaged in the commission of another capital felony or aggravated battery; (3) the rape was outrageously vile in that it involved torture, depravity of mind, or an aggravated battery to the victim. GA. CODE ANN. § 27.2534 (Supp. 1976).	Death penalty may be imposed upon defendant who commits murder provided at least one of ten statutorily defined aggravating circumstances is found. Three of the ten aggravating circumstances are the same aggravating circumstances that will justify a death sentence for rape. GA. CODE ANN. § 27.2534 (Supp. 1976).
Louisiana	Death penalty must be imposed for rape where one of the three following aggravating circumstances takes place: (1) female's utmost resistance is overcome by force; (2) female is prevented from resisting rape by threats of great and immediate bodily harm accompanied by apparent power of execution; (3) female is under the age of 12. LA. REV. STAT. ANN. § 14-42 (West Supp. 1976).	Death penalty must be imposed for first-degree murder, defined as murder where offender has specific intent to kill or commit great bodily harm and one of five aggravating circumstances is present. These are (1) murder is a certain kind of felony-murder; (2) victim is a fireman or policeman; (3) offender has a previous conviction of murder; (4) offender has intent to kill or harm more than one person; (5) offender offered or received something of value to perform the killing. LA. REV. STAT. ANN. § 14-30 (West Supp. 1976).

TABLE 1 — *Continued*

State	Rape	Murder
Mississippi	Death penalty must be imposed for rape of female under age of 12 by offender over the age of 18. MISS. CODE ANN. § 97-3-65 (Supp. 1975).	Death penalty must be imposed for capital murder, defined as (1) murder of peace officer or fireman; (2) murder by person under sentence of life; (3) murder perpetrated by explosive device; (4) murder for hire; (5) certain felony-murders; (6) murder of an elected official. MISS. CODE ANN. § 97-3-19, 21 (Supp. 1975).
North Carolina	Death penalty must be imposed for rape by offender over the age of 16 upon female under the age of 12 or upon any female who had resistance overcome by the use of a deadly weapon or by the infliction of serious bodily injury. N.C. GEN. STAT. § 14-21 (Supp. 1975).	Death penalty must be imposed for first-degree murder, defined as murder committed by poison, lying-in-wait, any other willful, deliberate and premeditated murder, or certain felony-murders. N.C. GEN. STAT. § 14-17 (Supp. 1975).
Oklahoma	Death penalty may be imposed for rape by male over 18 upon female under 14 or incapable because of lunacy of giving consent or upon any female where rape is accomplished by means of force overcoming her resistance or by threats of immediate great bodily harm accompanied by apparent power of execution. OKLA. STAT. ANN. tit. 21, § 1115 (West Supp. 1976).	Death penalty must be imposed for first-degree murder, defined as premeditated murder where one of ten specified aggravating circumstances are present. OKLA. STAT. ANN. tit. 21, § 701-3 (West Supp. 1976).
Tennessee	Death penalty must be imposed upon offender who rapes female under 12. TENN. CODE ANN. § 39-3702 (1975).	Death penalty must be imposed for first-degree murder, defined as premeditated murder or murder accompanied by one of nine aggravating circumstances. TENN. CODE ANN. § 39-2408 (1975).

TABLE 2. Rape

State	Citation	Maximum Sentence	Conduct Subject to Maximum[a]
Model Penal Code	§ 213.1	Life	1. Actor inflicts serious bodily injury or 2. Victim was not a voluntary social companion of actor upon the occasion of the crime, and had not previously permitted him sexual liberties.
Alabama	ALA. CODE tit. 14, § 395 (1959)	Life[b]	
Alaska	ALASKA STAT. 11.15.130 (1975)	20 years	
Arizona	ARIZ. REV. STAT. ANN. § 13.614 (Supp. 1976)	Life	
Arkansas	ARK. STAT. ANN. §§ 41-1803, 41-901(1)(a) (Supp. 1976)	Life	
California	CAL. PENAL CODE § 264, 264.1 (West 1970)	Life	1. Defendant inflicts great bodily injury on the victim, or 2. Defendant voluntarily acts in concert with another person to commit rape either personally or by aiding or abetting the other.
Colorado	COLO. REV. STAT. §§ 18-3-401–405, 18-1-105(1) (Supp. 1975)	50 years	1. Actor is physically aided or abetted by one or more other persons, or 2. Victim suffers serious bodily injury or 3. Actor is armed with a deadly weapon that is used to cause submission of the victim.
Connecticut	CONN. GEN. STAT. ANN. §§ 53a-70, 53a-35(b) (Supp. 1976)	20 years	

TABLE 2 — *Continued*

State	Citation	Maximum Sentence	Conduct Subject to Maximum[a]
Delaware	DEL. CODE tit. 11, §§ 764, 4205 (Supp. 1976)	Life	1. Defendant inflicts serious physical, mental, or emotional injury upon the victim, or 2. Victim was not the defendant's voluntary social companion on the occasion of the crime and had not previously permitted him sexual contact.
Florida	FLA. STAT. ANN. § 775.082 (West 1974)	Death	Person 18 years of age or older rapes a person 11 years of age or under.[c]
Georgia	GA. CODE ANN. § 27-2534 (1973)	Death	1. Defendant has a prior capital felony conviction, or 2. The rape was committed while the defendant was engaged in the commission of another capital felony or aggravated battery, or 3. The rape was outrageously vile in that it involved torture, depravity of mind, or an aggravated battery to the victim.
Hawaii	HAWAII REV. STAT. §§ 706-661, 707-730 (1976)	Life	1. Female is not defendant's voluntary social companion who had within previous 6 months permitted him sexual contact, or 2. Defendant inflicts serious bodily injury upon the victim, or 3. Victim is a female who is less than 14 years old, and defendant inflicts serious bodily injury.
Idaho	IDAHO CODE §§ 18-6101, 18-6104 (1948)	Life	
Illinois	ILL. ANN. STAT. ch. 38, § 11-1 (Smith-Hurd Supp. 1976)	Not less than 4 years[d]	
Indiana	IND. CODE ANN. §§ 35-13-4-3 (West 1975)	Life	Female is under 12 years of age.

TABLE 2 — *Continued*

State	Citation	Maximum Sentence	Conduct Subject to Maximum[a]
Iowa	IOWA CODE ANN. § 698.1 (West 1950)	Life	
Kansas	KAN. STAT. ANN. §§ 21-3502, 21-4501 (1974)	20 years	
Kentucky	KY. REV. STAT. ANN. §§ 510.040, 532.060 (Baldwin 1975)	Life	1. Victim is under 12 years old, or 2. Victim receives a serious physical injury.
Louisiana	LA. REV. STAT. ANN. § 14-42 (West Supp. 1976)	Death	1. Victim's resistance is overcome by force, or 2. Victim is prevented from resisting by threats of bodily harm, or 3. Victim is under 12 years of age.
Maine	ME. REV. STAT. ANN. tit. 17A, §§ 252, 1252(2)(A) (Pamphlet 1976)	20 years	
Maryland	MD. ANN. CODE art. 27, § 461 (1976)	Life	
Massachusetts	MASS. GEN. LAWS ANN. ch. 265, § 22 (West 1976)	Life	
Michigan	MICH. COMP. LAWS ANN. § 750.520b (Supp. 1976)	Life	1. Victim is under 13 years old, or 2. Actor is in position of authority over victim who is 13–16 years old, or 3. Act occurs in the commission of another felony, or 4. Actor is aided or abetted by another person and either the victim is mentally defective or the actor uses force, or 5. Actor is armed with a weapon, or 6. Actor threatens or actually uses force and causes personal injury to the victim.

TABLE 2 — *Continued*

State	Citation	Maximum Sentence	Conduct Subject to Maximum[a]
Minnesota	MINN. STAT. ANN. § 609.342 (West Supp. 1976)	20 years	1. Victim is under 13 years old; actor is more than 3 years older than victim, or 2. Victim is 13–16 years old; actor is more than 4 years older and in a position of authority over victim, or 3. Victim had a reasonable fear of imminent great bodily harm, or 4. Actor was armed with a dangerous weapon, or 5. Actor caused personal injury to victim.
Mississippi	MISS. CODE ANN. § 97-3-65 (Supp. 1975)	Death	Victim is under 12 years of age and actor is 18 years of age or older.
Missouri	MO. ANN. STAT. § 559.260 (Vernon Supp. 1976)	Not less than 2 years[d]	
Montana	MONT. CODE ANN. § 45-5-503 (1983)	40 years	1. Victim is less than 16 years old and offender is 3 or more years older, or 2. Offender inflicts bodily injury.
Nebraska	NEB. REV. STAT. § 28-408.3 (1975)	25 years	1. Actor overcomes victim by force, threat of force, coercion, or deception, or 2. Victim was mentally or physically unable to resist, or 3. Actor is more than 18 years old and victim is less than 16 years old.
Nevada	NEV. REV. STAT. § 200.363 (1967)	Life (without possibility of parole)	1. Substantial bodily harm results.

TABLE 2 — *Continued*

State	Citation	Maximum Sentence	Conduct Subject to Maximum[a]
New Hampshire	N.H. REV. STAT. ANN. § 632-A:2 (1975)	15 years	1. Actor overcomes victim with physical force, or 2. Actor overcomes victim with threats of physical force, or 3. Actor administers drugs to victim, or 4. Actor administers unethical medical treatment, or 5. Victim is mentally defective, or 6. Victim is unconscious or less than 15 years of age.
New Jersey	N.J. STAT. ANN. § 2A:138-1 (West 1969)	30 years	1. Victim is drugged, or 2. Actor is over 16 years old and victim is under 12 years old.
New Mexico	N.M. STAT. ANN. § 40A-9-21 (Supp. 1976), § 40A-29-3(A) (1972)	Life	1. Victim is under 13 years of age, or 2. Actor commits act by the use of force or coercion that results in great bodily harm or great mental anguish to the victim.
New York	N.Y. PENAL LAW §§ 130.35, 70.00 (McKinney 1975)	25 years	1. Actor commits act by forcible compulsion, or 2. Victim is physically helpless, or 3. Victim is less than 11 years old.
North Carolina	N.C. GEN. STAT. § 14-21 (Supp. 1975)	Death	1. Actor is more than 16 years of age and victim is a virtuous female child under the age of 12 years, or 2. Actor is more than 16 years of age and victim had her resistance overcome by the use of a deadly weapon or by the infliction of serious bodily injury to her.
North Dakota	N.D. CENT. CODE §§ 12.1-20-03, 12.1-32-01 (1976)	20 years	1. Actor inflicts bodily injury upon the victim, or 2. Victim is less than 15 years old, or 3. Victim is not a voluntary companion of the actor and has not previously permitted him sexual liberties.
Ohio	OHIO REV. CODE ANN. § 2907.02 (Page 1974)	Life	Victim is less than 13 years of age and is compelled to submit by force or threat of force.

TABLE 2 — *Continued*

State	Citation	Maximum Sentence	Conduct Subject to Maximum[a]
Oklahoma	OKLA. STAT. ANN. tit. 21, § 1115 (Supp. 1976)	Death	1. Act is committed by a male over 18 years of age upon a female under 14 years of age, or 2. Victim is incapable of giving consent because of lunacy, or 3. Act is accomplished by means of force or by means of threats of immediate and great bodily harm.
Oregon	OR. REV. STAT. §§ 163.375, 161.605 (1975)	20 years	1. Female is subjected to forcible compulsion by the male, or 2. Female is under 12 years of age, or 3. Female is under 16 years of age and is the male's sister, of the whole or of half blood, his daughter, or his wife's daughter.
Pennsylvania	18 PA. CONS. STAT. ANN. §§ 3121, 1103 (1973)	20 years	
Rhode Island	R.I. GEN. LAWS § 11-37-1 (1970)	Life	
South Carolina	S.C. CODE ANN. § 16-3-640 (Law. Co-op. 1977)	40 years	
South Dakota	S.D. COMP. LAWS ANN. § 22-22-5 (1975)	Not less than 10 years[d]	1. Female is under 10 years of age or is mentally defective, or 2. Victim's resistance is overcome by force.
Tennessee	TENN. CODE ANN. § 39-3702 (1975)	Death	Female is under 12 years of age.
Texas	TEX. PENAL CODE ANN. tit. 2, § 21.02 (Vernon 1975)	20 years	

TABLE 2 — *Continued*

State	Citation	Maximum Sentence	Conduct Subject to Maximum[a]
Utah	UTAH CODE ANN. § 76-5-405 (Supp. 1975)	Life	1. Actor causes serious bodily injury to victim, or 2. Actor compels submission by threat of kidnapping, death, or serious bodily injury, or 3. Victim is under 14 years of age.
Vermont	VT. STAT. ANN. tit. 13, § 3201 (1974)	20 years	
Virginia	VA. CODE § 18.2-61 (1975)	Life	
Washington	WASH. REV. CODE ANN. § 9.79.170 (Supp. 1975)	Not less than 20 years[d]	1. Actor uses or threatens to use a deadly weapon, or 2. Actor kidnaps the victim, or 3. Actor inflicts serious physical injury, or 4. Actor feloniously enters into the building or vehicle where victim is situated.
West Virginia	W.VA. CODE § 61-8B-3 (Supp. 1976)	20 years	
Wisconsin	WIS. STAT. ANN. § 944.01 (West 1958)	30 years	
Wyoming	WYO. STAT. § 6-63 (Supp. 1975)	Life	

[a] Unless otherwise stated, the conduct subject to the maximum is common law rape. Where aggravating circumstances in addition to common law rape must be found to authorize imposition of the maximum penalty, the aggravated circumstances are stated.

[b] The death penalty for rape has been set aside as a form of punishment in this state by the Supreme Court of Alabama. Tell v. State, 291 Ala. 86, 277 So. 2d 898 (1973). Since the death penalty has been eliminated from this section, the court is required to vacate and set aside sentences of death and substitute life imprisonment for the death sentence. Jackson v. State, 290 Ala. 130, 274 So. 2d 311 (1973).

[c] Under Florida procedure, the death penalty determination is totally discretionary. A death sentence will be imposed by the judge after consideration of the jury's recommendation. Pursuant to FLA. STAT. ANN. § 921.141(2)(b)-(c) (West Supp. 1976-77), the jury's recommendation will be based upon "whether sufficient mitigating circumstances exist . . . which outweigh aggravating circumstances found to exist." The statute then enumerates various aggravating and mitigating circumstances but sets no rule whatsoever as to when the death penalty must be or may not be imposed.

[d] Statute provides only for mandatory minimum sentence.

TABLE 3. Percentage of Rapists Sentenced to Death

Year	No. of Reported Rapes[a]	% of Reported Rapes That Resulted in Arrest	% of Persons Arrested Who Were Prosecuted for Rape	% of Persons Prosecuted Found Guilty of Rape	No. of Death Sentences Imposed for Rape	% of Those Convicted of Rape Who Received the Death Sentence[b]
1975	56,090	51	58	42	—	—
1974	55,210	51	60	35	17	.09
1973	51,000	51	76	36	7	.10
1972	46,430	57	73	32	8	.13
1971	41,890	55	70	35	7	.12
1970	37,270	56	70	36	9	.33
1969	36,470	56	62	34	9	.21
1968	31,060	55	73	40	9	.06
1967	27,100	61	74	37	3	.16
1966	25,330	62	78	40	7	.41
1965	22,470	64	72	40	20	.12
1964	20,550	67	77	40	5	.21
1963	16,400	69	79	39	9	.85

Source: CRIME IN THE U.S., UNIFORM CRIME REPORTS (1964–1975).

a Forcible rape is defined as the carnal knowledge of a female through the use of force or threat of force. Assaults to commit rape are also included, but statutory rape (without force) is not.

b These percentages were calculated from figures found in CRIME IN THE U.S., UNIFORM CRIME REPORTS (1964–1975).

TABLE 4.   Number of Rapists Executed, by Region

Year	No. of Death Sentences Imposed for Rape	No. of Sentences by Region				Executions for Rape
		North East	North Central	South	West	
1974	17	—	—	17	—	—
1973	7	—	—	7	—	—
1972	8	—	—	8	—	—
1971	7	—	—	7	—	—
1970	9	—	—	9	—	—
1969	9	—	—	9	—	—
1968	3	—	3	—	—	—
1967	7	—	—	7	—	—
1966	20	—	—	19	1	—
1965	4	—	—	4	—	4
1964	9	—	—	9	—	6
1963	9	—	—	9	—	2
1962	4	—	—	4	—	4
1961	21	—	1	20	—	8

Source: U.S. DEP'T OF JUSTICE, BUREAU OF PRISONS, NATIONAL PRISONER STATISTICS, CAPITAL PUNISHMENT 1962–1974.

NOTES

The author acknowledges his gratitude for the research assistance provided by Joseph S. Sabadish in preparing the tables and notes.

    1. *See* Gregg v. Georgia, 428 U.S. 153 (1976); Jurek v. Texas, 428 U.S. 262 (1976); Proffitt v. Florida, 428 U.S. 242 (1976).

    2. 375 U.S. 889 (1963) (Goldberg, J., dissenting).

    3. *See generally* M. MELTSNER, CRUEL AND UNUSUAL: THE SUPREME COURT AND CAPITAL PUNISHMENT (1973).

    4. 391 U.S. 510 (1968).

    5. That is, juries excluding all veniremen who stated that they were opposed to the death penalty or had conscientious scruples against voting for its imposition.

    6. 402 U.S. 183 (1971).

    7. *McGautha* actually involved two cases: *McGautha v. California*, which upheld the constitutionality of giving the jury standardless sentencing discretion in a capital case; and *Crampton v. Ohio*, a companion case, which upheld the constitutionality of the unitary trial procedure.

    8. 408 U.S. 238 (1972).

    9. *See* Gregg v. Georgia, 428 U.S. at 187–95. *See also* Woodson v. North

Carolina, 428 U.S. 280 (1976) (holding North Carolina statute that imposes mandatory death sentence upon conviction of first-degree murder to be in violation of the cruel and unusual punishment clause); Roberts v. Louisiana, 428 U.S. 325 (1976) (holding Louisiana statute imposing mandatory death sentence upon conviction of specified categories of first-degree murder to be similarly invalid). In *Gregg* the Court hinted that death sentences imposed pursuant to the unitary trial procedure upheld in *McGautha* might also be constitutionally invalid. *See* 428 U.S. at 190–95.

10. Gregg v. Georgia, 428 U.S. at 187 n.35.

11. *Id.*

12. Coker v. Georgia, 234 Ga. 555, 216 S.E.2d 782 (1975).

13. Packer, *Making the Punishment Fit the Crime*, 77 HARV. L. REV. 1071 (1964).

14. Note, *The Eighth Amendment, Beccaria, and the Enlightenment: An Historical Justification for the Weems v. United States Excessive Punishment Doctrine*, 24 BUFF. L. REV. 783, 807–15 (1975) [hereinafter referred to as BUFFALO Note].

15. C. BECCARIA, ON CRIMES AND PUNISHMENTS (W. Paolucci transl. 1963).

16. *See infra* text at notes 20–22.

17. Ullman v. United States, 350 U.S. 422, 450 (1956) (Douglas, J., dissenting). *See generally* BUFFALO Note, *supra* note 14, at 813–30.

18. *See* letter from Thomas Jefferson to Edmund Pendleton, August 26, 1776, in 1 THE PAPERS OF THOMAS JEFFERSON 505 (1950). For a partial text of the letter, see *infra* text at note 100.

19. *See* BUFFALO Note, *supra* note 14, at 819–26.

20. C. BECCARIA, *supra* note 15, at 13.

21. For example, it might be found that the death penalty or some other severe punishment might be necessary to achieve effective deterrence of some relatively minor offense.

22. C. BECCARIA, *supra* note 15, at 43–44.

The severity of punishment not only aggravates the likelihood that inhuman deeds will be committed, but also maintaining the essential proportion between the crime and the punishment becomes impossible because there is a limit to human endurance which necessarily measures the extremes of punishment as also impunity itself arises from the severity of the punishment as such cruelty is fatal to a constant system.

23. H. HART, PUNISHMENT AND RESPONSIBILITY 80 (1968).

24. Rudolph v. Alabama, 375 U.S. 889, 889–91 (1963) (Goldberg, J., dissenting).

25. Packer, *supra* note 13, at 1078.

26. *Id.* at 1079–81.

27. *See* H. PACKER, THE LIMITS OF THE CRIMINAL SANCTION 139–45 (1968).

28. H. HART, *supra* note 23, at 234.

29. *Id.*

30. *Id.* at 25.

31. *See* H. PACKER, *supra* note 27.

32. 217 U.S. 349 (1910).

33. *Id*. at 364.

34. *Id*.

35. The Court held that the guiding principle of the cruel and unusual punishment clause is "public opinion . . . enlightened by a humane justice." *Id*. at 378.

36. *Id*. at 366. Packer, *supra* note 13, at 1075, argues that *Weems* deals with the mode rather than the proportion of the punishment. However, the Court's analysis, see *infra* text at notes 37–43, as well as its invalidation of the entire penal statute (rather than merely the accessory provisions) makes it clear that it struck down the statute at least in part because it found the minimum term of imprisonment to be constitutionally disproportionate when considered in relation to the offense.

37. 217 U.S. at 366–67.

38. *Id*. at 377.

39. *Id*. at 380.

40. *Id*.

41. *Id*. at 380–81.

42. *Id*. at 381.

43. *Id*. at 382.

44. *See generally* Turkington, *Unconstitutionally Excessive Punishment: An Examination of the Eighth Amendment and the Weems Principle*, 3 CRIM. L. BULL. 145 (1967).

45. In part the proportionality doctrine's resurgence may be attributed to the Court's holding that the cruel and unusual punishment clause of the Eighth Amendment is applicable to the states through the Fourteenth Amendment. *See* Robinson v. California, 370 U.S. 660 (1962). Prior to this holding, the federal courts had few opportunities for applying the cruel and unusual punishment clause and the potential applicability of similar state clauses went largely unrecognized.

46. Some of the state constitutional provisions prohibit "cruel *or* unusual punishments." In practice this difference in wording appears to make little difference in defining the scope of the clause. *See, e.g.*, People v. Anderson, 6 Cal. 3d 628, 493 P.2d 880, 100 Cal. Rptr. 152 (1972) (holding that punishments that are either "cruel" *or* "unusual" are unconstitutional, but finding that the death penalty is both "cruel" and "unusual" and therefore meets both prongs of the test).

47. For example, in order to compare the punishment for the offense in question with punishments imposed for "more serious" offenses, it is obviously necessary to show where the offense in question ranks on a scale of seriousness.

48. *See* People v. Broadie, 37 N.Y.2d 100, 332 N.E.2d 338, 271 N.Y.S.2d 471 (1975) (upholding New York's statute imposing mandatory minimum terms of imprisonment upon conviction for possession and sale of drug offenses); People v. Wingo, 14 Cal. 3d 169, 534 P.2d 1001, 121 Cal. Rptr. 97 (1975) (upholding California statute imposing punishment of six months to life imprisonment upon conviction of assault by means of force likely to produce great bodily harm).

49. *See supra* text at notes 22–30.

50. Several recent cases have focused on the extent to which a punishment for a crime serves a valid penological purpose. *See Broadie*, 37 N.Y.2d 100, 332 N.E.2d at 344, 371 N.Y.S.2d at 478–79 (1975); People v. Lorentzen, 387 Mich. 167, 194 N.W.2d 827, 833 (1972). *See generally* Note, 44 FORDHAM L. REV. 637 (1975). However, none of these cases has suggested that a punishment that passes this test will necessarily be valid when measured against the disproportionality prong of the cruel and unusual punishment clause.

51. 8 Cal. 3d 410, 503 P.2d 921, 105 Cal. Rptr. 217 (1973).

52. CAL. CONST., art. I, § 17.

53. 8 Cal. 3d at 430, 503 P.2d at 934, 105 Cal. Rptr. at 230.

54. *Id*.

55. 483 F.2d 136 (4th Cir. 1973), *cert. denied*, 415 U.S. 983 (1974).

56. The West Virginia recidivist statute provided that anyone convicted three separate times of offenses "punishable by confinement in a penitentiary" should receive a mandatory sentence of life imprisonment. W. VA. CODE § 61-11-18 (1966).

57. 483 F.2d at 141.

58. *See* Downey v. Perini, 518 F.2d 1288, 1292 (6th Cir. 1975); Lorentzen, 387 Mich. 167, 194 N.W.2d 827, 831–32 (1972).

59. 438 F.2d 786 (4th Cir. 1970), *cert. denied*, 408 U.S. 942 (1972).

60. 438 F.2d at 788.

61. *Id*. at 793.

62. Workman v. Commonwealth, 429 S.W.2d 374 (Ky. 1968).

63. 429 S.W.2d at 378.

64. 8 Cal. 3d at 426, 503 P.2d at 931–32, 105 Cal. Rptr. at 227–28.

65. *See, e.g.*, Roberts v. Collins, 404 F. Supp. 119 (D. Md. 1975); Hobbs v. State, 253 Ind. 195, 252 N.E.2d 498 (1969); Dembowski v. State, 241 Ind. 250, 240 N.E.2d 815 (1968); Application of Cannon, 203 Or. 629, 281 P.2d 233 (1955).

66. 518 F.2d 1288 (6th Cir. 1975).

67. 518 F.2d at 1291–92.

68. *Id*. at 1292.

69. 483 F.2d 136 (4th Cir. 1973), *cert. denied*, 415 U.S. 983 (1974).

70. *See supra* text at note 56.

71. 483 F.2d at 142.

72. *Id*.

73. *In re* Lynch, 8 Cal. 3d 410, 435, 503 P.2d 921, 938, 105 Cal. Rptr. 217, 234 (1973).

74. *Id*. at 431, 503 P.2d at 935, 105 Cal. Rptr. at 231.

75. *See also In re* Foss, 10 Cal. 3d 910, 519 P.2d 1073, 112 Cal. 649 (1974) (invalidating statute providing that a twice-convicted (nonmarijuana) drug offender will be given a minimum sentence of 10 years' imprisonment without possibility of parole). *But see* People v. Broadie, 37 N.Y.2d 100, 332 N.E.2d 338, 371 N.Y.S.2d 471 (1975). *See supra* text of note 48.

76. In applying the Eighth Amendment to changing times, the courts are to be guided by "the evolving standards of decency that mark the progress of a maturing society." Trop v. Dulles, 356 U.S. 86, 100 (1958) (plurality opinion of

Warren, C.J.). *See* Gregg v. Georgia, 428 U.S. 153 (1976); Robinson v. California, 370 U.S. 660, 666 (1962).

77. 483 F.2d 136 (4th Cir. 1973), *cert. denied*, 415 U.S. 983 (1974).

78. *Id*. at 142. In subsequent cases, recidivist statutes imposing life sentences upon conviction of more serious crimes have been upheld. *See, e.g.*, Griffin v. Warden, 517 F.2d 756 (4th Cir. 1975) (upholding application of West Virginia statute where defendant was convicted of two burglaries and one grand larceny); Capuchino v. Estelle, 506 F.2d 440 (5th Cir. 1975) (upholding application of Texas habitual offender act).

79. 578 F.2d 1288 (6th Cir. 1975).

80. Defendant was charged with possession for sale and sale of a small amount of marijuana. *See Id*. at 1289.

81. *Id*. at 1291.

82. *See* Roberts v. Collins, 404 F. Supp. 119, 123 (D. Md. 1975).

83. Ralph v. Warden, 438 F.2d 786, 791–92 (4th Cir. 1976), *cert. denied*, 408 U.S. 942 (1972).

84. *Id*. at 791.

85. 428 U.S. 153 (1976).

86. The plurality held that one of the two basic prongs of the cruel and unusual punishment clause is that "the punishment must be not grossly out of proportion to the severity of the crime." *Id*. at 173 (plurality opinion of Stewart, J.).

87. *Id*. at 187.

88. *Id*.

89. This approach would supply some guidance in that it would presumably require the Court to seek out contemporary opinions as to whether there is a sufficient degree of equivalence between a particular punishment and a particular crime. *Cf*. Robinson v. California, 370 U.S. 660, 666 (1962) (holding that the applicable Eighth Amendment test is "contemporary human knowledge").

90. 428 U.S. at 175–84.

91. 428 U.S. 280 (1976).

92. *Id*. at 2984–90.

93. *See supra* text at notes 35–37 and note 35.

94. *See supra* text at notes 44–84.

95. 428 U.S. at 288; *see Gregg*, 428 U.S. at 175–84.

96. *Gregg*, 428 U.S. at 176.

97. *Woodson*, 428 U.S. at 292–93.

98. With respect to mandatory capital punishment, the Court gave considerable weight to historians' conclusions that "almost from the outset jurors reacted unfavorably to the harshness of mandatory death sentences." *Id*. at 289, *see id*. at 289 n.18.

99. *Gregg*, 428 U.S. at 179.

100. *Id*.

101. *Woodson*, 428 U.S. at 291–92.

102. *Id*. at 298–99.

103. *Gregg*, 428 U.S. at 182.

104. *See id*. "At the close of 1974 at least 254 persons had been sentenced to

death since *Furman*, and by the end of March, 1976, more than 460 persons were subject to death sentences." (Footnotes omitted.)

105. 428 U.S. at 293.

106. *Id.* at 295.

107. *Id.* at 296.

108. *See supra* text at notes 35–37, and note 35.

109. G. HASKINS, LAW AND AUTHORITY IN EARLY MASSACHUSETTS 142–54 (1960).

110. *See* letter from Thomas Jefferson to Edmund Pendleton, August 26, 1776, in 1 THE PAPERS OF THOMAS JEFFERSON 505 (1950).

111. 438 F.2d at 788.

112. MODEL PENAL CODE §§ 210.2, 210.6 (Proposed Official Draft 1962).

113. MODEL PENAL CODE § 213.1 (Proposed Official Draft 1962). The required aggravating circumstances are detailed *supra* in table 2.

114. MODEL PENAL CODE § 212.1 (Proposed Official Draft 1962) (kidnapping is a felony of the first degree unless the actor voluntarily releases the victim alive and in a safe place prior to trial).

115. MODEL PENAL CODE § 222.1 (robbery is first-degree felony when in the course of the theft actor purposely inflicts or attempts to inflict serious bodily harm on anyone).

116. MODEL PENAL CODE § 6.06 (Proposed Official Draft 1962).

117. For example, in Georgia, murder of a police officer or a firefighter is a capital felony; but rape of a police officer or firefighter is not in itself a capital crime.

118. For example, a capital sentence would be applicable if the murder were committed in the course of a felony or while the defendant was under a sentence of life imprisonment. *See* MISS. CODE ANN. § 97-3-19, 21 (1974).

119. *See* LA. REV. STAT. ANN. § 14-30-1 (West 1975).

120. It might be argued that such murders could be capital in Florida because they are "especially heinous, atrocious or cruel," FLA. STAT. ANN. § 921.141(6) (West Supp. 1976–77) and in Georgia because they are "outrageously or wantonly vile, horrible or inhuman in that they involve torture, depravity of mind, or an aggravated battery to the victim." GA. CODE ANN. § 27.2534.1(7) (Supp. 1975). However, the Florida Supreme Court has already narrowed the "especially heinous, atrocious or cruel" provision to mean a "conscienceless or pitiless crime which is necessarily torturous to the victim." State v. Dixon, 283 So. 2d 1, 9 (Fla. 1973). And the Supreme Court has indicated that a similarly narrow construction of Georgia's "outrageously vile" provision may be necessary to save the constitutionality of this section of the Georgia statute. *See Gregg*, 428 U.S. at 201.

121. *See In re* Lynch, 8 Cal. 3d 410, 426, 503 P.2d 921, 931–32, 105 Cal. Rptr. 217, 227–28 (1973).

122. 483 F.2d at 142. Of course, if *Hart's* approach were rigidly followed, it would be necessary to compare the application of Georgia's rape statute in a particular case with the operation of other rape statutes in effect in the country. *See supra* note 78.

123. That is, all seven statutes are suspect under a disproportionality analy-

sis. Actually, in four of the seven states—Louisiana, Mississippi, North Carolina, and Tennessee—the death penalty for rape provisions are clearly invalid because they provide for a mandatory capital sentence upon conviction. *See* Woodson v. North Carolina, 428 U.S. 280 (1976); Roberts v. Louisiana, 428 U.S. 325 (1976). In a fifth state, Oklahoma, the death penalty provisions delegate unstructured capital sentencing discretion to the jury and therefore appear clearly unconstitutional under *Furman*. Therefore, only Georgia and Florida have capital rape legislation that could possibly be valid.

124. 375 U.S. 889 (1963) (Goldberg, J., dissenting).

125. *Id*. at 889–90.

126. *See supra* text at note 83.

127. The worldwide trend toward abolition noted by Justice Goldberg also continues. Whereas in 1963 a United Nations survey showed that five of sixty-five foreign nations permitted the imposition of the death penalty for rape (see United Nations, Capital Punishment prepared by Marc Ancel, Justice of the French Supreme Court) 38, 71–75 [1962]), in 1975 a similar suvey showed that only three out of seventy-eight foreign countries retained the death penalty for rape. *See* U.N. Doc. E/5278 (1973), *reprinted in* 1975 U.N.Y.R. 575.

128. 428 U.S. 153, 179–81.

129. *Id*.

130. While seven states have statutory provisions making rape punishable by death, Oklahoma's statute was pre-*Furman*. *See supra* table 2.

131. *Gregg*, 428 U.S. at 181.

132. Prior to the Civil War, the Georgia penal code expressly applied to free white persons only. *See* Penal Code of 1811, § 67, printed in Lamar, Compilation of the Laws of Georgia 552 (1821). The penal code of 1811 provided that rape would be punished by imprisonment at hard labor for not less than seven nor more than sixteen years. *Id*. at 551.

133. Penal Code of 1816, §§ 33–34, Lamar, *supra* note 132, at 571.

134. Ga. Acts of 1811, No. 503, Lamar, *supra* note 132, at 797–800.

135. Ga. Acts of 1816, No. 508, § 1, Lamar, *supra* note 132, at 804.

136. Ga. Acts of 1866, No. 210.

137. Furman v. Georgia, 408 U.S. 238, 309 (1972) (Stewart, J., concurring).

138. Wolfgang & Riedel, *Rape, Racial Discrimination and the Death Penalty*, in H. Bedau & C. Pierce, Capital Punishment in the United States 105 (1976).

139. *Id*. at 111.

140. *Id*. at 111–12.

141. From a statistical study that considered the effect of many variables, Wolfgang and Riedel concluded that with respect to the crime of rape in the eleven southern states studied, "sentences of death have been imposed on blacks, compared to whites, in a way that exceeds any statistical notion of chance or fortuity . . . . [and that] the significant racial differentials found in the imposition of the death penalty are indeed produced by racial discrimination." *Id*. at 118–19.

142. *See supra* table 4.

143. Thus in Georgia there have apparently been only three death sentences

imposed for rape under the new statute. *See* Coker v. State, 234 Ga. 555, 216 S.E.2d 782 (1975); Hooks v. State, 233 Ga. 149, 210 S.E.2d 668 (1974); Eberheart v. State, 232 Ga. 247, 206 S.E.2d 12 (1974). Even a cursory persual of the reported appellate decisions indicates that there have been numerous rape convictions in which the defendant's life was spared despite the potential applicability of the capital sentencing provisions. *See, e.g.*, Atkins v. State, 236 Ga. 624, 225 S.E.2d 7 (1976) (rape was committed while defendant was engaged in kidnapping, another capital felony); Jones v. State, 235 Ga. 103, 218 S.E.2d 899 (1975) (same); Zilinmon v. State, 234 Ga. 535, 216 S.E.2d 830 (1975) (rape was committed while defendant engaged in commission of aggravated battery); Crowder v. State, 233 Ga. 789, 213 S.E.2d 620 (1975) (same); Hammock v. State, 233 Ga. 733, 213 S.E.2d 618 (1975) (same); Curtis v. State, 236 Ga. 362, 223 S.E.2d 721 (1976) (same).

144. 428 U.S. at 182.

145. *See supra* note 123.

146. Of the five, three are white and two black. Three were convicted under the Georgia statute and two under the Florida statute. Two other Georgia defendants, one white and one black, have been sentenced to death for rape and kidnapping.

Disproportionality and the Death Penalty: Update

Six months after the publication of this essay, the Court held in *Coker v. Georgia* [1] that death is a constitutionally disproportionate punishment for the crime of rape of an adult woman. In reaching this result, the Court applied some of the criteria identified in the essay. But the pivotal plurality opinion also stated that the Court's own judgment must be brought to bear on the question of disproportionality. [2] Applying that judgment, the Court concluded that death is a disproportionate punishment for rape because although rape is one of the most serious and reprehensible of all criminal offenses, nevertheless "in terms of moral depravity and of the injury to the person and to the public, it does not compare with murder, which does involve the unjustified taking of human life." [3]

Although the scope of the proportionality principle is still unclear, *Coker*'s analysis certainly suggests that imposition of the death penalty for any crime other than murder will be constitutionally suspect. With the possible exception of treason, murder is clearly the most serious of all peacetime offenses. Thus, *Coker*'s conclusion that rape "does not compare with murder" would seem to be applicable to crimes such as robbery, kidnapping, or even hijacking, and to dictate a conclusion that death as a punishment for these offenses is excessive.

Moreover, the Court's recent decision in *Enmund v. Florida* [4] demonstrates that even when a defendant is properly convicted of murder death may be a disproportionate punishment because of the particular circumstances of the offense. In *Enmund* the defendant was sentenced to death after it was established that he was an accomplice to a robbery in which two elderly people were killed. The Court held that in these circumstances death is not a valid penalty "for one who neither took life, attempted to take life, nor intended to take life." [5] The analysis leading to this result was interesting for several reasons. As in *Coker*, the Court based its conclusion on both objective indicators of societal acceptance and its own judgment. In dealing with objective indicators, the Court sought to determine not only the extent to which death is authorized as a penalty for the crime of being an accomplice to a felony-murder but also the extent to which juries actually impose death as a penalty for this offense. After meticulously examining the relevant data, the Court concluded that although about one-third of American jurisdictions would permit a death sentence for this offense, only a handful of those now on death row were actually sentenced to death for committing it. [6]

Turning to its own judgment as to the validity of the death penalty for the defendant's offense, the Court focused on whether imposing the death penalty would measurably contribute to either deterrence or retribution, the two principal justifications for capital punishment. In contrast to the deferential stance it adopted in *Gregg*,[7] the *Enmund* Court was not content to accept the legislative judgment on these issues. Rather, in dealing with the issue of deterrence, the Court relied on its own assessment of the evidence to conclude that the death penalty likely serves as a deterrent only in the narrow category of cases in which "murder is the result of premeditation and deliberation."[8] In dealing with the issue of retribution, the Court assessed the defendant's personal culpability. The majority concluded that

[p]utting the defendant to death to avenge two killings that he did not commit and had no intention of committing or causing does not measurably contribute to the retributive end of ensuring that the criminal gets his just deserts.[9]

Although *Enmund*'s holding is limited to the situation presented in that case, in view of Justice White's analysis the decision has potentially far-reaching implications. Taking the easiest case first, it is difficult to distinguish *Enmund* from a felony-murder case in which a defendant is sentenced to death after accidentally killing the victim during the perpetration of a felony. In assessing the *Enmund* defendant's moral culpability, Justice White mentioned that the defendant did not kill the victim; but he placed much greater emphasis on the defendant's lack of intent. After stating that "American criminal law has long considered a defendant's intention—and therefore his moral guilt—to be critical to 'the degree of—[his] criminal culpability'," Justice White concluded that

[f]or purposes of imposing the death penalty, [the defendant's] criminal culpability must be limited to his participation in the robbery, and his punishment must be tailored to his personal responsibility and moral guilt.[10]

If a defendant's intention is determinative of his "moral guilt," then a defendant who accidentally kills a victim during a robbery is no more culpable than one who participates in an armed robbery without intending or causing the death of anyone. Both defendants intended to commit a robbery and both presumably knew that they were creating a substantial risk of death or great bodily harm.[11] On the other hand, since neither defendant intended the death that in fact resulted, neither of them should be held morally accountable for it. Since, under *Enmund*, the penalty of death is reserved for situations in which the defendant is morally accountable for the death of another, it follows that death as a penalty is constitutionally excessive when the crime is the accidental killing of another during the course of a felony.

When *Enmund* is viewed more broadly, Justice White's focus on the issue of the defendant's intent indicates that the Court may be groping toward an important substantive limitation on capital punishment. His analysis suggests that the death penalty will be disproportionate for any offense in which the defendant did not intend the death of the victim. If the Court adopts this principle, the definition of intent to kill will become a critical constitutional issue, and the Court will have to deal with this issue in a variety of situations.[12] For example, suppose that an arsonist sets fire to a building, knowing that there are people asleep inside the building but hoping that they will escape without injury. If a victim dies as a result of the fire, did the arsonist intend her death?[13] Or suppose that a loan shark's enforcer brutally beats a victim, intending to cause him permanent injury. If the victim dies as a result of the beating, did the enforcer intend his death?

These examples raise the question whether, for Eighth Amendment purposes, a defendant's recklessness (or conscious disregard for a substantial risk to human life) can ever be equated with an intent to kill. Justice White did speak to this issue in *Lockett v. Ohio*[14] when, in a concurring opinion, he argued against allowing death as a penalty for conduct that

requires at most the degree of *mens rea* defined by the American Law Institute Model Penal Code as recklessness: conduct that is undertaken with knowledge that death is likely to follow.[15]

His view as to the minimum mens rea requirement was unequivocal:

I would hold that death may not be inflicted for killings consistent with the Eighth Amendment without a finding that the defendant engaged in conduct with the conscious purpose of producing death.[16]

If this view is accepted, it would have a profound impact on the administration of capital punishment. Few if any state death penalty statutes explicitly require a finding that the capital defendant have a "conscious purpose" to cause death.[17] If such a finding becomes constitutionally indispensable to a sentence of death, courts reviewing the validity of a death penalty would be required to scrutinize the record, evaluating particular jury instructions and/or findings by a judge to determine whether the finding required by the sentencer was in fact made.

The *Enmund* decision is also significant in that it may signal the Court's willingness to impose substantive limitations in other areas. In assessing the defendant's culpability, the Court emphasized that individualized judgment must be brought to bear upon the character of the offender as well as on the circumstances of the offense.[18] This suggests that there may be situations in which mitigating factors, such as the youth of the offender[19] or the quality of his background,[20] should preclude imposition of the death penalty regardless of the circumstances of the offense itself. *Enmund*'s analysis of objective indicators suggests that the most important factor in directing the Court's search for such limitations will be an analysis of jury performance. If, for example, it appears that juries rarely impose the death penalty upon defendants younger than eighteen,[21] the Court should at least seriously consider whether the death penalty is an excessive punishment for that category of defendants.

Finally, the analytical framework used by the *Enmund* majority may shape the approach to be adopted by the Court in the event that it reconsiders the constitutionality of our present system of capital punishment. In *Coker*, the Court stated that a punishment will be excessive if it *either* "makes no measurable contribution to acceptable goals of punishment" *or* is "grossly out of proportion to the severity of the crime."[22] In *Enmund*, however, it seemed to merge the two tests together, suggesting that the death penalty in that case was disproportionate because it did not contribute to acceptable goals of punishment.[23] More importantly, in assessing whether the penalty contributed to accepted penological goals, the *Enmund* majority considered only the goals of deterrence and retribution; and in determining whether those goals were promoted, the majority appeared to exercise a substantial measure of independent judgment, rather than deferring to the legislative determinations. Thus, if this example is followed, in passing on the ultimate constitutionality of the death penalty the Court will have to exercise its independent judgment to determine whether our system of capital punishment, as currently applied, makes a measurable contribution to the goals of deterrence or retribution.[24]

NOTES

1. 433 U.S. 584 (1977).
2. 433 U.S. at 597.
3. *Id.* at 598.
4. 102 S. Ct. 3368 (1982).
5. *Id.* at 3379.
6. *Id.* at 3376.
7. *See* 428 U.S. at 186–87.
8. 102 S. Ct. at 3377.
9. *Id.* at 3378.
10. *Id.*
11. As the dissent noted, *Enmund* may be read as holding that the death penalty *cannot* be constitutionally imposed when the only mental state estab-

lished is "the intent to commit an armed robbery coupled with the knowledge that armed robberies involve substantial risk of death or serious injury to other persons." 102 S. Ct. at 3391 (O'Connor, J., dissenting).

12. For a discussion of this issue, *see* Note, *Eighth Amendment—The Death Penalty and Vicarious Felony Murder: Nontriggermen May Not be Executed Absent a Finding of Intent to Kill*, 73 J. CRIM. L. & CRIMINOLOGY 1553, 1564–68 (1982) [hereinafter cited as Note, *Death Penalty and Nontriggermen*].

13. *See* Note, *Death Penalty and Nontriggermen, supra* note 12, at 1566, for a discussion of this hypothetical.

14. 438 U.S. 586 (1978).

15. 438 U.S. at 627–28 (White, J., concurring) (footnote omitted).

16. *Id.* at 628.

17. Some statutes do require that a capital defendant be convicted of first-degree murder in order to be eligible for the death penalty. *See, e.g.*, CAL. PENAL CODE § 190–190.4 (West Supp. 1981–82); MASS GEN. LAWS ANN. ch. 265, § 2 (West Pamphlet 1982); 18 PA. CONS. STAT. ANN. § 9711 (Supp. 1980). In some of these jurisdictions, first-degree murder is defined so as to include only intentional killings in which the defendant presumably does have a conscious purpose to cause death. *See, e.g.*, 18 PA. CONS. STAT. ANN. § 2502(a)(d) (Purdon Supp. 1978). In others, however, first-degree murder is defined broadly enough to include cases in which the defendant did not have a conscious purpose to kill. *See, e.g.*, CAL. PENAL CODE § 189 (West Supp. 1981–82) (including cases of felony-murder); MASS. GEN. LAWS ANN. ch. 265, § 2 (West Pamphlet 1982) (including murders perpetrated with "extreme atrocity or cruelty").

18. 102 S. Ct. at 3377.

19. *See* Edding v. Oklahoma, 455 U.S. 104 (1982) (declining to decide the constitutionality of imposing the death penalty on juvenile defendants).

20. For example, in terms of moral accountability, it may be questionable whether a severely retarded defendant could ever be viewed as deserving capital punishment. *See generally* Liebman & Shepard, *Guiding Capital Sentencing Discretion Beyond the "Boiler Plate": Mental Disorder as a Mitigating Factor*, 66 GEO. L.J. 757 (1978).

21. *See supra* note 19.

22. 433 U.S. at 592.

23. *See* 102 S. Ct. at 3377–78. This discrepancy is discussed in Note, *Death Penalty and Nontriggermen, supra* note 12, at 1562.

24. *See supra* "Introduction" at text accompanying notes 64–73, for a discussion of this issue.

Death-Qualified Juries:
The "Prosecution-Proneness"
Argument Reexamined

The Supreme Court's conclusion that the penalty of death is a unique penalty, "different in kind" from all other punishments,[1] is reflected in the Court's recent promulgation of procedural safeguards applicable only to defendants charged with capital offenses. For example, unlike ordinary defendants, those in capital cases have a right to be tried pursuant to a bifurcated proceeding in which the issues of guilt and punishment are separately considered;[2] moreover, if a capital verdict is returned, they cannot be precluded from offering any relevant evidence of mitigating circumstances to the sentencing judge or jury,[3] and they have significantly broader rights than other defendants to examine evidence used in making the sentence determination.[4] Ironically, however, the potential advantages created by these favorable procedures may be more than offset by a single disadvantage stemming from the mode of jury selection. In capital cases, unlike noncapital ones, the jury may be "death-qualified"; that is, in selecting the jury prior to the guilt phase of the proceedings, the prosecutor may be able to challenge for cause all those who state that they would automatically refuse to impose the death penalty in any capital case.[5]

What is the origin of the practice of death-qualification? And why does it place the capital defendant in a less advantageous position than the noncapital defendant? Both of these questions were considered nineteen years ago in a path-breaking article by Professor Walter Oberer.[6]

As Professor Oberer demonstrated, death-qualification was originally a by-product of the mandatory system of capital punishment formerly in effect in the United States.[7] Prior to the twentieth century, conviction of a crime for which the prescribed punishment was death automatically resulted in the imposition of the death penalty.[8] Under this system, of course, there was no division between a guilt and punishment phase; the jury's sole responsibility was to determine guilt, the death penalty automatically flowing from an affirmative finding on that issue. Accordingly, a juror with conscientious scruples against the death penalty might be inclined to avoid the imposition of capital punishment by refusing to find the defendant guilty of the capital charge regardless of the evidence. Thus, there was a danger that a defendant who was clearly guilty of a capital charge would nevertheless be acquitted or not convicted of that charge because of a juror's antipathy toward capital punishment.[9] Seeking to prevent this potential subversion of justice, most jurisdictions imposing capital punishment established by statute[10] or judicial ruling[11] that those with conscientious or religious scruples against the death penalty would not be permitted to serve as jurors in capital cases.[12]

By the middle of the twentieth century, however, mandatory capital punishment was replaced almost everywhere by discretionary capital punishment. Under this system, the jury would first decide whether the defendant should be found guilty of the capital charge and then, in either a bifurcated procedure (in which additional evidence bearing on the penalty could be presented to them)[13] or a unitary procedure (in which no additional evidence would be presented),[14] they would decide whether the death penalty should be imposed.

As Professor Oberer pointed out,[15] the justifications for a death-qualified jury under a discretionary system of capital punishment are less compelling than under a mandatory one. The state's legitimate interest in removing jurors whose aversion to capital punishment might lead them to vote contrary to their view of the evidence on the issue of guilt can certainly be secured by a less drastic means than the wholesale exclusion of all jurors with conscientious scruples against capital punishment.[16] Moreover, if the state truly contemplated that jurors in capital cases have freedom to accept or reject the death penalty on any basis whatever, as the discretionary capital sentencing statutes seem to imply,[17] it is not apparent why a juror's conscientious scruples against capital punishment or even her total unwillingness to vote for it in any case should incapacitate her from participation in the discretionary judgment.[18] Nevertheless, as Professor Oberer notes,[19] the effect of inertia was such that, with very few exceptions,[20] courts consistently held that the shift to discretionary capital punishment did not negate the prosecutor's right to a death-qualified jury.[21]

Why does the death-qualified jury place the capital defendant at a disadvantage when compared to noncapital defendants? Of course, the death-qualified jury is more likely to impose the death penalty, but this does not disadvantage capital defendants in relation to defendants for whom the death penalty is not at issue. As laid bare by Professor Oberer,[22] the central claim of unfairness to be made on behalf of capital defendants is that the death-qualified jury is "prosecution-prone" in the sense that it is more likely to *convict* than a non-death-qualified jury would be.[23] In support of this claim, Professor Oberer relied on psychological studies suggesting that individuals who are not opposed to the death penalty are generally more authoritarian in personality,[24] and thus are likely to be less humane and less receptive to arguments advocating a finding of innocence.[25] Subsequent psychological and sociological studies have supported this thesis;[26] there is now substantial empirical support for the conclusion that a death-qualified jury is more likely to convict than a non-death-qualified one.[27]

The question to be considered in this essay is whether the present practice of death-qualification is constitutional. More precisely, the essay will consider whether, prior to the beginning of the guilt phase of the proceedings, the prosecution may constitutionally exclude for cause prospective jurors who unequivocally state that they would automatically refuse to impose a sentence of death regardless of the evidence presented to them. This form of death-qualification is authorized by the first exception set forth in *Witherspoon v. Illinois*[28] and is apparently used in all but one of the thirty-five jurisdictions that currently retain capital punishment.[29] Not surprisingly, perhaps, the thesis of this essay is that criteria developed in recent Supreme Court decisions show this form of death-qualification to be unconstitutional.[30] In developing this thesis, the essay will include, first, an examination of the legal questions raised by the Court's decision in *Witherspoon*,[31] and then a demonstration of how more recent decisions, especially *Ballew v. Georgia*,[32] have placed the issues raised by *Witherspoon* in a new perspective.

The Legal Background: *Witherspoon* and Its Aftermath

The claim that a death-qualified jury is constitutionally biased with respect to the determination of guilt was presented to the Court in *Witherspoon v. Illinois*,[33] a murder case in which all individuals with conscientious scruples against capital punishment were excluded from the jury. While finding that this form of death-qualification resulted in the unconstitutional imposition of the death sentence,[34] the Court affirmed the defendant's murder conviction, holding that the empirical data presented by the defendant was "too tentative and fragmentary to establish that jurors not opposed to the death penalty tend to favor the prosecution in the determination of guilt."[35] Nevertheless, as Justice Black noted in his dissent, the Court seemed "[to go] out of its way" to suggest that development of firmer empirical data might result in a different ruling on this issue.[36] In this regard, footnote 18 of the Court's opinion seemed particularly significant.[37] In *Witherspoon*, the Court limited its holding by stating that it would not invalidate a death penalty imposed by a jury from which the only veniremen excluded were those who made it unmistakably clear that they would automatically vote against the death penalty.[38] Elsewhere, the Court intimated that the exclusion of these veniremen would not taint the subsequent penalty determination because "the resulting jury [would be] simply 'neutral' with respect to penalty."[39] Nevertheless, in footnote 18, the Court qualified this view as follows:

> Even so, a defendant convicted by such a jury in some future case might still attempt to establish that the jury was less than neutral with respect to *guilt*. If he were to succeed in that effort, the question would then arise whether the State's interest in submitting the penalty issue to a jury capable of imposing capital punishment may be vindicated at the expense of the defendant's interest in a completely fair determination of guilt or innocence—given the possibility of accommodating both interests by means of a bifurcated trial, using one jury to decide guilt and another to fix punishment. That problem is not presented here, however, and we intimate no view as to its proper resolution.[40]

This note certainly seems to hold considerable promise for the "prosecution-proneness" claim. It indicates that, despite *Witherspoon*'s narrowing of the permissible limits of death-qualification, empirical evidence may establish that a jury that is properly death-qualified under *Witherspoon* may still be "less than neutral with respect to guilt." Furthermore, it appears that a finding in favor of the defendant on this point would not necessarily be subordinated to the state's interest in obtaining a "neutral" death penalty determination; on the contrary, the Court seemed to suggest that the two interests could be accommodated by the simple expedient of providing one jury to determine guilt and a different one to assess the penalty. Under the circumstances, it was not altogether surprising that Justice Black read the note as "a thinly veiled warning to the States that they had better change their jury selection procedures or face a decision by this Court that their murder convictions have been obtained unconstitutionally."[41] Nevertheless, the portent perceived by Justice Black has not turned into fact. In the dozen years since *Witherspoon*, neither the Supreme Court nor any other court has held that a conviction rendered by a death-qualified jury is unconstitutional.[42] In view of the plethora of issues left unresolved by *Witherspoon*, this result is perhaps not altogether surprising. Although *Witherspoon* offered bright prospects to a defendant who could establish that a death-qualified jury was "less than neutral with respect to guilt," the Court offered little guidance as to how such a claim might be established. In addition, despite the encouraging innuendo in footnote 18,[43] the Court did not explain how a successful claim that a death-qualified jury was "less than neutral with respect to guilt" should be weighed against the state's interest in ensuring a neutral penalty determination.

Witherspoon did state that the evidence then before the Court was "too tentative and fragmentary to establish that jurors not opposed to the death penalty tend to favor the prosecution in the determination of guilt."[44] In the Court's view, the studies submitted for their consideration[45] were virtually worthless because the conclusions stated in them had neither appeared in the public domain nor been subjected to the scrutiny of cross-examination.[46] As noted previously, the Court did allude to the possibility of successfully using empirical evidence to establish some kind of constitutional claim.[47] However, it provided no guidance for assessing the probative worth of any particular form of empirical evidence.

The importance of this issue is heightened by the inherent uncertainty of evidence derived from the social sciences. As Professors Harry Kalven and Hans Zeisel have noted, the limitations on the efficacy of the social sciences in verifying an empirical proposition occur because "[s]ocial science more than natural science is forced to operate at a remove from the reality it studies. It must work, therefore, through a chain of inferences."[48] In other words, even the most well-designed social science experiment will only provide, at best, circumstantial evidence of the truth of the proposition it seeks to prove. Thus, in the present context, it is obviously impossible to study the actual impact of death-qualification in specific capital cases.[49] At best, the studies related to this problem will provide circumstantial evidence that will be a varying number of steps (or inferences) from the proposition at issue. With respect to the empirical evidence relating to a death-qualified jury, then, one question to be considered is the probative worth to be assigned to various types of evidence, all of which are some steps removed from irrefutable proof of the thesis under consideration.

At the time *Witherspoon* was decided, the relevant evidence actually in the public domain was substantially removed from the critical issue of whether a death-qualified jury would tend to be more favorable to the prosecution in determining guilt. At that time, there were published studies—not considered by the Court—that indicated that because certain personality traits often appeared in predictable groupings, people with punitive views could generally be classified as "authoritarian personalities," a classification that marked the individual as one holding ultraconservative views on a wide variety of issues.[50] These studies were significant because by providing at least preliminary support for Professor Oberer's conclusion that "human sympathy is hardly subject to nice compartmentalizations,"[51] they suggested a strong possibility that an individual's attitude toward capital punishment is likely to be associated with certain other significant views and attitudes.

Nevertheless, these studies did not constitute strong circumstantial proof of the prosecution-proneness hypothesis. Several steps in the circumstantial chain were missing, the first being some evidence that an individual's attitude toward the death penalty correlated with attitudes directly relevant to the jury decision-making process. For example, individuals with generally liberal attitudes (including an absolute refusal to impose the death penalty) might nevertheless be relatively pro-prosecution in their attitudes relating to the adjudication of guilt. Several post-*Witherspoon* studies sought to refute this possibility, however, by seeking to correlate attitudes toward the death penalty with attitudes toward issues that would appear to bear directly or indirectly on adjudicating guilt or innocence.[52] To date, the two broadest exercises of this kind are Professor Edmund Bronson's 1970 study, which elicited responses from prospective jurors in several counties of Colorado,[53] and a 1971 Harris Poll, which included results obtained from questioning a nationwide random sample of 2,068 subjects.[54] In the Bronson study, subjects were given questionnaires that asked whether they strongly opposed, opposed, favored, or strongly favored the death penalty.[55] They were then asked to pretend that they were serving on a jury and to indicate their agreement or disagreement with a series of statements, each of which was designed to appeal to subjects with a proneness to convict. Bronson's results showed a relationship of high statistical significance between the subjects' tendency to favor the death penalty and their agreement with each of the five following statements:

1)   If the police have arrested an individual and the district attorney has brought him to trial, there is good reason to believe that the man on trial is guilty.

2)   If the person on trial does not testify at his trial, there is good reason to believe that he is concealing guilt.

3)   Concerning the high level of violent crime in ghetto areas, this level of violent crime could be reduced if the courts would convict alleged lawbreakers more often.

4)   The courts are far too technical in protecting the so-called constitutional rights of those involved in criminal activity.

5)   The plea of insanity is a loophole allowing too many guilty men to go free.[56]

Although the clarity of some of these statements might be questioned,[57] Bronson's conclusion—that his results demonstrate a positive relationship between attitudes in favor of the death penalty and pro-prosecution attitudes toward issues relating to the determination of guilt[58]—appears to be unquestionably accurate.

The 1971 Harris Poll compared the attitudes of subjects who stated they would never impose the death penalty (and therefore could presumably be excluded for cause pursuant to *Witherspoon*'s first exception) and subjects who stated that they could impose the death penalty.[59] The results confirmed some of the findings reported by Bronson[60] and also showed that the "nonexcludable" subjects are significantly more likely than the "excludables" to trust the police,[61] to distrust the accused and his attorney,[62] and to disregard or slight legal principles that would ordinarily operate as safeguards for the accused.[63]

Of course, if the focus is on whether a death-qualified jury is more likely than a non-death-qualified one to convict, a significant inference must still be drawn before these "attitudinal" studies can be afforded weight. One must infer that a person's stated attitudes provide a valid indication of how she will perform when confronted with the necessity of acting as a juror in a trial-like situation. In this regard, the Bronson and Harris studies present some problems. While a person's expressed attitudes undoubtedly indicate to some extent how she would act in a particular situation,[64] it is well established that the more general the expressed attitude, the less reliable is a prediction that the subject will act in conformance with that attitude. Accordingly, when, as in the 1971 Harris Poll, a subject estimates the extent to which she would credit the testimony of an arresting officer or a defendant, the estimate may not be a very reliable indication of the extent to which the subject would actually credit the testimony of these witnesses in a trial. To obtain more reliable results, it would be desirable to conduct an experiment in which subjects evaluate the credibility of witnesses after actually observing them testify in a courtroom setting. If a study of this kind were to show that in comparison to the excludable subjects (i.e., those who could be excluded from a death-qualified jury), nonexcludables are more likely to credit police officers testifying for the prosecution and less likely to credit defendants, there would be a stronger basis for concluding that the difference between the two groups would be present when they are actually serving as jurors. One could, hence, more safely infer that the nonexcludables' different perception of credibility would translate into a generally increased tendency to convict.[65] Since no results from an experiment of this type have yet been reported, however, bridging the gap between subjects' stated attitudes and their expected behavior in an actual courtroom setting presents a significant problem.

To overcome this difficulty, experimenters have attempted to assess the critical relationship directly by studying jury behavior in either an actual or a simulated trial setting. Of course, there are potential difficulties with either approach. In seeking to correlate the attitudes and behavior of actual jurors, a major problem is that of controlling external stimuli. A juror's vote in any criminal case may be viewed as determined by a combination of external factors, including the nature of the prosecution's evidence, the skill of the attorneys, the impact of other jurors' expressed views, and myriad other matters; and internal factors, or more specifically the mindset with which each juror receives and evaluates the external stimuli. Both the internal and external factors are obviously important. Therefore, in order to develop a meaningful correlation between juror attitudes and behavior, it is necessary to have a reasonably large number of individuals exposed to the same or similar stimuli. Obviously, controlling the external stimuli for a large number of actual jurors is difficult. Our system operates so that no more than twelve jurors may participate in the decision of any criminal case. A simulated experiment, on the other hand, does have the advantage of being able to control almost completely the external stimuli to which a large number of subjects are exposed. The experimenter can make sure that all subjects acting as jurors in a simulated trial are exposed to the same evidence, the same argument of counsel, the same opportunity to deliberate, and so on. On the other hand, as will be elaborated later,[66] the disadvantage of a simulated experiment is that the differences between the simulation and reality may raise questions about whether the phenomenon detected in the experiment is one that also exists in reality.

Only one effort has been made to correlate the death penalty attitudes and behavior of actual jurors. In Professor Zeisel's study,[67] jurors who participated in criminal trials during 1954 and 1955 in Chicago and New York were asked how they voted on the first ballot of the case in which they participated and whether they had any conscientious scruples against the death penalty.[68] In addition, Zeisel made an ingenious attempt to ensure the presence of adequate external controls by asking for the vote on the first ballot of the entire jury of which each juror was a member.[69] Zeisel reasoned that the first ballot vote would be the most valid indicator of the overall strength of the prosecution's case. Thus, if the votes on the first ballot of five different cases were eleven guilty, one not guilty, it could be assumed that in all five cases the prosecution's case was very strong, presumably stronger than it would be in cases where the vote in favor of conviction was ten to two or less. Accordingly, jurors participating in those cases where the vote was eleven to one would be exposed to similar external stimuli at least in the sense that the strength of the prosecution's case would be roughly comparable in each instance.[70] In order to analyze results in cases where the strength of the prosecution's case was comparable, Zeisel grouped each individual's vote into one of eleven categories (determined by the total number of guilty votes on the entire jury's first ballot, with unanimous first ballot votes not being included). Zeisel found that in nine of the eleven groupings, jurors without scruples against the death penalty voted guilty more often than did jurors with scruples; moreover, in ten of the eleven groupings, the jurors without scruples voted not guilty less often than jurors with scruples.[71] Using standard statistical tests, Zeisel concluded that the odds were twenty-four to one that jurors without scruples against the death penalty were more likely than the scrupled jurors to vote guilty.[72]

Zeisel's study is uniquely valuable because it is the only one to successfully bridge the gap between attitudes and behavior by studying actual jurors. Nevertheless, the weight of Zeisel's evidence could be criticized on various grounds. First, since the data is now more than twenty-five years old, it may be questioned whether the relationships that were valid at that time are still valid today. Secondly, since the study was pre-*Witherspoon*, the jurors were not asked the question that would determine whether they would be ineligible to serve on a death-qualified jury today; they were merely asked whether they had scruples against imposing the death penalty, not whether they would automatically refuse to impose it regardless of the circumstances of the case before them. Finally, despite Zeisel's ingenious approach to controlling external stimuli, it could be argued that although the number of votes for conviction may generally reflect the overall strength of the prosecution's case, it permits wide variations in important aspects of the case. Accordingly, based on the results of this experiment, it is possible (though certainly not probable) that a disproportionate number of nonscrupled jurors were exposed to relatively unique circumstances (e.g., a particularly authoritarian judge) and that this disproportionate exposure had some impact on the results obtained.

In the simulated trial experiments the problem of controlling all relevant stimuli is solved by exposing all subjects to the same hypothetical cases. In each of the four experiments performed to date, all subjects were exposed to one or more hypothetical criminal cases and then asked to adjudicate the hypothetical defendant's guilt or innocence. Significantly, in all four experiments, the results have shown a positive correlation between views that survive death-qualification and a proneness to convict.[73] From a methodological standpoint the studies have various strengths and weaknesses. However, the confluence of results (evidencing a degree of consistency that is rare in social science literature) not only strengthens the empirical validity of each experiment[74] but diminishes the impact of the methodological deficiencies in each. Thus, the three experiments that presented subjects with written summaries of hypothetical cases and asked them to render a vote for guilt or innocence[75] could be criticized on the ground that because subjects may not become intensely involved in written summaries, their responses will not closely approximate the verdicts they would render if actually required to serve on a jury. However, corroborative results from both Professor Zeisel's study[76] and a more sophisticated simulated trial experiment conducted by Professor George Jurow[77] tend to indicate that the experiments conducted by written summary detect a phenomenon that is also present when the subjects are more intensely involved.

In Professor Jurow's experiment, 211 employees of Sperry-Rand Corporation were given tests to determine their attitudes toward capital punishment.[78] In addition, the subjects listened to audiotapes of two simulated murder trials,[79] and after hearing a simulated jury instruction from the judge in each case were given time to think about the case and then asked to find the defendant guilty or not guilty.[80] By this means Professor Jurow established some significant correlations between an individual's views on capital punishment and her performance in the mock trial experiments.[81] In particular, the experiment showed that with respect to both mock trials, subjects who would not be excludable for cause under *Witherspoon*[82] were more likely than the excludable subjects to return a verdict of guilty.[83]

Despite the relative sophistication of Jurow's experiment, his methodology could be criticized on various grounds. Exception could be taken to the sample used on the ground that 211 employees of Sperry-Rand do not accurately reflect the population from which an actual jury would be selected. On this particular point, Harris's nationwide survey of 2,068 subjects selected by random sampling techniques was far superior.[84] Further, objections could be made to the nature of the simulated trial. While listening to an audiotape would undoubtedly "involve" the subjects to a considerable extent, it might have been preferable to provide a videotape so that judgments made by the subjects might more closely approximate those demanded of actual jurors.[85] In addition, while the judge instructed the jury on the law,[86] the extent to which the instructions complied with actual jury instructions was not clearly stated;[87] to the extent that they deviated from actual charges, the subjects' understanding of the rules they were to apply could have been distorted.[88] Moreover, the audiotapes were each less than an hour long,[89] thus encompassing only a small fraction of the time a juror would typically be exposed to an actual murder trial; and since the mock jurors acted individually, they were completely removed from the influence of group participation that might affect the initial votes[90] as well as the final determination[91] of an actual jury. Furthermore, even if a mock trial experiment were to surmount all of these difficulties, it could still be faulted on the ground that it would "not be examining the actual behavior of jurors in a trial situation."[92] As Professor Jurow admitted, "no experiment can completely simulate a real life situation"[93] because a participant in a simulated trial experiment necessarily lacks a real juror's sense of the critical consequences that will turn upon the group's judgment.

Thus, despite the impressive strength and consistency of the multifarious empirical evidence relating to the death-qualified jury's proneness to convict, it is difficult to make any definitive statement about the probative quality of this evidence. As a result of the post-*Witherspoon* studies, the prosecution-proneness hypothesis has undoubtedly been strengthened. As Professor Girsh has recently pointed out, the studies have convincingly demolished the "banana ice cream" theory,[94] clearly establishing that one's attitude toward the death penalty is not an isolated phenomenon (as one's preference for banana ice cream might be) but rather is integrally related to other deeply held attitudes and values. Moreover, the studies show that the attitudes colored by one's view on the death penalty are attitudes that bear directly on the adjudicatory process in criminal trials and that the coloring is shaded almost uniformly in one direction:[95] nonexcludables (i.e., those eligible to serve on a death-qualified jury) tend to be more sympathetic to the prosecution than excludables.[96] And finally, studies of actual[97] and simulated[98] jury behavior confirm these results by showing that when presented with an actual decision-making situation, nonexcludables are significantly more likely than excludables to render a judgment in favor of the prosecution. In view of this significant accumulation of data, it is perhaps unduly facile to take the position, asserted by several courts, that the present body of empirical data is still "too tentative and fragmentary" to alter the conclusion arrived at by the Court in *Witherspoon*.[99] Nevertheless, the problems with the experiments alluded to above[100] make it obvious that the studies are indeed operating at a remove from reality; there are gaps in our knowledge that have not been and probably can never be completely filled by these or any other studies. Thus, based on the scant guidance supplied by the *Witherspoon* case itself, the probative quality of the empirical evidence is unclear.[101]

Quite aside from the problem of evaluating the empirical evidence, there is the question of defining the applicable legal standard: What must the empirical evidence show to establish that the death-qualified jury is non-neutral with respect to the determination of guilt? *Witherspoon* did provide some guidance on this point. The Court intimated that "non-neutrality as to guilt"—the key phrase of note 18—would be established if a defendant could show that death-qualification "results in an unrepresentative jury on the issue of guilt or substantially increases the risks of conviction."[102] However, the meaning of these terms is far from self-evident. The term "unrepresentative jury" connotes a situation in which a cognizable group within the community has been excluded from jury service. Therefore, one might interpret this phrase as inviting the defendant to establish the constitutional claim by showing either that individuals excluded because of their opposition to capital punishment are themselves a "cognizable group" within the community[103] or that the exclusion of these individuals results in a constitutionally impermissible underrepresentation of some other "cognizable group" within the community, such as blacks, women, or people of a particular religious faith.[104] Under existing authority, establishing either of these claims on the basis of currently available empirical data would be difficult.[105]

Because of the context in which the phrase appears, however, "an unrepresentative jury on the issue of guilt" might more appropriately be read as defining a jury that, in comparison to one accurately representing the community, is tilted toward the prosecution in the sense that, to paraphrase Justice Stewart, it is "uncommonly willing" to find a defendant guilty.[106] Interpreted in this manner,[107] the "unrepresentative jury on the issue of guilt" phrase closely parallels the more explicit phrase to which it is conjoined. The "unrepresentative jury" phrase shows that a jury that has a disproportionate tendency to convict creates constitutional problems; the conjoining phrase, "substantially increase the risks of conviction," adds the logical corollary. If a particular jury is "uncommonly willing" to convict, it would seem to follow that the "risks of conviction" for a defendant facing that jury are "substantially increased." So viewed, the conjoining phrases indicate that a jury's "non-neutrality" or prosecution-proneness can be determined by analyzing either the jury's internal attitudes or its potential findings. If the jury is shown to have views that establish that it is "uncommonly willing" to convict, or if it can be established that the "risks of conviction" for a defendant facing that jury are "substantially increased," the jury's "non-neutrality" will be demonstrated. Interpreted in this manner, *Witherspoon*'s dicta define the area of inquiry but do not establish a substantive standard. Although the Court speaks of an "unrepresentative jury on the issue of guilt," it does not define a "representative jury on the issue of guilt." Therefore, it fails to establish a benchmark against which a jury's propensity to convict may be measured. Moreover, phrases such as "substantially increased" are obviously ambiguous. Accordingly, the problem of determining how much "prosecution-proneness" is too much, or, more precisely, when a death-qualified jury's increased propensity to convict makes it "unrepresentative" with respect to the guilt determination or "substantially increases the risks of conviction" is one which is not resolved by *Witherspoon*.

This issue was brought into sharp focus by the Fifth Circuit's decision in *Spinkellink v. Wainwright*.[108] In *Spinkellink* the court assumed for the purposes of argument that "a death-qualified jury is more likely to convict than a non-death-qualified jury";[109] nevertheless, the court stated that this "indicates only that a death-qualified jury might favor the prosecution and that a non-death-qualified jury might favor the defendant. The pivotal question, therefore, is which appearance most closely reflects reality."[110]   Without actually addressing this "pivotal question," the court concluded that the death-qualified jurors involved in the trial could not be "branded prosecution-prone" because "they indicated only that they would be willing to perform their civic obligations as jurors and obey the law."[111] In short, the court determined that in the absence of a finding of actual "bias" on the part of one or more members of the death-qualified jury, that jury cannot be considered "non-neutral" (or prosecution-prone) within the meaning of *Witherspoon*.

Spinkellink's analysis is fatally defective because it totally ignores the significance of *Witherspoon*'s dicta. As noted above,[112] *Witherspoon*'s dicta imply that a death-qualified jury's attitudes and conviction propensity must be measured against some benchmark; that is, the pertinent qualities of the death-qualified jury must be compared with those of a jury that can properly be viewed as constituting the constitutional norm, or in *Witherspoon*'s words, a jury that is "representative" with respect to the issue of guilt. *Spinkellink*'s analysis indicates that the "representative" jury that is to serve as the benchmark may be any jury in which none of the jurors is "biased."[113] But this is absurd. *Witherspoon*'s analysis clearly indicates that a "representative" jury is one that in some sense represents the community. As *Spinkellink* recognizes,[114] "bias" is a legal standard authorizing exclusion of prospective jurors who have certain fixed opinions relating to the matter they are about to try. Accordingly, there is no necessary connection between a jury of "unbiased" jurors and the degree to which the jurors selected are representative of the community. Therefore, a jury of "unbiased" jurors cannot possibly be considered to be a "representative" jury in the sense contemplated by *Witherspoon*.[115]

Spinkellink's misdirected analysis highlights the importance of refining *Witherspoon*'s meaning. What is the "representative" jury that serves as the benchmark against which the death-qualified jury's performance must be measured? And what differences between the death-qualified jury and the benchmark will be sufficient to establish the death-qualified jury's "non-neutrality"? The first question can probably be answered more easily than the second. *Witherspoon*'s logic suggests that the benchmark against which the death-qualified jury should be measured is the non-death-qualified jury used in noncapital cases. This jury is a logical benchmark because it is used in the vast majority of criminal cases, and it is "representative" of the community in the sense that it is surrounded by procedures designed to ensure that it will be selected from a fair cross section of the community.[116] No better benchmark could be found.

The difficulty of the second question may be seen by refining it so as to ask how much of an "increase in the risks of conviction" will be enough to be considered "substantial" within the meaning of the second part of the applicable test. Based on an analysis of *Witherspoon*'s dicta,[117] it has been argued that any perceptible change in the jury's propensity toward conviction should be sufficient to meet the standard.[118] However, on this point, the implications of *Witherspoon*'s dicta are far from clear.[119] A "substantial increase" could mean any increase of substance, but it could mean any number of other things as well. Like other aspects of *Witherspoon*'s analysis of the prosecution-proneness issue, this phrase is a chameleon, one that is laced with ambiguity. Accordingly, the lower courts' reluctance to invalidate the death-qualified jury on the basis of *Witherspoon* alone is not surprising.[120]

The Significance of *Ballew v. Georgia*

Although it does not deal with the issue of prosecution-proneness, the Court's decision in *Ballew v. Georgia*[121] sheds considerable light on problems relating to that issue that were raised but not resolved by *Witherspoon*. In *Ballew* the Court unanimously concluded that the trial of a Georgia misdemeanor defendant before a jury of only five persons constituted a denial of the defendant's right to trial by jury guaranteed by the Sixth and Fourteenth Amendments. In an opinion authored by Justice Blackmun, five members of the Court expressly justified this result on the basis of a careful evaluation of the published statistical and sociological data bearing upon various attributes of juries composed of different numbers.[122]

The Blackmun opinion began its analysis by noting that under *Williams v. Florida*,[123] a decision upholding the constitutionality of six-person juries, a jury's purpose of providing a safeguard between the accused and the prosecutor or judge[124] is fulfilled when the group serving as jury is "of sufficient size to promote group deliberation, to insulate members from outside intimidation, and to provide a representative cross-section of the community."[125] In considering the five-person jury's ability to fulfill these functions, the majority evaluated empirical data relating to three separate but intertwined areas of concern: first, that smaller juries will lead to less effective group deliberation;[126] second, that smaller juries will skew the accuracy and consistency of jury verdicts[127] to the disadvantage of the defense;[128] and third, that reducing jury size reduces the extent to which juries will represent minority groups within the community.[129] In finding that the reduction to a five-person jury creates problems in each of these areas, the Court relied on a number of different types of studies. On some points, the majority relied on principles derived from psychological studies of groups in general rather than studies of juries. It used these general principles to infer that "progressively smaller juries are less likely to foster group deliberation,"[130] and it partially supported the conclusion that smaller juries are likely to disfavor the defense by noting that "group theory suggests that a person in the minority will adhere to his position more frequently when he has at least one other person supporting his argument."[131] With respect to other points, the Court purported to rely on results obtained by various types of statistical analysis. In order to show that reducing jury size reduced community representation, the Court relied on established probability theory to show the extent to which selecting six members instead of twelve from a random population would reduce the probability that the group chosen would contain one or two members of a minority group comprising 10 percent of the random population.[132] On the other hand, the two statistical studies cited by Justice Blackmun[133] as casting doubt on the accuracy of results reached by five-person juries and as suggesting an imbalance to the detriment of the defense were considerably more complicated. Each of these studies was premised on certain critical but debatable assumptions about the way individual jurors interact and about the realities and values of the criminal justice system.[134] Significantly, the Court took pains to comment on one of these assumptions; noting that the Nagel and Neff study assumed that the harm of convicting an innocent person was ten times as great as the harm of acquitting a guilty one,[135] it characterized this assumption as "perhaps not unreasonable"[136] and proceeded to discuss with apparent approval findings that were predicated on it.[137]

The Court also weighed data emanating from simulated trial experiments studying the performance of six- and twelve-person juries.[138] In this area, two of Professor Saks's findings[139] were apparently accorded substantial weight. First, in evaluating the accuracy and consistency of verdicts rendered by five-person juries, the Court relied on Saks's finding that when presented with two specific simulated trials, twelve-person juries were more consistent than six-person ones in arriving at the same verdict;[140] and second, the Court noted that the statistical studies' predictions concerning the extent to which reduction to a six-member jury reduces minority representation on the jury were closely corroborated by Saks's findings.[141] On the other hand, the empirical studies tending to show insubstantial differences between twelve- and six-person juries were criticized by the Court on the basis of their methodological deficiencies.[142] The Court made two particularly interesting points in its discussion of methodological considerations. In criticizing studies that compare the aggregate results of cases tried before juries of different sizes, the Court noted that the aggregation of data risks "masking case-by-case differences in jury deliberations"[143]—i.e., perhaps hiding or obscuring significant differences that might appear if individual cases or smaller categories of cases were compared.[144] Even more significantly, while acknowledging that disparities between results reached by juries of different sizes will "appear in only small percentages,"[145] the Court nevertheless emphasized that this small percentage of cases will be of vital concern because maintaining "a properly functioning jury system" is most essential "when the case is close, and the guilt or innocence of the defendant is not readily apparent."[146]

Having evaluated the data, the Court proceeded to a discussion of the applicable legal standards. Interestingly, to the extent the empirical evidence considered by the Court was directed to a specific legal issue, it was directed to comparing the efficacy of twelve-person juries and six-person juries; none of it was specifically concerned with the functioning of five-person juries. Nevertheless, while admitting that it discerned no clear line separating six-member juries from five-member ones,[147] the Court reaffirmed *Williams*'s holding that six-person juries are constitutionally valid[148] but concluded that reducing jury size below six impaired the purpose and functioning of the criminal trial jury to a constitutional degree.[149] The basis for this conclusion was that "the assembled data raise substantial doubt about the reliability and appropriate representation of panels smaller than six."[150] As this observation implies, the Court did not purport to accept the data's conclusions as irrefutable proof or to base its decision on any single aspect of the data. Instead, the Court specifically noted that its conclusion of constitutional impairment was based on the "combined" effect of the problems indicated by the studies.[151]

The Court indicated that in determining whether the Sixth Amendment right to jury trial has been infringed, the magnitude of the individual interest at stake must be taken into account. The Court considered the government's argument that a lesser number of jurors should be sufficient in misdemeanor trials than in felony trials, but rejected it on the ground that the Court could not conclude that "there is less need for the imposition and the direction of the sense of the community in this case than when the state has chosen to label an offense a felony."[152]

Having found a "constitutional impairment" of the defendant's Sixth Amendment right to jury trial, the Court proceeded to "consider whether any interest of the state justifies the reduction."[153] The two interests asserted by the state were financial savings and reduced court time.[154] While admitting that reducing jury size does produce substantial financial benefits,[155] the Court found that the savings resulting from a reduction from six to five members "would be minimal."[156] With respect to the second asserted interest, the Court relied on empirical studies to conclude that it is questionable whether even the reduction in jury size from twelve to six members produces significant savings in court time.[157] Finding the state's justifications to be insignificant, the Court held Georgia's use of the five-person jury to be constitutionally invalid.

The *Ballew* majority's approach to the problem presented in that case certainly appears to represent a significant advance in the Supreme Court's use of evidence derived from the social sciences.[158] However, it would be foolish to assume that the majority's mode of analysis, undoubtedly shaped to some extent by the special characteristics of the issue before it, can be easily applied to other situations in which proof of an empirical proposition may have constitutional significance. Nevertheless, the majority's approach to the issue presented in *Ballew* is relevant to the prosecution-proneness issue in that it not only sheds light on some of the issues left unresolved by *Witherspoon* but also, by refining the contours of Sixth Amendment jurisprudence, establishes a new means of approaching that issue.

First, *Ballew* establishes that the benchmark to be used in evaluating an aberrant type of jury trial is, in fact, the type of jury trial normally used in criminal cases. Thus, the five-person jury is measured against the traditional twelve-person jury. This confirms that in confronting the prosecution-proneness issue the death-qualified jury must be compared with the non-death-qualified jury.

Secondly, *Ballew*'s approach to the empirical data is significant in several respects. Its analysis of the statistical and sociological data indicates that when an empirical proposition is at issue, the Court will make a common sense evaluation of the total body of published empirical data bearing on that issue. In making this evaluation, the Court will take account of methodological deficiencies in particular studies, but will not exclude studies from consideration merely because a study may be operating at several "removes" from the proposition at issue or is premised on certain debatable assumptions. In other words, to establish that a phenomenon exists, it is not necessary to establish the last link in a chain of proof. Valid conclusions concerning five-person juries can be drawn from studies of six-person juries or studies of small groups generally. Thus, *Ballew*'s approach indicates that the combined effect of the empirical data relating to prosecution-proneness must be intelligently weighed to determine whether the phenomenon revealed by those studies is one that is likely to exist in reality.

This last point deserves elaboration. Although the *Ballew* majority cited numerous figures and conclusions that appear in studies the Court discussed, it would underestimate *Ballew*'s analysis to suggest that the majority intended to rely on the magnitude of the reported results to establish that Sixth Amendment interests are constitutionally impaired. After evaluating the studies, the Court concluded that the reduction to five-person juries "create[s] a substantial threat to Sixth and Fourteenth Amendment guarantees." The majority certainly did not say that the studies proved any particular difference between five- and twelve-person juries. This indicates that the studies' conclusions about the *degree* to which reduction in jury size reduces the jury's ability to perform its essential functions were relevant only in that they indicated a likelihood that the jury's ability to perform these functions would in fact be reduced and that the reduction would not be minimal.

If *Witherspoon*'s dicta is interpreted in light of *Ballew*, it should follow that, for example, the question of whether a death-qualified jury "substantially increases the risks of conviction" should turn on whether the empirical data indicates that there is a likelihood that death-qualified juries will convict more often than non-death-qualified ones, and that this difference, if it exists, will not be minimal. To apply *Ballew* in this manner might be somewhat incautious, however, since *Ballew* also suggests that a jury's disproportionate conviction-proneness is only one aspect of its inability to perform its essential functions. Yet *Ballew* does clearly provide a yardstick for determining whether the Sixth Amendment jury trial right is infringed; accordingly, the death-qualified jury's combined impact on the jury's ability to fulfill its three vital functions should be scrutinized.

Finally, *Ballew* indicates that when the empirical evidence is sufficient to show that aberrant state procedure constitutes a "substantial threat" to a defendant's Sixth Amendment guarantee of an impartial jury trial, the validity of the procedure must be determined by balancing the appropriate interests involved. However, the nature of this balancing process may be more complex than the Court explicitly indicates. In determining whether the state procedure threatens impairment of the "purpose and functioning of the jury in a criminal trial" to a constitutionally significant degree, the Court explains that it will weigh the magnitude of the individual interest at stake;[159] then, if the requisite degree of impairment is found, it will determine whether any interest of the state justifies the risk imposed.[160]

Yet if this is really a complete and accurate description of the process employed, it is somewhat difficult to explain the Court's reaffirmation of *Williams*'s holding that a six-person jury is constitutional. If the two-step balancing process described in *Ballew* is indeed the relevant test, *Williams*'s cursory reaffirmation would have to be based on a conclusion that reducing jury size to five impairs the purpose and functioning of the jury to a constitutional degree, but reducing to six does not.[161] However, this conclusion seems inconsistent with the Court's analysis of the empirical evidence. The principal empirical results cited by *Ballew* came from studies comparing the functioning of twelve- and six-person juries; thus, the Court based its finding that the five-person jury impaired constitutional concerns on empirical conclusions relating to six-person juries. This approach could still be consistent with a finding that reduction to six does not impair constitutional concerns if the Court had indicated some basis for believing that there is a discernibly greater impact on constitutional concerns when the reduction is to five members instead of six. However, the Court made no such suggestion, but rather expressly admitted that it could not "discern a clear line between six members and five."[162] Thus, a judgment that reduction to a five-member jury impairs constitutional concerns seems almost inevitably to involve an implied finding that reduction to a six-member jury does the same.

Of course, the Court's analysis could also mean that even though there is no "clear line" between the effects created by reduction to six as opposed to reduction to five, constitutional adjudication sometimes necessitates arbitrary line drawing; and in this case, the Court's evaluation of the empirical data leads it to draw the line so as to hold that the effects created by reduction of jury size to six are not sufficient to impair constitutional concerns, but that any greater effects *will* be sufficient. But this explanation is obviously incomplete. Since, as the Court admits, nothing in the available data suggests that juries of five will be qualitatively different from juries of six, why does the Court draw the line where it does? Almost certainly, unstated considerations, such as *stare decisis* and a concern for not disrupting state systems of justice, played a part in the Court's choice. The *Williams* decision upholding the constitutionality of six-person juries was promulgated in 1971. Presumably, some states relied on that decision in altering their procedure.[163] To overrule *Williams* or even to suggest that it was ripe for reconsideration could have a rather unsettling effect on state systems of criminal justice, not only undermining the states' reliance on that particular decision but also impairing their confidence in the stability of other favorable constitutional rulings.[164] On the other hand, the disruptive effect of invalidating the constitutionality of the five-person jury will be relatively minimal; no state can assert any justifiable reliance on the legitimacy of the practice,[165] and few states will even be affected by the new ruling because, as Justice Blackmun noted,[166] only two states had instituted this novel procedure at the time of *Ballew*.

Institutional concerns, such as *stare decisis*, could be viewed simply as state interests to be weighed in the balance once the existence of a substantial threat to the Sixth Amendment interest is shown. However, as a rule, institutional interests cannot be easily accommodated into a court's balancing process; these interests are in essence considerations (often intangible) that cause a court to feel more or less comfortable about deciding a particular issue in a particular way. Therefore, in this context, institutional interests might best be viewed as shaping the stance a court will or should adopt when considering a Sixth Amendment issue.

However, whether the problem is perceived exactly in this way is not of crucial importance to resolving the prosecution-proneness issue. The significant implication of *Ballew* is that three distinct sets of interests must be considered: first, death-qualification's impact on the jury's ability to fulfill the functions defined by *Ballew*; second, any state interests that might be asserted to justify death-qualification; and third, any institutional concerns that might bear on this issue. After assessing the strength of these interests, application of the balancing test seemingly used by *Ballew* should determine the constitutionality of the death-qualified jury.

Applying *Ballew*'s Principles to the "Prosecution-Proneness" Issue

Death-Qualification's Impact on the Jury's Ability to Fulfill Its Functions

In light of *Ballew*, evaluation of the empirical data relating to prosecution-proneness must be concerned with death-qualification's combined impact on the jury's deliberations, accuracy, and representative quality.[167] Moreover, in keeping with *Ballew*'s approach, death-qualification's impact in any one of these areas will be weighed in the balance despite the fact that the impact in that area would not in itself be sufficient to create a constitutional impairment.[168] The empirical evidence indicates that death-qualification has at least one important effect on the jury's deliberations. One aspect of "effective group deliberation" that *Ballew* identified as "critical" was the "counterbalancing of various biases" among different members of the jury.[169] In this regard, Harris's 1971 study of the attitudes held by individuals who absolutely oppose the death penalty is significant. As noted earlier,[170] one of this study's findings was that individuals' views on the death penalty are correlated with their attitudes toward various aspects of the criminal justice system. In some cases, the differences between the expressed attitudes of the excludable and nonexcludable subjects was quite marked. In particular, it appeared that the latter would be significantly more likely than the former to distrust the defense attorney,[171] to trust the prosecutor,[172] to credit the testimony of police officers,[173] and to disregard or slight constitutional principles and rules of law that tend to favor the defendant.[174] These findings indicate that if one were to draw a bell-shaped curve representing the distribution of attitudes favorable or unfavorable to the defense in relationship to the determination of guilt, those eligible to serve on a death-qualified jury would be disproportionately in the right-hand portion of the curve, i.e., in the area representing views that are relatively unfavorable to the defense. In other words, excluding the excludables is almost equivalent to lopping off a portion of the bell-shaped curve located at the end of the spectrum where relatively pro-defense views are represented. Obviously, the effect of eliminating these views will be to reduce the extent to which views relatively unfavorable to the defense will be counterbalanced. In view of the magnitude of some of the differences found by Harris,[175] the impact of this phenomenon would not appear to be minimal.

With respect to the second area of concern, the jury's capacity to reflect an accurate cross-section of the community, the studies indicate that death-qualification pursuant to a post-*Witherspoon* test will have a disproportionate effect on certain segments of the population. In particular, studies show that opposition to capital punishment is significantly more prevalent in blacks than whites[176] and in women than men.[177] Since *Ballew* appeared to be especially concerned about procedures that would reduce minority representation on juries,[178] gauging death-qualification's potential impact on black representation may be particularly important. According to the 1971 Harris Poll, death-qualification pursuant to *Witherspoon*'s first exception would eliminate 35 percent of all blacks but only 21 percent of all whites.[179] Reliance on these figures indicates that if blacks originally comprised 10 percent of the eligible jury population, the expected effect of death-qualification would be to reduce their proportion to 8.4 percent.[180] The government might argue that this effect is minimal because the chances that a randomly selected death-qualified jury will have one or two members from a minority group comprising 8.4 percent of the community is substantially greater than the chances that a randomly selected six-person jury will have one or two members from a minority group comprising 10 percent of the community.[181] However, because death-qualification does not produce a reduction in jury size, the two sets of figures cannot really be compared. Even though it may be true that in the context of jury deliberations, two members of a minority group will often be more than twice as effective as one member would be,[182] common sense as well as elementary mathematics still suggests that when the jury size diminishes from twelve to six, the impact either one or two minority members will have upon the rest of the jury will naturally increase. The point is, unlike reduction in jury size, death-qualification does not give potential minority jurors anything in exchange for the fact that it significantly reduces the likelihood that they will serve on a jury. Accordingly, death-qualification's impact on the representative quality of the jury, especially its impact on black representation, should be given significant weight.

Ballew's final area of concern relates to the "accuracy" or "consistency" of jury verdicts. As the Court implicitly recognized,[183] this concern would appear to be the most crucial. To some extent, the jury's other two functions are significant only as means to this end. The jury's ability to deliberate effectively and to reflect a cross-section of the community are important primarily because they will lead to jury verdicts that more accurately reflect the judgment of the community and more closely approximate the goal of producing the optimal mixture of factually accurate verdicts.[184] Accordingly, the empirical data that bears on death-qualification's impact on jury "accuracy" or "consistency" should be scrutinized with particular care.

In the real world, of course, there is no way of determining whether a jury verdict is accurate.[185] At best, the empirical data can provide some indication of the alteration in the normal pattern of jury verdicts that may be produced by an aberrant procedure such as death-qualification or reduction of jury size. Even providing an accurate gauge of this alteration is difficult, however, because, as previously emphasized,[186] no experiment can duplicate exactly the effects produced in the real world. Nevertheless, of the various methods that might be used to study the effects produced, those that undoubtedly operate at the "nearest remove from reality" are either examination of actual jury behavior or simulated trial experiments in which the effect of the aberrant procedure may be gauged by comparing results obtained pursuant to it with those obtained as a result of normal practice.[187]

In finding that reducing jury size threatens to impair the accuracy and consistency of jury verdicts, *Ballew* gave weight to results from two simulated trial experiments performed by Professor Saks. In the first of these, college students divided into groups of six and twelve determined the guilt or innocence of a defendant based on their reading of a mock trial transcript;[188] in the second, there were two significant modifications: the mock juries were composed of former jurors rather than college students, and instead of reading a transcript, the subjects viewed a videotape of a mock trial.[189] As Saks noted, the results obtained[190] suggested that whether the evidence pointed toward guilt or innocence (as judged by an average representative of the community), twelve-person juries would more consistently return verdicts in accordance with the weight of the evidence.

Of the several simulated experiments relating to death-qualification,[191] the Jurow experiment[192] is the one most comparable to that performed by Saks. Like Saks, Jurow conducted two mock trial experiments;[193] however, the two sets of experiments differed in that both of Jurow's mock trials were presented by audiotape and all of his subjects deliberated individually rather than in groups.[194] One of the most pertinent of Jurow's findings was that in both experiments, the excludable subjects (i.e., those who would be subject to exclusion pursuant to *Witherspoon*'s first exception) had a lesser tendency to convict than the nonexcludable ones.[195]

The fact that Saks's subjects deliberated in groups, whereas Jurow's subjects (and those in the other simulated trial experiments relating to death-qualification) deliberated individually, might appear to be significant. It could mean that Saks's findings relate to differences between different types of potential juries but Jurow's (and the other experimental results) relate only to differences between potential jurors who are either excludable or nonexcludable under the *Witherspoon* test; because the latter experiments relate to an individual's conviction propensity, they are one step further removed from the constitutional issue to which they are relevant.

However, this step can be bridged. Very reliable data suggests that there is a strong relationship between an individual juror's conviction propensity and a jury's conviction propensity. In particular, Kalven and Zeisel's extensive study of jury trials reveals that at least in general terms, the probability of a particular jury verdict may be calculated on the basis of the individual juror's vote on the first ballot.[196] Since the first ballot is likely to occur early in the deliberations, it may be assumed that a juror's vote on this ballot generally reflects her own view of the appropriate verdict.[197] Therefore, since there is apparently a strong correlation between an average juror's propensity to convict and an average jury's propensity to convict, results from simulated experiments like Jurow's can be used to infer differences in the conviction propensities of death-qualified and non-death-qualified juries.

In two important respects, the death-qualification experiments' results are far more compelling than the data reported by Saks. First, as Professor Saks candidly admitted,[198] his findings, while certainly suggestive, were not statistically significant.[199] On the other hand, results reported by the death-qualification studies are in some cases highly statistically significant;[200] and when experiments measuring the same phenomenon are considered together, the statistical significance of the combined results is overwhelming.[201] Moreover, the confluence of results not only strengthens the empirical validity of each experiment but also dissipates the force of methodological objections one might raise against any one of them. Thus, the experiments indicate that the same phenomenon is present regardless of whether the simulation techniques employed are highly sophisticated[202] or relatively unsophisticated,[203] regardless of whether only two experiments[204] or more[205] are used, and regardless of whether the subjects employed in the study accurately reflect the population from which a jury would be drawn[206] or not.[207] And finally, the results obtained by Professor Zeisel through questioning of actual jurors[208] provides another important link in the chain of evidence by suggesting that the phenomenon identified by the simulated experiments is one that is, in fact, translated into reality. By any reasonable standard, then, the empirical evidence that demonstrates a death-qualified jury's disproportionate proneness to convict is of far stronger probative quality than Saks's finding that verdicts rendered by twelve-person juries are more consistent than those rendered by six-person juries.

In response to this point, the government might concede that the empirical evidence establishes that the death-qualified jury is more likely than a non-death-qualified one to convict, but still argue that in view of the magnitude of the differences reported by the most carefully performed studies, this finding of conviction-proneness is minimal. For example, in the Jurow experiment the exclusion of those subjects not eligible to serve on a death-qualified jury would increase the percentage of subjects voting for conviction by 1.1 percent (from 43.6 percent to 44.7 percent) in the first mock trial and by 1.7 percent (from 58.3 percent to 60.0 percent) in the second one.[209] In comparison to the differences reported by Saks,[210] so the argument would go, these differences are minimal.

However, this argument misconceives the thrust of *Ballew*'s analysis in two important respects. First, *Ballew* quite properly eschewed any attempt at quantification.[211] Undoubtedly, the majority recognized that in most cases even the best social science experiments will be able to detect only the presence of a phenomenon, not its magnitude.[212] Thus, Saks's results can be taken as some evidence that twelve-person juries will be more consistent in their verdicts than six-person juries; Jurow's results (taken in conjunction with the corroborative results obtained from other studies) constitute substantially stronger evidence that a death-qualified jury is more likely to convict than a non-death-qualified one. However, neither set of results can be taken as revealing the magnitude of the phenomenon as well as the likelihood of its existence.[213]

Moreover, in view of *Ballew*'s overall analysis, the magnitude of differences detected by the prosecution-proneness experiments cannot be considered minimal. By implicitly accepting the hypothesis that the conviction of an innocent defendant is much more harmful than the acquittal of a guilty one,[214] *Ballew* underlined its commitment to avoiding a variance in jury verdicts that operates to the "detriment of . . . the defense."[215] Moreover, the court was emphatic in expressing its lack of concern with percentages. Justice Blackmun explicitly stated that it is in the "small percentag[e]" of cases "[w]hen the case is close, and the guilt or innocence of the defendant is not readily apparent" "that the jury trial right has its greatest value."[216]

The differences detected by the prosecution-proneness experiments are directly related to these two concerns. If the results accurately reflect the differences that exist in reality, it appears that the effect of death-qualification will not be to increase every capital defendant's chances of conviction by a small amount, but rather to magnify significantly the danger of conviction for defendants in a few close cases, while leaving the great majority of defendants' chances unaffected. To illustrate, if death-qualification has the effect of producing a 1 percent increase in the proportion of eligible prospective jurors who would vote for conviction in a particular close case,[217] this means that in the particular capital case involved, it can be expected that out of 100 prospective jurors, 1 who would have voted for acquittal will be replaced by 1 who will vote for conviction. The chance that a jury of 12 will contain the juror representing this "swing" vote is approximately one in eight.[218] Thus, death-qualification may have an impact in only about one-eighth of all close capital cases.[219] However, its impact in this small group of cases may be enormous because in a close case (where by definition the eligible jury population will be quite evenly divided between guilt and acquittal), the vote on a randomly selected jury's first ballot is likely to be nearly evenly divided,[220] and when it is, the change of a single juror's vote may obviously be determinative.[221] Moreover, unlike the impact of a reduction in jury size,[222] when the change to a death-qualified jury will have an effect on the outcome, it will *always* be to the detriment of the defense. Accordingly, since death-qualification will apparently infringe on jury verdict accuracy in both the manner and types of cases that most concerned the *Ballew* majority, this infringement can hardly be considered minimal.

In summary, the empirical data indicates that death-qualification will have some impact in all of the areas of concern identified by *Ballew*. "Effective group deliberation" may be impaired because of death-qualification's tendency to remove people whose attitudes may tend to counteract biases held by those who are eligible to serve on a capital jury. The extent to which the jury accurately reflects a cross-section of the community will be altered because death-qualification will have a disproportionate effect on discrete groups within the population, particularly blacks. Finally, and perhaps most significantly, death-qualification impairs jury verdict accuracy, for in some of those close cases in which the jury's determination of guilt or innocence may properly be expected to be hanging in the balance, death-qualification will have the effect of shifting the pendulum to the detriment of the defense. Viewed in the light of the concerns articulated by *Ballew*, these findings would appear sufficient to establish that the death-qualified jury constitutes a "substantial threat" to a defendant's Sixth Amendment guarantee of an impartial jury trial.

Weighing State Interests That Might Be Asserted as Justifications for Death-Qualification

The basic state interest that may be asserted in support of maintaining a death-qualified jury is the interest in securing, as *Witherspoon* characterized it, a "neutral" determination as to whether or not the death penalty should be imposed.[223] When a state provides that in certain cases capital punishment may be imposed pursuant to articulated criteria that must be weighed by the jury in making a death penalty determination, it does have a legitimate interest in ensuring that all members of the jury will actually weigh the death penalty decision in accordance with the articulated guidelines. In light of this interest, the state may justifiably assert that individuals who clearly state that they would absolutely refuse to consider the imposition of the death penalty in any case should not be permitted to participate in the penalty determination. Assuming this assertion is accepted as a legitimate justification,[224] the question presented is whether the state also has a legitimate justification for excluding individuals who would make the same statement at the guilt phase of the proceedings.[225]

Witherspoon seemed to assume that in a bifurcated trial proceeding, the state interest in a "neutral" penalty determination and the defendant's interest in a "neutral" guilt determination could be accommodated by the simple expedient of providing "one jury to decide guilt and another to fix punishment."[226] Nevertheless, a state might assert two justifications for choosing to exclude non-death-qualified jurors at the guilt phase rather than at the penalty phase.

First, the state might assert that the inclusion of non-death-qualified jurors at the guilt stage jeopardizes its interest in securing a proper verdict because a juror's adamant opposition to capital punishment (together with her knowledge that in the event of a capital verdict she would be excluded from the death penalty determination) might lead her to "nullify" the law by voting against a capital verdict despite her contrary view of the evidence. In dealing with this issue, it is important to focus precisely on the means the state may employ to secure its interest. Assuming that some substantial proportion of those who would automatically vote against the imposition of capital punishment at the penalty phase would also seek to nullify the possibility of capital punishment at the guilt stage,[227] the real question is whether the remedy of excluding all prospective jurors who fall within *Witherspoon*'s first exception is an appropriate one. In view of the defendant's significant Sixth Amendment interests, rough and approximate rules of thumb may not constitutionally be used to exclude "broad categories of persons from jury service" in lieu of determining their particular fitness to serve.[228] *Witherspoon* itself demonstrates that when veniremen are being excluded for opposition to the death penalty, the exclusionary rule must be shaped precisely to correspond with the government's legitimate interest.[229] In order to eliminate prospective jurors who would nullify at the guilt stage to avoid a possible death sentence, it is only necessary to exclude all those whose views on capital punishment "would prevent them from making an impartial decision as to the defendant's *guilt*."[230] As the Court stated in *Witherspoon*[231] and held in *Lockett v. Ohio*,[232] veniremen who respond affirmatively to this inquiry may properly be excluded for cause. If a venireman responds in the negative, there is no more reason for assuming that she will in fact nullify than there is for assuming that one who states that she is opposed to capital punishment but will consider imposing it will in fact refuse to impose the death penalty in any case. Since *Witherspoon* indicates that a juror's qualification to serve must be determined on the basis of the statement made in the voir dire,[233] exclusion pursuant to *Witherspoon*'s second exception is a sufficient but finely tuned means of safeguarding the state's interest in excluding nullifiers. There is certainly no basis for concluding that *all* prospective jurors who fall within the first *Witherspoon* exception also fall within the second exception;[234] accordingly, the assertion that exclusion pursuant to the first exception is necessary to protect against potential nullifiers cannot be supported.

Second, a state might assert that by retaining death-qualification at the guilt phase, it will avoid administrative inconvenience. That is, exchanging the present system for one in which death-qualification is postponed until the penalty phase will necessitate loss of time and expense. In assessing the strength of this interest, it should be noted that in *Ballew* the Court dismissed the claimed savings in cost and efficiency as "little or no justification" for the reduction to five-member juries.[235] In the present situation, these potential savings would appear to be even less. Whereas *Ballew* was dealing with a procedure applied in all criminal misdemeanor cases, a state's system of death-qualification will be at issue only in capital cases. While exact figures are not available, it seems fair to assume that in most jurisdictions misdemeanor jury trials will be much more frequent than jury trials in potential capital cases. Therefore, this procedural change will have potential impact in a relatively small number of cases.

Moreover, the number of cases in which death-qualification at the penalty phase will actually occur will be even smaller because in order to reach this point, a confluence of three events is required. First, the guilt jury must actually reach a verdict;[236] second, that verdict must be one that authorizes the possible imposition of capital punishment;[237] and third, the prosecutor must decide that he actually desires to death-qualify the penalty jury.[238] If any of these events does not take place, the elimination of the need for any death-qualification will effect an obvious saving of cost and efficiency.

What of the cases in which death-qualification at the penalty phase will actually be necessary? In view of the presence of alternate jurors (and the trial judge's discretionary authority to provide for additional alternates in cases where they may be required),[239] death-qualification at the penalty phase should not often necessitate selection of a new penalty jury. In many cases, excluded jurors could merely be replaced by alternates.

In those rare cases in which selection of a new penalty jury will actually be required, the necessity for inquiring into matters other than death-qualification will presumably make the time expended in selection longer than that which would be consumed by death-qualifying the original jury at the guilt phase. Moreover, the selection of a new penalty jury will lengthen the total time of trial. The new jury's ignorance of the evidence relating to guilt will make it necessary for the parties to reintroduce any evidence that could bear on the penalty determination. However, the increases in court time necessitated by these problems could be minimized. Since the state has wide discretion to provide rules that will expedite jury selection,[240] the time consumed in selecting a new penalty jury need not be significant; and the burden of presenting evidence from the guilt phase to the new penalty jury could be substantially mitigated by the simple expedient of videotaping the guilt phase of the proceedings and showing the material portions of this videotape to the new penalty jury.[241]

In summary, the only legitimate governmental justifications for maintaining death-qualification (pursuant to *Witherspoon*'s first exception) at the guilt phase rather than the penalty phase of the proceedings relate to cost and efficiency. Moreover, the total savings in cost and efficiency should not be significant. The total number of jury trials in capital cases is relatively small, the number of these cases in which death-qualification at the penalty phase will mandate selection of a new penalty jury will be even smaller, and in those few cases the state can institute procedures that will minimize the extent to which the change will increase jury man-hours or burden the courts. Viewed in light of the priorities articulated by *Ballew*, then, the governmental justifications for death-qualifying the jury at the guilt phase are too insubstantial to be afforded any significant weight.

Balancing the Interests

In applying the balancing test used in *Ballew*, it is not sufficient to weigh merely the extent to which the death-qualified jury threatens impairment of the Sixth Amendment jury trial right against the governmental justifications for retaining the death-qualified jury. In addition, both the magnitude of the individual interest at stake[242] and the institutional interests that bear on the propriety of retaining or discarding the procedure in question[243] must also be considered.

The individual interests at stake are certainly greater in this case than they were in *Ballew*. In *Ballew* the Court indicated that labeling a crime a misdemeanor or a felony would not change the nature of the individual interest.[244] However, when a defendant's life is at stake—as it is when the death-qualified jury is used—it is not a question of labeling. As the Fifth Circuit said in *Marion v. Beto*,[245] "[t]he magnitude of a decision to take a human life is probably unparalleled in the human experience of a member of a civilized society."[246] At least since *Powell v. Alabama*,[247] the Supreme Court has demonstrated an undeviating commitment to the principle that the need for accurate fact-finding is greater in capital cases than in any other type of case.[248] Accordingly, the individual interest at stake weighs heavily against retaining the death-qualified jury. There can be no stronger individual interest than that of avoiding an improper conviction in a case in which the defendant's life is at stake.

At first glance, institutional considerations relating to stability appear to weigh strongly in favor of retaining the death-qualified jury. A decision invalidating the current practice of death-qualification would undoubtedly have a more disruptive effect on state systems of criminal procedure than the Court's decision in *Ballew*. Whereas the five-member jury was a relatively new practice that at the time of *Ballew* was in effect in only two states, death-qualification in some form has been in effect for more than a century,[249] and death-qualification pursuant to the *Witherspoon* exceptions is presently used in all but one of the thirty-five jurisdictions that authorize the imposition of capital punishment.[250] To be sure, in view of *Witherspoon*'s dictum, a ruling invalidating the death-qualified jury would not directly contravene the principle of *stare decisis*. The Court explicitly explained that the narrow scope of its 1968 ruling was based on the inadequacies in the empirical data then before it.[251] Nevertheless, states might reasonably argue that in detailing the scope of its holding, *Witherspoon* implicitly authorized the form of death-qualification that is now in effect, and that during the twelve intervening years the Court has provided no hint that this practice might be unconstitutional. Thus, eliminating or altering the death-qualified jury would be disruptive in that it would have a widespread impact that would infringe on legitimate reliance interests.

On the other hand, because of the pronounced shift in doctrine effected by the Court's capital punishment decisions,[252] a claim of justifiable reliance on the validity of a procedure employed in capital cases seems very weak. Since 1976, the administration of capital punishment has entered a new era in which past assumptions about the validity of previously employed procedures are no longer sound. For example, in *Gardner v. Florida*,[253] a 1977 decision, the Court broke with past precedent[254] by holding that a judge could not impose a death sentence on the basis of a confidential presentence report unless the contents of the report were first disclosed to the defense.[255] The Court took pains to emphasize that in light of the post-1972 awareness of the magnitude of the interest involved when a defendant's life is at stake, a heightened concern has emerged for maintaining procedures that appear to and in fact do afford fairness and rationality to capital defendants.[256] The lesson of cases like *Gardner* is that when questions that touch on whether the death penalty will be imposed are at issue, disturbing the law is appropriate because of the evolving recognition of the increased protection that must be afforded to capital defendants.

Indeed, in light of this evolving principle, eliminating the death-qualified jury in capital cases might be viewed as removing an anomaly from our system of justice. Capital defendants should have more stringent safeguards and protections than noncapital ones; yet, because of the death-qualified jury, capital defendants are apparently placed at a disadvantage at an extremely critical stage of the proceedings—at the stage, in fact, that requires the factual determinations on which a possible capital verdict will depend. Because the presence of this anomaly seems inconsistent with the goal of providing procedures that appear to and in fact do afford fairness and rationality to capital defendants, the institutional interest of upholding the legitimacy of an entrenched practice may not be relied on by the government. Instead, the real institutional interests at stake combine with the other interests identified by *Ballew* to point strongly in favor of a ruling invalidating the death-qualified jury.

Conclusion

The theory that the death-qualified jury places the capital defendant at a disadvantage with respect to the determination of guilt is not a new one. In fact, even before Professor Oberer expounded on the theory's empirical foundation, prosecutors in capital cases apparently operated on the assumption that it was correct.[257] In *Witherspoon v. Illinois*, the

Supreme Court took note of this theory, and, while not invalidating the form of death-qualification that is currently in use, in effect invited capital defendants to prove on the basis of sound empirical data that it is unconstitutional. In response to *Witherspoon*'s invitation, several studies produced new data that significantly strengthened the claim that the death-qualified jury is prosecution-prone. However, because *Witherspoon* failed to provide the criteria under which empirical evidence of prosecution-proneness could be transformed into a successful constitutional attack, the legal significance of these studies was problematic, at least until the Court's decision in *Ballew v. Georgia*.

In *Ballew* the Court appeared to articulate the necessary criteria, indicating that when a state procedure allegedly infringes on a defendant's Sixth Amendment right to jury trial, the Court will examine the relevant empirical evidence to determine the extent to which the procedure impairs the jury's ability to fulfill three essential functions: to deliberate effectively, to represent an accurate cross-section of the community, and to provide accurate and consistent verdicts. In the event it finds these functions impaired to a constitutional degree, the Court will balance the infringement of the defendant's Sixth Amendment rights against any state interests that may be asserted as justification for the infringement. The burden of this essay is that applying the criteria articulated in *Ballew* necessitates a conclusion that the form of death-qualification presently employed in capital cases constitutes a violation of a defendant's rights under the Sixth and Fourteenth Amendments.

Of course, there is always some danger in applying constitutional principles beyond their immediate context. Since the criteria developed in *Ballew* are couched in terms of determining the scope of the Sixth Amendment right to jury trial, they would seem to be applicable to the present issue. Yet the constitutionality of the death-qualified jury is indubitably a different issue from the one present in *Ballew*. The type of empirical evidence bearing on the two claims is different, the legal terrain in which the two claims are presented is different, and the ramifications of a ruling invalidating the constitutionality of each practice are undoubtedly different. The argument here has been that these factors actually weigh in favor of a ruling invalidating death-qualification. This conclusion, however, is somewhat speculative because the considerations involve imponderables that cannot be calibrated with precision. At the very least, though, the implications of *Ballew* suggest—not only to the Supreme Court, but also to other courts and legislatures—that the constitutionality of the death-qualified jury is an issue ripe for reconsideration. The relevant empirical data should be weighed to determine whether this practice impermissibly prejudices the rights of capital defendants. If, as the Supreme Court has indicated, the conclusion that death is a punishment different in kind from all other punishments has committed our society to the ideal of providing fair and rational procedures that will fully safeguard the rights of capital defendants, then examination of the relevant data should lead to the conclusion that the death-qualified jury, as it presently exists, should be eliminated from our system of justice.

NOTES

The author expresses his appreciation to Professor John Decani of the University of Pennsylvania, Department of Statistics, for his advice and assistance in dealing with statistical data, and to Kim Eaton for her valuable research assistance.

1. Gregg v. Georgia, 428 U.S. 153, 188 (1976) (plurality opinion of Stewart, J.); Furman v. Georgia, 408 U.S. 238, 306 (1972) (concurring opinion of Stewart, J.).

2. While not expressly imposing a constitutional rule to this effect, *Gregg*'s pivotal plurality opinion noted that the constitutional concerns expressed by *Furman* "are best met by a system that provides for a bifurcated proceeding. . . ." 428 U.S. at 195. States wishing to maintain capital punishment have accepted this hint. Every state statute that authorizes the imposition of capital punishment provides that capital defendants will be tried in a bifurcated procedure. *See, e.g.*, FLA. STAT. ANN. § 921.141 (West Cum. Supp. 1978); N.C. GEN. STAT. § 15A-2000 (Cum. Supp. 1977).

3. *See* Lockett v. Ohio, 438 U.S. 586 (1978).

4. *See* Gardner v. Florida, 430 U.S. 349 (1977).

5. *See* Witherspoon v. Illinois, 391 U.S. 510, 522 n.21 (1968). For a fuller discussion of this aspect of *Witherspoon*, see *infra* text at note 36.

6. *See* Oberer, *Does Disqualification of Jurors for Scruples Against Capital Punishment Constitute Denial of Fair Trial on Issue of Guilt?* 39 TEX. L. REV. 545 (1961).

7. *Id*. at 549–52.

8. *See id*. at 549; Bye, *Recent History and Present Status of Capital Punishment in the United States*, 17 J. CRIM. L. 234, 236 (1926).

9. *See* Woodson v. North Carolina, 428 U.S. 280, 293 (1976). *See generally* Mackey, *The Inutility of Capital Punishment: A Historical Note*, 54 B.U.L. REV. 32 (1974).

10. *See* Knowlton, *Problems of Jury Discretion in Capital Cases*, 101 U. PA. L. REV. 1099, 1106 (1953).

11. *See, e.g.*, United States v. Puff, 211 F.2d 171 (2d Cir.), *cert. denied*, 347 U.S. 963 (1954).

12. *See generally* Oberer, *supra* note 6, at 550 nn.25 & 26.

13. *See, e.g.*, PA. CONS. STAT. ANN. Stat. 19, § 1621 (1959) (no longer in force).

14. *See, e.g.*, OHIO REV. CODE ANN. §§ 2901.01 (1962) (no longer in force).

15. *See* Oberer, *supra* note 6, at 550–51.

16. For a further discussion of this point, see text at notes 219–26 *infra*.

17. As *Witherspoon* noted, under the discretionary system of capital punishment the jury making the penalty determination was "[g]uided by neither rule nor standard" in exercising its discretion as to whether the death penalty should be imposed. 391 U.S. at 519.

18. *But see Witherspoon*, 391 U.S. at 520 (suggesting that the presence of jurors who would not consider voting for the death penalty might thwart the state's interest in a "neutral" penalty determination).

19. *See* Oberer, *supra* note 6, at 551.

20. At the time of Professor Oberer's article, only two states—Iowa and South Dakota—did not allow challenges for cause to be made against potential jurors holding scruples against the death penalty. *Id.* at 557–58.

21. *See, e.g.*, Piccott v. State, 116 So. 2d 626 (Fla. 1959). However, the Court's decision in *Witherspoon* did narrow the prosecutor's right to a death-qualified jury. For a delineation of *Witherspoon*'s holding, see *infra* note 36 and accompanying text.

22. See Oberer, *supra* note 6, at 555.

23. The claim is not, of course, that a death-qualified jury will be more likely than a non-death-qualified one to convict in all situations. Obviously, myriad other factors, including the quality of the evidence presented in the case, the skill of the opposing counsel, and the attitude of the trial judge, may have a more significant effect on a defendant's chances than whether or not the jury is death-qualified. Moreover, assuming all other factors are equal, the claim is not that every death-qualified jury will be more likely to convict than every non-death-qualified one; rather, it is simply that assuming all other factors are held constant, the substitution of a death-qualified jury for a non-death-qualified one in any group of criminal cases will increase the proportion of convictions obtained from that group.

24. *See* Oberer, *supra* note 6, at 552 n.36 (citing ADORNO, FRENKEL-BRUNSWICK, LEVINSON, & SANFORD, THE AUTHORITARIAN PERSONALITY (1950)).

25. *See* Oberer, *supra* note 6, at 552, 565 n.87.

26. For an excellent summary of the relevant studies relating to this issue, see Girsh, *The Witherspoon Question: The Social Sciences and the Evidence*, 35 NLADA BRIEFCASE 99 (1978).

27. *See generally* Girsh, *supra* note 26, at 125.

28. *See* 391 U.S. at 522 n.21.

29. *See infra* note 250.

30. The constitutionality of death-qualification pursuant to *Witherspoon*'s second exception is not considered in this essay. Thus, it will be assumed that prior to the commencement of the guilt phase, the prosecution may properly exclude all prospective jurors who unequivocally state that "their attitude toward the death penalty would prevent them from making an impartial decision as to the defendant's *guilt*." 391 U.S. at 522–23 n.21.

31. 391 U.S. 510 (1968).

32. 435 U.S. 223 (1978).

33. 391 U.S. 510 (1968).

34. *Id*. at 522. The Court fully delineated the scope of its holding in a footnote. *Id*. at 522–23 n.21. *See also infra* text at notes 38–39.

35. 391 U.S. at 517.

36. *Id*. at 539 (Black, J., dissenting).

37. *Id*. at 520 n.18. *See infra* text at note 40.

38. 391 U.S. at 522 n.21. This is often referred to as the "first *Witherspoon* exception"; the second *Witherspoon* exception, also delineated in the footnote, applies to veniremen who make it unmistakably clear "that their attitude toward the death penalty would prevent them from making an impartial decision as to the defendant's *guilt*." *Id*. (emphasis in original).

39. *Id*. at 520.

40. *Id*. at 520 n.18.

41. *Id*. at 539 (Black, J., dissenting).

42. In Lockett v. Ohio, 438 U.S. 586, 596 (1978) the Court assumed *"arguendo*, that *Witherspoon* provides a basis for attacking the conviction as well as the sentence in a capital case," but held that exclusion of veniremen who made it unmistakably clear that their views on capital punishment would render them unable to comply with the law was proper because these veniremen fell within the second *Witherspoon* exception. Thus, while the Court has decided that excluding veniremen pursuant to *Witherspoon*'s second exception will not taint a capital conviction, it has not reconsidered the issue addressed in this essay—that is, whether exclusion of veniremen pursuant to *Witherspoon*'s first exception can constitutionally taint a conviction.

For recent lower court rulings rejecting the prosecution-proneness claim, *see, e.g.*, Spinkellink v. Wainwright, 578 F.2d 582 (5th Cir. 1978). *But cf.* Grigsby v. Mabry, 483 F. Supp. 1372 (E. D. Ark. 1980) (expressing conclusion that "the exclusion of those who unalterably oppose the death penalty may affect guilt determination," *id*. at 1388, but holding only that defendant is entitled to an evidentiary hearing on the prosecution-proneness claim). *See generally* White, *The Constitutional Invalidity of Convictions Imposed by Death-qualified Juries*, 58 CORNELL L. REV. 1176, 1181 n.26 (1973).

43. *See supra* text at note 40.

44. 391 U.S. at 517.

45. Three unpublished studies were "submitted" to the Court only in the sense that two of them were cited in the petitioner's brief and one in his petition for writ of certiorari. *See id*. at 517 n.10.

46. The Court in Witherspoon noted that

we can only speculate . . . as to the precise meaning of the terms used in those studies, the accuracy of the techniques employed, and the validities of the generalizations made. Under these circumstances, it is not surprising that the *amicus curiae* brief filed by the NAACP Legal Defense and Educational Fund finds it necessary to observe that, with respect to bias in favor of the prosecution on the issue of guilt, the record in this case is "almost totally lacking in the sort of factual information that would assist the Court."

Id. at 517 n.11. *See generally* Girsh, *supra* note 26, at 99; White, *supra* note 42, at 1179–80.

47. *See supra* text at note 40.

48. See H. KALVEN & H. ZEISEL, THE AMERICAN JURY 11 (Phoenix ed. 1971).

49. In any given case, it would obviously be impossible to compare the performance of a death-qualified and non-death-qualified jury because our system of justice does not permit simultaneous judgments to be returned by two juries deliberating on the same case.

50. *See, e.g.,* Boehm, *Mr. Prejudice, Miss Sympathy and the Authoritarian Personality: An Application of Psychological Measuring Techniques to the Problem of Jury Bias*, 1968 WIS. L. REV. 734. *See generally* Oberer, *supra* note 6, at 565 n.87.

51. Oberer, *supra* note 6, at 552.

52. *See* LOUIS HARRIS & ASSOC., STUDY NO. 2016, at Question 15 (1971) (on file at NAACP Legal Defense and Educational Fund, 10 Columbus Circle, Suite 2030, New York, N.Y. 10019 [hereinafter cited as 1971 Harris Poll]); Jurow, *New Data on the Effect of a "Death-Qualified" Jury on the Guilt Determination Process*, 84 HARV. L. REV. 567, 584 (1971); Bronson, *On the Conviction Proneness and Representativeness of the Death-Qualified Jury: An Empirical Study of Colorado Veniremen*, 42 U. COLO. L. REV. 1 (1970).

For a discussion of the extent to which the study results (published versus unpublished) may be judicially recognized by the Court, see *infra* note 101.

53. Bronson, *supra* note 52.

54. 1971 Harris Poll, *supra* note 52, at 1.

55. Bronson, *supra* note 52, at 8.

56. *Id.* at 7 (footnote omitted).

57. For example, the terms "good reason" in statements 1 and 2 and "too many" in statement 5 are open-ended terms that could be subject to widely different interpretations. Moreover, in using the term *guilty* or *guilt*, the author does not distinguish between legal and factual guilt. Thus, a subject with a knowledge of the criminal justice system might justifiably conclude that statement 1 is true in the sense that there is "good reason" (i.e., substantial cause) to believe that an arrested defendant is *factually* guilty; another subject might view the statement solely from the perspective of a juror and conclude that it sets forth an improper statement of law.

58. Bronson, *supra* note 52, at 9.

59. 1971 Harris Poll, *supra* note 52, at Questions 6–11, 13.

60. For example, the poll used the following more carefully crafted question to reexamine subjects' view of the insanity defense: "In most cases the jury should ignore a defense of insanity because it is a loophole that allows too many guilty people to go free." *Id.* at Question 11. The poll found that those who could vote for the death penalty were significantly more likely than those who could never vote for it to agree with this statement (67 percent agree, 28 percent disagree, as compared to 57 percent agree, 35 percent disagree).

61. When asked how much they would trust the testimony of the policeman who made the arrest in a criminal case the answer "a lot" was given by 56 percent of those who could vote for the death penalty but only by 47 percent of those who could never vote for it. *Id.* at Question 6.

62. Thirty percent of those who could never vote for the death penalty said they would trust what the defendant said "a lot," as compared with 27 percent of those who could vote for the death penalty. *Id*. at Question 6. Thirty-seven percent of those who could vote for the death penalty but only 27 percent of those who could never vote for it said they thought that (in comparison to the prosecutor), the "defense attorney is a man who is better skilled at playing tricks in the courtroom than in seeking justice." *Id*. at Question 10.

63. When asked how they would respond as jurors in a criminal case when confronted with a defendant who did not take the witness stand in his own defense, 28 percent of those who could never vote for the death penalty said they would not find him innocent; 34 percent of those who could vote for the death penalty said the same. When asked for their response if the defendant made a confession but the judge wouldn't let it be introduced because the defendant had no lawyer there when he made it, 31 percent of those who could never vote for the death penalty said they would not find the defendant innocent, as compared to 41 percent of those who could vote for the death penalty. When asked for their response if they had read a newspaper article that stated that the defendant had committed the crime charged, disregarding hypothetical instructions from the judge to ignore the article, 15 percent of those who could vote for the death penalty said they would not find the defendant innocent; 12 percent of those who could never vote for the death penalty said the same. *Id*. at Question 13.

64. Perhaps the best illustration of this correlation is the rather remarkable accuracy of "polls" that ask subjects how they are going to vote in a coming presidential election. Since 1948, the results taken from polls conducted within a few days prior to the election have been accurate within a few percentage points.

65. Although no figures are available, it is undoubtedly true that jurors' evaluations of the credibility of crucial witnesses (such as arresting officers and defendants) will often play a critical part in determining whether they will vote for conviction or acquittal.

66. *See infra* text at notes 85–93.

67. H. Zeisel, Some Data on Juror Attitudes Towards Capital Punishment (1968).

68. *Id*. at 27.

69. *Id*.

70. Of course, in each of the five cases the prosecution's case might be strong for different reasons. In one, the evidence of guilt might be simply overwhelming, in another the jury might have been strongly influenced by the judge's pro-prosecution charge, in still another the defense counsel's ineptness might have contributed substantially to the outcome. These differences could have some impact upon Zeisel's findings.

71. H. Zeisel, *supra* note 67, at 28–29.

72. *Id*. at 32.

73. *See infra* notes 75, 78–83.

74. In statistical terms, when two or more separate studies produce results that point in the same direction, it becomes less likely that the results of any one study are due to chance.

75. In the Wilson study subjects were presented with brief written descrip-

tions of the facts presented to the jury in five criminal cases. The subject was then asked to assume that he was a member of the jury deciding each of the cases and, on the basis of the facts and his interpretation and evaluation of them, to vote guilty or not guilty in each of the cases. W. Wilson, Belief in Capital Punishment and Jury Performance (1968) (unpublished manuscript). In the Goldberg study subjects were presented with written descriptions of sixteen simulated cases in which a defendant was accused of causing death or injury to another and were asked "to decide the guilt or innocence of the defendant and the sentence in each case based on the summary of the evidence presented." Goldberg, *Toward Expansion of Witherspoon: Capital Scruples, Jury Bias, and Use of Psychological Data to Raise Presumptions in the Law*, 5 HARV. C.R.-C.L. REV. 53, 59–60 (1969). In the Harris survey subjects were presented with four cards, each card presenting the definition of a criminal offense and facts that arguably supported a conviction for that offense, and were asked to vote guilty or not guilty on the basis of this information. 1971 Harris Poll, *supra* note 52, at Question 15. *See* Edison, *The Empirical Assault on Capital Punishment*, 23 J. LEGAL EDUC. 2, 14 (1970).

76. *See* H. ZEISEL, *supra* note 67.

77. *See* Jurow, *supra* note 52.

78. *Id.* at 577.

79. *Id.* at 581.

80. *Id.* at 582.

81. *Id.* at 583.

82. The subjects who would presumably be excludable for cause under *Witherspoon* were those who in response to a set of alternatives chose the following: "I could not vote for the death penalty regardless of the facts or circumstances of the case." *Id.* at 599. This statement apparently falls within the standard of exclusion articulated by the Court in *Witherspoon. See supra* text at note 38.

83. Jurow, *supra* note 52, at 583–85.

84. When the subjects of the Jurow study are compared to those selected through the approved sampling techniques used in the 1971 Harris Poll, *supra* note 52, it appears that the following groups were underrepresented: blacks, women, people with low incomes, people with limited education, and non–Roman Catholics. *See* White, *supra* note 42, at 1183.

85. Videotape would appear to have at least two important advantages over audiotape. First, the opportunity to observe the performances in the simulated script would undoubtedly increase the subjects' ability to make judgments on questions of credibility and their sense that such judgments are indispensable to reaching a verdict. Second, visual exposure to characters performing in a courtroom setting would be likely to increase both their sense of identification with the characters in the simulated performance and their sense of involvement in the task assigned to them.

86. Jurow, *supra* note 52, at 608, 611.

87. *Id.*

88. For example, in the first simulated trial, an expert witness gave important evidence relating to a "paraffin" test. *Id.* at 607. In an actual case, but not

apparently in Jurow's experiment, the judge would give the jury detailed guidelines to apply in weighing the expert's testimony.

89. *Id.* at 581.

90. Professor Jurow pointed out this problem, noting that "the effects of the group process and, for example, the influence of authoritarian personalities upon the group process are as yet unexplored." *Id.* at 596.

91. The Kalven and Zeisel study of jury trials indicates that the chances of ultimate conviction or acquittal are closely correlated to the number of votes for conviction or acquittal on the first ballot. *See infra* note 196. However, as the authors admit, there will be some deviations from this general pattern. *See* H. KALVEN & H. ZEISEL, *supra* note 48, at 488.

92. Cohen, *Comments on the Scrupled-Juror Problem*, 23 J. LEGAL EDUC. 21, 23 (1970).

93. Jurow, *supra* note 52, at 596. *See generally* Orne, *On the Social Psychology of the Psychological Experiment: With Particular Reference to Demand Characteristics and their Implications*, 17 AM. PSYCHOLOGIST 776 (1962); Rosenthal, *On the Social Psychology of the Psychological Experiment: The Experimenter's Hypothesis as Unintended Determinant of Experimental Results*, 51 AM. SCIENTIST 268 (1963).

94. *See* Girsh, *supra* note 26, at 100. The comparison between a "preference" for the death penalty and a preference for "banana ice cream" was first made in one of the amicus briefs presented in *Witherspoon. See* Amicus Brief filed by NAACP Legal Defense and Educational Fund at 40, Witherspoon v. Illinois, 391 U.S. 510 (1968).

95. In all of the literature, there are apparently no findings that point in the opposite direction—that is, there is no showing that those who are opposed to the death penalty will have some attitudes that are relatively favorable to the prosecution with respect to the determination of guilt.

96. *See supra* text at notes 52–63.

97. *See supra* text at notes 67–72.

98. *See, supra* text at notes 73–83.

99. *See, e.g.*, United States *ex rel.* Townsend v. Twomey, 452 F.2d 350 (7th Cir. 1972), *rev'g* 322 F. Supp. 158 (N.D. Ill. 1971).

100. *See supra* text at notes 72–73, 84–93.

101. A related problem pertains to the extent to which the study results may be judicially recognized by the Court. Except for the Wilson study, *supra* note 75 and portions of the 1971 Harris Poll, *see* White, *supra* note 142, at 1181, 1185–86, all of the study results have been published in scholarly journals. The Court has never clearly articulated the extent to which it will judicially recognize either published or unpublished studies, but it would appear certain that the former are entitled to greater weight than the latter. In *Witherspoon* the Court noted that the unpublished studies submitted in that case would not be afforded significant weight because the Court would be left to speculate on "the terms used in those studies, the accuracy of the techniques employed, and the validity of the generalizations employed." 391 U.S. at 517 n.11. It would seem that in order to alleviate fully the concerns expressed by the Court in that footnote, the author of a study would actually have to appear as a witness and be subject to cross-

examination concerning the study's methodology and results. An alternative procedure would be to have an expert witness testify to a study's results after examining its methodology and findings. To date, courtroom hearings of these types have been rare. If they occur, an author or expert witness's availability for cross-examination should render the question whether a study has been published or not virtually irrelevant. Whether a study is published or unpublished, certainly its author (and presumably also an expert in the field who is familiar with the study) can be cross-examined concerning its methodology and results.

Where no witness appears to present empirical results, published studies should be considered superior to unpublished ones if only because their presence in the public domain gives authorities in the field an opportunity to attack their findings and methodology. However, unpublished studies that have been relied on by authorities in the field should be entitled to some weight because presumably they would not be relied on unless the authorities found them to be reasonably reliable. Both the Wilson and Harris results have been relied on by authorities in the field. *See* Girsh, *supra* note 26, at 100, 102.

102. 391 U.S. at 517.

103. The question of what constitutes a "cognizable group" within the community is itself one on which there are divergent lines of authority. *See generally* Zeigler, *Young Adults as a Cognizable Group in Jury Selection*, 76 MICH. L. REV. 1045, 1057–61 (1979). The Court has long recognized that when a member of an identifiable minority group (such as a black) is on trial, the systematic exclusion of that minority group is unconstitutional because it creates a potential for bias against the minority defendant. *See, e.g.*, Hernandez v. Texas, 347 U.S. 475 (1954) (Mexicans); Strauder v. West Virginia, 100 U.S. 303 (1879) (blacks). In *Hernandez* the Court defined a "cognizable group" in the following terms:

> Throughout our history differences in race and color have defined easily identifiable groups which have at times required the aid of the courts in securing equal treatment under the laws. But community prejudices are not static, and from time to time other differences from the community norm may define other groups which need the same protection. Whether such a group exists within a community is a question of fact.

347 U.S. at 478. In Peters v. Kiff, 407 U.S. 493 (1972), the Court expanded the definition of a "cognizable group" by holding that where blacks are systematically excluded from jury service, a white defendant as well as a black one will have standing to complain of a constitutional violation. Three members of the majority explicitly premised this holding on the view that "when any large and identifiable segment of the Community is excluded from jury service, the effect is to remove from the jury room qualities of human nature and varieties of human experience, the range of which is unknown and perhaps unknowable." 407 U.S. at 503 (plurality opinion of Marshall, J., joined by Douglas, J., and Stewart, J.). Under the test, those who automatically refuse to impose the death penalty might be seen as a "cognizable group" because they bring to the jury room at least a perspective on capital punishment that appears to reflect a unique view of humanity. On the other hand, lower court decisions have interpreted the test as requiring "a common thread which runs through the group, a basic similarity in attitudes or ideas or experience which is present in members of the group and

which cannot be adequately represented if the group is excluded from the jury selection process. *See, e.g.*, United States v. Suzman, 337 F. Supp. 140, 143 (S.D.N.Y.), *aff'd*, 468 F.2d 1245 (2d Cir. 1972), *cert. denied*, 410 U.S. 973 (1973). Obviously, establishing such a "common thread" in the present case (or in any other) is almost impossible because of the difficulty in showing that the excludables (i.e., veniremen who may be eliminated pursuant to the first *Witherspoon* exception) have a broad spectrum of attitudes that are not shared by at least a substantial proportion of the nonexcludables. *See generally* Zeigler, *supra*, at 1071.

104. Based on the presently available data, the strongest claim of this nature is that death-qualification results in an underrepresentation of blacks. The 1971 Harris Poll showed that nationwide, exclusion pursuant to *Witherspoon*'s first exception results in the exclusion of 35 percent of all blacks and only 21 percent of all whites. 1971 Harris Poll, *supra* note 52, at Question 3d. Assuming that in a particular community blacks comprise 10 percent of the eligible jury population, eliminating the above percentages of blacks and whites would reduce the proportion of blacks eligible for jury duty to 8.4 percent. *See infra* note 180. Based on present doctrine, this degree of disparity would not appear to be sufficient to establish a prima facie case of discrimination against blacks in jury selection. *Compare, e.g.*, Swain v. Alabama, 380 U.S. 202 (1965) (evidence that black males comprise 26 percent of the male population over twenty-one but only 10 to 15 percent of the grand and petit juries over a substantial period of time insufficient to establish a prima facie case) *with* Sims v. Georgia, 389 U.S. 404 (1967) (where blacks comprise 24.4 percent of the population but only 4.7 percent of the grand jury list and 9.8 percent of petit jury list, a prima facie showing of discrimination is established). However, it has been argued that "[a] distinction should be made between a selection process which leads to an initial underrepresentation of black veniremen, and one which allows the direct exclusion of a disproportionate number of apparently qualified potential black jurors." White, *supra* note 42, at 1195. Where the disproportionate exclusion of blacks occurs for a reason that has some relationship to their blackness, arguably no disproportionate exclusion should be tolerated. *Cf.* Alexander v. Louisiana, 405 U.S. 625, 630 (1972) (holding that no "statistical" showing of a prima facie case of racial discrimination is required when jury selection procedures are not "racially neutral" in that the use of a "questionnaire and . . . information card provided a clear and easy opportunity for racial discrimination"). In the present case, the arguable basis for connecting blacks' disproportionate exclusion with their blackness is that "[b]lacks are disproportionately opposed to capital punishment because over the years a disproportionate number of blacks have been executed." *Id*.

105. *See supra* notes 103–04.

106. 391 U.S. at 521.

107. The language of the phrase, focusing as it does on the jury's failure to represent the community on the *issue of guilt*, supports this interpretation. In addition, *Witherspoon*'s holding, *see supra* notes 33–38, was explicitly premised on the determination that a jury "[c]ulled of all who harbor doubts about the wisdom of capital punishment," 391 U.S. at 520, does not represent the community with respect to the penalty determination because it is a jury that is "uncom-

monly willing to condemn a man to die." 391 U.S. at 521. In the context of this analysis, it is quite natural to assume that when the Court speaks of an "unrepresentative jury on the issue of guilt," it is contemplating a jury that is "uncommonly willing" to find a defendant guilty.

108. 578 F.2d 582 (5th Cir. 1978).

109. *Id.* at 594.

110. *Id.*

111. *Id.*

112. *See supra* text at notes 106–08.

113. "In the instant case a reading of the transcript of the voir dire examination demonstrates that those veniremen who were chosen to be jurors in no way indicated that they were biased for the prosecution or against the defendant." 578 F.2d at 594.

114. *See* 578 F.2d at 594.

115. Moreover, *Spinkellink*'s determination that an attack on the death-qualified jury must be premised on a claim that the jury is actually "biased" renders *Witherspoon*'s carefully phrased dictum irrelevant. Obviously, if the jury is "biased" within the traditional meaning of that term, the defendant need not premise his constitutional claim on the implications of *Witherspoon*'s language but can establish a Sixth Amendment violation on the basis of settled pre-*Witherspoon* authority. *See, e.g.*, Irvin v. Dowd, 366 U.S. 717, 722–23 (1961).

116. *See generally* Taylor v. Louisiana, 419 U.S. 522, 527–30 (1975).

117. *See* 391 U.S. at 518 (citing Glasser v. United States, 315 U.S. 60, 84–86 (1942)).

118. *See* White, *supra* note 42, at 1199–200.

119. Although *Witherspoon* cited the portion of *Glasser* that places a strong stamp of disapproval on "[t]endencies, no matter how slight" in the direction of a selection process that favors the prosecution, the *Glasser* dictum was not quoted, and it was not cited as placing a gloss on the "substantially increases the probabilities of conviction" language but only as defining the standard of impartiality demanded of a juror in her role as "arbiter of the punishment to be imposed." 391 U.S. at 518.

120. With the exception of Ballew v. Georgia, 435 U.S. 223 (1978), post-*Witherspoon* cases have not shed much additional light on the prosecution-proneness issue. However, one important development should be noted. In *Witherspoon* the prosecution-proneness claim presented to the Court was that convictions returned by death-qualified juries are in violation of the due process clause. As a result of the Court's holding in Duncan v. Louisiana, 391 U.S. 145 (1968), the due process clause of the Fourteenth Amendment now incorporates the Sixth Amendment right to jury trial; accordingly the current prosecution-proneness argument can be premised on the claim that a death-qualified jury violates a defendant's Sixth Amendment right to jury trial. The Court has indicated that in the context of jury selection, the Sixth Amendment imposes more exacting requirements than the Fourteenth Amendment. *Compare* Taylor v. Louisiana, 419 U.S. 522 (1976) *with* Hoyt v. Florida, 368 U.S. 57 (1961).

121. 435 U.S. 223 (1978).

122. Although concurring with the Court's judgment on the constitutional

issue, three members of the Court criticized the majority for its heavy reliance on sociological data, particularly when "neither the validity nor the methodology employed by the studies cited was subjected to the traditional testing mechanisms of the adversary process." 435 U.S. at 246 (Powell, J., concurring, joined by Rehnquist, J., and Burger, C.J.). In response, the majority opinion justified its reliance on the studies by noting, "[w]e have considered them carefully because they provide the only basis, besides judicial hunch, for a decision about whether smaller and smaller juries will be able to fulfill the purpose and functions of the sixth amendment." *Id.* at 232 n.10. The Court also noted that there was precedent for considering the results of published studies that have not been tested in a courtroom proceeding. *Id.*

123. 399 U.S. 78 (1970).

124. *See* Duncan v. Louisiana, 391 U.S. 147, 156 (1968) (defining a jury's constitutional function in these terms).

125. Ballew, 435 U.S. at 237 (citing *Williams*, 399 U.S. at 100).

126. 435 U.S. at 232.

127. *Id.* at 234.

128. *Id.* at 236.

129. *Id.*

130. *Id.* at 232.

131. *Id.* at 236.

132. *Id.* at 237 (relying on Lempert, *Uncovering "Nondiscernible" Differences: Empirical Research and the Jury-Size Cases*, 73 Mich. L. Rev. 643, 687–88 (1975).

133. *See* Nagel & Neff, *Deductive Modeling to Determine an Optimum Jury Size and Fraction Required to Convict*, 1975 Wash. U.L.Q. 933. Friedman, *Trial by Jury: Criteria for Convictions, Jury Size and Type I and Type II Errors*, 26-2 Am. Stat. 21 (April 1972).

134. For example, one critical assumption of the Nagel & Neff study was that "above 95 percent of the defendants tried by juries are in fact guilty and about 5 percent are innocent." Nagel & Neff, *supra* note 133, at 943.

135. *See id.* at 946.

136. 435 U.S. at 234.

137. *Id.*

138. *Id.*

139. *See* M. Saks, Jury Verdicts (1977).

140. 435 U.S. at 235.

141. *Id.* at 237 n.27 (citing M. Saks, *supra* note 139, at 90).

142. *Id.* at 237.

143. *Id.*

144. After noting two examples in which statements of overall results (e.g., judges held for plaintiffs 59 percent of the time, juries held for plaintiffs 56 percent of the time) obscured more substantial differences (judges and juries disagreed in 22 percent of the cases), the Court emphasized that "the averages masked significant case-by-case differences that must be considered when evaluating jury function and performance." *Id.* at 238.

145. *Id.* at 239.

146. *Id.* at 237.

147. *Id.* at 239.

148. *Id.*

149. *Id.*

150. *Id.*

151. *Id.* at 242.

152. *Id.* at 241. In a footnote the Court further expounded on the insignificance of the misdemeanor "label" by noting that "the nature of the substance of the misdemeanor charges against petitioner supports the refusal to distinguish between felonies and misdemeanors. The application of the community's standards and common sense is important in obscenity trials where juries must define and apply local standards." *Id.* at 241 n.33.

153. *Id.* at 243.

154. *Id.* at 244.

155. *Id.*

156. *Id.*

157. *Id.* While acknowledging that the empirical data relating to this point is mixed, *id.* at 244 n.40, the Court appeared to give special credence to one study's conclusion that "[t]otal trial time did not diminish, and court delays and backlogs improved very little," *id.* at 244 (citing and relying on Pabst, *Statistical Studies of the Costs of Six-Man versus Twelve-Man Juries*, 14 WM. & MARY L. REV. 326, 327 (1972).

158. For earlier examples of the Court's use of sociological data in determining issues relating to the Sixth Amendment right to jury trial, *see, e.g.*, Williams v. Florida, 399 U.S. 78 (1970); Duncan v. Louisiana, 391 U.S. 145 (1968).

159. *See supra* text at note 152.

160. *See supra* text at notes 153–57.

161. Theoretically, this result could also be based on a conclusion that the state interests justifying a reduction to six are greater than the interests justifying a reduction to five. However, a conclusion of this sort would be patently absurd. If anything the state's interests in cost and efficiency will be stronger when the reduction is to the lower number.

162. 435 U.S. at 244.

163. For example, in 1977 Wisconsin changed from the mandatory twelve-member jury in criminal cases to a discretionary one; the parties can agree on a lesser number than twelve, but not less than six. *See* WIS. STAT. ANN. § 756.096 3(a) (West 1979). For an analysis of state decisions dealing with post-*Williams* legislative reductions of jury size, see Note, *Right to Trial by Jury—Number of Jurors*, 47 A.L.R.3d 895 (1976).

164. For a recent comment on the value of *stare decisis, see, e.g.*, Jim Rose, Warden v. Mitchell, 443 U.S. 545 at 594 (1979) (Stevens, J., dissenting): "The doctrine of *stare decisis* is not a strait jacket that forecloses reexamination of outmoded rules. The doctrine does, however, provide busy judges with a valid reason for refusing to remeasure a delicate balance that has tipped in the same direction every time the conflicting interests have been weighed."

165. In support of its claim that the five-person jury was above the constitutional minimum, Georgia asserted its reliance on *Williams*'s statement that "[W]e

have no occasion in this case to determine what minimum number can still constitute a 'jury,' but we do not doubt that six is above that minimum." Williams v. Florida, 399 U.S. 78, 91 n.28 (1970). However, *Ballew* properly rejected this strained emphasis on semantics. *See* 435 U.S. at 244.

166. *See* 435 U.S. at 244.

167. *See supra* text at note 151.

168. *See* 435 U.S. at 242.

169. *Id*. at 234. *Ballew* noted that reduction of jury size also impaired "group deliberations" in that the reduction adversely affected the jury's collective memory, its capacity for self-criticism, and the likelihood that a particular jury member will make an important contribution. *Id*. at 232. The existing studies have not attempted to measure death-qualification's potential impact in these areas. However, the studies do indicate that the authoritarian bent of individuals who will survive death-qualification tends to make them disproportionately rigid in their attitudes. *See* Jurow, *supra* note 52, at 585; Boehm, *supra* note 50, at 740. It may not be unreasonable to infer that this rigidity may adversely affect these individuals' capacity for self-criticism. However, neither study specifically measured this quality.

170. *See supra* text at notes 59–63.

171. Subjects were asked whether they agreed or disagreed with the statement that "[d]efense [a]ttorneys are more likely to be dishonest because they are always trying to get criminals off." Fifty-one percent of those who could vote for the death penalty agreed with the statement, compared with only 43 percent of those who could never vote for the death penalty. 1971 Harris Poll, *supra* note 52, at Question 9.

172. Thirty-three percent of those who could vote for the death penalty said they would trust what the prosecuting attorney had to say "a lot," as did 27 percent of those who could never vote for the death penalty. *Id*. at Question 6.

173. Concerning their trust of what the arresting officer had to say, 56 percent of those who could vote for the death penalty, compared to 47 percent of those who could never vote for it, said they would trust him "a lot." *Id*. at Question 6.

174. *See supra* note 63.

175. *See supra* notes 171–74.

176. According to the 1971 Harris Poll, *supra* note 52, at Question 3a, 52 percent of the blacks questioned opposed capital punishment, compared to 33 percent of the whites. *See also* Smith, *A Trend Analysis of Attitudes Toward Capital Punishment, 1936–1974, reprinted in* STUDIES OF SOCIAL CHANGE SINCE 1948 (J. Davis ed. 1976) (showing by means of charts that at all time periods between 1953 and 1974 blacks were significantly more opposed to capital punishment than whites).

177. Harris found that 42 percent of the women surveyed opposed the death penalty in comparison to 30 percent of the men. 1971 Harris Poll, *supra* note 52, at Question 3a. In the Bronson study, 57.1 percent of the women and 42.9 percent of the men strongly opposed capital punishment. Bronson, *supra* note 52, at 22.

178. "The Court repeatedly has held that meaningful community participa-

tion cannot be attained with the exclusion of minorities or other identifiable groups from jury service." 435 U.S. at 236–37.

179. 1971 Harris Poll, *supra* note 52, at Question 3d.

180. This figure may be arrived at as follows:

p = percentage of eligible black jurors before *Witherspoon* exclusions
x = percentage of eligible black jurors excluded
y = percentage of eligible white jurors excluded
p' = percentage of eligible black jurors after *Witherspoon* exclusions

$$p' = \frac{p - (px)}{1 - [(1-p) \cdot y] - [p \cdot x]}$$

$$p = .10, x = .35, y = .21$$

$$p' = \frac{.10 - [(.35)(.10)]}{1 - [(.21)(.90)] - [(.35)(.10)]}$$

$$p' = .084 \text{ or } 8.4\%$$

181. *Ballew* noted that "if a minority group constitutes 10% of the community, 53.1% of randomly selected six-member juries could be expected to have no minority representative among their members, and 89% not to have two." 435 U.S. at 237. On the other hand, if a minority group constitutes 8.4 percent of the community, 65.1 percent of randomly selected twelve-member juries could be expected to have no minority representatives and 73.3 percent not to have two. These figures were computed by Professor John DeCani as follows:

p = chances that at least one member of x group will be selected in n selections
x = proportion of x group to total population
p = $(1-x)^n$
let n = 12
x = 8.4% or 0.084
p = $(.916)^{12} = .349$ or 34.9%
$1-p$ = 65.1%
$p(Y)$ = probability of selecting y in n selections
y = number from minority group selected for jury,
n = number of selections made (i.e., size of jury),

$$p(y) = \frac{n!}{y!\,(n-y)!}\ p^x(1-p)^{\,n-x}$$

y = 2 or more
n = 12
$p(1)$ = 0.384
$p(2)$ = $1 - p(1) - p(0)$
$p(2)$ = 0.267
$1-p(y)$ = 0.733

182. *See* 435 U.S. at 236 (noting that "group theory suggests that a person in the minority will adhere to his position more frequently when he has at least one other person supporting his argument").

183. The Court's priorities appear to be reflected in its statement that "a properly functioning jury system will insure evaluation by the sense of the community and will also tend to insure accurate factfinding." 435 U.S. at 238. In addition, while *Ballew* was undoubtedly concerned with the impact of a reduction in jury size on the jury's ability to represent the community, it devoted even more attention to issues relating to "accuracy" and "consistency." *See* 435 U.S. at 232.

184. In determining the "optimal" mixture of factually accurate verdicts, an assumption must be made concerning the relative harm of an innocent person's conviction versus a guilty person's acquittal. If the former is considered to be ten times as harmful as the latter, then obviously the "optimal" mixture will not be merely the fewest number of "erroneous" results but a mixture of "erroneous" results that is weighted heavily toward minimizing the erroneous conviction of an innocent person.

185. As Professor Saks has noted, "unlike problem-solving tasks used in much research on decision-making, the jury's task is one in which there exists no objective criterion against which to compare the decisions of differently structured juries. The 'true' verdict can never be known. If it were, there would be no need for a jury decision." M. Saks, *supra* note 139, at 14.

186. *See supra* text at note 93.

187. *See supra* text at notes 67–83.

188. M. Saks, *supra* note 139, at 66.

189. *Id*.

190. *Id*. at 86. Excluding "hung juries," the results tabulated by Saks showed that in the first experiment, twelve-person juries reached the same verdict (acquittal) 83 percent of the time, whereas six-person juries reached the same verdict (acquittal) only 69 percent of the time; in the second experiment (in which the evidence was weighted more strongly in favor of guilt), twelve-person juries reached the same verdict (conviction) 71 percent of the time, whereas six-person juries reached that same verdict only 57 percent of the time. *Id*. at 86.

191. *See supra* text at notes 73–83.

192. *See* Jurow, *supra* note 52.

193. *Id*. at 581.

194. *Id*. at 582.

195. *Id*. at 584. Specifically, in the first mock trial (involving a "liquor store hold up"), the proportion of excludables and nonexcludables voting for conviction was 33.3 percent and 44.7 percent respectively; in the second mock trial (involving a "rape-murder"), the figures were 42.9 percent and 60.0 percent. Eliminating the excludable subjects would increase the proportion of votes for conviction by 1.1 percent (from 43.6 percent to 44.7 percent) in the "liquor store hold up" trial and by 1.7 percent (from 58.3 percent to 60.0 percent) in the "rape-murder" trial. Jurow, *supra* note 52, at 583.

196. Based on extensive empirical findings, the authors conclude that when there is an initial majority either for conviction or for acquittal, the jury in roughly nine out of ten cases decides in the direction of the initial majority. Only with extreme infrequency does the minority succeed in persuading the

majority to change its mind during the deliberation. But this is only to say that *with very few exceptions the first ballot decides the outcome of the verdict*. H. KALVEN & H. ZEISEL, *supra* note 48, at 488 (emphasis in original).

197. For example, jurors who disclosed the progress of deliberations in the celebrated murder prosecution of Juan Corona revealed that while most of the evidence in the case was discussed prior to the initial ballot, real conversation or analysis was impeded because "most of the jurors were anxious to know where everyone else stood before expressing their own views." *See* V. VILLASENOR, JURY: THE PEOPLE VS. JUAN CORONA 63 (1977).

198. M. SAKS, *supra* note 139, at 88.

199. "Statistical significance" is a mathematical concept that enables a researcher to state the likelihood that the results of a particular study could have been due to chance variations and do not reflect differences which exist in reality. Statistical significance is conventionally reported in "p" levels. Thus, "$p=.05$" means that the particular finding that is reported could have occurred by chance only five times in a hundred. In general, results are characterized as "statistically significant" when $p \leq .05$. *See generally* Q. MCNEMOR, PSYCHOLOGICAL STATISTICS (4th ed. 1969).

200. Application of conventional statistical tests shows the statistical significance of the results obtained from the various simulated experiments to be as follows: (1) For Goldberg's results, *supra* note 75, showing that based on their votes in sixteen cases "scrupled" subjects are less likely to convict than "nonscrupled" ones $p \leq .08$; (2) For Wilson's results, *supra* note 75, showing that based on their votes in six cases, "scrupled" subjects are less likely to convict than "nonscrupled" ones, $p \leq .02$; (3) For Harris's results, *supra* note 52, showing that in each of four cases nonexcludable subjects are more likely to convict than excludable ones, $p \leq .01$ as to three of the cases (typewriter robbery; manslaughter, assaulting an officer) and $p \leq .10$ as to the fourth one (automobile larceny); (4) For Jurow's results, *supra* note 52, showing that in two cases nonexcludable subjects are more likely to convict than excludable ones, $p \leq .34$ as to Case I and $p \leq .13$ as to Case II.

201. For example, if Jurow's and Harris's findings pertaining to nonexcludable subjects' increased propensity to convict are taken together, the combined significance level of p is less than .04 as to Jurow's Case I and less than .009 as to Jurow's Case II.

202. *See* Jurow, *supra* note 52.

203. *See* 1971 Harris Poll, *supra* note 52; Goldberg, *supra* note 75; Wilson, *supra* note 75.

204. *See* Jurow, *supra* note 52.

205. *See, e.g.*, Goldberg, *supra* note 75 (sixteen simulated cases used); Wilson, *supra* note 75 (six cases used).

206. *See* 1971 Harris Poll, *supra* note 52; and *supra* text at note 84.

207. *See* Jurow, *supra* note 52; and *supra* text at note 84.

208. *See* H. ZEISEL, *supra* note 67.

209. *See supra* note 195.

210. *See supra* note 190.

211. *See supra* text following note 158.

212. The concept of statistical significance is relevant here. The fact that a study's results are statistically significant establishes that it is unlikely that the results pointed in the indicated direction occurred as a matter of chance; it does not establish that the *magnitude* of the differences obtained did not occur as a result of chance.

213. Of course, when a study produces statistically significant results, statistical tests can under some circumstances produce additional conclusions relating to the magnitude of the differences involved. However, these conclusions will generally be relatively imprecise. *See, e.g.*, H. ZEISEL, *supra* note 67, at 32 (based on statistical tests, "odds are 4 to 1 that the difference in the percentage points of Guilty votes will fall somewhere between 4 and 17 percentage points, in the indicated direction") (footnote omitted).

214. *See supra* text at notes 135–37.

215. 435 U.S. at 236.

216. *Id.* at 237–38.

217. In Jurow's two simulated experiments death-qualification's effect would be to produce a 1.1 percent increase in the eligible subjects voting for conviction in one case and a 1.7 percent increase in the other. *See supra* text at note 209.

218. This figure is obtained by adding the sum of the chances of choosing the "swing" juror in each of twelve random selections, keeping in mind that the population decreases by one with each selection. Thus, the sum of 1/100, 1/99 . . . 1/90, 1/89 equals 12.7 percent.

219. As a case becomes "clearer" in the sense that the evidence is weighed more heavily in favor of either the prosecution or the defense, the more likely all jurors (both those who could never vote for the death penalty and those who could vote it) will be to vote in the direction of the evidence. Hence, the "clearer" the case, the less impact death-qualification will be likely to have upon the number of jurors voting for conviction.

220. For example, if it is assumed that three-fifths of the eligible jury population would vote for conviction on the first ballot, the chances that there will be exactly six or seven votes for conviction on the first ballot are approximately two in five. This result, which was worked out by Professor DeCani, is arrived at as follows:

p	= average probability of conviction
m	= total number of jurors
x	= number of votes for conviction
Prob(x)	= $m!\,/\text{Prob}\,(x) = m!/x!(m-x)!\,p^x(1-p)^{m-x}$, $x=0, 1, \ldots, n$
p	= $3/5$ $m = 12$ $x = 7$
Prob(7)	= .2270
Prob(6)	= .1766
Prob(6 or 7)	= Prob(6) + Prob(7) = .4036

221. If it is accepted that the jury will vote in accordance with the outcome of the first ballot 90 percent of the time, then a change from five to six or six to seven votes for guilty on the first ballot is obviously likely to have a decisive impact on the defendant's chances.

222. Based on Saks's experiments, it appears that in cases in which the evidence favors the prosecution, reduction in jury size will be likely to favor the defense by reducing the "consistency" with which the jury will vote in the direction of the evidence. *See* M. SAKS, *supra* note 139, at 88.

223. *See* 391 U.S. at 520.

224. In opposition to this assertion, defendant might argue that excluding from the penalty determination all individuals who are absolutely opposed to the death penalty is in violation of the cruel and unusual punishment clause of the Eighth Amendment. Recent Supreme Court decisions indicate that the jury's ability to " ' maintain a link between contemporary community values and the penal system'," Woodson v. North Carolina, 428 U.S. 280, 295 (1976) (plurality opinion) (quoting *Witherspoon*, 391 U.S. at 515) has become an essential ingredient of any death sentencing procedure under the Eighth Amendment. In 1976 the Court held mandatory death penalty statutes unconstitutional, *Woodson*, Roberts v. Louisiana, 428 U.S. 325 (1976); on the ground that they were incompatible with "contemporary values," *Woodson*, 428 U.S. at 295, as demonstrated by the results of discretionary jury sentencing. In Gregg v. Georgia, 428 U.S. 153, 206 (1976), the Court plainly relied on the notion that juries' reflections of contemporary community attitudes in regard to the propriety of capital punishment would keep infliction of the death penalty in line with the evolving standards of decency that are the measure of the Eighth Amendment. The Court saw the jury's role as reflecting developing values not only on the question whether the death penalty should be inflicted at all, but also on the narrower question whether capital punishment is appropriate for "certain kind[s] of murder case[s]." *Id.* Defendant could argue that juries selected with the systematic exclusion of every venireman who would automatically refuse to vote for the death penalty would not adequately represent the community's attitude toward the death penalty; and, therefore, since this vital "link between contemporary community values and the penal system," *Witherspoon*, 391 U.S. at 519 n.15, is severed, juries selected pursuant to this form of death-qualification cannot possibly perform the vital constitutional function assigned to capital juries by the Court's decisions in *Gregg, Woodson*, and *Roberts*.

225. If death-qualification pursuant to *Witherspoon*'s first exception occurred at the penalty phase rather than the guilt phase, it is possible that different individuals would be excluded because the jurors' immediate proximity to the capital trial they participated in would be likely to color their response to the death-qualification inquiry. However, if anything, this consideration would be likely to favor the state by resulting in the exclusion of some jurors whose statements that they would automatically refuse to impose the death penalty in any case might be produced by their view of the case they had just participated in rather than their general views on capital punishment.

226. 391 U.S. at 520 n.18.

227. Although the history of capital punishment certainly includes instances of juror nullification, *see supra* note 9, it is not clear to what extent jurors absolutely opposed to the death penalty might "nullify" when adjudicating guilt pursuant to the current nonmandatory systems of capital punishment. In claiming that this problem is in fact a substantial one, the state might rely on an aspect of

the Bronson study in which subjects were asked to express their approval or disapproval of the following hypothetical action:

> Mr. Jones is on a jury deliberating on a case of first degree murder. If the man on trial is found guilty, he will go to the electric chair. If he is found not guilty, he will go free. Mr. Jones believes that the man on trial *is guilty*; however, he does not vote him guilty because he doesn't believe in capital punishment.

Bronson, *supra* note 52, at 11. Bronson found that of the sixty-five subjects who were "strongly opposed" to capital punishment (and therefore might most probably be subject to exclusion pursuant to *Witherspoon*'s first exception), only 49.2 percent actually disapproved of juror Jones's action; 9.2 percent strongly approved of it, 21.5 percent approved, and the rest were undecided (these figures represent corrections of a printing error in Bronson's original text). Of course, these figures do not really provide a good indication of the magnitude of the "nullification" problem. Quite aside from the fact that Bronson's question focused on a case where the death penalty was mandatory rather than imposed pursuant to a weighing of aggravating and mitigating circumstances, the primary problem with Bronson's results is that they measure merely the subject's evaluation of someone else's conduct, not their best estimate as to how they would react in the same situation. It is quite possible that subjects who approve or even strongly approve of juror Jones's action would nevertheless not feel that they would act in the same way themselves.

228. Duren v. Missouri, 439 U.S. 357, 369 (1979). *Accord*, Taylor v. Louisiana, 419 U.S. 522, 534–35 (1975).

229. In *Witherspoon* it was assumed that the government has a legitimate interest in excluding all veniremen who because of their opposition to capital punishment would automatically refuse to consider the imposition of the death penalty in any case or would be unable to make an impartial decision about the defendant's guilt. 391 U.S. at 522–23 n.21. From the state's point of view, one means of securing the exclusion of all such veniremen is to remove every venireman who expresses conscientious scruples against imposing the death penalty. Nevertheless, the Court rejected this sweeping approach in favor of a finely tuned inquiry directed to determining whether particular veniremen made it "unmistakably clear" that they in fact had the view that would justify their exclusion. *Id*.

230. 391 U.S. at 523 n.21.

231. *Id*.

232. 438 U.S. 586, 596 (1978).

233. *See supra* note 38 and accompanying text.

234. Obviously, a venireman can consistently and properly take the position that she will treat the guilt and penalty determinations as completely separate stages of the proceedings.

235. 435 U.S. at 244.

236. A jury might fail to reach a verdict both in cases where the jury deliberations break down or fail to create an agreement and in ones where the trial itself is aborted prior to the commencement of jury deliberations.

237. In other words, the defendant must be convicted of the capital charge. In most jurisdictions the capital charge is either murder, *see, e.g.*, GA. CODE

ANN. § 26-1101 (1977), or some more narrowly defined category of murder, *see, e.g.*, TEX. PENAL CODE ANN. § 19.03 (Vernon 1974).

238. In some cases in which a capital verdict is returned, the prosecutor will determine that the state's interests will not be advanced by a death sentence. Obviously, in those cases the prosecutor would have no reason to death-qualify the penalty jury.

239. *See, e.g.*, PA. R. CRIM. PROC. 1108(a) (1975).

240. *See, e.g.*, Ristaino v. Ross, 424 U.S. 589, 594 (1976): *"[v]oir dire* 'is conducted under the supervision of the court, and a great deal must, of necessity, be left to its sound discretion.' " (quoting Connors v. United States, 158 U.S. 408, 413 (1895)).

241. Moreover, using two juries rather than one might have compensating advantages. The new system would reduce the hardship incurred by any one person serving as a juror (since participating in just the guilt phase or just the penalty phase of the proceedings would presumably be less time-consuming than participating in both), and this might not only increase individual jurors' ability to concentrate but also reduce the possibility that aborted proceedings might occur as a result of juror problems.

242. *See supra* text at note 152.

243. *See supra* text at notes 162–67.

244. *See supra* note 152 and accompanying text.

245. 434 F.2d 29 (5th Cir. 1971).

246. *Id.* at 32.

247. 287 U.S. 45 (1932) (holding indigent defendant in state capital case has constitutional right to effective counsel). Between *Powell* and Gideon v. Wainwright, 372 U.S. 335 (1963), the indigent defendant had an absolute right to the appointment of counsel only in capital cases. *See, e.g.*, Betts v. Brady, 316 U.S. 455 (1942).

248. For a classic explanation of the Court's differing approach to capital and noncapital cases, see Stein v. New York, 346 U.S. 156, 196 (1953): "When the penalty is death, we, like state court judges, are tempted to strain the evidence and even, in close cases, the law in order to give a doubtfully condemned man another chance." *See also* Reid v. Covert, 354 U.S. 1, 77 (1957) (Harlan, J., concurring). *Cf.* Corbitt v. New Jersey, 439 U.S. 212, 217 (1978) (distinguishing New Jersey's "non vult" statute from the statute involved in Jackson v. United States, 390 U.S. 570 (1968), principally on the ground that the death penalty was not involved).

249. *See supra* text at notes 7–12.

250. Maryland is the one jurisdiction that does not permit death-qualification pursuant to *Witherspoon*'s first exception in capital cases. *See* MD. CTS. & JUD. PROC. CODE ANN. § 8-210(c) (1974). For cases allowing death-qualification of the jury pursuant to *Witherspoon*'s first exception, *see, e.g.*, Rowbotham v. State, 542 P.2d 610 (Okla. Crim. App. 1975); State v. Avery, 286 N.C. 459, 212 S.E.2d 142 (1975); State v. Elliot, 25 Ohio St. 2d 249, 267 N.E.2d 806 (1971); State v. Wilson, 57 N.J. 39, 269 A.2d 153 (1970); Thomas v. Leeke, 257 S.C. 491, 186 S.E.2d 516 (1970); Commonwealth v. Rightnour, 435 Pa. 104, 253 A.2d 644 (1969).

251. *See supra* text at notes 35–40.

252. Prior to 1972, the prevailing system of capital punishment was one in which the jury that returned a capital verdict would make an unguided discretionary judgment as to whether a death sentence should be imposed. In 1972, the Court held that a sentence of death imposed pursuant to this system of capital punishment is in violation of the cruel and unusual punishment clause of the Eighth Amendment. Furman v. Georgia, 408 U.S. 238 (1972). In 1976 the Court made it clear that *Furman* should not be interpreted as holding that the death penalty itself is unconstitutional but rather that it was the delegation of standardless capital sentencing discretion to the jury that rendered death penalties imposed pursuant to that procedure constitutionally invalid. *See* Gregg v. Georgia, 428 U.S. 153, 188–96 (1976). At the same time, the Court further refined the constitutional requirements of a system of capital punishment by holding that mandatory systems are unconstitutional, *see* Woodson v. North Carolina, 428 U.S. 280 (1976) (holding North Carolina statute that imposes mandatory death sentence upon conviction of first-degree murder to be in violation of the cruel and unusual punishment clause); Roberts v. Louisiana, 428 U.S. 325 (1976) (holding Louisiana statute imposing mandatory death sentence upon conviction of specified categories of first-degree murder to be similarly invalid), and by delineating the procedural safeguards that must apparently be incorporated into a constitutionally valid discretionary system. *See Gregg*, 428 U.S. at 190–93. In subsequent cases, the Court has further refined and articulated these requirements. *See, e.g.*, Lockett v. Ohio, 438 U.S. 586, 604 (1978) (holding that in "all but the rarest kind of capital cases," the sentencer may "not be precluded from considering *as a mitigating factor*, any aspect of a defendant's character or record and any of the circumstances of the offense that the defendant proffers as a basis for a sentence less than death") (footnotes omitted); Gardner v. Florida, 430 U.S. 349 (1977) (holding that a judge could not impose a death sentence on the basis of a confidential presentence report unless the contents of the report were first disclosed to the defense).

253. 430 U.S. 349 (1977).

254. In Williams v. New York, 337 U.S. 241 (1949), the Court affirmed the constitutionality of a death sentence imposed by a trial judge on the basis of material in a presentence report that was supplied by witnesses whom the defendant had no opportunity to confront or cross-examine. In addition to noting one factual distinction between *Williams* and *Gardner*, 430 U.S. at 356, the Court also emphasized that *Williams*'s rationale should no longer be controlling because the "Court has acknowledged its obligation to re-examine capital-sentencing procedures against evolving standards of procedural fairness in a civilized society." 430 U.S. at 357 (plurality opinion of Stevens, J.) (footnote omitted).

255. 430 U.S. at 361 (plurality opinion of Stevens, J.).

256. *Id.* at 358.

257. Prosecutors have a long tradition of seeking to obtain a death-qualified jury even though they have no intention of asking the jury to impose the death penalty. *See, e.g.*, Oberer, *supra* note 6, at 555.

Death-Qualified Juries: Update

The preceding essay was published in 1980. Since then, some very significant empirical data relating to the prosecution-proneness issue has not only been published[1] but also tested by cross-examination in adversary proceedings. In at least two recent cases, courts have considered the prosecution-proneness claim on the basis of a record that included all the relevant empirical data, including new research relating to juror voting behavior, juror attitudes, demographic characteristics, and differences in juror evaluation of evidence. As the California Supreme Court indicated, the research methods used in conducting the new studies were generally outstanding. In fact, the flaws in the earlier studies that sprang from methodological problems were almost entirely eliminated. With the addition of the data gleaned from these studies, the experts who testified were able to give the clearest picture of the effects of death-qualification that has ever been presented to a court.

The first of these two cases was *Hovey v. Alameda County*.[2] After meticulously examining the record before it in *Hovey*, the California Supreme Court essentially concluded that the prosecution-proneness thesis was established. In the court's view, the studies demonstrated that a death-qualified jury is more likely to vote for conviction than a non-death-qualified one. Nevertheless, the court refused to invalidate California's system of death-qualification because it found that the studies did not fully answer the relevant legal question. Under California law, the defendant in capital cases is allowed to exclude all potential jurors who would automatically vote in favor of the death penalty upon a capital defendant's conviction of a capital offense. Thus, in testing the prosecution-proneness hypothesis in California, the relevant comparison is between the jury used in noncapital cases and one in which both individuals who would automatically vote in favor of the death penalty and those who would automatically vote against it are excluded. This comparison was never explored in the studies. Because of this defect, the California Supreme Court held that defendant failed to meet his burden of establishing the non-neutrality of the California death-qualified jury.[3]

The second of the two cases is *Grigsby v. Mabry*.[4] In *Grigsby* the record presented to the federal district judge was similar to the record presented in *Hovey* except that a somewhat different group of experts testified and additional empirical data relating to the number of "automatic death penalty" jurors (i.e., the group who would automatically vote in favor of the death penalty in the event that defendant was convicted of a capital crime) was presented. Like the California Supreme

Court, the federal district court concluded that the prosecution-proneness thesis was established. In contrast to *Hovey*, however, *Grigsby* actually reversed the defendant's conviction,[5] holding that convictions
imposed by a death-qualified jury are unconstitutional. The court specifically rejected the prosecution's contention that the exclusion of "automatic death penalty" jurors undermined the validity of the defendant's
claim. Based on its assessment of the pertinent data, the court concluded
that "the number of those who would automatically vote for the death
penalty . . . is negligible when compared to those who would never
under any circumstances vote for the death penalty."[6] Moreover, the
court indicated that excluding "automatic death penalty" jurors could
not undermine the defendant's claim in any event. The court held that
convictions imposed by a death-qualified jury are unconstitutional on
two grounds. First, "[death-qualification] denies the accused a trial by a
jury representative of a cross-section of the community; and second, it
creates juries that are conviction-prone."[7] As the court recognized, the
first of these conclusions is not in any way dependent on a finding that
the number of "automatic death penalty" jurors is negligible in comparison to the number of "automatic life imprisonment" jurors. Rather, as
the court emphasized, excluding "automatic death penalty" jurors further diminishes the representative quality of the jury.[8]

Both *Hovey* and *Grigsby* are extremely significant decisions. The
Hovey opinion is particularly noteworthy because of its lucid exposition
of the social science data. Using helpful charts as a visual aid, the court
provides an analysis of the existing empirical data that is thorough and
sophisticated, yet at the same time entirely accessible to interested lawyers or lay people. Moreover, despite its result, the *Hovey* opinion provides an analysis that strongly supports the prosecution-proneness thesis.
In the course of its opinion, the court gives painstaking attention to the
various methodological objections to the empirical studies asserted on
behalf of the government. With the exception of the claim that the studies fail to take account of the exclusion of the "automatic death penalty"
jurors, all of the government objections are found to be without merit.
Thus, despite the ultimate rejection of the claim presented in that case,
the *Hovey* opinion delivers a severe blow to the practice of death-qualifying the jury. Based on the court's analysis, only one more link in the
chain of empirical data is needed to establish the death-qualified jury's
unconstitutionality. If it can be shown that the "automatic death penalty" group comprises only an insignificant portion of the population, the
California Supreme Court, unless it disavows the reasoning of *Hovey*,
will be required to hold that the death-qualified jury used in that state is
unconstitutional.

Grigsby has the potential to be an even more far-reaching decision than *Hovey*. As in *Hovey*, the court's analysis of the social science data is lucid and penetrating. Unlike *Hovey*, however, *Grigsby* is the first clear precedent for holding that the death-qualified jury is unconstitutional. Moreover, since the government has already appealed the federal district court's ruling, *Grigsby* may eventually set the stage for a ruling on this issue by the United States Supreme Court.

The different results in *Hovey* and *Grigsby* stem entirely from the differing significance that each court attached to the exclusion of the "automatic death penalty" jurors. As both courts indicate, prospective jurors may be divided into five groups: (1) the "automatic death penalty group," comprised of people who as jurors would automatically vote for the death penalty if defendant is convicted of a capital offense; (2) the "favor the death penalty group," which favors the death penalty but will not vote to impose it in every case; (3) the "indifferent group," which neither favors nor opposes the death penalty; (4) the "oppose the death penalty" group, which opposes the death penalty but will not automatically vote against it in every case; and (5) the "automatic life imprisonment" group, which will automatically vote against the death penalty in every case. Based on its evaluation of the data, *Hovey* concluded that jurors selected from the first four groups would be more likely to convict a capital defendant than jurors selected from all five groups. Nevertheless, the California Supreme Court also concluded that it was not clear that jurors selected from the middle three groups (i.e., excluding the "automatic death penalty" group as well as the "automatic life imprisonment" group) would be more conviction-prone than jurors selected from all five groups. *Grigsby*'s basis for rejecting the latter conclusion was its finding that "the number of those who would automatically vote for the death penalty . . . is negligible when compared to those who would never under any circumstances vote for the death penalty."[9]

Common sense, as well as the limited empirical data presented to the two courts,[10] suggests that *Grigsby*'s finding is accurate. Given the strength of the abolition movement, it is not surprising that a substantial segment of the population, perhaps between 15 and 20 percent,[11] belong in the "automatic life imprisonment" group. On the other hand, as Justice White suggested in *Adams v. Texas*,[12] the existence of people belonging to an "automatic death penalty" group remains largely hypothetical. Even people who strongly favor the death penalty are seldom in favor of imposing it in every capital case. To fit within the "automatic death penalty" group, a prospective juror would have to not only be in favor of imposing the death penalty to every defendant convicted of a capital offense but also be willing to state in advance of trial that she would not even be willing to consider the possibility of sentencing a convicted capital defendant to life imprisonment. There may indeed be people whose commitment to the biblical admonition "an eye for an eye" would lead them to make this type of statement. But it seems indisputable that this group is small in comparison to those whose opposition to capital punishment would lead them to state that they would automatically vote against the death penalty in every capital case.[13]

Furthermore, as *Grigsby* indicates, it seems incongruous to recognize that there is a positive correlation between views in favor of the death penalty and predisposition toward conviction and yet at the same time hold that the tilt toward the prosecution produced by excluding those whose adamant opposition to capital punishment renders them least likely to convict may be exactly counterbalanced by excluding another group whose views in favor of capital punishment identifies them as those most likely to favor the prosecution. Even if the two groups were comparable in size, eliminating both of them would not have the same effect as eliminating neither of them. Rather, as *Grigsby* recognizes, eliminating the two groups profoundly alters the composition of the potential jury pool. The resulting jury is likely to be more homogeneous. There is less likely to be a clash of sharply opposing viewpoints and more likely to be a consensus. This change favors the prosecution. Because juries in criminal cases are more likely to convict than acquit, eliminating those jurors who are most likely to acquit penalizes the defense more than eliminating the jurors who are most likely to convict would penalize the prosecution. In particular, removing the former group reduces the defendant's chances of obtaining a hung jury, a result which is anathema to the prosecution but often a principal objective of the defense. Thus, in at least one important respect, death-qualifying a jury has the same effect as reducing its size: "[The] data suggests that the verdicts of jury deliberation in criminal cases will vary . . . and that the variance amounts to an imbalance to the detriment of one side, the defense."[14]

Moreover, as *Grigsby* emphasizes, death-qualification does more than impair effective group deliberation. It removes from jury service people whose views on capital punishment give them a distinct perspective on issues related to the determination of guilt. When important voices from the community are not present in the jury room, the extent to which a jury represents the judgment of the community is suspect. In *Ballew v. Georgia* the Supreme Court emphasized that an essential purpose of the right to jury trial is to ensure participation by a representative cross-section of the community in the determination of a criminal defendant's guilt.[15] In view of this paramount concern, it seems appropriate to conclude that eliminating two distinct points of view from the jury denies the defendant's right to a jury that is representative of the community. Accordingly, *Grigsby*'s analysis of this issue seems correct.

The ultimate impact of *Hovey* and *Grigsby* cannot be foreseen at this time. Because of its result, *Hovey*'s impact to date has been fairly minimal. To the extent that they discuss the empirical evidence, the post-*Hovey* opinions in other states appear to accept the California Supreme Court's analysis of the record in *Hovey*.[16] Because of *Hovey*'s discussion of the "automatic death penalty" jurors, however, following *Hovey* does not necessarily lead to a holding that the death-qualified jury is unconstitutional. To date, no case except *Grigsby* has taken that position.

Grigsby, of course, is too new a decision to have had any impact. If the district court's ruling is upheld on appeal, then it will undoubtedly have a significant effect. But even if the *Grigsby* decision is reversed, the lower court's lucid exposition of the empirical data and its persuasive analysis of the legal issues may cause future courts to adopt a new perspective when assessing the constitutional validity of the death-qualified jury.

NOTES

1. *See* Ellsworth & Fitzgerald, *Due Process v. Crime Control: Death-Qualification and Jury Attitudes*, 8 LAW & HUM. BEHAV. 31 (1984); Thompson, Cowan, Ellsworth, & Harrington, *Death Penalty Attitudes and Conviction Proneness: The Translation of Attitudes Into Verdicts*, 8 LAW & HUM. BEHAV. 95 (1984); Cowan, Thompson, & Ellsworth, *The Effects of Death-Qualification on Jurors: Predisposition to Convict and the Quality of Deliberation*, 8 LAW & HUM. BEHAV. 53 (1984). Ellsworth, Bukaty, Cowan, & Thompson, *The Death-Qualified Jury and the Defense of Insanity*, 8 LAW & HUM. BEHAV. 81 (1984); Kadane, *After Hovey: A Note on Taking Account of the Automatic Death Penalty Jurors*, 8 LAW & HUM. BEHAV. 115 (1984).

2. 28 Cal. 3d 1, 168 Cal. Rptr. 128, 616 P.2d 1301 (1980).

3. 28 Cal. 3d at 65, 168 Cal. Rptr. at 171, 616 P.2d at 1345.

4. No. PB-C-78-22 (E.D. Ark. Aug. 5, 1983).

5. In *Grigsby*, three defendants, Grigsby, Holsey, and McCree, were before the court. Since the defendant Grigsby had died and the defendant Holsey did not properly raise the issue, the court reversed only one conviction—that of the defendant McCree.

6. *Grigsby*, No. PB-C-78-22 at 62.

7. *Id.* at 1.

8. *Id.* at 58.

9. *Id.* at 67.

10. In a follow-up to her principal study, Professor Phoebe Ellsworth contacted twenty-two of the twenty-three subjects who stated that they "strongly favored" the death penalty. All twenty-two indicated that they "would be will-

ing to consider voting for life imprisonment or death depending on the evidence." 168 Cal. Rptr. at 173, 616 P.2d at 1345. In addition, the Jurow study, which was part of the record presented in *Hovey*, indicated that 2.4 percent of the subjects in that study indicated that they would impose the death penalty in any case where the law permitted it. *See* Jurow, *New Data on the Effect of a "Death-Qualified" Jury on the Guilt Determination Process*, 84 HARV. L. REV. 567, 583, 599 (1971). *See also* Kadane, *supra* note 1.

11. The most recent survey, see Ellsworth & Fitzgerald, *supra* note 1 at 42, found that 17.2 percent of the Alameda County population would be excluded for jury service by death-qualification. Earlier surveys concluded that an even higher percentage of the population would be excluded. *See, e.g.,* White, *The Constitutional Invalidity of Convictions Imposed by Death-qualified Juries*, 58 CORNELL L. REV. 1176, 1178 n.12 (1973) (noting that in the 1971 Harris Poll 23 percent of the population stated that they would refuse to vote for the death penalty under any circumstances).

12. *See* 448 U.S. 38, 49:

Despite the hypothetical existence of the juror who believes literally in the Biblical admonition "an eye for an eye," . . . it is undeniable . . . that such jurors will be few indeed as compared with those excluded because of scruples against capital punishment.

13. *See supra* note 12.

14. Ballew v. Georgia, 435 U.S. 223, 236 (1978).

15. *See* 435 U.S. at 230.

16. *See* State v. Peyton, 29 Wash. App. 701, 630 P.2d 1362, 1367–68 (1981) (follows *Hovey*, focuses on automatic death penalty issue); State v. Bartholemew, 98 Wash. 2d 173, 654 P.2d 1170 (1982) (same); State v. Mitchell, 611 S.W.2d 223, 230 (Mo. 1981) (concurring opinion) (relies on *Hovey*); State v. Mercer, 618 S.W.2d 1, 16–17 (Mo. 1981) (dissenting opinion) (same); Justus v. Commonwealth, 222 Va. 667, 283 S.E.2d 909 (1981) (evidence held not properly in record, but follows *Hovey*, relying on automatic death penalty issue); Commonwealth v. Story, 497 Pa. 273, 288–92, 440 A.2d 488, 495–98 (dissenting opinion) (same); Fielden v. State, 437 N.E.2d 986 (Ind. 1982) (accepts *Hovey*'s conclusions on studies).

Police Trickery in Inducing
Confessions

Use of trickery or deceit in the questioning of criminal suspects is a staple of current police interrogation practices. The prevalence of this technique is attested to not only by its frequent appearance in reported cases,[1] but also, and perhaps more significantly, by the central importance it is given in police interrogation manuals.[2] For example, Inbau and Reid's widely read manual, *Criminal Interrogation and Confessions*,[3] outlines twenty-six specific techniques to be used in interrogating a suspect;[4] most of these techniques will inevitably involve some form of deception because they require an officer to make statements that he knows are untrue or to play a role that is inconsistent with his actual feelings.[5] The effectiveness of these techniques is amply documented by the authors as they recount case after case in which a strategic lie or a timely false show of sympathy was instrumental in leading a suspect to confess.[6]

A conscientious police officer (or one with an unusually high degree of legal sensitivity) might wonder, however, exactly what if any limit the Constitution places on the admission of confessions obtained by deceitful interrogation techniques. If this officer attempted to discover the answer in the opinions of the United States Supreme Court, he would encounter grave difficulties. Dictum in *Miranda v. Arizona*[7] indicates that police are precluded from using trickery to induce a waiver of a suspect's Fifth and Sixth Amendment rights.[8] Moreover, in applying the established rule that only voluntary statements can be admitted into evidence at a criminal trial, the Court has excluded confessions obtained through deception[9] and expressed judicial distaste for certain deceptive practices.[10] Nevertheless, the conscientious officer would find that the Court has neither held nor even indicated that any particular type of police trickery would in and of itself render a resulting confession inadmissible.

In the absence of definitive guidance from the Supreme Court, the conscientious police officer might naturally refer to the principles that are lucidly expressed in the Inbau and Reid police manual. The benchmark to be used in judging the permissibility of deceptive practices is simply stated: "Although both 'fair' and 'unfair' interrogation practices are permissible, nothing shall be done or said to the subject that will be apt to make an innocent person confess."[11] Although Inbau and Reid offer no catalogue of prohibited practices,[12] the test does provide a clear and direct focus. At first blush, the test acts as a substantial safeguard for the innocent suspect; in addition, it is supported by plausible moral and pragmatic justifications,[13] as well as by considerable state court authority.[14]

Unfortunately, however, the Inbau-Reid test is not wholly consistent with Supreme Court doctrine. First, the Court's voluntariness standard does not focus solely on the reliability of a particular confession; rather, it also requires a determination that the means of obtaining the confession were consistent with our accusatorial system of criminal justice.[15] Even the guilty person has the right to demand that his guilt be demonstrated by the state. Therefore, examination of the "totality of the circumstances" must reveal that a suspect's statement was "the product of his free and rational choice."[16] In order to protect more fully the suspect's freedom of choice, the Court has held that certain coercive interrogation techniques result in an "involuntary" confession as a matter of law, irrespective of the likelihood that they did or could produce a *false* confession and irrespective of their effect on the actual defendant before the court. Thus, in *Ashcraft v. Tennessee*,[17] Justice Black, speaking for the Court, found that an unbroken thirty-six-hour interrogation was "so inherently coercive that its very existence is irreconcilable with the possession of mental freedom."[18]

In addition to the concern for freedom of choice, the modern voluntariness standard has a fairness component. In *Spano v. New York*,[19] for example, the Court expressed concern not only with excluding confessions obtained by potentially coercive methods but also with ensuring that the police "obey the law while enforcing the law."[20] The Court's disapproval of the police tactics employed in *Spano* and a number of other cases[21] indicates that in deciding when the police are "obeying the law," the Court will measure the police conduct against certain basic standards of fairness that are fundamental to our system of justice.[22] Consequently, even reliable confessions should be inadmissible when they are induced by modes of police trickery that are inconsistent with basic notions of fairness.

Moreover, the impact of the Fifth and Sixth amendments on police interrogation practices must be considered. *Malloy v. Hogan*[23] held that the Fifth Amendment privilege against self-incrimination is applicable to the states, and *Miranda v. Arizona*[24] established that it applies at the station house. *Miranda* holds that suspects subjected to custodial interrogation have an absolute right to remain silent,[25] that the police must give them certain warnings to ensure protection of this right,[26] and that a suspect must be given a "continuous opportunity" to exercise these rights.[27] In short, *Miranda* holds that for reasons drawn from the Fifth Amendment privilege, suspects subjected to custodial interrogation must be afforded the protection provided by the warnings not only at the beginning of the interrogation, but also throughout the interrogation process.[28]   In addition, the Court's recent holding in *Brewer v. Williams*[29] indicates that quite aside from the protections provided by *Miranda*, some suspects subjected to police interrogation have an independent Sixth Amendment right to an attorney.[30] Accordingly, any police practice that undermines the protections provided by either *Miranda* or the Sixth Amendment right to an attorney should be constitutionally impermissible.

To summarize, then, an officer who wants to comply with the constitutional limits on the use of trickery in inducing confessions must be concerned with more than simply avoiding tricks that are likely to induce false statements. In addition, he must curb the use of trickery that has the effect of rendering the resulting confession involuntary or that negates the effect of protections provided by the Fifth and Sixth amendments.

These general principles, however, do not provide the concrete guidance needed to determine the legitimacy of particular police practices. Regrettably, other authoritative sources do not provide much additional assistance. The draftsmen of the American Law Institute's Model Code of Pre-Arraignment Procedure considered the problem of trickery in police interrogation[31] but failed to issue any definitive guidelines. The model code currently offers only general restatements of the existing law,[32] and two somewhat cryptic statements suggesting that statements obtained through the use of "unfair" police trickery should be inadmissible.[33]

This cautious approach is certainly understandable. The effect of police trickery cannot be considered in a vacuum. Trickery that is relatively innocent in one context might have a devastating effect on certain suspects when employed in a different setting. The multiplicity of available interrogation practices renders the articulation of clear rules extremely difficult.   The fact that suspects have different degrees of sensitivity and resistance to deceptive tactics inevitably hampers the development of a comprehensive approach to the problem. Finally, the subtle messages that can be communicated through changes in vocal inflection and nonverbal communication pose a formidable fact-finding task for the Court. These and other problems support the conclusion that it is inappropriate to attempt to promulgate comprehensive guidelines relating to the permissible limits on police trickery in inducing confessions.[34]

Nevertheless, there is a need to provide more meaningful guidance to the police and lower courts. The thesis of this essay is that it is possible to identify certain interrogation tactics that are likely to create an unacceptable risk of depriving the suspect of his constitutional rights.

The first part of the essay is a detailed examination of the constitutional limitations on the admissibility of confessions; it will introduce a per se approach that strikes a tolerable balance between the competing interests of predictability and flexibility. In the remainder of the essay it will be demonstrated that several widely used interrogation tactics should be prohibited on such a per se basis.

The context in which these categories of deception are considered will be primarily one in which the suspect's Fifth or Sixth Amendment rights, or both, are applicable but have been validly waived.[35] There are two reasons for focusing the analysis in this manner. First, although the Supreme Court has indicated that an effective waiver of the *Miranda* and *Brewer*[36] rights cannot be achieved through police trickery,[37] the restrictions on police deception in the postwaiver situation are less than clear.[38] Second, the police manuals advise law enforcement officials to obtain a waiver before employing any of the suggested interrogation tactics.[39] The lack of clear constitutional standards and the apparent police belief that deception is appropriate in this context suggest the need for a detailed examination of the legitimacy of police trickery in this area.

Constitutional Limitations on Police Trickery

The Current Status of *Miranda*

As has already been noted,[40] the *Miranda* requirements are calculated to ensure adequate Fifth Amendment protection for suspects subjected to custodial interrogation. Custodial interrogation was defined as questioning by police officers "after a person has been taken into custody or otherwise deprived of his freedom of action in a significant way."[41] The Supreme Court provided that at the beginning of such interrogation, in the absence of "other procedures which are at least as effective in apprising accused persons of their right of silence and in assuring a continuous opportunity to exercise it,"[42] the interrogating officer must advise the suspect that he has a right to remain silent, that anything he says can be used against him, and that he has a right to have retained or appointed counsel present at the interrogation.[43] Moreover, the Court stated that a suspect may waive these rights, "provided the waiver is made voluntarily, knowingly, and intelligently."[44] As noted above,[45] the Court emphasized that even after an initial waiver, the suspect has a continuing opportunity to assert the right to remain silent or the right to an attorney at any point prior to the completion of the interrogation.[46]

The Burger Court has limited *Miranda* in important respects.[47] For present purposes, two limitations are particularly significant. First, by its decisions in *Beckwith v. United States*[48] and *Oregon v. Mathiason*,[49] the Court appears to have restricted its definition of "custodial interrogation" to situations that involve "coercive environments" similar to those considered by the Court in *Miranda* itself.[50] Thus, unless a suspect is actually subjected to the coercive pressures generated by involuntary restraints and interrogation in a police stationlike atmosphere,[51] *Miranda* seems to be inapplicable.

Second, the Court concluded in *Michigan v. Tucker*[52] that the use in a criminal trial of statements obtained in violation of *Miranda* does not in itself violate the Fifth Amendment privilege. The Court perceived the *Miranda* warnings as a prophylactic rule devised to ensure that statements are voluntarily made.[53] Under *Tucker*, statements obtained in violation of *Miranda* will generally be inadmissible,[54] but their use by the prosecution will not violate the Fifth Amendment unless there is a violation of the traditional voluntariness test.[55] *Tucker*, in effect, equates the privilege against self-incrimination with voluntariness, a test that was not designed to ensure the suspect's awareness of his constitutional rights.[56] In short, it can be inferred from this decision that the Court has rejected interpreting *Miranda* to provide a constitutionally mandated guarantee that suspects will be afforded the opportunity for intelligent exercise of the right to remain silent at each point in the interrogation.[57] Nevertheless, although the *Tucker* Court viewed the *Miranda* warnings as a prophylactic device rather than a constitutionally mandated procedure, the scope of the protection afforded by the *Miranda* warnings was not altered.

In order to comprehend fully the limitations that *Miranda* imposes on police interrogation tactics in the postwaiver context, it is necessary to examine more precisely the requirement that the suspect be permitted to reassert the right to silence and the right to counsel. It should first be recalled that the purpose of the warnings is to reduce the possibility of coercion throughout the interrogation process. If the *Miranda* warnings are to serve this necessary prophylactic function effectively, police trickery that distorts their meaning or vitiates their effect should render a resulting confession inadmissible. No one would argue that a specific verbal denial of the possibility of reassertion is a permissible interrogation tactic. However, as will be demonstrated below,[58] certain types of police misconduct achieve the same result without explicit misrepresentation of the law. If the reassertion right is to have any real content, the police should be required to desist from any trickery that significantly distorts the meaning and effect of the *Miranda* warnings.

The Independent Right to an Attorney

The aforementioned narrowing of the situations in which the *Miranda* warnings are required definitely enhances the significance of the interrogated suspect's independent right to an attorney that was enunciated in *Brewer v. Williams*.[59] In *Williams*, the Court found it unnecessary to reach a claim that the pretrial police interrogation of the defendant violated *Miranda*.[60] Rather, the Court held that the defendant was "deprived of a different constitutional right—the right to the assistance of counsel."[61] Reaffirming *Massiah v. United States*,[62] the Court held that "the right to counsel granted by the Sixth and Fourteenth Amendments means at least that a person is entitled to the help of a lawyer at or after the time that judicial proceedings have been initiated against him."[63]

As a result of the *Williams* decision, suspects subjected to police interrogation may assert violations of either *Miranda* or the separate Sixth Amendment right. A detailed examination of the interrelationship between the Fifth and Sixth Amendment rights is beyond the scope of this essay.[64] *Williams*, however, leaves unanswered two questions that are particularly significant in determining the right-to-counsel doctrine's applicability to police trickery in inducing confessions. First, when does the right to counsel attach? And second, to what extent does the existence of the right depend upon the suspect's assertion of it?

Williams establishes that the right to counsel attaches *at least* at the formal beginning of the adversary process. Of course, unless the right attaches at an earlier point, *Williams* would exert no influence on the vast amount of police interrogation that occurs before the suspect is formally arraigned. For that reason, interpreting the "at least" language is crucial to an understanding of the constitutional limitations on police trickery. Earlier cases, including not only *Escobedo v. Illinois*,[65] which arguably has little precedential value,[66] but also *United States v. Hoffa*,[67] have apparently operated on the assumption that in this context the suspect's Sixth Amendment right comes into effect at the point of arrest.[68] More recent cases, such as *Williams*,[69] *United States v. Mandujano*,[70] and *Kirby v. Illinois*,[71] may indicate that the Court is now leaning toward a rule under which the Sixth Amendment right to counsel will never come into effect prior to the formal initiation of criminal charges;[72] however, at least with respect to police interrogation, the question remains open.

In the context of police interrogation, the *Hoffa* and *Escobedo* approach appears to be correct. At the point of formal arrest, the police are likely to be as committed to prosecution as they will be when charges are formally brought. Because the police objectives and tactics are likely to be identical at the arrest and postarraignment stages, interrogation following arrest should be viewed as a part of the adversary process and therefore as the event that triggers the suspect's Sixth Amendment rights. *Kirby*'s holding that the Sixth Amendment right to counsel at a pretrial confrontation commences only after the initiation of formal proceedings is distinguishable because, unlike the situation in *Kirby*, pretrial interrogation may involve the privilege against self-incrimination. Even when it takes place in a noncustodial setting, pretrial interrogation has the potential effect of forcing an individual "to be made the deluded instrument of his own conviction"[73] in violation of the Fifth Amendment privilege. Because of this critical interplay between the Fifth and Sixth Amendments,[74] insofar as police interrogation is concerned the suspect's Sixth Amendment right to an attorney should attach at the point of formal arrest.

In considering the extent to which the existence of the suspect's independent right to counsel depends on his assertion of it, three different situations should be analyzed: (1) when, as in *Williams*, the suspect has asserted the right and is represented by counsel; (2) when the right has attached and the suspect has not had the opportunity to assert or waive it;[75] and (3) when there has been an initial waiver of the right.[76]

On its facts, the holding in *Williams* extends only to the first situation—at the time of the interrogation, the defendant was represented by counsel. Significantly, however, the Court attached no importance to the fact that Williams had already asserted his right to an attorney. Rather, the Court emphasized that "once adversary proceedings have commenced against an individual, he has a right to legal representation when the government interrogates him."[77] In fact, the Court explicitly stated that "the right to counsel does not depend on a request by the defendant."[78] Thus, the second situation appears to be within the reasoning of *Williams*.

The third case—when the suspect has specifically declined to exercise his right to counsel—is undoubtedly the most difficult one. In *Williams*, the Court made it clear that a suspect may waive his right to an attorney, provided that waiver meets the standards of intentionality and awareness promulgated in *Johnson v. Zerbst*.[79] The real question is whether the suspect's initial waiver precludes him from reasserting the right. In the *Miranda* context, an initial waiver does not have this effect.[80] Although distinctions might be drawn between the *Miranda* protections and the independent right to counsel,[81] there is good reason to require that both rights be capable of reassertion. Whether the suspect changes his mind about the need for an attorney in order to protect his right against self-incrimination (in which case *Miranda* rights are applicable) or to protect his chances at the forthcoming trial (as in the *Williams* and *Massiah* situations), he should be allowed a continuous opportunity to assert his right. The right to a fair trial is no less fundamental than the Fifth Amendment privilege, and the right to have counsel present during the interrogation protects both constitutional interests with equal force. Like *Miranda* rights, the Sixth Amendment right to have counsel present at postarrest interrogation should be continuously available to the suspect.[82]

The Current Definition of an Involuntary Confession

As Justice Harlan noted in his *Miranda* dissent, the Court has infused the concept of voluntariness "with a number of different values."[83] Justice Harlan focused on the three paramount concerns that have shaped the test of admissibility: first, an abhorrence of convictions based on unreliable confessions;[84] second, a feeling that police practices used to obtain confessions should not impose intolerable pressure on the will of individual suspects;[85] third, a belief that such practices should not be contrary to the standards of fairness that are fundamental in our system of justice.[86] A quick review of the court's development of these three strands of voluntariness is helpful in understanding their relevance to the problem of police trickery.[87]

Early state court cases tended to focus almost exclusively on the reliability interest.[88] This emphasis was probably attributable to the shocking factual settings of the early Supreme Court confession cases.[89] Writing for a unanimous Court in *Ward v. Texas*,[90] Justice Byrnes poignantly inveighed against the police practices that left the defendant in that case "willing to make any statement that the officers wanted him to make."[91] In addition, Justice Byrnes pointed to previous cases in which the Court had invalidated convictions obtained under circumstances that raised severe questions about their reliability.[92]

In *Rogers v. Richmond*,[93] however, the Court considered the relationship between reliability and voluntariness and sharply distinguished between the two concepts. The Court held that the probable truth of a confession, i.e., its reliability, could not be used to support a finding of voluntariness.[94] Justice Frankfurter, writing for the majority, emphasized that the voluntariness standard protects interests other than reliability; in particular, he noted, it forbids the use of coerced confessions to convict a defendant.[95] Thus, although the test is not framed in terms of reliability, it provides some assurance that a confession admitted into evidence is the product of the suspect's perception of the event and not the result of police coercion.

The second strand of the voluntariness test conditions admissibility on a finding that the confession was a product of the suspect's free and rational choice.[96] Because of the case-by-case nature of the inquiry, it is impossible to do more than delineate the various factors that the Court has weighed in determining whether a particular confession was the product of impermissible coercion.[97] As Justice Goldberg recognized in *Haynes v. Washington*,[98] the test requires that the Court assess the effect of police practices on the "mind and will of an accused,"[99] and determine the point at which the pressures created are so great that the accused's will may be properly considered to be "overborne."[100] As will be discussed below,[101] the unpredictability of the voluntariness test greatly limits its usefulness as a legal standard for the control of police trickery in interrogation.

A third important component of the involuntariness test relates to the Court's assessment of the fairness or legitimacy of the police tactics employed.[102] In view of the applicable line of authority,[103] a determination of voluntariness may not be based merely on a judgment that the suspect retained some minimal capacity to resist police efforts to induce a confession. Rather, as Justice Harlan's *Miranda* dissent noted, the police must be barred from exerting "a degree of pressure [on] an individual which unfairly impairs his capacity to make a rational choice."[104]

The Need for Per se Rules

In fashioning a constitutional doctrine concerning the admissibility of suspects' confessions, a court must inevitably do more than merely decide the extent to which police trickery may be tolerated in a free society. In addition, it must structure the resulting legal rules in a way that recognizes the institutional realities of the criminal justice system. In particular, a court must take into account the infinite variety of suspects' personality patterns and police interrogation practices. On one level, because criminal suspects do not possess uniform personality characteristics, a court must decide the extent to which the appropriate tests will be tailored to accommodate particular criminal suspects' individual responses to police pressure. In other words, should a court apply a subjective or objective test, or something in between? A distinct but closely related problem concerns the extent to which a court should prohibit particular interrogation techniques through the promulgation of per se rules (i.e., prohibiting a certain tactic or category of tactics). As will be demonstrated below, the extent to which a per se approach is adopted will have important consequences on police behavior and judicial review.

The pertinent question in the objective-subjective controversy can be rephrased: Should the courts focus primarily on the police conduct itself and attempt to measure its likely effect on a typical person who is in the suspect's position or should the courts focus exclusively on the *actual* impact of the police conduct on the *particular* suspect who is before the court? An objective approach clearly generates more meaningful guidance for the police and lower courts than its subjective counterpart. Under the latter approach, when the legitimacy of an interrogation tactic varies with the strengths and weaknesses of a particular suspect, an interrogating officer cannot predict the judicial response to the use of a given tactic with any degree of precision. When the dimensions of constitutional standards are so ill defined, the danger must increase that the police will conduct their interrogations without regard for the constitutional rights of the suspect. Similarly, the subjective approach provides little guidance to the courts. If the question in every case is the effect on a particular suspect, precedent is likely to be of little importance. To the extent possible, therefore, both from the perspectives of law enforcement and judicial administration, courts should develop legal rules that limit interrogation tactics by objective standards.

In fact, Professor Yale Kamisar's 1963 study demonstrates that although Supreme Court opinions often purport to engage in a subjective inquiry, "much more often than not, if not always, when the Court considers the peculiar, individual characteristics of the person confessing, it is only applying a rule of *inadmissibility*. 'Strong' personal characteristics rarely, if ever, 'cure' forbidden police methods; but 'weak' ones may invalidate what are generally permissible methods."[105] The Court's determination of whether the standard was met was based in part on its evaluation of the effect that the police tactics employed would have on a typical person in the position of the suspect subjected to the interrogation, and in part on its assessment of the fairness of the tactics employed.[106]

The second question—the extent to which the courts should prohibit particular interrogation tactics through per se rules as opposed to considering the totality of the circumstances—has not been resolved in a way that provides satisfactory guidance for courts and law enforcement officials. In assessing the legality of police interrogation tactics, the pre-*Escobedo* cases generally did not rely on per se rules. Recognizing that the impact of police practices on an individual may not be considered in a vacuum, the Court considered the impact of the pressures generated by police tactics in light of their probable cumulative effect.[107] In a few extraordinary situations, the Court indicated that using a particular police practice would be sufficient in itself to render a resulting confession involuntary.[108] However, for the most part, the Court insisted on determining voluntariness through a meticulous examination of the "totality of circumstances."[109]

By the early sixties, however, experience had demonstrated that the "totality of circumstances" test was an ineffective means of preventing unacceptable police pressures. The inadequacy of the test is partially attributable to the imperfection of the applicable fact-finding procedure.[110] As Professor Kamisar has recently demonstrated, in most cases the traditional litigation process is simply inadequate to determine either the extent or the quality of police pressure applied to individual criminal suspects.[111] Beyond that, however, the "totality of circumstances" test's fatal flaw is its failure to generate precedents that can serve as guidelines for the police and the lower courts.

The failure to formulate rules that apply beyond limited factual settings has had important consequences. Police are most likely to view as legitimate effective interrogation tactics that have not been expressly prohibited.[112] Moreover, in analyzing the myriad circumstances surrounding an interrogation, trial judges unfortunately are tempted to defer to the judgment of the police.[113] Finally, appellate courts may quite legitimately defer to lower court findings of voluntariness, particularly because they are at least partially factual; and also because due to the innumerable circumstances that generally are involved, it is unlikely that any given case will be controlled by a prior Supreme Court decision.[114] The net result is that in many cases the courts effectively defer to the police and make their judgment of the legitimacy of interrogation tactics the decisive one.

Per se rules prohibiting certain categories of police tactics obviously provide better guidance for the police and increased protection for suspects. Accordingly, the framing of the constitutionally mandated rules limiting police trickery should be undertaken with awareness of these realities. The inquiry envisioned in this essay requires that a court take an additional conceptual step after determining that a given interrogation tactic violates the *Miranda* or *Williams* guarantees or results in a coerced confession: whenever possible, the court should identify the objectionable characteristic that emerges from its scrutiny of the facts surrounding an invalid interrogation. If that infirmity creates an unacceptable risk of infringing the typical suspect's constitutional rights, the court should hold that such police conduct is illegal per se. Although the objectionable police conduct may conceivably occur in myriad forms and various settings, a per se rule would require that police officers design their interrogation techniques to avoid the proscribed conduct in all situations. Although it is impossible to develop prospectively a complete catalogue of prohibited tactics, in this essay the suggested objective approach and conceptual framework will be used to identify several police tactics that create an unacceptable risk of infringing the typical suspect's constitutional rights. Before beginning this task, however, it is necessary to define the standard of probability implicit in the phrase "unacceptable risk" and to specify the degree of subjectivity envisaged in this approach.

The per se rules should prohibit police conduct that is *likely to render* a resulting confession involuntary or to undermine the effect of required *Miranda* warnings or a suspect's independent right to an attorney. Although law enforcement interests rule out a lesser burden of proof (e.g., *possibly render*), the fundamental nature of the suspect's constitutional rights mandates a sensible allocation of the risk of error. This standard of probability (i.e., *likely to render*) is preferable to requiring a demonstration that the conduct in question invariably or nearly always results in violations. Police should not engage in conduct that is likely to induce a coerced confession or negate constitutional protections (even though it may not invariably do so) because obviously a high risk exists that significant harm (in terms of unlawfully obtained confessions or improper coercion) will ensue. Therefore, prophylactic rules designed to deter the police from engaging in conduct with such a probable effect are appropriate.

In formulating per se rules of this type, a court should not consider police conduct in a vacuum. The likelihood that particular conduct will coerce confessions or undermine Fifth or Sixth Amendment protections depends not only on the content of the conduct but also on its probable effect on a specific suspect. Particularly in the case of psychologically oriented interrogation techniques, conduct that might be totally innocuous when employed in an ordinary interrogation situation may, under certain special circumstances, be likely to have a devastating psychological impact on a suspect. Therefore, the per se rules should be formulated not in terms of prohibiting specific police conduct as such, but as prohibiting police conduct that is likely to have certain types of effects on suspects.[115]

For example, if it is determined that the tactic of challenging a suspect's dignity should be prohibited,[116] in deciding whether this per se rule applies a court will have to consider whether a person in the suspect's position (given the individual characteristics of the suspect known to the police)[117] would feel that the police conduct was a challenge to his dignity.[118] If it is found that the police tactic induces such a feeling, operation of the per se rule will render any resulting confession automatically inadmissible. However, if the court finds that when viewed from the perspective of a reasonable person in the position of the interrogating officer, the tactic does not constitute a challenge to the suspect's dignity, the per se rule will be inapplicable. Thus, the per se rules will of necessity be phrased in terms of conduct and its likely effect, the latter of which introduces a limited degree of subjectivity into the test.

Obviously, the development and application of per se rules will involve the court in difficult judgments. In determining whether police conduct will be likely to have a particular impact on the typical suspect, the court may have to perform the difficult task of placing itself in the shoes of the suspect as viewed by the interrogating officer. However, given the complexity of the interests at stake, any principled approach in this area inevitably will involve difficult judgments. When compared to the more subjective version of the "totality of circumstances" test, the proposed approach will provide increased clarity in that the police and courts will at least be informed of specific danger zones; that is, they will have notice that tactics that have certain predictable effects are forbidden. The proposed approach has the virtue of allowing the courts to take account of the complex interrelationship between police conduct and its effect on individual suspects while at the same time enabling them to decide cases in a way that will provide concrete guidance for the future.

Evaluation of Certain Police Interrogation Tactics

This section of the essay will include a description of certain categories of interrogation tactics that can validly be subjected to per se prohibitions. No attempt will be made to discuss every widely employed tactic or to develop a general theory that would be applicable to every technique. For the sake of organizational clarity, tactics that create problems primarily because of their potential negation of the *Miranda* protections (or the independent right to counsel) will be discussed first, and tactics that should be prohibited because of their coercive effects will be treated second.

Deception about Whether an Interrogation Is Taking Place

A form of deception that totally undermines the Fifth or Sixth Amendment protections available to an individual occurs when the police deceive a suspect about whether an interrogation is taking place.[119] A classic example of this type of deception occurred in *Massiah v. United States*.[120] In *Massiah*, the defendant and his confederate Colson were arrested and indicted for possession of narcotics aboard a United States vessel. After both were released on bail, Colson, without defendant's knowledge, agreed to cooperate with the government in their efforts to obtain further information relating to the offense.[121] Equipped with a transmitter that broadcasted conversations held in his automobile to another government agent, Colson engaged in a lengthy conversation with defendant; at defendant's trial, incriminating statements made by him during the course of this conversation were introduced into evidence. The Court held the statements inadmissible on the ground that they were obtained in violation of the protections afforded the defendant by his Sixth Amendment right to counsel.[122]

Of course, the deception used in *Massiah* did not deprive the defendant of his right to an attorney in any ordinary sense. As Professors Arnold Enker and Sheldon Elsen have pointed out, "so far as the record in *Massiah* reveals, [the defendant] may very well have consulted with his counsel before talking to Colson."[123] Indeed, nothing indicates that the government did anything to prevent him from having his attorney present when he met with Colson in the car.[124] What the government did was not to deprive the defendant of his right to counsel, but rather to render that right useless by not disclosing that the conversation with Colson was, in effect, a part of an adversary process in which an attorney's presence was necessary. Thus, as the Court implicitly recognized, the key to the violation in *Massiah* was the fact that due to the governmental deception, at the time the defendant made his incriminating statements to Colson he "did not even know that he was under interrogation by a government agent."[125] Due to this deception, the Sixth Amendment protection that should have been available to defendant was effectively defeated. A practice that makes the suspect unaware that the police are interrogating him, and therefore is likely to remove from his consideration the question whether he should have counsel present, clearly creates an unacceptable risk of infringement of the suspect's constitutional rights. This interrogation technique, therefore, should be the subject of a per se prohibition.

The per se prohibition against deception that defeats the suspect's Sixth Amendment right by deceiving him about whether an interrogation is taking place should not be limited to postindictment interrogation (which is the extent of the holding of *Massiah*), but should also be extended to similar conduct that occurs after formal arrest.[126] This stratagem is as likely to be effective in the period *between* arrest and indictment as it is afterward. Further, the per se proscription should apply whether or not the suspect has initially waived his right to an attorney. As was noted previously,[127] the government must afford the suspect a continuous opportunity to assert his right to an attorney throughout the interrogation process. Deception about whether an interrogation is taking place, however, negates this opportunity. When a suspect is deceived about whether the government is seeking to elicit incriminating evidence from him,[128] he obviously has little basis on which to assess or reassess the question whether he needs the assistance of counsel during this phase of the adversary process. Therefore, even if the suspect has initially waived his right to an attorney, police deception about whether an interrogation is currently taking place should also be impermissible per se.

Even if the Court holds that the suspect's right to an attorney is not triggered at the point of arrest,[129] admissions obtained as a result of post-arrest deception about whether an interrogation is taking place should be held inadmissible on the ground that the use of this tactic is inherently unfair. Close examination of the relative strengths of the suspect and the police in this context demonstrates the desirability of extending the fairness strand of voluntariness doctrine to prohibit this practice.[130]

In order to understand the suspect's perspective, it must be noted that he is invariably confined in some manner when this deception is perpetrated.[131] Professor George Dix has pointed out that surreptitious attempts to elicit incriminating disclosures place considerable pressure to confess on any confined suspect. As Dix states, "Mere confinement might increase a suspect's anxiety, and he is likely to seek discourse with others to relieve this anxiety. That search, of course, may make him more susceptible to an undercover investigator seeking information about the offense for which the suspect has been arrested."[132] Confinement of the suspect increases the power of the police in an important respect. Because the suspect's ability to select people with whom he can confide is completely within their control,[133] the police have a unique opportunity to exploit the suspect's vulnerability. In short, the police can ensure that if the pressures of confinement lead the suspect to confide in anyone, it will be a police agent. In view of the government's control over the suspect's channels of communication, it is blatantly unfair to allow the government to exploit the suspect's vulnerability by trickery of this type.

Indeed, in one respect the deception in the "jail plant" situation is more invidious than that involved in *Spano v. New York*,[134] the seminal case dealing with the fairness strand of voluntariness doctrine.[135] In *Spano*, the defendant adamantly resisted police efforts to obtain a statement until he was confronted by Bruno, a fledgling officer who was also defendant's childhood friend, and who by telephone had persuaded Spano to surrender to the police. Pursuant to instruction from his superiors, Bruno falsely told the defendant that his "telephone call had gotten him [Bruno] into trouble, that his job was in jeopardy, and that loss of his job would be disastrous to his three children, his wife and his unborn child."[136] After assuming this role four times within the period of an hour, Bruno's deception successfully elicited a confession.

Although the Court held that the confession was involuntary based on the totality of the circumstances,[137] the majority opinion's marked distaste for Bruno's conduct indicated that the use of such a stratagem might in itself invalidate the resulting confession. To be sure, the deception employed in *Spano* can be distinguished from that of the typical jail plant situation. First, it is significant that Bruno was a longtime friend of the defendant, as opposed to a previously unknown cellmate. Second, in contrast to the typical jail plant situation, the defendant in *Spano* was explicitly and persistently urged to confess in order to avert dire consequences for his friend.[138] The presence of these additionally coercive elements in *Spano* undoubtedly intensified the pressure placed on the defendant to make an incriminating statement.

However, the broader "illegal methods"[139] language in *Spano* suggests that the Court was concerned more with deception than coercion. When the potential for deception is the focus of comparison, the conventional jail plant ploy emerges as the more objectionable interrogation tactic. In *Spano*, the defendant at least knew that his "friend" was a police officer and that his goal was to obtain a confession. By contrast, the suspect exposed to the "jail plant" is deceived completely about his cellmate's identity and purpose. The deception perpetrated in *Spano* unfairly weakened the suspect's ability to resist the police efforts to obtain a confession; the trickery of the jail plant ploy affords the suspect no opportunity to apply his powers of resistance because the peril of speaking is hidden from him. Accordingly, the fairness aspect of *Spano* should be expanded to prohibit this practice.

Once a general category of trickery has been deemed prohibited per se, a similar technique (especially one arguably within the same category) can be analyzed by comparing it to the tactic already proscribed. To be successful, such a comparison will involve the difficult definitional problems inherent in framing or applying legal rules. In the context of this type of deception, the analysis may be expected to involve distinguishing between impermissible deception about whether an interrogation is taking place and a permissible failure to disclose relevant information. Many of the tactics used in the course of an ordinary interrogation may have the effect of making a suspect forget that the police are seeking to elicit incriminating evidence.[140] Presumably, however, when a suspect has been informed of the police officer's intention to interrogate him and has consented, the police will not be required to preface every attempt to elicit incriminating statements[141] with a reminder to the suspect that they are continuing to interrogate him. On the other hand, the government obviously should not be permitted to argue that no deception occurred in *Massiah* because the defendant never happened to ask Colson whether he was acting as an undercover agent for the government. In between these two extremes, this analysis will involve close comparisons: the adoption of a per se rule will not eliminate the necessity of difficult line-drawing.

People v. Ketchel,[142] which involved an interrogation tactic analogous to deception about whether interrogation is taking place, provides an opportunity to demonstrate the suggested approach. In *Ketchel*, three defendants were arrested for robbery and murder. After talking with them for twenty minutes about the crimes, the police left the three suspects together in a room, after telling them that they were " 'free' to talk."[143] The room had in fact been wired to record the conversation. During the conversation, two of the defendants expressed the possibility that the room might be bugged.[144] Nevertheless, all three of them proceeded to make incriminating statements. In holding that these statements were properly admissible at the defendants' trials, the court applied the traditional voluntariness test[145] and found that "[t]he prior police statements as to the free use of the room could not have been such 'as to overbear [defendants'] will to resist and bring about confessions not freely self-determined' . . . because [defendants] themselves suspected their conversations *were* overheard."[146] Thus, the court implied that police trickery with respect to whether an interrogation is taking place will not be impermissible so long as the suspect subjected to such trickery is aware of the *possibility* that such trickery is being employed.

This approach is misdirected and should not be incorporated into an analysis of a suspect's Sixth Amendment rights. As noted above, a subjective approach that focuses on the effect of police practices on a particular defendant does not provide effective guidance to the police and courts.[147] Moreover, even if a totally objective approach is not adopted, as long as a defendant is actually deceived, it should not matter whether he was totally deceived, or partially deceived in that he recognized the possibility of deception. After all, anyone who considers the matter will know that there is *always* some possibility of governmental deception. A suspect's constitutional rights should not turn upon the degree of cynicism he expresses.[148]

If it has first been established that deception about whether an interrogation is taking place is impermissible per se,[149] under the suggested approach the question in a case like *Ketchel* should be whether the failure to disclose the fact that the room was bugged can be equated with that deception. In light of *Massiah*, impermissible deception can obviously take place without any overt misstatement. Deception in this context would appear to occur whenever the government fails to disclose to the suspect that it has changed the situation to make it contrary to an ordinary person's reasonable expectations about interrogation. An ordinary person in Massiah's position would not reasonably expect that his friend was acting as a government agent; similarly, an ordinary person occupying the position of the defendants in *Ketchel* would not reasonably expect that the room in which they were conversing was bugged. Because governmental deception of this nature is likely to lead an arrested suspect to believe that no interrogation is taking place, incriminating statements obtained by failing to disclose that a room is bugged should likewise be inadmissible per se.

Deception That Distorts the Meaning of the *Miranda* Warnings

When the *Miranda* protections are applicable, deception that defeats them definitely occurs when police trickery leads the suspect to believe that the *Miranda* warnings are totally inapplicable. For example, if in the course of an interrogation following a valid waiver, the suspect is questioned by a new officer who tells him that he no longer has a right to remain silent or that statements he makes cannot be used against him, statements made by the suspect in response would clearly be inadmissible.[150]

If *Miranda* is more than an empty formality, statements or tricks that significantly distort the meaning of the warnings should similarly be barred. For example, telling a suspect who has initially waived his rights that statements he makes to the officers will actually benefit him in a reduction of the charge[151] appears to conflict with the meaning of the first two *Miranda* warnings. The suspect might naturally infer that although he may have some technical right to remain silent, the right is not a meaningful one in that in reality it is in his best interest to talk. At the same time, he may feel that although his statement can be used against him, that is not nearly as important as the fact that it can be used in his favor. Direct distortion of this magnitude obviously vitiates the effect of the *Miranda* warnings,[152] thus resulting in a violation of the principle that requires that the warnings remain in effect (or at least not be negated by police conduct) throughout the interrogation.

At least some degree of distortion of the *Miranda* warnings occurs whenever the police make a misstatement that relates to the legal effect of the suspect's exercise of his right to remain silent. For example, if after warning the suspect of his rights and obtaining a valid waiver, the police tell the suspect that one of his confederates is going to make an accusatory statement in his presence, and this statement can be used against him unless he denies it,[153] this incorrect statement of law[154] adds an important caveat to the *Miranda* warnings. In effect, the suspect is told, "You have a right to remain silent, but in the context of your particular situation, exercising that right will produce damaging evidence that will be used against you." This addition to the *Miranda* warnings so distorts their meaning that it significantly undermines their effect. A substantial likelihood exists that during the remainder of the interrogation, the suspect, confronted with this information, will base his decision whether or not to assert his constitutional right to remain silent on the mistaken premise that his silence can be used against him. The interrogator's distortion of the *Miranda* warnings creates an unacceptable risk that the ordinary suspect will be deprived of the protection afforded by them. Therefore, statements obtained as a result of these types of misstatements should be inadmissible per se.

Of course, the police may indirectly achieve distortion of the *Miranda* warnings' meaning without making any misstatements of the law. This may occur when the police verbally impress upon the suspect that it is really in his own best interest for him to talk and tell the truth. For example, the Inbau-Reid manual recommends that the interrogator should inform "the suspect that even if he were your own brother (or father, sister, etc.), you would still advise him to speak the truth."[155]

The validity of practices that indirectly distort the *Miranda* warnings may be tested by comparing their likely effect to the results of direct distortion of the *Miranda* warnings, already the subject of a per se proscription under the suggested analysis. Statements of this type undercut the effect of *Miranda* warnings just as effectively as direct distortions of the warnings' legal scope. After all, the typical criminal suspect is not interested in abstract propositions of law; he wants to know what the score is. He may well believe that because the police are the ones who gave him the *Miranda* warnings, they can be expected to know their value. If the police advise him that it is really in his best interest to make a full disclosure, the suspect is likely to believe them, and as a result the effect of the *Miranda* warnings will be essentially negated. Although the inherent limitations of a system that initially entrusts the protection of the suspect's constitutional rights to the police must be acknowledged, a minimal circumscription of the police's adversarial role is necessary if *Miranda* is to have any content. If we are to attribute constitutional significance to verbal warnings by the police, it is only logical that we attach equal weight to police statements that predictably vitiate the warnings' desired effect. Thus, consistent with the policy against directly undermining the effect of the *Miranda* warnings, their indirect distortion, for example by means of advice to the suspect that it is in his own best interest to make a full disclosure, should also be prohibited per se.

Deception That Distorts the Seriousness of the Matter under Investigation

A slightly different form of trickery occurs when, after having given the suspect his *Miranda* warnings, the police misrepresent the seriousness of the offense. A typical example of this occurs when an interrogating officer falsely informs a murder suspect that the victim is still alive.[156] In analyzing whether this type of trickery impermissibly undermines the effect of the *Miranda* warnings, it is first necessary to determine whether the suspect must be informed of the nature of the charges about which he is being questioned before he may validly waive his *Miranda* rights.

Lower courts generally have held that the interrogating officer need not inform the suspect of the specific nature of the charges involved in order to obtain a valid waiver.[157] The Supreme Court's present view on this issue, however, is not clear. In the landmark case of *Johnson v. Zerbst*,[158] the Court equated waiver of a constitutional right with "an intentional relinquishment or abandonment of a known right or privilege."[159] In cases involving the waiver of trial counsel or of the right to trial, this standard has been held to mean that there can be no valid waiver unless the defendant has fairly full information relating to the consequences of the waiver.[160] Thus, when waiver of these rights is at issue, precise information relating to the nature of the charges against the defendant is clearly required.[161]

In *Schneckloth v. Bustamonte*,[162] a recent case involving waiver of Fourth Amendment rights, the Court noted in passing that when the suspect's Fifth Amendment privilege is in effect at the station house, the "standards of *Johnson* were . . . found to be a necessary prerequisite to a finding of a valid waiver."[163] In view of the development that *Johnson* has undergone in the right-to-trial and right-to-counsel contexts, this language can easily be relied on to require that a suspect be informed of the precise nature of the charges about which he is being questioned as a prerequisite to waiver of his *Miranda* rights.

Other elements of the Court's recent analysis of the concept of waiver, however, could be used to support an opposite result. In *Schneckloth*, the Court indicated that two considerations are of particular importance in determining the applicable standard of waiver: first, the extent to which the right at stake bears on the integrity of the fact-finding process;[164] second, the degree of structure that inheres in the context in which the waiver is sought.[165] Either of these considerations could be used to dilute the applicable standard of waiver in the *Miranda* context. Compared to the courtroom environment in which the rights to counsel and jury trial are waived, the custodial interrogation setting is relatively unstructured. In light of its analysis in *Schneckloth*, the Court may find that it is "unrealistic" to impose additional requirements beyond delivery of the *Miranda* warnings.[166] Moreover, although *Schneckloth* properly recognized that the *Miranda* rights do have a bearing on the determination of guilt or innocence,[167] other post-*Miranda* decisions evince a perception on the part of the Court that statements obtained in violation of *Miranda* may be introduced into evidence without jeopardizing the integrity of the fact-finding process.[168] Therefore, in keeping with the doctrine of variable waiver articulated in *Schneckloth*,[169] the Court might be expected to hold that a suspect may validly waive his rights under *Miranda* even though he was not informed of the precise nature of the charges forming the subject matter of the interrogation.

Even if the Supreme Court ultimately holds that disclosure of the charge is not a prerequisite to a valid waiver of *Miranda* rights, however, this will not mean that after obtaining a valid waiver without such disclosure police officers may then misrepresent the seriousness of the charge in order to eliminate any remaining resistance in the suspect. Because the *Miranda* rights must be capable of reassertion at any point in the interrogation process,[170] the mere existence of a waiver does not immunize subsequent police misrepresentation. On the contrary, misrepresenting the seriousness of the charge cripples the suspect's capacity to reassess the desirability of asserting the rights outlined in the warnings. The presence of inaccurate information about the legal consequences that will accompany ill-considered speech achieves as pernicious an effect as direct distortion of the *Miranda* warnings. Although many doubtlessly constitutional methods of police trickery distort the suspect's perception of his predicament, it is sophistry to make rigid distinctions between the suspect's abstract understanding of his legal rights and his concrete ability to make effective use of them. Principled resolution of this problem requires some analysis of the significance of the particular factual distortion in terms of the suspect's ability to exercise the *Miranda* rights.

Whatever balance a court would strike in other areas, the effect of misrepresentation of the charge cannot be overestimated. If suspects ever engage in the type of rational deliberation implicit in a system that depends on warnings, it is a virtual certainty that their perception of the potential punishment will assume critical importance in deciding whether or not to confess. Indeed, with the exception of deception about whether interrogation is taking place,[171] it is difficult to imagine trickery that exerts a more devastating effect on the suspect's ability to use his constitutional rights meaningfully. By distorting the suspect's understanding of his legal predicament, police misrepresentation of the charge is very likely to dissipate the effect of the *Miranda* warnings substantially. It therefore creates an unacceptable risk that the suspect will not be able to exercise his constitutional rights effectively. Accordingly, trickery of this type should be impermissible per se.

"A Pretended Friend Is Worse":[172] The Assumption of Nonadversarial Roles by Interrogating Officers

According to Royal and Schutt's treatise on police interrogation, "[r]esistance to the disclosure of [incriminating] information is considerably increased . . . if something is not done to establish a friendly and trusting attitude on the part of the subject."[173] Accordingly, the interrogating officer will often assume a nonadversarial role in which the suspect will perceive him not as an officer who is attempting to elicit incriminating information, but rather as a friend or counsellor who is truly concerned with the suspect's welfare.[174] For example, in *State v. Reilly*,[175] the chief interrogating officer manipulated the situation so that the eighteen-year-old suspect would view the officer almost as a father.[176] In *State v. Biron*,[177] one of the interrogating officers assumed the role of religious counsellor by speaking to the suspect as a fellow Catholic and enlightening him about the values of confession.[178] Similar examples of a role switch appear, or are at least hinted at[179] in many other cases.[180]

In some cases, the suspect's perception of the officer as a friendly figure will create extreme pressures to confess. In the *Reilly* case, for example, it is apparent that the suspect's inordinate desire to gain the acceptance of the interrogator whom he perceived as a father figure[181] compelled him not only to make a statement, but also to try with pathetic eagerness to confess to those details that he sensed the police were seeking.[182] In light of this example,[183] it may be concluded that when the interrogator's shift to a nonadversarial role is highly effective or when the suspect is extraordinarily sensitive to such tactics, a real danger exists that the shift will induce a false confession.[184]

The more pervasive danger, however, is that the interrogator's assumption of a nonadversarial role will negate the effect of the second *Miranda* warning. The point of telling the suspect that anything he says can be used against him is to sharpen his awareness of his position. As the *Miranda* majority stated: "[T]his warning may serve to make the individual more acutely aware that he is faced with a phase of the adversary system—that he is not in the presence of persons acting solely in his interest."[185] As Royal and Schutt suggest,[186] when the police effectively assume a nonadversarial role, the essential awareness if likely to be dissipated. The suspect's belief that he is talking to a friend or counsellor who has his best interests at heart will cause him to forget that he is involved in an adversarial interrogation in which his constitutional protections are of vital importance.[187] Accordingly, in order to avoid this negation of the protection provided by the second *Miranda* warning, the device of seeking to elicit incriminating information through the assumption of a nonadversarial role should be barred.[188]

Tricks That Take on the Character of Threats or Promises

In an early interpretation of the Fifth Amendment privilege, the Court concluded that one category of police tactics will automatically render a resulting confession involuntary. The 1897 case of *Bram v. United States*[189] laid down the rule that in order to be free and voluntary within the meaning of the Fifth Amendment privilege, a confession must be one that was "not . . . extracted by any sort of threats or violence, nor obtained by any direct or implied promises, however slight."[190] Although the *Bram* rule originally applied only to the federal government,[191] the Supreme Court explicitly noted in *Brady v. United States*[192] that *Malloy v. Hogan's*[193] incorporation of the Fifth Amendment privilege made it fully applicable to the states.[194]

The *Bram* doctrine's impact on deceptive police practices depends, of course, on the interpretation given to the terms "threats" and "promises." Under a broad interpretation, many police interrogation tactics might be held to constitute implicit threats or promises in the sense that their objective is to make the suspect believe that his situation will be improved in some way if he does confess, or that it will become worse if he does not. On the other hand, some lower courts have been quite adept at interpreting *Bram* in a narrow way that virtually strips the doctrine of its vitality.[195] In view of the Court's reaffirmation of *Bram* in *Brady*,[196] principled application of the doctrine is necessary.

Interpreting the *Bram* doctrine depends on two interrelated and particularly difficult questions. The first concerns the extent to which the terms of a promise or threat must be articulated; the second involves specification of the type of detriments or benefits that legitimately may be offered to a suspect. Both problems present themselves in a variety of contexts. For example, the *Miranda* opinion describes a deceptive practice recommended by the O'Hara manual: "The accused is placed in a line-up, but this time he is identified by several fictitious witnesses or victims who associated him with different offenses. It is expected that the subject will become desperate and confess to the offense under investigation in order to escape from the false accusations."[197] In this situation, because the police make no statement of any kind to the suspect, one could argue that no express or implied threat has been made. Nevertheless, the purpose of the charade is clear. In effect, the police say to the suspect, "Confess to the crime you are charged with, or you will find yourself being prosecuted for crimes that you did not commit."[198]

The interrogation of John Biron[199] included a number of instances in which the benefits of confessing (or detriments of not confessing) were suggested but not clearly delineated. Biron was an eighteen-year-old youth who was accused of participating in a felony-murder with one or two other teenagers. At one point, one of the interrogating officers said to him: "The thing you want to remember is that there's two of you involved and you're both to blame. But if you don't tell the truth, and the other one does, it puts more blame on your part."[200]   Another officer employed a metaphor to make essentially the same point:

Right up to your ears you're implicated. That hole is getting bigger, you're digging it deeper. You're the fellow who's going to determine how long you're going to be buried. . . . You're the one guy who's got the shovel; you're the one fellow who's digging the hole. You just figure out how deep you want to dig that hole, how far down you want to bury yourself; and you just keep right on digging. Of course, if you would start telling the truth, we could throw a little of that dirt back in, and make it a little shallower.[201]

Although neither officer referred specifically to the suspect's legal liability, it appears that the first officer's reference to "blame" was not limited to moral culpability, and the significance of the second officer's metaphor is obvious. The impression created by these officers was that the suspect would maximize his time of incarceration if he did not confess, but might obtain a reduced sentence if he did.

In other situations, the police may attempt to induce a confession by offering the possibility of benefits that do not involve reduction of legal liability. The benefits offered the suspect may be tangible, such as an opportunity to talk with a spouse[202] or a chance to receive medical treatment,[203] or intangible, such as an assuagement of guilt feelings or a promise of greater respect from the interrogating officer. In the *Biron* interrogation, for example, one officer continually urged the suspect to "get it off [his] chest" in order to "feel better."[204] The same officer repeatedly told the youth, first by implication, and then explicitly, that the officer would "respect [the suspect] a lot more" if he "told the truth."[205]

In determining the appropriate scope of the *Bram* doctrine, the doctrine's underlying rationale must be explored. As Justice White implied in *Brady*[206] and as Justice Harlan noted in his dissent in *Miranda*,[207] *Bram* reflects a judgment that certain types of threats or promises are likely to "apply a degree of pressure to an individual which unfairly impairs his capacity to make a rational choice."[208] In the case of threats or promises of the type involved in *Bram* (i.e., those that relate to the suspect's status in the criminal justice system),[209] the basis for this judgment is not difficult to perceive—it is simply improper for the police to place a price tag on the right to remain silent in a context in which the bargain offered to the suspect is likely to prove illusory.[210] Moreover, this type of pressure is likely to exert substantial influence on the suspect's will. Although the bargain may in fact be illusory, the stress engendered by the custodial interrogation setting is likely to diminish significantly the suspect's ability to evaluate its worth. In some cases, this kind of pressure could very easily cause an innocent person to confess,[211] and in any case, such tactics materially increase the likelihood that an ensuing decision to confess will be a result of this outside pressure rather than a consequence of a rational decision stemming from the suspect's owner inner motives.

Because of these considerations, the *Bram* doctrine should apply whether or not the threat or promise is explicitly articulated, as long as the police suggestion is likely to induce a suspect to believe that his legal position (in terms of potential charges, periods of incarceration, or collateral consequences pertaining to his relationship with the criminal justice system)[212] will improve if he confesses or deteriorate if he remains silent. A police statement to the suspect that by "telling the truth" he can "throw a little dirt back in, and make [the hole] a little shallower" distorts the suspect's decision-making process no less than a direct statement that he will spend less time in prison if he confesses. In fact, the former type of statement may have greater impact. The sinister implications of the suggestive metaphor may infuse the suspect's situation with added terror and further decrease the probability that he can determine rationally whether he wants to make a particular statement.

The extent to which the *Bram* rule should be extended to prohibit threats or promises that do not touch on the suspect's legal status is problematic. Even when the inducement has little or no bearing on the suspect's relationship to the criminal justice system, pressures of coercive magnitude may be created. It is indisputable, however, that not all threats and promises carry the same risk of constitutional infirmity. Police tactics that take on the character of threats or promises obviously occur in a multiplicity of forms. In addition, the impact of the tactics varies widely with the sensitivity of the suspect and the strength of the particular inducement. In view of these factors, and because the suggested per se approach calls for a delineation of relatively specific practices that create an unacceptable risk of constitutional deprivation, one might argue that a literal reading of the *Bram* rule is inappropriate.

The rejection of a per se rule for this type of deception can only be justified, however, if the alternative—the totality of the circumstances test—offers meaningful protection against impermissibly coercive threats and promises. Justice White's majority opinion in *Brady* suggests that the *Bram* rule reflects a judgment that the totality of the circumstances test is unworkable in this context. In *Brady*, the Court upheld the validity of a guilty plea in a situation in which exercise of the right to trial would have subjected the defendant to the possibility of the death penalty. Distinguishing *Bram*, the Court emphasized that the presence of counsel could dissipate "the possibly coercive impact of a promise of leniency."[213] The majority explicitly endorsed the *Bram* rationale, however, in language that bordered on describing it as a per se rule:

Bram is not inconsistent with our holding. . . . *Bram* dealt with a confession given by a suspect in custody, alone and unrepresented by counsel. In such circumstances, even a mild promise of leniency was deemed sufficient to bar the confession, not because the promise was an illegal act as such, but because defendants at such times are too sensitive to inducement and the possible impact on them too great to ignore and too difficult to assess.[214]

Although Justice White's reference to "leniency" might imply that he was limiting his analysis to promises that relate to the suspect's status within the criminal justice system, his conclusion concerning the unworkability of the totality of the circumstances test cannot be limited to promises of that character. Promises and threats involving tangible benefit and detriment obviously vary in terms of coercive effect, as do promises of leniency. Although many promises and threats are less coercive than "even a mild promise of leniency," the difficulty of assessing the effect on the suspect subjected to the interrogation suggests that with respect to this issue the totality of the circumstances test does not provide effective protection for the suspect's constitutional rights.

In addition to the concerns expressed by Justice White in *Brady*, no apparent societal interest supporting the use of threats and promises during interrogation is sufficiently compelling to justify the painstaking effort required by the totality of the circumstances test. It is by no means clear that the employment of such tactics achieves law enforcement gains that outweigh the coercive effects that are engendered. In the context of a type of deception that has a variable likely effect, unless some significant societal interest in such police conduct exists, the suspect's constitutional privilege against self-incrimination is better protected by a per se rule. In summary, although threats and promises of tangible benefits made by police during interrogation in order to elicit a confession vary significantly in terms of coercive effect, they are properly the subject of a per se proscription.

When the police merely suggest to the suspect that a confession will make him feel better or cause them to respect him more, there is no reason to exclude the confession as involuntary. Indeed, the Supreme Court in *Bram* indicated that a confession probably would not be invalidated if the benefit that induced it "was that of the removal from the conscience of the prisoner of the merely moral weight resulting from concealment."[215] This judgment is proper. Within our constitutional framework, confessions that stem from inner pressures such as a desire to relieve one's conscience or a desire to be respected are clearly voluntary.[216] The fact that police trickery may play a part in magnifying these pressures is not in itself sufficient basis to conclude that such tactics should be forbidden on a per se basis. In such cases, it is preferable to employ traditional voluntariness methodology to exclude the relatively rare confessions that are the result of impermissible coercion.

Repeated Assurances That the Suspect Is Known to Be
Guilty

In the *Biron* interrogation, one of the interrogators prefaced his questioning by saying, "I suppose they've told you what you're suspected of doing: *What we already know that you've done*."[217] The device of
impressing the suspect with the interrogators' certainty of his guilt was
continually employed throughout the interrogation.[218] In view of the
recommendations contained in the police manuals, this is hardly surprising. One of the principal directives in the Inbau-Reid manual is that the
interrogator should "Display an Air of Confidence in the Subject's
Guilt."[219] In elaborating, the authors note that "[a]t various times during the interrogation the subject should be reminded that the investigation has established the fact that he committed the offense; that there is
no doubt about it; and that, moreover, his general behavior plainly
shows that he is not now telling the truth."[220]

In justifying this technique, the authors state that it is "not apt to
induce a confession of guilt from an innocent subject."[221] However, Professor Edwin Driver's examination of social psychological data casts
doubt on this assertion. The evidence indicates that "when an individual
finds himself disagreeing with the unanimous judgment of others regarding an unambiguous stimulus, he may yield to the majority even though
this requires misreporting what he sees or believes."[222] The psychological pressures of custodial interrogation undoubtedly weaken the defenses
of many criminal suspects.[223] A significant danger exists that, confronted with positive assurances of their guilt from authority figures[224]
who appear to have a full knowledge of the facts,[225] they will not only
"yield to the majority judgment," but adopt the facts that are suggested
to them.[226]

Moreover, the repeated assurances of the suspect's guilt are expressly
designed to impress on him the futility of resistance.[227] In effect, the
suspect is being told, "We know you are guilty; so why not admit it?" In
identifying the coercive attributes of the interrogation techniques employed in *Culombe v. Connecticut*,[228] Justice Frankfurter particularly
emphasized the fact that the interrogating officers continually impressed
upon the defendant that their sole purpose was to obtain a confession of
guilt,[229] thus indicating a judgment that this type of pressure is likely to
have a particularly debilitating effect on the suspect. The cumulative
pressures of custodial interrogation and repeated assurances of the suspect's guilt are of sufficient magnitude to justify the conclusion that they
create an unacceptable risk of an involuntary confession. Accordingly,
the use of this tactic should be forbidden per se.

The "Mutt and Jeff" Routine

One of the classic deceptive practices recommended in the police manuals is the so-called Mutt and Jeff routine. Although this routine has many variations, its basic elements are simple. Jeff, the friendly interrogator, begins the questioning. After Jeff employs a friendly, sympathetic approach for a period of time, Mutt (the unfriendly interrogator) appears and "berate[s] the subject."[230] Jeff then resumes his sympathetic approach.[231] The act may be developed in various ways: the two interrogators may stage an argument in front of the suspect;[232] the suggestion may be made that the suspect will be left with Mutt if he does not cooperate with Jeff;[233] or the same interrogator may assume both roles.[234] One important element common to all the variations, however, is that Mutt will display hostility toward the suspect and make demeaning comments about him. In one variation, the Mutt character may refer to the suspect "as a rather despicable character."[235] Alternatively, if the same interrogator acts out both roles, he may "get up from his chair" and address the suspect as follows: "Joe, I thought that there was something basically decent and honorable in you but apparently there isn't. The hell with it, if that's the way you want to leave it; I don't give a damn."[236]

By labeling one variant of the Mutt and Jeff routine an interrogation "ploy,"[237] and then condemning the use of "patent psychological ploys,"[238] the *Miranda* majority implied that the use of this strategy may be inherently coercive. Such a judgment could stem from the implications of Mutt's hostility.[239] After Jeff, the suspect's only ally, deserts him, a real risk arises that he will perceive Mutt's angry statements as a threat of physical mistreatment.[240] In evaluating the significance of this risk, the context in which the hostility is exhibited must be considered. A suspect who has already spent some time in the debilitating atmosphere of the police station growing increasingly anxious about his fate is confronted by an authority figure who with obvious hostility conveys to him the message that he is no good. What visions might this raise in the mind of the already frightened suspect? The suspect does not know that the police will not mistreat him. He does know that he is within their absolute control and that they have the capacity to hurt him in many ways. When he hears an apparently angry officer voice the opinion that he is worthless, it requires little imagination for him to conclude that the officer will treat him in accordance with this estimation. Inbau and Reid assert that Mutt's berating of the suspect helps induce a confession because Jeff's sympathetic treatment becomes more effective.[241] The increased effectiveness of Jeff's treatment, however, can be attributed to the suspect's desire to avoid any further dealings with Mutt and the threat that his manner portends.[242] In short, the risk that the suspect will perceive a threat of mistreatment in Mutt's display of hostility is simply too great to tolerate.

A second reason exists for prohibiting the use of this tactic. The intimidating potential of the Mutt and Jeff routine is magnified by the demeaning message that it conveys to the suspect: "You are no good unless you confess." Significantly, Inbau and Reid conclude that the most effective variation on the Mutt and Jeff theme occurs when the same officer enacts both roles.[243] When an officer who has offered friendship and support to the suspect suddenly changes his mind and tells him that he is not a decent person, the impact on the suspect's ability to resist police efforts to induce a confession is likely to be significant.

Empirical evidence supports this conclusion. Professor Driver's survey of the psychological evidence indicates that the procedures of arrest and detention can temporarily induce shame and humiliation in nearly anyone,[244] and will create strong pressure to assuage those feelings.[245] If this is true, interrogation practices that exacerbate those feelings and suggest that only confession can alleviate them, undoubtedly exert extreme pressure on the suspect's decision-making process. When the demeaning message is conveyed with the potent force of the Mutt and Jeff technique, a significant likelihood exists that an involuntary confession will be the result. Given the implicit threat of force and the potentially coercive challenge to dignity that the Mutt and Jeff routine fosters, it is reasonable to conclude that it should be the subject of a per se proscription.

Although the Mutt and Jeff routine is a particularly coercive interrogation tactic and not all challenges to the suspect's honor or dignity will result in the same level of coercion, the use by law enforcement officers of any tactic that challenges a suspect's honor or dignity raises a fundamental question for our system of criminal justice. Despite the rudimentary development of a fairness component in voluntariness doctrine,[246] the Supreme Court has never explicitly endorsed the very basic proposition that criminal suspects have a right to be treated in a manner that reflects a concern for their dignity as human beings. It appears, however, that a basic postulate of the Fifth Amendment is a concern for protecting the dignity of the individual.[247] Interrogation tactics that are calculated to make the suspect feel that he is not a decent or honorable person unless he confesses constitute direct assaults on that dignity. More than thirty years ago, the Court intimated that stripping a suspect of his clothes in order to induce a confession was impermissible.[248] In light of our increased sensitivity to the effect of psychological tactics, practices that are calculated to strip individuals of their self-respect should be equally objectionable. Accordingly, such interrogation techniques should be barred as inherently unfair.

Conclusion

Without coherent guidelines, the conscientious interrogating officer who wants to comply with the law but still be effective in properly securing admissible confessions is placed in an impossible position. The deceptive practices recommended by the police manuals are undoubtedly effective, and based on existing case law, few if any of them are clearly illegal. On the other hand, the permissibility of police trickery may not be determined solely by asking whether the trickery in question is likely to induce an unreliable confession, as the manuals suggest. The protections provided by the *Miranda* warnings, the Sixth Amendment right to an attorney, and the modern version of the voluntariness test limit the types of deceptive practices that the police may employ. This essay has been an attempt to demonstrate that effective protection of these constitutional rights can only be achieved through the formulation of per se rules—that is, whenever the practice under scrutiny creates an unacceptable risk that the ordinary suspect's constitutional rights will be infringed, the practice should be proscribed. Application of this analysis to several widely employed interrogation tactics results in a finding that they should be absolutely prohibited. Although the development and application of such guidelines will undoubtedly challenge the institutional competence of the courts,[249] vigorous judicial scrutiny of police trickery in interrogation is essential if the criminal justice system is truly to operate within constitutional confines.

NOTES

I am particularly indebted to Professor Yale Kamisar of the University of Michigan Law School for his interest, his guidance (including the many helpful suggestions he made upon reading an earlier draft of this essay), and his legal writings, which have illuminated this area of the law for the past two decades. I am also indebted to Professor Louis B. Schwartz of the University of Pennsylvania Law School for his helpful criticism on an earlier draft of this essay, and to David Cicola for his excellent research assistance.

1. In three of the most recent Supreme Court cases dealing with the admissibility of confessions, it appears that the confessions were obtained at least in part by police trickery. *See* Brewer v. Williams, 430 U.S. 387 (1977) (confession obtained after deeply religious murder suspect heard "Christian burial" speech); Oregon v. Mathiason, 429 U.S. 492 (1977) (per curiam) (confession obtained after police falsely told suspect that his fingerprints had been found at the scene of the crime); Michigan v. Mosley, 423 U.S. 96 (1975) (confession obtained after

police falsely told suspect that another suspect had named him as the gunman). In *Williams*, the police trickery was not discussed because the Court found a violation of the suspect's Sixth Amendment right to counsel. 430 U.S. at 397–98. In *Mathiason* and *Mosley*, the Court noted that the validity of the police conduct was not within the scope of its review. 429 U.S. at 495–96; 423 U.S. at 99. For recent lower court cases in which it appears that police trickery was used to obtain confessions, see, for example, United States *ex rel.* Galloway v. Fogg, 403 F. Supp. 248 (S.D.N.Y. 1975) (police misrepresented to the suspect the extent to which other persons had implicated him); Moore v. Hopper, 389 F. Supp. 931 (M.D. Ga. 1974), *aff'd mem.*, 523 F.2d 1053 (5th Cir. 1975) (police falsely told murder suspect that murder weapon had been recovered); State v. Cobb, 115 Ariz. 484, 566 P.2d 285 (1977) (police falsely told robbery suspect that his fingerprints were found at the scene of the crime); People v. Groleau, 44 Ill. App. 3d 807, 358 N.E.2d 1192 (1976) (police falsely told murder suspect that victim was still alive).

2. *See* CRIMINAL INVESTIGATION AND INTERROGATION (rev. ed. S. Gerber & O. Schroeder 1972); F. INBAU & J. REID, CRIMINAL INTERROGATION AND CONFESSIONS (2d ed. 1967); C. O'HARA, FUNDAMENTALS OF CRIMINAL INVESTIGATION (4th ed. 1978); F. ROYAL & S. SCHUTT, THE GENTLE ART OF INTERVIEWING AND INTERROGATION (1976); C. VAN METER, PRINCIPLES OF POLICE INTERROGATION (1973). For an indication of the extent to which these tactics are in fact used, see Sterling, *Police Interrogation and the Psychology of Confession*, 14 J. PUB. L. 25, 41–43, 52–57 (1965).

3. F. INBAU & J. REID, *supra* note 2.

4. *Id.* at 26–108.

5. For an excellent general discussion of the definition of deception and lying, see S. BOK, LYING: MORAL CHOICE IN PUBLIC LIFE (1978).

6. *See* F. INBAU & J. REID, *supra* note 2, at 42, 49.

7. 384 U.S. 436 (1966).

8. *Id.* at 476.

9. Massiah v. United States, 377 U.S. 201 (1964) (tape of incriminating statements made to confederate who was acting under cover for prosecution held inadmissible as interrogation violative of Fifth and Sixth Amendments); Spano v. New York, 360 U.S. 315 (1959) (lies by police officer who was suspect's childhood friend were one element in finding that confession was obtained by means violative of due process); Leyra v. Denno, 347 U.S. 556 (1954) (confession induced by psychiatrist who was introduced to the suspect as the medical doctor whom he had requested held inadmissible as involuntary).

10. *See* Miranda v. Arizona, 384 U.S. 436, 449–55 (1966); Spano v. New York, 360 U.S. 315, 323 (1959).

11. F. INBAU & J. REID, *supra* note 2, at 218.

12. Leaving aside any quibbles one might have with the standard of certainty provided by the term "apt," neither the test as stated nor the remainder of the manual informs an interrogating officer of the types of interrogation techniques that are "apt" (or likely) to induce a false confession.

13. F. INBAU & J. REID, *supra* note 2, at 217–18.

14. *See, e.g.*, Canada v. State, 56 Ala. App. 722, 725, 325 So. 2d 513, 515,

cert. denied, 295 Ala. 395, 325 So. 2d 516 (1976) (tricks acceptable unless "likely" to produce false confessions); R.W. v. State, 135 Ga. App. 668, 671, 218 S.E.2d 674, 676 (1975) ("test in determining voluntariness is whether an inducement, if any, was sufficient, by possibility, to elicit an untrue acknowledgment of guilt"); Commonwealth v. Baity, 428 Pa. 306, 315, 237 A.2d 172, 177 (1968) (trick permissible as long as it has "no tendency to produce a false confession").

15. *See infra* notes 83–104 and accompanying text.

16. Greenwald v. Wisconsin, 390 U.S. 519, 521 (1968) (per curiam).

17. 322 U.S. 143 (1944).

18. *Id.* at 154.

19. 360 U.S. 315 (1959).

20. *Id.* at 320.

21. Watts v. Indiana, 338 U.S. 49, 55 (1949) (plurality opinion of Frankfurter, J.) ("Protracted, systematic and uncontrolled subjection of an accused to police interrogation . . . is subversive of the accusatorial system."); Malinski v. New York, 324 U.S. 401, 418 (1945) (Frankfurter, J., concurring) (despite prosecutor's justification of the police procedures as necessary, delaying arraignment and questioning suspect while he was naked was "so below the standards by which the criminal law . . . should be enforced as to fall short of due process of law").

22. *See generally* Paulsen, *The Fourteenth Amendment and the Third Degree*, 6 STAN. L. REV. 411, 431 (1954).

23. 378 U.S. 1 (1964).

24. 384 U.S. 436 (1966).

25. *Id.* at 444. Of course, in view of the post-*Miranda* cases, it is by no means clear that the privilege applies at the station house in all situations. *See infra* text accompanying notes 53–62.

26. 384 U.S. at 444.

27. *Id.*

28. The Court was adamant that the suspect be afforded an opportunity to reassert his rights even though he had initially waived them. *See infra* text accompanying notes 44–47. In order to safeguard the suspect's "continuous opportunity" to change an initial decision not to assert his rights, one state supreme court held that the warnings must be repeated if the nature of the interrogation process has caused a dissipation of their effect. *See* Commonwealth v. Wideman, 460 Pa. 699, 334 A.2d 594 (1975). However, several courts have held that even a break in the interrogation process of two or three days did not mandate restatement of the warnings. Y. KAMISAR, W. LAFAVE, & J. ISRAEL, MODERN CRIMINAL PROCEDURE 578 (4th ed. 1974).

29. 430 U.S. 387 (1977).

30. *Id.* at 397–98.

31. MODEL CODE OF PRE-ARRAIGNMENT PROCEDURE, §§ 140.2, 140.4, 140.6, 150.2 (Proposed Official Draft 1975).

32. *Id.* at §§ 140.2 ("No law enforcement officer shall attempt to induce an arrested person to make a statement by indicating that such person is legally obligated to do so.") & 140.6 ("No law enforcement officer shall take any action

which is designed to, or which under the circumstances creates a significant risk that it will, result in an untrue incriminating statement by an arrested person.").

33. No law enforcement officer shall attempt to induce an arrested person to make a statement or otherwise cooperate by . . . (b) any other method which, in light of the person's age, intelligence and mental and physical condition, unfairly undermines this ability to make a choice whether to make a statement or otherwise cooperate.

Id. at § 140.4.

If a law enforcement officer induces an arrested person to make a statement in the absence of counsel which deals with matters that are so complex or confusing that, in light of such person's age, intelligence, and mental and physical condition, there is a substantial risk that such statement may be misleading or unreliable or its use may be unfair, such statement shall not be admitted in evidence against such person in a criminal proceeding.

Id. at § 150.2(9).

34. For an elaboration of the reasons in support of this conclusion, see Bator & Vorenberg, *Arrest, Detention, Interrogation and Rights to Counsel: Basic Problems and Possible Legislative Solutions*, 66 COLUM. L. REV. 62, 73–74 (1966).

35. That is, the suspect has been given his *Miranda* warnings or has been informed of his right to an attorney and soon thereafter has made statements or taken action that under existing law would constitute a valid waiver of his rights. As will be demonstrated more fully below, the Fifth and Sixth Amendments and the voluntariness requirement provide continuing protection to the suspect, even after an initial waiver.

36. 430 U.S. 387 (1977).

37. The *Miranda* majority stated: "[A]ny evidence that the accused was threatened, tricked, or cajoled into a waiver will, of course, show that the defendant did not voluntarily waive his privilege." Miranda v. Arizona, 384 U.S. 436, 476 (1966). In *Brewer v. Williams*, the Court explicitly stated that the stringent waiver standard first formulated in *Johnson v. Zerbst* applied to waiver of the right to counsel. Brewer v. Williams, 430 U.S. 387, 404 (1977) (quoting Johnson v. Zerbst, 304 U.S. 458, 464 (1938)). *See infra* notes 78–80 and accompanying text. Accordingly, the *Miranda* prohibition on trickery in inducing a waiver would appear to apply with equal force in the *Williams* context.

38. Professors Kamisar, LaFave, and Israel have pointed to the uncertainty in this area of the law. Y. KAMISAR, W. LaFAVE & J. ISRAEL, *supra* note 28, at 589–90.

39. According to one widely used manual, "all but a very few of the interrogation tactics and techniques presented in our earlier [pre-*Escobedo*, pre-*Miranda*] publication are still valid if used after the recently prescribed warnings have been given to the suspect under interrogation, and after he has waived his self-incrimination privilege and his right to counsel." F. INBAU & J. REID, *supra* note 2, at 1, *quoted in* Y. KAMISAR, W. LaFAVE, & J. ISRAEL, *supra* note 28, at 589.

40. *See supra* text accompanying notes 26–28.

41. Miranda v. Arizona, 384 U.S. 436, 444 (1966).

42. *Id.* at 467.

43. *Id.* at 444.

44. *Id.*

45. *See supra* text accompanying notes 27 & 28.

46. *Miranda*, 384 U.S. at 445.

47. For an excellent critical analysis of the post-*Miranda* cases, see Stone, *The Miranda Doctrine in the Burger Court*, 1977 SUP. CT. REV. 99.

48. 425 U.S. 341 (1976) (questioning of suspect in private house held not to require *Miranda* warnings).

49. 429 U.S. 492 (1977) (per curiam) (private questioning of a suspect, who came to police station "voluntarily" at officer's request, held not to require *Miranda* warnings).

50. As Professor Stone has noted, "Mathiason was questioned in a police station behind closed doors, he was on parole, and he was informed, not just that he was being investigated, but that the police already believed him to be guilty." Stone, *supra* note 47, at 154. Despite the similarity between the coercive pressures confronting Mathiason and those confronting the *Miranda* defendants, the Supreme Court summarily concluded that *Miranda* did not apply because it was concerned with custodial interrogation and "[i]t was *that* sort of coercive environment to which Miranda by its terms was made applicable, and *to which it is limited.*" 429 U.S. at 495 (latter emphasis added).

51. In Orozco v. Texas, 394 U.S. 324 (1969), the Court held that *Miranda* applied when the defendant was arrested at his home. However, in light of *Beckwith* and *Mathiason*, the current vitality of *Orozco* is questionable.

52. 417 U.S. 433 (1974). For an incisive analysis of *Tucker*, see Stone, *supra* note 47, at 115–25.

53. 417 U.S. at 444: "The Court recognized [in *Miranda*] that these procedural safeguards were not themselves rights protected by the Constitution but were instead measures to insure that the privilege against compulsory self-incrimination was protected."

54. *But see* Harris v. New York, 401 U.S. 222 (1971) (holding that statements obtained in violation of *Miranda* may be admissible for the purpose of impeaching the defendant's credibility).

55. [Respondent's] statements could hardly be termed involuntary as that term has been defined in the decisions of this Court. . . . [T]he police conduct at issue here did not abridge respondent's constitutional privilege against compulsory self-incrimination, but departed only from the prophylactic standard laid down by this court in *Miranda* to safeguard that privilege.

417 U.S. at 445–46.

56. In determining the issue of a confession's "voluntariness," the Court has indicated that police failure to advise the suspect of his right to remain silent or his right to counsel will be afforded significant, but not decisive, weight. *See, e.g.*, Schneckloth v. Bustamonte, 412 U.S. 218, 249 (1973) ("voluntariness is a question of fact to be determined from all the circumstances, and while the suspect's knowledge of a right to refuse is a factor to be taken into account, the

prosecution is not required to demonstrate such knowledge as a prerequisite to establishing a voluntary consent.").

57. For an argument favoring this interpretation of *Miranda*, see Dix, *Mistake, Ignorance, Expectation of Benefit, and the Modern Law of Confessions*, 1975 Wash. U.L.Q. 275, 331–36.

58. *See infra* notes 150–88 and accompanying text.

59. 430 U.S. 387 (1977).

60. *Id.* at 397–98. The Court also found it unnecessary to reach defendant's claim that his confession was involuntary. *Id.*

61. *Id.*

62. 377 U.S. 201 (1964).

63. 430 U.S. at 398.

64. For an extraordinarily perceptive analysis of this interrelationship, see Kamisar, Brewer v. Williams, Massiah, *and* Miranda: *What is "Interrogation"? When Does It Matter?*, 67 Geo. L.J. 1 (1978).

65. Escobedo v. Illinois, 378 U.S. 478 (1964). *Escobedo* held that the suspect's Sixth Amendment right to an attorney comes into effect as soon as he becomes the "focus" of the police investigation. *Id.* at 490–91.

66. *See, e.g.*, Kirby v. Illinois, 406 U.S. 682, 689 (1972) (plurality opinion of Stewart, J.) ("The Court has limited the holding of *Escobedo* to its own facts . . . .").

67. 385 U.S. 293 (1966).

68. In *Hoffa*, the Court appeared to base its conclusion that the surreptitious governmental interrogation did not violate the suspect's Sixth Amendment right to counsel on the fact that the defendant had not yet been arrested. *Id.* at 310.

69. 430 U.S. at 398–99 (dictum). In justifying its decision, the Court particularly emphasized that judicial proceedings were initiated against the defendant at the time of the interrogation. Moreover, the Court's prominent citation of *Kirby v. Illinois* may be significant in view of *Kirby*'s holding that in the context of a preindictment show-up defendant's right to counsel did not attach until judicial proceedings had been initiated against him.

70. 425 U.S. 564, 581 (1976) (plurality opinion of Burger, C.J., joined by White, J., Powell, J., and Rehnquist, J.) (finding on the basis of *Kirby* that a grand jury target being questioned by the grand jury has no right to the presence of counsel because "[n]o criminal proceedings had been instituted against [him], hence the Sixth Amendment right to counsel had not come into play.").

71. 406 U.S. 682 (1972) (holding that the right to counsel did not apply to a preindictment show-up).

72. *See generally* Kamisar, *supra* note 64, at 83.

73. 2 W. Hawkins, A Treatise of Pleas of the Crown 595 (8th ed. London 1824) (1st ed. London 1716–21), *quoted in* Culombe v. Connecticut, 367 U.S. 568, 581 (1961) (plurality opinion of Frankfurter, J.). Although Frankfurter quoted Hawkins with the avowed purpose of identifying one of the principles imbedded in due process (or fundamental justice), it is apparent that the privilege against self-incrimination protects the same interest. It is worth noting that *Culombe* antedated Malloy v. Hogan, 378 U.S. 1 (1964), which held that the Fifth Amendment applies to the states.

74. *See* United States v. Mandujano, 425 U.S. 564, 602–03 (1976) (Brennan, J., concurring).

75. *See, e.g.*, United States v. Satterfield, 558 F.2d 655 (2d Cir. 1976) (statement of accused held inadmissible when prosecution failed to meet the "heavy burden" of showing a knowing waiver of the right to counsel although the accused had not requested an attorney).

76. *See, e.g.*, United States v. Putnam, 557 F.2d 1181 (5th Cir. 1977).

77. *Williams*, 430 U.S. at 401.

78. *Id.* at 404.

79. "[I]t was incumbent upon the State to prove 'an intentional relinquishment or abandonment of a known right or privilege.' " *Id.* (quoting Johnson v. Zerbst, 304 U.S. 458, 464 (1938)).

80. *See supra* note 28 and accompanying text.

81. Unlike the independent Sixth Amendment right, the *Miranda* protections are needed to shield the suspect from police coercion. Because the coercive influences of the custodial setting may quickly operate to overcome an individual's will, affording the individual subjected to these influences a continuous opportunity to assert his rights may be particularly important.

82. With respect to a defendant's right to an attorney at trial, lower court cases have indicated that an initial waiver of the right will not preclude a subsequent assertion of it unless the assertion will "disrupt orderly procedure." *See* Arnold v. United States, 414 F.2d 1056, 1059 n.1 (9th Cir. 1969) (dictum), *cert. denied*, 396 U.S. 1021 (1970). *Accord*, Fields v. State, 507 S.W.2d 39 (Mo. App. 1974).

83. 384 U.S. at 507.

84. *See infra* text accompanying notes 88–95.

85. *See infra* text accompanying notes 96–101.

86. *See supra* text accompanying notes 19–22.

87. The history and development of the voluntariness standard have been recounted in greater detail elsewhere. *See generally* O. STEPHENS, THE SUPREME COURT AND CONFESSIONS OF GUILT (1973); Bator & Vorenberg, *supra* note 34; Kamisar, *A Dissent from the* Miranda *Dissents: Some Comments on the "New" Fifth Amendment and the Old "Voluntariness" Test*, 65 MICH. L. REV. 59 (1966); Kamisar, *What Is an Involuntary Confession?* 17 RUTGERS L. REV. 728 (1963) [hereinafter cited as *Involuntary Confessions*]; Paulsen, *supra* note 22; *Developments in the Law—Confessions*, 79 HARV. L. REV. 935 (1966) [hereinafter cited as *Developments in the Law*].

88. *See generally Developments in the Law, supra* note 87, at 964–69.

89. In a 1963 article, Professor Kamisar drew the following conclusions about the role that the reliability interest has played in voluntariness doctrine:

Although what the court is *prepared* to do cannot adequately be explained in this manner, *on their facts*, the *decided* cases can be viewed as an application of two "reliability" standards: First, taking into account the personal characteristics of the defendant and his particular powers of resistance, did the police methods create too substantial a danger of falsity? Second, without regard to the particular defendant, are the interrogation methods utilized in this case . . . sufficiently likely to cause a significant number of

innocent persons to falsely confess, that the police should not be permitted to proceed in this manner?
Involuntary Confessions, supra note 87, at 755 (emphasis in original).
    90. 316 U.S. 547 (1942).
    91. *Id*. at 555.
    92. Justice Byrnes stated:
        This Court has set aside convictions based upon confessions extorted from ignorant persons who have been subjected to persistent and protracted questioning, or who have been threatened with mob violence, or who have been unlawfully held incommunicado without advice of friends or counsel, or who have been taken at night to lonely and isolated places for questioning.
Id. (citing Vernon v. Alabama, 313 U.S. 547 (1941); Lomax v. Texas, 313 U.S. 544 (1941); White v. Texas, 310 U.S. 530 (1940); Canty v. Alabama, 309 U.S. 629 (1940); Chambers v. Florida, 309 U.S. 227 (1940); Brown v. Mississippi, 297 U.S. 278 (1936); Wan v. United States, 266 U.S. 1 (1924)).
    93. 365 U.S. 534 (1961).
    94. *Id*. at 543–45.
    95. *Id*. at 540–41.
    96. *See, e.g.*, Culombe v. Connecticut, 367 U.S. 568, 602 (1961) (plurality opinion of Frankfurter, J.); United States v. Mitchell, 322 U.S. 65, 68 (1944). *See generally Developments in the Law, supra* note 87, at 973–84.
    97. *See generally Developments in the Law, supra* note 87, at 973–83.
    98. 373 U.S. 503 (1963).
    99. *Id*. at 515.
    100. *See, e.g.*, Lynumn v. Illinois, 372 U.S. 528, 534 (1963) ("We have said that the question in each case is whether the defendant's will was overborne . . . ."); Spano v. New York, 360 U.S. 315, 323 (1959) ("We conclude that petitioner's will was overborne by official pressure, fatigue and sympathy falsely aroused after considering all the facts . . . ."). *See generally Developments in the Law, supra* note 87, at 973.
    101. *See infra* text accompanying notes 107–14.
    102. *See supra* text accompanying notes 19–22.
    103. *See Spano*, 360 U.S. 315, and cases cited *supra* in note 21.
    104. 384 U.S. at 507 n.4 (quoting Bator & Vorenberg, *supra* note 34, at 73).
    105. *Involuntary Confessions, supra* note 87, at 758 (emphasis in original).
    106. *See generally id*.
    107. *See, e.g.*, Culombe v. Connecticut, 367 U.S. 568, 601–02 (1961); Spano v. New York, 360 U.S. 315, 321, 323 (1959).
    108. In Ashcraft v. Tennessee, 322 U.S. 143, 154 (1944), the Court held that thirty-six hours of continuous interrogation was "inherently coercive." The strong implication was that when questioning of that duration occurs, the effect of other factors need not be considered. Moreover, even the *Ashcraft* dissent recognized that "violence *per se* is an outlaw," 322 U.S. at 160 (Jackson, J., dissenting), thus implying that any statement induced by violence or threat of violence would be automatically inadmissible. *Accord*, Payne v. Arkansas, 356 U.S.

560, 567 (1958); Ward v. Texas, 316 U.S. 547, 555 (1942); Brown v. Mississippi, 297 U.S. 278, 286 (1936).

109. *See generally Developments in the Law, supra* note 87, at 973–84.

110. *See generally* Amsterdam, *The Supreme Court and the Rights of Suspects in Criminal Cases*, 45 N.Y.U. L. REV. 785, 806–09 (1970).

111. *See* Kamisar, *Foreword: Brewer v. Williams—A Hard Look at a Discomfiting Record*, 66 GEO. L.J. 209, 234–35 (1977).

112. Despite the *Miranda* opinion's evident distaste for a number of the tactics contained in the Inbau-Reid manual, *see* 384 U.S. at 449–55, the revised edition (published one year after *Miranda*) advised the police to continue using the same tactics. *See* F. INBAU & J. REID, *supra* note 2, at 1. Obviously, the authors reasoned that tactics not specifically prohibited could continue to be employed. This perhaps illustrates the validity of Justice Jackson's observation, made in the Fourth Amendment context, to the effect that "officers interpret and apply themselves and will push to the limit" constitutional doctrines expounded by the Supreme Court. *See* Brinegar v. United States, 338 U.S. 160, 182 (1949) (Jackson, J., dissenting).

113. One of the most striking recent examples of this appears in State v. Reilly, No. 5285 (Conn. Super. Ct. Apr. 12, 1974), *vacated*, 32 Conn. Supp. 349, 355 A.2d 324 (1976). *See infra* text accompanying notes 175 and 176. In addition to employing the psychological techniques described below, the police held the immature eighteen-year-old suspect incommunicado, allowed him at most a few hours' sleep and no hot food, and interrogated him for virtually twenty-six continuous hours in order to obtain his confession. Based on a plethora of Supreme Court cases, the confession would appear to be clearly inadmissible. *See, e.g.*, Ashcraft v. Tennessee, 322 U.S. 143 (1944), discussed *supra* at note 108. Nevertheless, the lower court admitted it.

114. For an illustration of the highly deferential attitude that may plausibly be adopted by an appellate court, see Mincey v. Arizona, 98 S. Ct. 2408, 2422–23 (1978) (Rehnquist, J., concurring in part and dissenting in part). *See also* Ashcraft v. Tennessee, 322 U.S. 143, 156–58, 170–73 (1944) (Jackson, J., dissenting).

115. It should be emphasized, however, that the Court's assessment of the officer's intent or good faith should not affect the application of a per se rule. If it is determined that the officer's conduct was in fact likely to have the proscribed effect on the suspect, the absence of conscious wrongdoing on the officer's part should be constitutionally irrelevant.

116. *See infra* notes 245–48 and accompanying text.

117. This factor must be taken into account because the guidelines are ultimately designed to regulate police conduct. If the police engage in conduct that from their perspective would appear innocuous, but in fact is likely to have a devastating effect on the suspect, the conduct should not become the subject of a per se rule. However, when innocent conduct induces a confession that is involuntary under traditional doctrine, the confession must of course be excluded. *See* Townsend v. Sain, 372 U.S. 293, 308–09 (1963) (benign purpose of interrogating officer does not validate a confession that is in fact involuntary). A confession should also be held invalid, although not on a per se basis, if it is obtained by innocent police conduct that impermissibly vitiates the effect of *Mi-*

randa warnings or the independent right to counsel. Such a result could be obtained under the traditional methodology.

118. For example, in Brewer v. Williams, 430 U.S. 387 (1977), the interrogating detective's "Christian burial" speech and his use of the word "Reverend" in addressing the suspect would be likely to challenge the dignity of a deeply religious person, but would have little effect on the dignity of an ordinary person. Because the detective was aware of the suspect's deep religious convictions, 430 U.S. at 392, the speech could properly be characterized as a challenge to the suspect's dignity.

119. Actually, in light of the post-*Miranda* narrowing of *Miranda*'s applicability, *see supra* notes 47–57 and accompanying text, it is likely that the suspect has no Fifth Amendment protection when this form of deception occurs. Because the suspect is unaware that interrogation is taking place, it is likely that the "custodial interrogation" element of *Miranda* would not be met. *See supra* text accompanying notes 47–57. Therefore, the point at which the Sixth Amendment right attaches assumes critical importance. In this essay the argument has been that the Sixth Amendment right should be triggered at the point of formal arrest. *See supra* notes 64–74 and accompanying text. However, if the right does not come into effect until after a suspect is formally charged, the police may use undercover agents or private citizens to obtain statements from suspects who are in police custody and who have asserted their *Miranda* rights but have not yet been formally charged. For lower court cases dealing with this issue, see, for example, Commonwealth v. Bordner, 432 Pa. 405, 247 A.2d 612 (1968) (statements inadmissible when police engaged defendant's parents to elicit incriminating statements from him while he was in the hospital); State v. Travis, 116 R.I. 678, 360 A.2d 548 (1976) (statements inadmissible when police placed undercover policeman in defendant's cell shortly after his arrest and defendant had already refused to talk to police before seeing an attorney).

120. 377 U.S. 201 (1964).

121. *Id.* at 202.

122. *Id.* at 205–06.

123. Enker & Elsen, *Counsel for the Suspect*: Massiah v. United States *and* Escobedo v. Illinois, 49 MINN. L. REV. 47, 56 n.32 (1964).

124. *Id.*

125. 377 U.S. at 206.

126. The argument here has been that the Sixth Amendment right should be triggered at the point of formal arrest. *See supra* notes 64–74 and accompanying text.

127. *See supra* notes 79–81 and accompanying text.

128. This would appear to be the appropriate definition of interrogation in the *Massiah-Williams* context, as opposed to the definition of custodial interrogation within the meaning of *Miranda*. One recent circuit court case has held that in view of *Williams*'s language relating to the meaning of interrogation, *Massiah*'s proscription only applies when the undercover agent engages in direct questions or inquiries, and not when he engages the defendant in conversation with the purpose of eliciting incriminating responses. Wilson v. Henderson, 584 F.2d 1185 (2d Cir. 1978), *petitions for rehearing and rehearing en banc denied*, 590

F.2d 408 (2d Cir. 1979). As Professor Kamisar's recent article demonstrates, this is an improper interpretation of *Williams*. Kamisar, *supra* note 64, at 5–44 & *passim. Accord,* Henry v. United States, 570 F.2d 544 (4th Cir. 1978).

129. Professor Kamisar has predicted that *Williams* will not be extended to interrogation that occurs before the initiation of formal adversary proceedings. *See* Kamisar, *supra* note 64, at 83.

130. For a brief discussion of this aspect of voluntariness doctrine, see *supra* notes19–22 and accompanying text.

131. Under ordinary circumstances, before an arrested suspect can be released, the charges against him must be dropped or he must be brought before a judicial officer for the commencement of formal adversary proceedings. If the charges are dropped and the suspect is released, the Sixth Amendment right to counsel probably does not apply to subsequent police interrogation. Although the argument in this essay has been that the right should attach at the point of arrest, it is likely that dropping the charge would negate the effect of the prior arrest for purposes of applying *Williams*. The Court has held that even though the police may continue to focus on the suspect as a target of their investigation, they are not required to arrest a suspect, and thereby possibly trigger his Sixth Amendment rights, simply because they have sufficient evidence to take that step. Hoffa v. United States, 385 U.S. 293, 310 (1966). Accordingly, in cases in which the suspect is not confined, he would not be protected by the Sixth Amendment, even though deception about whether he is being interrogated may in fact occur.

132. Dix, *Undercover Investigations and Police Rulemaking*, 53 TEXAS L. REV. 203, 230 (1975). Professor Dix suggests that a *Miranda*-type barrier should preclude use of the "jail plant" tactic. *Id.* Professor Kamisar has argued cogently to the contrary. *See* Kamisar, *supra* note 64, at 61–69.

133. Justice Marshall's dissent from a denial of cert. in Miller v. California, 392 U.S. 616, 616 (1968), noted this aspect of confinement. In *Miller*, an undercover police agent testified at defendant's trial about conversations they had engaged in while they shared a cell prior to the defendant's arraignment. In a per curiam opinion, the Court dismissed the writ of certiorari as improvidently granted. Justice Marshall, and the three justices who joined in his opinion, would have extended *Massiah* to exclude the agent's testimony. Justice Marshall argued that "[i]ndeed, in one respect at least, this is a clearer case than *Massiah*: unlike the defendant there, who had been released on bail, petitioner was in custody without bail, with a consequent lack of freedom to choose her companions." *Id.* at 624.

134. 360 U.S. 315 (1959).

135. *See supra* notes 19–22 and accompanying text.

136. 360 U.S. at 323.

137. *Id.* at 321.

138. The coercive nature of this tactic can be explained by the fact that it takes on the character of a threat. For a discussion of the legitimacy of the use of threats and promises during interrogation, see *infra* notes 189–217 and accompanying text.

139. 360 U.S. at 320–21.

140. For example, it is said that in order to create a rapport that will encourage the disclosure of incriminating information, it is desirable to "[e]stablish confidence and friendliness by talking for a period about everyday subjects. In other words, 'have a friendly visit.' " *See* F. ROYAL & S. SCHUTT, *supra* note 2, at 61–62. Obviously, the purpose of the "friendly visit" is to distract the suspect from the fact that an interrogation is taking place. *See generally* Kamisar, *supra* note 111.

141. The Court apparently adopted this definition of "interrogation" in Brewer v. Williams, 430 U.S. 387, 399–400 (1977). *See supra* note 128.

142. 59 Cal. 2d 503, 381 P.2d 394, 30 Cal. Rptr. 538 (1963), *rev'd en banc*, 63 Cal. 2d 859, 409 P.2d 694, 48 Cal. Rptr. 614 (1966). After retrial on the penalty issue, the Supreme Court of California voided the confessions on the authority of Escobedo v. Illinois, 378 U.S. 478 (1964). People v. Ketchel, 63 Cal. 2d 859, 868, 409 P.2d 694, 699, 48 Cal. Rptr. 614, 619 (1966).

143. 59 Cal. 2d at 521, 381 P.2d at 402, 30 Cal. Rptr. at 546.

144. *Id.*, 381 P.2d at 403, 30 Cal. Rptr. at 547.

145. The case was originally decided before *Massiah* or *Miranda*.

146. 59 Cal. 2d at 521, 381 P.2d at 403, 30 Cal. Rptr. at 547 (emphasis in original).

147. *See supra* notes 99–106 and accompanying text.

148. *Cf.* Amsterdam, *Perspectives on the Fourth Amendment*, 58 MINN. L. REV. 349, 384 (1974) ("[N]either *Katz* nor the fourth amendment asks what we expect of government. They tell us what we should demand of government.").

149. *See supra* text accompanying notes 119–27.

150. *Cf.* Commonwealth v. Dunstin, 373 Mass. 612, 368 N.E.2d 1388 (1977), *cert. denied*, 435 U.S. 943 (1978) (incriminating statements held inadmissible when guard told defendant that only statements made under oath at trial could be used against him); Commonwealth v. Hale, 467 Pa. 293, 356 A.2d 756 (1976) (results of tests by police psychiatrist held inadmissible when psychiatrist told accused before testing that the test results would be used only at sentencing).

151. *Cf.* Fillinger v. State, 349 So. 2d 714 (Fla. Dist. Ct. App. 1977) (confession held involuntary because defendant was told that if she cooperated the state attorney would be so informed before establishing the amount of the bond upon which she was to be held); State v. Biron, 266 Minn. 272, 123 N.W.2d 392 (1963) (confession held inadmissible when given after suspect was told that his confession might lead to a juvenile court trial instead of one in criminal court). The contents of the tape recording made of the six-hour Biron interrogation are discussed below. *See infra* text accompanying notes 199–201 & 217.

152. *Cf.* Commonwealth v. Singleton, 439 Pa. 185, 189–90, 266 A.2d 753, 754–55 (1970) (holding that delivering the second *Miranda* warning by telling suspect that "any statement he gave could be used '*for*, or against him' at trial" is impermissible because it "vitiates the intended impact of the warning" (emphasis added) (footnote omitted)).

153. *Cf.* State v. Braun, 82 Wash. 2d 157, 509 P.2d 742 (1973) (police told accused that codefendant's confession would be admissible against him if repeated in his presence). Of course, the police may convey the same message to

the suspect tacitly without misinforming him of the effect of his failure to deny. *Cf. infra* text accompanying note 155.

154. The Court has made it clear that once the *Miranda* warnings have been given, the defendant's silence may not be used against him under any circumstances. *See* Doyle v. Ohio, 426 U.S. 610 (1976).

155. F. INBAU & J. REID, *supra* note 2, at 60.

156. *See, e.g.*, People v. Groleau, 44 Ill. App. 3d 807, 358 N.E.2d 1192 (1976); State v. Cooper, 217 N.W.2d 589 (Iowa 1974). *See also* Y. KAMISAR, W. LaFAVE, & J. ISRAEL, *supra* note 28, at 571.

157. *See, e.g.*, United States v. Anderson, 533 F.2d 1210, 1212 n.3 (D.C. Cir. 1976); Collins v. Brierly, 492 F.2d 735 (3d Cir.), *cert. denied*, 419 U.S. 877 (1974); United States v. Campbell, 431 F.2d 97 (9th Cir. 1970); People v. Prude, 66 Ill. 2d 470, 363 N.E.2d 371, *cert. denied*, 434 U.S. 930 (1977); People v. Pereira, 26 N.Y.2d 265, 258 N.E.2d 194, 309 N.Y.S.2d 901 (1970). *Contra*, Schenk v. Ellsworth, 293 F. Supp. 26 (D. Mont. 1968). *Cf.* Commonwealth v. Dixon, 475 Pa. 17, 379 A.2d 553 (1977) (suspect must be informed of the "transaction" that gave rise to his detention and interrogation).

158. 304 U.S. 458 (1938).

159. *Id.* at 464.

160. *See* Boykin v. Alabama, 395 U.S. 238 (1969) (right to trial); Minor v. United States, 375 F.2d 170 (8th Cir.), *cert. denied*, 389 U.S. 882 (1967) (waiver of trial counsel).

161. In the case of waiver of the right to trial, it has been held that the defendant must demonstrate a clear understanding of the charges against him. Henderson v. Morgan, 426 U.S. 637 (1976). In addition, the defendant must have a "full understanding of what the plea connotes and of its consequence." Boykin v. Alabama, 395 U.S. 238, 244 (1969). When the defendant waives his right to counsel, he must understand not only the charges and statutory offenses against him, but also the possible punishments, defenses, and mitigating circumstances, and any facts "essential to a broad understanding of the whole matter." Von Moltke v. Gillies, 332 U.S. 708, 724 (1948) (plurality opinion of Black, J.). *See generally* Note, *The Right of an Accused to Proceed Without Counsel*, 49 MINN. L. REV. 1133, 1141–45 (1965).

162. 412 U.S. 218 (1973).

163. *Id.* at 240.

164. *Id.* at 242.

165. *Id.* at 243–45. For a critical examination of this aspect of *Schneckloth*, see Spritzer, *Criminal Waiver, Procedural Default and the Burger Court*, 126 U. PA. L. REV. 473, 477–80 (1978).

166. In most cases, of course, it would not be any more difficult for the police to inform the suspect of the charges they are investigating than it is for them to deliver the warnings required by *Miranda*. There might be some cases, however, in which defining the precise nature of the charges under investigation would be difficult. *See, e.g.*, Commonwealth v. Tatro, 76 Mass. App. Ct. Adv. Sh. 568, 346 N.E.2d 724 (1976) (homicide charges not contemplated at time accused was questioned about robbery because cause of victim's death had not yet been determined).

167. *See Schneckloth*, 412 U.S. at 240: "The [*Miranda*] Court made it clear that the basis for decision was the need to protect the fairness of the trial itself . . . ."

168. *See, e.g.*, Hass v. Oregon, 420 U.S. 714 (1975); Harris v. New York, 401 U.S. 222 (1971).

169. *See supra* text accompanying notes 164 and 165.

170. *See supra* note 28 and accompanying text.

171. *See supra* notes 119–49 and accompanying text.

172. Spano v. New York, 360 U.S. 315, 323 (1959). Both *Spano* and Leyra v. Denno, 347 U.S. 556 (1954), lend some preliminary support to the conclusion advanced in this section. In both cases the Court invalidated confessions obtained by police interrogators who purported to speak to the defendants in a nonadversarial capacity. In *Leyra*, the police psychiatrist who obtained the confession told the defendant he was a doctor who was going to help him with his headaches. 347 U.S. at 559. In *Spano*, a police officer told defendant (who had been his childhood friend) that his job would be in jeopardy if the defendant did not confess, and that loss of his job would be disastrous to his three children, his wife, and his unborn child. 360 U.S. at 323. Although the Court clearly expressed its disapproval of the deceptive practice employed, *id.*, it considered the use of the childhood friend as just "another factor which deserves mention in the totality of the situation," *id.*, and held that this practice combined with other factors in the case to overbear defendant's will, *id.* Thus, the Court did not go so far as to indicate that the deceptive practice alone was sufficient to invalidate the confession.

173. F. ROYAL & S. SCHUTT, *supra* note 2, at 61–62, *quoted in* Kamisar, *supra* note 111, at 209.

174. This tactic is closely related to deception about whether an interrogation is taking place. *See supra* notes 119–50 and accompanying text. Although the assumption of a nonadversarial role may not totally negate the suspect's awareness that he is the subject of a police interrogation, the effective employment of this stratagem will substantially diminish his perception that particular questions are in fact part of the interrogation.

175. No. 5285 (Conn. Super. Ct. Apr. 12, 1974), *vacated*, 32 Conn. Supp. 349, 355 A.2d 324 (1976). *See* J. BARTHEL, A DEATH IN CANAAN (1976). This excellent account of the murder case in which Peter Reilly was convicted of manslaughter but eventually exonerated contains substantial portions of the tape-recorded police interrogation of Reilly. *See id.* at 39–130.

176. *See, e.g., id.* at 85:

S: [interrogator]: Have you ever felt close enough to someone that you could really trust them?

    . . . .

P: [suspect]: Nope . . . yes, excuse me. I do have someone that I could speak to like that. That would be Aldo Beligni.

S. Let's you and I try something. You try to feel about me . . .

P: Like a father?

S: Like somebody who's really interested in you, and then . . .

P: Well, I do already. That's why I come out with all this.

177. 266 Minn. 272, 123 N.W.2d 392 (1963). A six-hour tape-recording of the interrogation conducted in *Biron* is on file in the libraries of the University of Michigan and University of Minnesota Schools of Law [hereinafter cited as *Biron* Tapes]. The case is discussed in Kamisar, *Fred E. Inbau: "The Importance of Being Guilty,"* 68 J. CRIM. L. & CRIMINOLOGY 182, 184, 185 nn.19 & 20 (1977). The author expresses his gratitude to Professor Kamisar for making portions of the tapes available to the University of Pittsburgh School of Law.

178. Actually, it might be more accurate to say that the officer attempted to assume the role of a priest figure. Excerpts from the tape disclose that after the suspect asked to see a priest, Hawkinson, an interrogator who had previously exhibited courtesy and restraint in his dealings with the suspect, entered and the interrogation proceeded as follows:

H: Mike was telling me that you'd like to see a priest. Is that true?
S: Yes.
H: I'm Catholic, too. I can appreciate that. Any particular one that you'd like to see?
S: No.
H: I think you realize you'll feel a lot better—
S: Yeah, that's true.
H: If you did do it, and you tell about it. I think you know that. It's just like when you go to confession, if you make a good clean confession, well, you feel good, received the next morning. My name is Hawkinson but I am a Catholic, a convert many years ago. In fact this Sunday night, I'm going out to King's house on a retreat for two days.

179. In cases such as *Reilly, Biron*, and State v. Miller, 76 N.J. 392, 388 A.2d 218 (1978), *see infra* note 180, in which the interrogation is actually recorded, examples of an interrogating officer's switch to a nonadversarial role are much more apparent than in nonrecorded cases. This tends to support Professor Kamisar's argument that our traditional litigational tools are simply not calculated to elicit all of the constitutionally relevant facts of secret police interrogation. *See* Kamisar, *supra* note 111.

180. *See* Davis v. North Carolina, 384 U.S. 737, 750–51 (1966) (defendant confessed immediately after officer who was friend of family said a short prayer on his behalf); Spano v. New York, 360 U.S. 315 (1959) (defendant urged to confess by officer who had in fact been a boyhood friend); *Miller* (officer told defendant that the murderer was not a criminal who deserved punishment, but a person in need of medical care, and that he would do all he could to help if the defendant spoke about the incident). *Cf.* State v. Thompson, 287 N.C. 303, 214 S.E.2d 742 (1975), *modified*, 428 U.S. 908 (1976) (defendant's father, who was a police sergeant, urged defendant to cooperate with sheriff during interrogation on murder charges).

181. The extent of Reilly's feeling of dependence was fully revealed when he twice inquired of the interrogator if there was a possibility that he might come to live with the officer and his family. J. BARTHEL, *supra* note 175, at 98, 117–18, 127.

182. *See, e.g., id.* at 83, 91:
S: What about a knife, Pete? Remember using a knife?

P: I don't, but a straight razor thing registers.

S: And a knife, Pete.

P: Maybe. Could you give me the details? . . .

. . . .

I mean, was there a knife mark?

S: Pete, you know very well why I won't answer that question. 'Cause you're not being honest . . . . You're trying to maneuver me and trick me into telling you facts that you already know. I know the facts.

P: Well, if you would give me some hints . . . .

183. The evidence discovered later that led to the ultimate dismissal of Reilly's case appears to establish conclusively that his confession was false. *See* Reilly v. State, 32 Conn. Supp. 349, 355 A.2d 324, 333–39 (1976), *vacating* No. 5285 (Conn. Super. Ct. Apr. 12, 1974). Moreover, during the course of the interrogation, Reilly said that he must have raped his mother, *id.* at 119, a statement that was patently false because no rape was alleged to have occurred.

184. Under Professor Kamisar's analysis, such a danger should in itself operate to render involuntary all confessions induced as a result of this particular stratagem. *See Involuntary Confessions, supra* note 87, at 753–55.

185. 384 U.S. at 469.

186. *See supra* text accompanying notes 172 & 173.

187. *Miranda*, 384 U.S. at 467–69.

188. If it is determined that the suspect (given his characteristics that are known to the police) would be likely to view the interrogating officer as a friend, father figure, religious counsellor, or any other nonadversarial figure, this per se rule would be violated. The fact that the officer was actually manifesting his true concern for the suspect would, of course, be constitutionally irrelevant because the officer's bona fides would not mitigate the potential destruction of the protections afforded by *Miranda*. *See supra* note 115.

189. 168 U.S. 532 (1897).

190. *Id.* at 542–43.

191. In state cases, post-*Bram* confessions that were clearly given in exchange for direct promises of leniency by the police were found not to be in violation of the Fourteenth Amendment. *See, e.g.*, Stein v. New York, 346 U.S. 156 (1953) (confession held voluntary when given in exchange for promise that accused's father would be released from jail and brother would not be disciplined for parole violation).

192. 397 U.S. 742 (1970).

193. 378 U.S. 1 (1964).

194. *Brady*, 397 U.S. at 753.

195. *See, e.g.*, United States v. Ferrara, 377 F.2d 16 (2d Cir.), *cert. denied*, 389 U.S. 908 (1967) (confession voluntary when obtained after federal agent told accused that he would probably be released on reduced bail if he cooperated).

196. 397 U.S. at 754. *See infra* text accompanying notes 213 & 214.

197. C. O'HARA, FUNDAMENTALS OF CRIMINAL INVESTIGATION 105–06 (1956), *quoted in* Miranda v. Arizona, 384 U.S. 436, 453 (1966).

198. A study of interrogation practices in New Haven indicated that the police have conveyed this same type of message to suspects in post-*Miranda*

cases. *Interrogations in New Haven: The Impact of* Miranda, 76 YALE L.J. 1519, 1546 (1967) [hereinafter cited as *Interrogations in New Haven*].

199. *See supra* notes 177–80 and accompanying text.

200. *Biron* Tapes, *supra* note 177.

201. *Id.*

202. Haynes v. Washington, 373 U.S. 503 (1963) (confession held involuntary when suspect was held incommunicado for sixteen hours, and police refused to allow him to talk to his wife unless he confessed).

203. *See* United States *ex rel.* Collins v. Maroney, 287 F. Supp. 420, 422 (E.D. Pa. 1968) (statement by narcotics addict in withdrawal held involuntary when given after promise of treatment by physician).

204. *Biron* Tapes, *supra* note 177.

205. *Id.* Remarks of this type may be improper because they tend to place the officer in a nonadversarial role, *see supra* text accompanying notes 172–88, or because they are implicit attacks on the suspect's dignity, *see infra* text accompanying notes 243–48.

206. 397 U.S. 742, 754 (1970).

207. 384 U.S. 436, 507 (1966) (Harlan, J., dissenting).

208. *Id.* at 507 & n.4 (quoting Bator & Vorenberg, *supra* note 34, at 73).

209. In *Bram*, the accused was told by a detective that another crewman had seen him commit the murder, 168 U.S. at 562, and that he should tell the detective if he had an accomplice in order to avoid "[having] the blame of this horrible crime on your own shoulders." *Id.* at 564. The Court interpreted the first of these statements as a threat, and the second as an offer of a benefit. *See* Dix, *supra* note 57, at 288–89.

It is not always impermissible for the government to offer a legal benefit in exchange for a decision not to exercise a constitutional right. For instance, the court's legitimization of plea bargaining allows this type of bargain to be struck when a defendant's right to trial is at issue. *See Brady*, 397 U.S. at 753–54. *See generally* Alschuler, *The Supreme Court, the Defense Attorney, and the Guilty Plea*, 47 U. COLO. L. REV. 1 (1975).

210. Promises made in the context of custodial interrogation are likely to prove illusory because an unaided suspect lacks the capacity to evaluate the actual value of any express or implied commitment made by the police. Thus, in *Brady* the Court distinguished plea bargaining from the *Bram* doctrine on the ground that in the former case, the defendant is represented by an attorney who can fully advise him of the value of any bargain offered. *See supra* note 196. It should be noted that based on this rationale, the *Bram* doctrine might not apply to a situation in which a suspect subjected to custodial interrogation is in fact represented by counsel.

211. This is especially true when, as is often the case, the implied promise of leniency is combined with police assurance that the suspect has little chance of escaping conviction if he goes to trial. For example, in the *Biron* case, the police repeatedly told the suspect not only that they knew he was guilty, *see infra* text accompanying notes 217 & 218, but also that he would be found guilty (because he would be unable to convince a judge and jury of his innocence!), and then suggested to him that he might be able to escape trial as an adult if he confessed.

See Biron Tapes, *supra* note 177. Confronted with this choice of alternatives, an innocent suspect might very reasonably decide that it would be in his best interest to confess.

212. *E.g.*, a promise that the suspect's bail will be set at a lower figure in the event he makes an incriminating statement. *See* United States v. Ferrara, 377 F.2d 16, 17 (2d Cir.), *cert. denied*, 389 U.S. 908 (1967) (distinguishing *Bram*, court held confession obtained after a promise of reduced bail voluntary under all the circumstances). Empirical evidence indicates that this type of inducement is offered to suspects quite frequently. *See Interrogations in New Haven, supra* note 198, at 1545.

213. 397 U.S. at 754.

214. *Id.*

215. 168 U.S. at 564.

216. *Cf.* Culombe v. Connecticut, 367 U.S. 568, 576 (1961) (plurality opinion of Frankfurter, J.): "However, a confession made by a person in custody is not always the result of an overborne will. The police may be midwife to a declaration naturally born of remorse, or relief, or desperation, or calculation."

217. *Biron* Tapes, *supra* note 177 (emphasis added).

218. *Id.*

219. F. INBAU & J. REID, *supra* note 2, at 26–31.

220. *Id.* at 28.

221. *Id.* at 29.

222. Driver, *Confessions and the Social Psychology of Coercion*, 82 HARV. L. REV. 42, 51–52 (1968).

223. *See id.* at 60.

224. The police manuals advise the interrogating officers to try to appear to the suspects as figures who command respect. *See, e.g.*, F. INBAU & J. REID, *supra* note 2, at 18.

225. *Id.* at 13–17.

226. *See* Driver, *supra* note 222, at 51–53. State v. Reilly, No. 5285 (Conn. Super. Ct. Apr. 12, 1974), *vacated*, 32 Conn. Supp. 349, 355 A.2d 324 (1976), provides a striking example of this phenomenon. After the police repeatedly told him they knew he did it, *see, e.g.*, J. BARTHEL, *supra* note 175, at 84, he at one point unequivocally adopted the details that they suggested to him. *Id.* at 124.

227. F. INBAU & J. REID, *supra* note 2, at 30.

228. 367 U.S. 568 (1961).

229. *Id.* at 631 (plurality opinion of Frankfurter, J.). The same factor was identified as potentially coercive in earlier cases. *See* Spano v. New York, 360 U.S. 315, 323–24 (1959); Malinski v. New York, 324 U.S. 401, 407 (1945).

230. F. INBAU & J. REID, *supra* note 2, at 62.

231. *Id.* at 63.

232. *Id.* at 62.

233. *See* C. O'HARA, *supra* note 197, at 104, *quoted in* Miranda, 384 U.S. at 452.

234. F. INBAU & J. REID, *supra* note 2, at 62.

235. *Id.*

236. *Id.* at 63.

237. 384 U.S. at 452.

238. *Id.* at 457.

239. Before describing the practice, the Court noted that it involves "a show of some hostility." *Id.* at 452.

240. Inbau and Reid take pains to note that "the second (unfriendly) interrogator should resort only to verbal condemnation of the subject; under no circumstances should he ever employ physical abuse or threats of abuse or other mistreatment." F. INBAU & J. REID, *supra* note 2, at 63. However, the authors' inclusion of this warning at this point is in itself significant—it reveals a recognition that when a police officer verbally abuses a suspect, there is a substantial danger that to the suspect the abuse may take on the attributes of a threat.

241. *Id.* at 63.

242. The *Reilly* case contains an example of the Mutt and Jeff routine with the chief interrogating officer acting out both roles. After Reilly stated that he was really not sure of the facts he was admitting, the interrogator, who was previously friendly and supportive, *see, e.g., supra* note 176, said to Reilly:

O.K. I don't want you to play any more headgames with us. And if you want to play this way, we'll take you and lock you up and treat you like an animal . . . . And I think it's about time that you sat up in that chair and you faced us like a man and you realize that trying to talk to two state policemen like they're two goddamn idiots, it's not gonna work.

J. BARTHEL, *supra* note 175, at 109.

243. *See* F. INBAU & J. REID, *supra* note 2, at 63.

244. *See* Driver, *supra* note 222, at 58.

245. *Id.* at 58–59.

246. *See supra* text accompanying notes 19–22.

247. *See Miranda*, 384 U.S. 436 at 457; Culombe v. Connecticut, 367 U.S. 568, 581–82 (1961) (plurality opinion of Frankfurter, J.). *See generally* L. LEVY, ORIGINS OF THE FIFTH AMENDMENT 431–32 (1968).

248. Malinski v. New York, 324 U.S. 401, 407 (1945).

249. The adoption of this approach will undoubtedly require procedural innovation to ensure its effective implementation. Most significantly, Professor Kamisar's suggestion of mandatory recording of police interrogations should be adopted. *See* Kamisar, *supra* note 111, at 236–43.

Waiver and the Death Penalty:
The Implications of *Estelle v. Smith*

Sometimes the most interesting aspects of a Supreme Court opinion lie beneath its surface. An unarticulated premise or language that is not fully developed may contain the seeds of a new principle that has the potential to germinate and later reshape constitutional doctrine. In recent years opinions dealing with procedural aspects of the death penalty have been among the most likely to contain such seeds.[1] The Court's decision in *Estelle v. Smith*[2] provides another example of this phenomenon.[3] Buried in the Court's opinion are two unarticulated principles that could have wide ramifications. Exploring these principles will be the primary focus of this essay.

Even on the surface, the decision in *Smith* is significant and surprising. Identifying trends in Supreme Court doctrine is always hazardous, but since the early seventies, the Burger Court has shown a strong distaste for the doctrine established by the Warren Court in its landmark decision of *Miranda v. Arizona*.[4] Beginning with *Harris v. New York*,[5] a case decided during Chief Justice Burger's first term on the Court, it adopted a posture that was unsympathetic to constitutional claims predicated upon application of the *Miranda* decision.[6] Language from *Miranda* was rejected as dicta[7] or was interpreted so as to result in a rejection of the particular *Miranda* claim before the Court.[8] Moreover, the Court not only refused to extend *Miranda* to new situations,[9] but strongly intimated that application of *Miranda* would be confined to the particular coercive environment involved in that case.[10]

During 1980, the Court decided two cases that to some degree ameliorated the concerns of those who favor prophylactic constitutional limitations on police tactics used to induce confessions. While rejecting a *Miranda* claim on its facts, *Rhode Island v. Innis*[11] to some extent resuscitated *Miranda* by defining *interrogation* within the meaning of *Miranda* in relatively broad terms.[12] Also, *United States v. Henry*[13] provided additional protection to arraigned or indicted defendants by adopting a surprisingly liberal interpretation of the Sixth Amendment right to counsel.[14] Nevertheless, with one relatively minor exception,[15] the Burger Court's record of refusing to hold "a single item of evidence inadmissible on authority of *Miranda*"[16] was still intact until *Smith* was decided on May 18, 1981.[17]

Against this backdrop, the Court's decision appears surprising. In *Smith* a majority of the Court went out of its way to decide a *Miranda* issue in favor of the defendant. Moreover, as an independent basis for decision, the Court unanimously concluded that the defendant's Sixth Amendment right to an attorney was violated. The Court's analysis of the *Miranda* issue in *Smith* constitutes an extension of *Miranda* and, apparently, a shift in the Burger Court's view of the underpinnings of that doctrine. While less clear, the Court's analysis of the Sixth Amendment issue is also doctrinally significant in that, at least in the context of the situation presented in *Smith*, it appears to redefine the nature of the Sixth Amendment right.

In dealing with the Fifth and Sixth Amendment issues, the Court placed relatively little emphasis on the fact that they arose in the context of a capital case. Nevertheless, examination of the majority's analysis suggests that its implications will have special significance for capital defendants. Specifically, the implications touch on the safeguards applicable when a capital defendant's waiver of constitutional rights is at issue. They suggest, first, that a valid waiver under *Miranda* cannot take place unless the capital defendant is informed that he is charged with an offense carrying a possible sentence of death, and, second, that at least in situations where a capital defendant's Fifth and Sixth Amendment rights are both applicable, consultation between the capital defendant and his attorney will be a prerequisite to a valid waiver of his Sixth Amendment right. In order to explore these implications of *Smith*, it is necessary to begin by explaining the circumstances presented in that case and then go on to consider the implications of the Court's two lines of constitutional analysis.

The Decision in *Smith v. Estelle*[18]

Defendant Ernest Smith was indicted in Texas for murder, arising from his participation in an armed robbery in which his accomplice shot and killed a grocery store clerk.[19] The state of Texas announced its intention to seek the death penalty.[20] Thereafter, the trial judge informally, and apparently without notice to the defense attorney,[21] ordered the prosecuting attorney to arrange a psychiatric examination of Smith by Dr. James P. Grigson in order to determine his competency to stand trial.[22] After interviewing Smith in jail for approximately ninety minutes, Dr. Grigson filed a report with the court in which he expressed the opinion that Smith was competent to stand trial.[23]

Since Smith was being tried as a capital defendant, Texas law required that his case be tried in a bifurcated proceeding that includes a guilt phase and a penalty phase. If the jury finds the defendant guilty of a capital offense,[24] a separate sentencing proceeding is conducted before the same jury. At the penalty phase, if the jury affirmatively answers three questions relating to issues on which the state has the burden of proof beyond a reasonable doubt, the judge must impose the death penalty.[25] One of the three critical questions the jury must determine is "whether there is a probability that the defendant would commit criminal acts of violence that would constitute a continuing threat to society."[26]

Smith was convicted of murder, a capital offense.[27] At the beginning of the sentencing hearing, the state rested, subject to the right to reopen. The defense then called three lay witnesses: two relatives who testified to Smith's good reputation and character, and the owner of a gun he possessed during the robbery, who testified to Smith's knowledge that the gun would not fire because of a mechanical defect.[28] The state then called Dr. Grigson as a rebuttal witness.

Prior to trial, Smith's counsel had obtained an order requiring the state to disclose the witnesses it planned to use both at the guilt stage and, if known, at the penalty phase.[29] Subsequently, the trial court granted a defense motion to bar the testimony, during the state's case-in-chief, of any witness whose name did not appear on that list.[30] Dr. Grigson's name was never placed on the witness list.[31] Despite defense counsels' objection that defendant had not received notice of the possibility of Dr. Grigson's testimony, the judge permitted the psychiatrist to present expert testimony on the issue of Smith's future dangerousness.[32]

Dr. Grigson's testimony on this issue was striking and devastating. On the basis of his ninety-minute examination, he offered a positive expert opinion that Smith was "a very severe sociopath," that "he [was] going to go ahead and commit other similar or same criminal acts if given the opportunity to do so," that there is no treatment or medicine that "in any way at all modifies or changes this behavior," and that his sociopathic condition "will only get worse."[33] Cross-examination of Dr. Grigson was not beneficial to the defendant; on the contrary, in the course of supporting his conclusion that Smith had "no remorse or sorrow for what he has done," Dr. Grigson was able to testify to and place his own interpretation on a particularly incriminating statement allegedly made by Smith during the course of the psychiatric interview.[34]

The jury answered the three questions submitted to them in the affirmative, and, as required by law, the judge imposed the death penalty. In the Texas courts, the only challenge to Dr. Grigson's testimony was that his name had not been listed as a witness in compliance with the defendant's motion that the state list all of the witnesses to be used in its case-in-chief. The Texas Supreme Court ruled that there was no violation because Dr. Grigson testified as a rebuttal witness at the penalty trial and thus did not come within the terms of defendant's motion.[35] The death penalty imposed by the lower court was affirmed.[36]

Defendant raised several additional challenges to Dr. Grigson's testimony in its motion for a writ of habeas corpus.[37] After full consideration of the state court record, the federal district court held that the use of Dr. Grigson's testimony without proper notice to defense counsel violated Smith's Sixth and Fourteenth Amendment rights to the effective assistance of counsel as well as his Eighth Amendment right to present mitigating evidence at the penalty trial,[38] and that the procurement of Dr. Grigson's testimony (through the psychiatric examination) was in violation of Smith's Fifth Amendment privilege against self-incrimination.[39] In affirming the issuance of the writ, the Fifth Circuit agreed that both the use and the procurement of Dr. Grigson's testimony was unconstitutional.[40] The court found that the state's failure to provide adequate notice to the defense of Dr. Grigson's testimony was in violation of the disclosure principles suggested by the Supreme Court in *Gardner v. Florida*,[41] a case that was predicated on interpretations of both the due process clause and the Eighth Amendment cruel and unusual punishment clause.[42] With respect to the procurement of Dr. Grigson's testimony, the Fifth Circuit went further than the district court, holding that under the circumstances the introduction of Dr. Grigson's testimony at the penalty trial was in violation of both Smith's Fifth Amendment privilege against self-incrimination[43] and his Sixth Amendment right to an attorney.[44]

In an opinion authored by Chief Justice Burger, the Supreme Court affirmed[45] the appellate decision. However, despite the lower court's extensive consideration of a narrower ground for decision,[46] the Court addressed the Fifth Amendment claim on the merits and resolved it in the defendant's favor, holding that under the circumstances involved in *Smith*, the defendant was entitled to *Miranda* warnings prior to the psychiatric examination.[47] In addition, as an independent ground of decision, the six-member majority also decided the Sixth Amendment issue in the defendant's favor.[48] In two separate opinions, the three remaining justices concurred on Sixth Amendment grounds without reaching the Fifth Amendment issue.[49]

Implications of the Court's Fifth Amendment–*Miranda* Analysis

The majority began their analysis of the Fifth Amendment issue by focusing on whether the Fifth Amendment privilege is applicable in the context presented in *Smith*. The state argued that the privilege was inapplicable for two reasons: first, it should not apply when the evidence in question is being used only to determine punishment after conviction and not to establish guilt;[50] and second, it should not apply to the psychiatric evidence presented in *Smith* because the defendant's communications to Dr. Grigson were nontestimonial.[51]

In rejecting the state's first argument, the Court did not state that the Fifth Amendment privilege will apply to all statements obtained from a defendant for the purpose of determining his penalty.[52] Instead, the majority focused on the fact that the particular penalty involved in *Smith* was the "ultimate penalty of death."[53] Drawing on other decisions imposing strict procedural protections where the death penalty is at issue,[54] the Court stated that in view of "the gravity of the decision to be made at the penalty phase, the State is not relieved of the obligation to observe fundamental constitutional guarantees."[55] Thus, the Court's holding that the Fifth Amendment privilege was applicable at the penalty stage of the proceedings appears to be predicated on the fact that the death penalty is at issue in those proceedings. This analysis suggests not only that the death penalty is of a different magnitude than other punishments, but also that one should view the death penalty determination as a separate stage of the adversary process—one in which the issue at stake is quite distinct from that involved in the guilt phase of the trial.[56]

The majority also rejected the state's claim that statements made by Smith to Dr. Grigson during the psychiatric interview were nontestimonial.[57] The Chief Justice found that the issue in *Smith* was not analogous to that in cases involving voice exemplars,[58] handwriting exemplars,[59] lineups,[60] or blood samples[61] because Dr. Grigson's diagnosis was not based simply on his observations of Smith, but rather was premised in large part on "statements [Smith] made, and remarks he omitted,"[62] during the course of the psychiatric interview. Thus, the Court found the Fifth Amendment privilege to be applicable "because the State used as evidence against [Smith] the substance of his disclosures during the pretrial psychiatric examination."[63]

Having determined that the Fifth Amendment applied, the Court went on to conclude that the defendant was entitled to *Miranda* warnings prior to the psychiatric examination. In view of its prior holdings, the Court's analysis was striking.

Given the Court's recent treatment of *Miranda*, there would appear to be strong arguments against applying it to a psychiatric interview, especially one conducted for the purpose of determining competency to stand trial. The underlying premise of the *Miranda* decision was that because of the atmosphere at a police station and the tactics employed by police interrogators there, police interrogation of an individual in custody is inherently coercive.[64] Based on that premise, the Court concluded that warnings to the individual are necessary to ensure that statements obtained from him are a product of his free choice,[65] or, in other words, are not compelled from him in violation of the Fifth Amendment privilege. Thus, in order to apply *Miranda* to the present situation it would appear to be necessary to show that the coercive atmosphere present in a psychiatric examination of a defendant in custody is the same as or similar to the inherently coercive atmosphere that *Miranda* found to be present in a custodial police interrogation.

On the basis of empirical evidence, one can certainly argue that psychiatric interviews are sufficiently analogous to police interrogations to be considered inherently coercive within the meaning of *Miranda*.[66] However, as noted previously,[67] prior to the *Smith* case, the Burger Court had evidenced an extreme reluctance to apply *Miranda* to new situations. For example, in *United States v. Mandujano*[68] four members of the Court in a plurality opinion by Chief Justice Burger maintained that a "putative" defendant appearing before the grand jury was not entitled to *Miranda* warnings.[69] In distinguishing this situation from the custodial police interrogation at issue in *Miranda*, the plurality read *Miranda* as focusing on a particular type of coercive setting, one which "was seen by the Court as police 'coercion' derived from 'factual studies [relating to] police violence and the 'third degree' . . . physical brutality—beating, hanging, whipping—and to sustained and protracted questioning incommunicado in order to extort confessions.' "[70] Because the environment confronting a grand jury witness is obviously different, the plurality refused to extend *Miranda* to this situation.[71]

On other occasions, the Court as a whole has evidenced a similar disposition to confine *Miranda* to the type of custodial interrogation that was particularly involved in the situations before the Court in that case.[72] The Court's per curiam decision in *Oregon v. Mathiason*[73] is particularly noteworthy.[74] In *Mathiason* the defendant was on parole when he was contacted by a police officer investigating a burglary. In response to a note left at his apartment by the officer, defendant phoned the officer and agreed to meet with him later that afternoon at the State Patrol Office.[75] The officer met defendant in the hallway, took him into his office and closed the door. Without advising him of his *Miranda* rights, the officer told the defendant that the police believed he was involved in the burglary, and falsely stated that his fingerprints had been found at the scene.[76] After some further discussion, defendant confessed.[77] The Oregon Supreme Court held that *Miranda* warnings were required because the "interrogation took place in a 'coercive environment'."[78] The Supreme Court, however, reversed. Based on the particular facts involved,[79] the per curiam majority held that at the time of his confession, defendant was not "in custody 'or otherwise deprived of his freedom of action in any significant way.' "[80] Having found that *Miranda* was not directly applicable, the Court was emphatic in refusing to consider the possibility of extending *Miranda* to an analogous form of coercive environment.[81] After reiterating that *Miranda* was concerned with custodial interrogation, the Court declared that "[i]t was *that* sort of coercive environment to which *Miranda* by its terms was made applicable, and to which it is limited."[82]

Based on these authorities, it would appear that before the Court would apply *Miranda* to the psychiatric examination involved in *Smith* it would have to conclude that the potential for coercion in that setting is equivalent to (or, perhaps, exactly the same as) that involved when a defendant in custody is subjected to interrogation by the police. However, the Court never specifically addressed this issue.[83] Instead, it summarily concluded that "[t]he considerations calling for the accused to be warned prior to custodial interrogation apply with no less force to the pretrial psychiatric examination at issue here."[84] In equating the psychiatric examination with custodial police interrogation, the Court did not focus on the potentially coercive atmosphere involved, but rather on the defendant's lack of awareness of the incriminatory dangers:

During the psychiatric evaluation, [defendant] assuredly was "faced with a phase of the adversary system" and was "not in the presence of [a] person acting solely in his interest." . . . Yet he was given no indication that the compulsory examination would be used to gather evidence necessary to decide whether, if convicted, he should be sentenced to death. He was not informed that, accordingly, he had a constitutional right not to answer the questions put to him.[85]

Thus, in the custodial setting,[86] the government psychiatrist's failure to inform the defendant about the stakes involved in the interview was enough to constitute a violation of *Miranda*.

The shift from evaluating the coercive potential of the particular context in which the defendant is questioned to focusing on the defendant's awareness of the incriminatory potential of his responses obviously will reach beyond the context of the *Smith* case. The Court unambiguously spelled out one potential effect of the decision when it stated: "That [defendant] was questioned by a psychiatrist designated by the trial court to conduct a neutral competency examination, rather than by a police officer, government informant, prosecuting attorney is immaterial."[87] This statement, which is entirely consistent with the rest of the Court's analysis, seems to indicate that *Miranda*'s requirements will apply when any agent of the government seeks to question a defendant in custody. If this reading of *Smith* is correct, one important practical consequence is that the government will be effectively barred from using undercover agents to obtain incriminating statements from defendants who are arrested and in custody but not yet arraigned.[88] As Professor Kamisar has vividly demonstrated,[89] there is a strong argument against concluding that questioning of a defendant by a "jail plant" government agent is inherently coercive within the meaning of *Miranda*.[90] Nevertheless, based on *Smith*'s analysis, a government jail plant who was seeking to obtain incriminating information from a defendant in custody but not yet arraigned[91] would be required to give the defendant some form of meaningful *Miranda* warnings[92] before he would be allowed to ask him questions about his offense or engage in any speech or conduct that would constitute "interrogation" within the meaning of *Rhode Island v. Innis*.[93]

In line with the shift toward making sure that the defendant is aware that he is being confronted with a phase of the adversary process, the Court's discussion of the actual warnings required is extremely interesting. Although the majority clearly held that Dr. Grigson was required to warn defendant in order to render the results of the psychiatric exam admissible in the penalty proceeding, it did not specify the precise nature of the warnings required. Significantly, the Court never stated that merely giving the defendant the warnings required by *Miranda* would suffice. On the contrary, in its apparent articulation of a holding on the Fifth Amendment issue, the Court implied that the familiar warnings would not be enough: "Because [defendant] did not voluntarily consent to the pretrial psychiatric examination after being informed of his right to remain silent and *the possible use of his statements*, the State could not rely on what he said to Dr. Grigson to establish his future dangerousness."[94] What warning would be sufficient to alert the defendant as to "the possible use his statements?" Earlier in its opinion, the Court appeared to speak directly to this issue when it stated that the defendant "was given no indication that the compulsory examination would be used to gather evidence necessary to decide whether, if convicted, he should be sentenced to death."[95] This certainly implies that, at least in the context of a case like *Smith*, a simple warning to the defendant that "anything you say can be used against you" would be insufficient. Instead, the defendant would have to be specifically warned that if he were convicted of a capital offense, the jury in a penalty proceeding could use statements made by him in the psychiatric examination to decide whether to sentence him to death.

Of course, the implications of this aspect of the *Smith* opinion are not clear. The reference to a death penalty warning requirement is not essential to the Court's holding.[96] In the context of Smith, one could read Chief Justice Burger's reference to the warning as simply identifying one means by which the defendant could be enlightened as to the possible use that might be made of his disclosures to the psychiatrist.[97]

Under this narrow reading of the majority's language, a death penalty warning would not be required so long as the defendant was otherwise alerted as to the incriminatory potential of his disclosures to the government agent.[98] Thus, in cases where the defendant had notice that the psychiatrist or other government agent would possibly testify for the government at the penalty phase of the proceedings, no specific warning that statements made by the defendant could be used to decide "whether, if convicted, he should be sentenced to death," would be required. And in cases where the psychiatrist or other government agent was merely going to testify against the defendant at his capital trial, no death penalty warning of any kind would be mandated.

This narrow interpretation of *Smith*, however, runs against two central threads of the Court's analysis. As has already been noted,[99] *Smith* effected an important change in the *Miranda* doctrine in that it shifted the focus away from the question whether the particular environment confronting the defendant was inherently coercive and toward the issue whether the defendant was made adequately aware of the adversary interests at stake. In addition, *Smith* was consistent with the Court's other recent death penalty decisions in that it emphasized the unique character of the punishment of death. The Court made it clear that the adversary consequences involved at the penalty phase are not only of a greater magnitude than those involved in any noncapital sentencing determination, but are also distinct from the adversary consequences involved at the guilt phase of the trial.[100]

Both of these principles bear upon the doctrine of waiver. In *Miranda* itself the Court stated that in order to establish a valid waiver the government must satisfy the heavy burden of demonstrating that "the defendant knowingly and intelligently waived his privilege against self-incrimination."[101] Subsequent decisions, especially the Court's analysis in *United States v. Washington*,[102] suggested that the Court might no longer be willing to apply this strict doctrine of waiver in the *Miranda* context.[103] *Smith*'s shift in focus revitalizes the doctrine, however, by making it clear that at least in certain contexts, a warning that enlightens the defendant as to the nature of the adversary interests at stake will be indispensable to a valid waiver of *Miranda* rights.

Of course, one need not read *Smith* as holding that such a warning is indispensable to a valid waiver under *Miranda* in all cases.[104] The Court's emphasis on the unique nature of the adversary interests involved at the death penalty hearing[105] does suggest, however, that a differentiation must be made between a defendant's knowledge that the prosecution may use his statement against him to secure the death penalty and his knowledge that the prosecution may use it against him for any other purposes. If the defendant's statement is to be used against him in the penalty phase of a capital trial, then knowledge that the statement may be used for this purpose should be essential to a valid waiver under *Miranda*. A capital defendant who lacks such knowledge will not be aware of the true nature of the adversary interests involved.

This analysis does not in itself prove that a capital defendant should necessarily be entitled to a death penalty warning. Assuming that a capital defendant's awareness of the nature of the adversary interests at stake is indispensable to a valid waiver, it does not follow that the defendant must be specifically informed as to the nature of those interests. An alternative approach would be to require that the defendant's awareness of the nature of the adversary interests at stake be litigated on a case-by-case basis. On this point, *Smith*'s reference to the fact that the defendant was not given a death penalty warning is perhaps significant.[106] Since the court could have simply stated that there was no basis for concluding that the defendant in *Smith* would be aware that his statement might be used against him at his penalty trial, the majority's choice of language suggests that in this particular context, it may be inclined to eschew a case-by-case approach, opting instead for the imposition of a warning requirement.

If one can properly read *Smith*'s language in this way, the Court's judgment seems wise. Litigating a defendant's knowledge is difficult in any situation. In the present context, it would appear to be particularly unproductive because in most cases the only evidence that would likely bear significantly on the relevant issue would be the circumstances surrounding the defendant's arrest, including anything the officers might have said to him at that time. But unless the defendant was alerted in some way to the fact that he was charged with a capital offense, it is unlikely that his knowledge about the potential use of his statement could be inferred from the circumstances of his arrest. Given the complexity of capital punishment legislation[107] as well as the rarity with which the death penalty is actually imposed,[108] it is not appropriate to conclude that defendants charged with capital offenses are cognizant of the possibility of a death sentence when they are not so informed by the government.[109] Therefore, one should not dismiss *Smith*'s reference to a death penalty warning requirement as surplusage. At least when the government seeks to obtain statements from a custodial defendant for use in penalty proceedings at which the imposition of the death penalty will be a possibility, requiring such a warning as a prerequisite to the statement's admissibility is entirely consistent with the premises that undergird *Smith*'s analysis.

The case in which the government agent is seeking to obtain a defendant's statement for use in the guilt stage of a capital trial is somewhat more problematic. One might argue that the defendant's statement is being introduced merely to establish guilt, and, therefore, even if a special death penalty warning is applicable in cases where a defendant's statement is going to be used against him at the penalty stage, it is not applicable in this situation. However, this argument is too formalistic; it does not take into account the underlying purpose of the death penalty warning. The additional warning is needed when the defendant must be made aware of the true character of the adversary interests at stake—that is, when he must be informed that he is confronted with not merely a stage of the adversary process, but a stage at which his words could lead to his own execution.[110] The defendant's need for this information is equally present whether his statement is to be introduced against him at the guilt or penalty phase of a capital trial. In both cases, his words may lead to his execution. Indeed, if the prosecution introduces the defendant's statement at the guilt phase and the jury convicts the defendant of a capital offense, the jury will in fact consider the defendant's statement at the penalty phase. The same jury deliberates at both the guilt and penalty phase, and in deciding the penalty issue it will inevitably and quite properly consider any of the evidence admitted at the guilt stage that bears upon the relevant issues at stake in the penalty stage.

Moreover, with respect to securing a capital defendant's constitutional protections, the Court has already virtually obliterated any distinction between the guilt and penalty phase of a capital trial. In reiterating that stricter procedural requirements must be met in capital trials than in ordinary cases, the Court in *Beck v. Alabama*[111] unambiguously stated[112] and implicitly held that the same high standard of scrutiny applies whether the procedure involved relates to the guilt or penalty determination.[113] It should follow that if a capital defendant is entitled to the special protection afforded by a warning relating to the potential use of his incriminating statements at the penalty phase of his capital trial, the same protection should be provided to a capital defendant who is confronted with the possibility of being incriminated by his own statements at the guilt phase of the trial. Therefore, at least in cases in which the death penalty is actually imposed, the death penalty warning requirement should apply to statements that are obtained for use against defendants at the guilt stage of their capital trials.[114]

Smith's Sixth Amendment Implications

The Court also concluded, as an independent basis for its decision, that the defendant's Sixth Amendment right to counsel was violated. The Court's brief discussion of the Sixth Amendment issue was cryptic but potentially significant.

In placing its decision on Sixth Amendment grounds, the Court reaffirmed the principle that the defendant's Sixth Amendment right to an attorney provides the defendant with different and broader protection than *Miranda*'s guarantee of a right to have counsel present at a government interrogation.[115] The Court indicated that the defendant's Sixth Amendment right was applicable in *Smith* because adversary proceedings against the defendant had commenced[116] and because Dr. Grigson's examination of the defendant "proved to be" a critical stage of the proceedings.[117] The majority then proceeded to explain why defendant's Sixth Amendment right was violated.

> Defense counsel, however, were not notified in advance that the psychiatric examination would encompass the issue of their client's future dangerousness, and [defendant] was denied the assistance of his attorneys in making the significant decision of whether to submit to the examination and to what end the psychiatrist's findings could be employed.[118]

This language appears to alter the scope of the Sixth Amendment right in two respects. First, it redefines the nature of the right to an attorney. For at least the past decade, the Sixth Amendment right to an attorney at pretrial proceedings was generally taken to mean the right to have an attorney present at those proceedings.[119] The Sixth Amendment right recognized in *Smith*, however, was the defendant's right to the assistance of an attorney in making the decision whether to submit to the pretrial proceedings—in that case, a psychiatric exam.[120] Because the Court emphasized that the defendant needed the attorney's advice in order to decide whether to invoke his Fifth Amendment privilege,[121] it is logical to interpret *Smith* as providing defendants with the right to counsel's assistance in decision making whenever the Sixth Amendment right applies in a context where the defendant's invocation of the Fifth Amendment privilege is potentially applicable. This reading of *Smith* will clarify the meaning of the Sixth Amendment right in cases where the government seeks to elicit incriminating statements from defendants by using undercover informers.[122] In these cases the government will not satisfy the defendant's Sixth Amendment right by somehow arranging to have the defendant's attorney present at the time the surreptitious attempt to elicit disclosures takes place.[123] Rather, the defendant's Sixth Amendment right will entitle him to an attorney's advice as to whether he should submit to the government attempt to elicit information. By putting the Sixth Amendment right on this basis, the Court ensures the defendant's awareness of the government's efforts to obtain information and thereby eliminates the possibility that the government through deception may negate the effect of the Sixth Amendment right.

Second, the Court's approach appears to modify the doctrine of

Sixth Amendment waiver. Although the Court noted that it was not holding that the defendant was precluded from waiving his Sixth Amendment right,[124] its emphasis on counsel's right to advance notification[125] seems to mean that, at least in the situation involved in *Smith*, the government could not circumvent the defendant's Sixth Amendment protection by merely informing the defendant of his right to an attorney and obtaining a personal waiver of that right from him; instead, it appears that some consultation between the defendant and his attorney would ordinarily be indispensable to a valid waiver of the Sixth Amendment right.[126]

If this reading of *Smith* is correct, then there is some need to reconcile this aspect of *Smith* with the Court's analysis in *Brewer v. Williams*.[127] In *Williams* the Court dealt with a situation in which the police obtained incriminating disclosures from a defendant after he had been arraigned and was represented by counsel. The Court held that the use of the defendant's incriminating disclosures at trial was in violation of the defendant's Sixth Amendment right to an attorney.[128] However, the Court emphasized that it was not holding that the defendant "*could not*, without notice to counsel, have waived his rights under the Sixth and Fourteenth Amendments"[129] but only that no such waiver took place under the actual facts of *Williams*.[130] Significantly, the four dissenting justices found that the defendant did in fact waive his Sixth Amendment right;[131] and in a concurring opinion, a fifth justice read the Court as explicitly holding that the defendant's Sixth Amendment right "may be waived, after it has attached, without notice to or consultation with counsel."[132]

Several possible approaches could be taken in reconciling the conflicting principles expounded by the Court in *Williams* and *Smith*. The broadest approach would be to read *Smith*'s doctrine of Sixth Amendment waiver as replacing the *Williams* analysis. A broad reading of *Smith* would appear consistent with the ethical precept, implicitly articulated by the Court in *United States v. Henry*, that the government should not seek to communicate with a defendant represented by an attorney in the absence of the attorney's consent.[133] Nevertheless, to disregard *Williams*'s explicit discussion of the requirements of a Sixth Amendment waiver might be somewhat incautious, especially in view of the vehemence with which the waiver issue was discussed by the various opinions in that case.

A more limited approach is to distinguish the situations in *Smith* and *Williams* on the basis of the particular facts involved in each case. Among the various distinctions one could draw, three seem potentially relevant. First, at the time the government sought to obtain the information from the defendant, the defendant's attorney was accessible to the government in *Smith* but not in *Williams*;[134] second, *Smith* involved a psychiatric examination, whereas *Williams* involved police interrogation;[135] and third, *Smith*, but not *Williams*,[136] was a capital case in which the evidence obtained by the government was used to lead to a sentence of death.

The difference of attorney accessibility in *Smith* and *Williams* could lead to a rule that takes into account whether it is feasible for the government to arrange for attorney-client consultation immediately prior to the time when it seeks to obtain incriminating disclosures. Thus, one could read *Smith* as requiring notice to the attorney as a prerequisite to waiver only in cases where such notice is feasible. *Williams*, then, would mean that when notice to the attorney is not feasible, the defendant could waiver his Sixth Amendment right on his own without first consulting with his attorney.

There are two difficulties with this rule. First, the defendant's access to his attorney is a matter that will inevitably be subject to governmental manipulation. Since the government has total discretion as to when it will seek to elicit disclosures from the defendant, it can elect to make such an attempt at a time when the defendant's attorney will not be physically accessible.[137] Moreover, the issue of access or feasibility really seems to bear little relationship to the question of waiver.[138] If the defendant's constitutional right is of such a nature that consultation with an attorney is indispensable to a valid waiver, this rule should apply regardless of whether it is feasible for the government to arrange for consultation between the defendant and his attorney at the particular time in question.

The rule of Sixth Amendment waiver suggested in *Smith* could be limited to cases in which the government is seeking to conduct a psychiatric examination. The justification for drawing the line at this point would be that the decision whether the defendant should submit to a psychiatric examination is one that is "difficult . . . even for an attorney" in that it involves considerations of trial strategy as well as an evaluation of the propensities of the particular psychiatrist involved.[139] Because the decision involved is so complex and so clearly beyond the understanding of ordinary defendants, there might be grounds for saying that most defendants would need to consult with an attorney before they could appreciate the value of receiving an attorney's advice on this decision.

However, there are also problems with this analysis. First, the Court has never held that a defendant's appreciation of the value of receiving an attorney's advice is essential to a valid Sixth Amendment waiver.[140] Moreover, if this approach were adopted, there is really no basis for concluding that defendants would be less likely to understand the value of receiving an attorney's advice about whether they should consent to a psychiatric exam than they would the value of receiving an attorney's advice about whether they should agree to participate in a more traditional form of government interrogation. A defendant's lack of familiarity with the psychiatric exam would likely heighten his caution, thus reducing the probability that he would willingly rely on his own judgment. On the other hand, there is a greater possibility that a defendant's familiarity with traditional police questioning would lead him to underestimate the value of receiving an attorney's advice before making his own decision whether to waive his constitutional rights. Thus, in this latter situation, there is at least an equal risk that a defendant would fail to appreciate the value of consulting with an attorney before making a decision whether to waive his Fifth and Sixth Amendment rights.

The final approach to distinguishing the cases is to hold that the rule suggested in *Smith* will apply only in capital cases.[141] The primary rationale for adopting this distinction would be that in capital cases the courts must tighten the safeguards relating to waiver because the potential application of the death penalty is itself a factor that will distort the defendant's decision-making process.[142]

The Court has implicitly recognized this principle in other contexts. In *Fay v. Noia*[143] one of the issues before the Court was whether the defendant had made an intelligent waiver of his right to appeal his state conviction for murder.[144] The defendant had been convicted of first-degree murder and sentenced to life imprisonment.[145] He failed to appeal his state court conviction. At his habeas corpus hearing, it was established that he was aware of his right to appeal.[146] However, his attorney testified that an important consideration in the defendant's decision not to exercise his right of appeal was his "fear that if successful he might get the death sentence if convicted on a retrial."[147] The Court found that under these circumstances the validity of the defendant's waiver was vitiated by the fact that he was confronted with "the grisly choice whether to sit content with life imprisonment or to travel the uncertain avenue of appeal which, if successful, might well have led to a retrial and death sentence."[148] The Court declined to hold that the injection of the death penalty into the decision-making process would negate the possibility of waiver in all circumstances.[149] Nevertheless, the Court's analysis makes it clear that whenever the possibility of the death penalty is a factor that may distort the defendant's decision-making process, stricter standards of waiver are appropriate.[150]

If the interjection of the death penalty would tend to impair rational decision making in the context involved in *Noia*, it would be even more likely to do so at the pretrial stage when the defendant is likely to lack orientation as to the operation of the system and certainly has not yet had an opportunity to assess the considerations relevant to a waiver of his constitutional rights. As in *Noia*, a defendant's fear of the death penalty might cause him to waive his constitutional rights without rationally weighing the risks involved.[151] On the other hand, a defendant with ambivalent feelings toward the death penalty would be equally ill equipped to make a rational judgment about whether he should waive his constitutional rights.[152] In view of these concerns, it is only a modest step to hold, as *Smith* suggests, that a capital defendant who is represented by an attorney can not waive his Sixth Amendment right at a pretrial stage unless he first consults with his attorney.

Indeed, based on preexisting Sixth Amendment doctrine, it would appear that the rule suggested by *Smith* should be pushed at least one step further. If the basis for the rule is that the death penalty vitiates the defendant's ability to make an uncounselled choice about whether to assert his Sixth Amendment right, then the rule should not be limited to cases in which the defendant is actually represented by counsel. The defendant's need for consultation is certainly the same regardless of whether he happens to be represented by counsel. Accordingly, the rule should apply to all cases in which a capital defendant's Sixth Amendment right is in effect.

In *Henry v. United States*[153] the Court held that an indicted defendant's Sixth Amendment right was in effect at a time when he was not yet represented by counsel.[154] *Henry*'s holding combined with the *Brewer v. Williams* dicta[155] appears to establish that the Sixth Amendment right attaches at least at the point of arraignment, whether or not the defendant is in fact represented by counsel.[156] Therefore, *Smith*'s suggested rule should mean at least that with respect to pretrial proceedings at which a Fifth Amendment privilege against self-incrimination is applicable, the capital defendant who has been arraigned can not waive his Sixth Amendment right to an attorney unless he is first permitted to consult with an attorney.

Conclusion

Although *Smith* appears to address the constitutional issues without giving significant weight to the fact that they are presented in the context of a capital case,[157] the case is best understood as the Court's latest attempt to ensure procedural fairness for capital defendants. Viewed in this framework, *Smith*'s result is not surprising. Nevertheless, the Court decided the case on remarkably broad grounds. Instead of focusing on the lack of reliability of procedures unique to *Smith*,[158] the Court developed new protections for capital defendants by reaching out to decide the case on Fifth and Sixth Amendment grounds.

When *Smith* is perceived as extending the procedural protections afforded capital defendants, the interplay between the Court's Fifth and Sixth Amendment holdings becomes particularly interesting. The Court's Fifth Amendment analysis suggests that if the prosecution plans to introduce a defendant's statements against him in any case that in fact results in the imposition of the death penalty, a specific warning of this possible consequence will be a prerequisite to a valid waiver of his *Miranda* rights. On the other hand, under the best reading of the majority's Sixth Amendment analysis, once that same defendant's Sixth Amendment right to counsel attaches, he cannot waive it without first consulting with an attorney. Thus, while the majority's Fifth Amendment analysis intimates that a defendant's knowledge that the prosecution may use his statement to obtain a death sentence will be indispensable to a knowing waiver of his Fifth Amendment privilege, the Court's Sixth Amendment analysis implies that this same knowledge will be likely to distort the defendant's decision-making ability. Under such circumstances the defendant must consult with an attorney before he can intelligently evaluate his need for the assistance of counsel in deciding whether to assert his Fifth Amendment privilege.

A possible explanation for the difference between the two rules is that the Court is applying a stricter standard of waiver when the defendant's Sixth Amendment right, rather than his *Miranda* right, is at issue.[159] The Court's decisions holding that the former guarantee provides broader protection than the latter would provide some support for adopting a dual standard.[160] Nevertheless, it seems inappropriate to allow this kind of distinction to control. In the present context, the critical focus should be on the impact the death penalty will have on a capital defendant's decision-making capacity. If knowledge that the death penalty is a possible consequence distorts the rationality of a defendant's decision making, the same distortion will occur whether the decision making takes place prior to the time when the Sixth Amendment right attaches or afterwards.[161] Indeed, when the police give *Miranda* warnings (including the death penalty warning) to an unrepresented defendant who has not yet been arraigned, the distorting effect of the death penalty is likely to be at its peak. Therefore, it seems anomalous to hold that this defendant can personally waive his Fifth Amendment privilege, but a similar defendant who has been arraigned will have to consult with an attorney before he will be in a position to make the same decision.

To remove this anomaly, it is not necessary for the Court to discard its two-track system under which the Sixth Amendment right to an attorney affords a defendant broader protection than *Miranda*. Rather, it merely needs to focus explicitly on defining the standards of waiver courts are to apply in capital cases. On this point, the *Smith* opinion appears to have two important insights: (1) a defendant's knowledge that the death penalty is a possible consequence of his decision to disclose information is indispensable to a valid waiver of *Miranda* rights; and (2) defendants who know they are facing a possible death penalty are ill equipped to make an unaided pretrial decision that may determine whether they shall live or die. *Smith* strongly suggests that the first insight will be translated into a constitutional rule that will require that capital defendants be given a death penalty warning before they are allowed to waive their *Miranda* rights. To translate *Smith*'s second insight into an appropriate constitutional rule, it would be desirable to hold that capital defendants must be afforded an opportunity to consult with an attorney before they will be allowed to waive their Fifth Amendment privilege. By placing the rule of waiver on this basis rather than keying it to the attachment of the defendant's Sixth Amendment right, the Court would focus directly on the relevant issue—that is, ensuring that the defendant's decision making is rational. This approach will more nearly fulfill the Court's articulated objective of establishing procedures that appear to and in fact do afford fairness and rationality to capital defendants.[162]

NOTES

I wish to thank Yale Kamisar of the University of Michigan Law School and my colleague Tom Gerety for their helpful comments on an earlier draft of this article, and Linda Tobin for her valuable research assistance.

1. One explanation for this may be that in deciding such cases the Court will necessarily be torn between a desire for establishing a procedural rule that will have due regard for the interests of law enforcement and a concern for providing procedural fairness for capital defendants. Unless the Court chooses to establish special procedural protections for capital defendants, Beck v. Alabama, 447 U.S. 625 (1980), the attempt to resolve this conflict is likely to create a degree of ambivalence in the Court's analysis.

2. 451 U.S. 454 (1981).

3. For other examples, *see, e.g.*, Lockett v. Ohio, 438 U.S. 586 (1978); Witherspoon v. Illinois, 391 U.S. 510 (1968). For a comment on the seeds contained in *Lockett, see* Hertz & Weisberg, *In Mitigation of the Penalty of Death: Lockett v. Ohio and the Capital Defendant's Right to Consideration of Mitigating Circumstances*, 69 CAL. L. REV. 317 (1981). For an extensive discussion of the

hidden implications of *Witherspoon, see* Gillers, *Deciding Who Dies*, 129 U. PA. L. REV. 1 (1980).

4. 384 U.S. 436 (1966).

5. 401 U.S. 222 (1971). For an incisive analysis of the Court's decision in *Harris, see* Dershowitz & Ely, *Harris v. New York: Some Anxious Observations on the Candor and Logic of the Emerging Nixon Majority*, 80 YALE L.J. 1198 (1971).

6. This trend was identified by commentators. In 1977, Professor Stone's incisive analysis of twelve of the Burger Court's post-*Miranda* decisions led him to conclude that the court was embarked on a gradual dismantling of *Miranda. See* Stone, *The Miranda Doctrine in the Burger Court*, 1977 SUP. CT. REV. 99, 169. In 1978, Professor Kamisar, in his classic analysis of the Court's decision in Brewer v. Williams, 430 U.S. 387 (1977), foresaw even more portentous signs for supporters of *Miranda*. Based on his analysis of the various opinions in Brewer, Professor Kamisar suggested that the Court might be prepared to jettison *Miranda* and replace it with a modified version of the Sixth Amendment rule established by the Warren Court in its 1964 decision of Massiah v. United States, 377 U.S. 201 (1964). Kamisar, Brewer v. Williams, Massiah, *and* Miranda: *What is "Interrogation"? When Does it Matter?*, 67 GEO. L.J. 1 (1978), *reprinted in* Y. KAMISAR, POLICE INTERROGATIONS AND CONFESSIONS 139–224 (1980) [hereinafter cited as POLICE INTERROGATION AND CONFESSIONS].

7. 401 U.S. at 224 (rejecting dicta that statements obtained in violation of *Miranda* may not be used for the purpose of impeachment).

8. Michigan v. Mosley, 423 U.S. 96, 100–07 (1975) (interpreting *Miranda*'s command that "the interrogation must cease" when the suspect indicates that he "wishes to remain silent" so as to allow the police to resume interrogating a defendant who asserted his right to remain silent under the particular circumstances involved in that case. For an incisive analysis of *Mosley*, see Stone, *supra* note 6, at 129–37.

9. United States v. Mandujano, 425 U.S. 564 (1976) (discussed *infra* in text accompanying notes 68–71).

10. Oregon v. Mathiason, 429 U.S. 492 (1977) (discussed *infra* in text accompanying notes 73–82).

11. 446 U.S. 291 (1980).

12. *See infra* note 93. *See generally* White, *Interrogation Without Questions*: Rhode Island v. Innis *and* United States v. Henry, 78 MICH. L. REV. 1209, 1224–36 (1980).

13. 447 U.S. 264 (1980). *See infra* text accompanying note 153.

14. *See generally* White, *supra* note 12, at 1236–41.

15. In Tague v. Louisiana, 444 U.S. 469 (1980) the Court in a per curiam decision held that in a case where "no evidence at all was introduced to prove that [the defendant] . . . knowingly and intelligently waived his rights before making [an] . . . inculpatory statement," *id* at 471, the statement was inadmissible because the prosecution failed to satisfy its burden of proving a waiver of the defendant's *Miranda* rights. *Id*

16. Stone, *supra* note 6, at 100.

17. In Edwards v. Arizona, 451 U.S. 477 (1981), a case decided on the same

day as *Smith*, the Court ruled that a defendant's statement was obtained in violation of *Miranda* because the police failed to honor his invocation of his right to
have an attorney present at questioning. Because the analysis applied in *Edwards* was foreshadowed by the majority and concurring opinions in Michigan v.
Mosley, 423 U.S. 96 (1975), *Edwards*'s ruling cannot be considered as unexpected
as the Court's application of *Miranda* in *Smith*.

18. 451 U.S. 454 (1981).

19. *Id.* at 456.

20. *Id.* at 456.

21. *Id.* at 456, 458 n.5, 471 n.15.

22. *Id.* at 456–57. In fact, defendant never challenged his competency to
stand trial. *Id.* at 457 n.1.

23. Under Texas law, the crime of murder in the course of committing a
robbery is a capital offense. TEX. PENAL CODE ANN. 5, § 19.03(a)(2), (b)
(Vernon 1974).

24. TEX. CRIM. PROC. CODE ANN. § 37.071 (Vernon 1981).

25. *Id.*

26. 451 U.S. at 458. As Professor Black has observed, the implications of
this question are troubling because "[t]he concept of the existence of a
'probability' 'beyond a reasonable doubt' is and can only be puzzling—even
mind-boggling—to a jury or to anybody." Black, *Due Process for Death: Jurek
v. Texas and Companion Cases*, 26 CATH. U.L. REV. 1, 4 (1976).

27. 451 U.S. at 457.

28. *Id.* at 458.

29. *Id.* at 459.

30. *Id.* at 458.

31. *Id.*

32. *Id.*

33. *Id.*

34. *Id.* In response to the question "[w]hat . . . was the most important
thing that . . . caused you to think that [Smith] . . . is a severe sociopath," Dr.
Grigson testified as follows:

> He told me that this man named Moon looked as though he was going to
> reach for a gun, and he pointed his gun toward Mr. Moon's head, pulled the
> trigger, and it clicked—misfired, at which time he hollered at Howie, appar-
> ently his other partner there who had a gun, "Watch out, Howie. He's got a
> gun." Or something of that sort. At which point he told me—now I don't
> know who shot this man, but he told me that Howie shot him, but then he
> walked around over this man who had been shot—didn't . . . check to see if
> he had a gun nor did he check to see if the man was alive or dead. Didn't
> call an ambulance, but simply found the gun further up underneath the
> counter and took the gun and the money. This is a very—sort of cold-
> blooded disregard for another human being's life. I think that his telling me
> this story and not saying, you know, "Man, I would do anything to have that
> man back alive. I wish I hadn't just stepped over the body." Or you know,
> "I wish I had checked to see if he was all right" would indicate a concern,
> guilt, or remorse. But I didn't get any of this.

Id. at 465 n.9.

35. Smith v. State, 540 S.W.2d 693, 699 (Tex. 1976).

36. *Id.* at 700.

37. Smith v. Estelle, 445 F. Supp. 647 (N.D. Tex. 1979).

38. *Id.* at 658–61.

39. *Id.* at 661–64.

40. Smith v. Estelle, 602 F.2d 694 (5th Cir. 1979).

41. 430 U.S. 349 (1977).

42. *Id.* at 362 (plurality opinion of Stevens, J.); *id.* at 364 (White, J., concurring).

43. 602 F.2d at 708-09.

44. *Id.* at 709.

45. Estelle v. Smith, 451 U.S. 454 (1981).

46. The Court could have affirmed the Fifth Circuit decision on due process–Eighth Amendment grounds, holding that the government violated the principle articulated in *Gardner* when it failed to disclose to defendant the fact that Dr. Grigsby was going to testify as a witness against him. In addition, the majority could have joined the concurring opinions in deciding the case on Sixth Amendment grounds without reaching the Fifth Amendment issue.

47. 451 U.S. at 466–69.

48. *Id.* at 471.

49. *Id.* at 474 (Stewart, J., concurring) (joined by Powell, J.); *id.* at 474 (Rehnquist, J., concurring). Justice Rehnquist could be viewed as dissenting from the majority's analysis of the Fifth Amendment issue. After stating that he would not "consider the Fifth Amendment issues and cannot subscribe to the Court's resolution of them," *id.* at 474, he went on to consider the possible application of *Miranda* and concluded that "Particularly since it is not necessary to decide this case, I would not extend the *Miranda* requirements to cover psychiatric examinations such as the one involved here," *id.* at 476.

50. *Id.* at 462.

51. *Id.* at 463.

52. Lower courts have generally held that the privilege is not applicable to statements obtained from defendants for noncapital sentencing. *See, e.g.*, Moore v. State, 83 Wis. 2d 285, 265 N.W.2d 540 (1978).

53. 451 U.S. at 462.

54. The Court cited Green v. Georgia, 442 U.S. 95 (1979); Presnell v. Georgia, 439 U.S. 14 (1978); Gardner v. Florida, 430 U.S. 349 (1977). 451 U.S. at 463.

55. *Id.*

56. The same point is also suggested by the Court's earlier statement that "[j]ust as the Fifth Amendment prevents a criminal defendant from being made 'the deluded instrument of his own conviction,' Culombe v. Connecticut, [367 U.S. 568, 581 (1961)] . . . quoting 2 Hawkins Pleas of the Crown 595 (8th ed. 1824), it protects him as well from being made the 'deluded instrument' of his own execution." 451 U.S. at 462.

Moreover, in Bullington v. Missouri, 451 U.S. 430 (1981), the Court explicitly articulates this same point and makes it the central tenet of its analysis. In *Bullington*, the defendant was twice tried under Missouri's bifurcated capital sentencing procedure. At the first trial, he was convicted of capital murder and sentenced to life imprisonment. After this conviction was reversed, he was subjected to a second trial in which the jury not only again convicted him of capital murder but also imposed a sentence of death. In holding that this death penalty was imposed in violation of the double jeopardy clause of the Fifth Amendment, the Court reasoned that under the procedure employed by the state, the penalty phase of the proceedings "resembled and, indeed, in all relevant respects was like the immediately preceding trial on the issue of guilt or innocence. It was itself a trial on the issue of punishment so precisely defined by the Missouri statutes." *Id.* at 438. Accordingly, the Court concluded that "[b]ecause the sentencing proceeding at [defendant's] . . . first trial was like the trial on the question of guilt or innocence, the protection afforded by the Double Jeopardy Clause to one acquitted by a jury also is available to him, with respect to the death penalty, at his retrial." *Id.* at 446.

57. *Id.* at 463–65.

58. In United States v. Dionisio, 410 U.S. 1 (1973), the Court held that the compelled production of voice exemplars would not violate the Fifth Amendment privilege, since the exemplars were to be used only for identification purposes and not for their communicative content.

59. In Gilbert v. California, 388 U.S. 263 (1967), the Court concluded that a handwriting exemplar not offered for the content of what is written is an identifying physical characteristic outside the protection of the privilege against compulsory self-incrimination.

60. In United States v. Wade, 388 U.S. 218 (1967), the Court held that lineups are nontestimonial and thus not within the protection of the Fifth Amendment privilege.

61. In Schmerber v. California, 384 U.S. 757, 765 (1966), the Court found that extraction and chemical analysis of a blood sample from defendant involved no "shadow of testimonial compulsion."

62. 451 U.S. at 464.

63. *Id.* at 465. Throughout its opinion, the Court emphasized that it was not holding that the Fifth Amendment privilege was applicable to all psychiatric examinations. The majority specifically stated that if the state had used the statements made to Dr. Grigson merely for the purpose of determining defendant's competency to stand trial, no Fifth Amendment issue would have arisen. *Id.* In addition, the majority intimated that a different issue would have been presented if testimony based on a defendant's statements made in the course of a psychiatric examination were introduced to rebut psychiatric testimony offered by the defendant for the purpose of establishing a defense of insanity. *Id.* In a footnote, the Court added that the court of appeals left open " 'the possibility that a defendant who wishes to use psychiatric evidence in his own behalf [on the issue of future dangerousness] can be precluded from using it unless he is [also] willing to be examined by a psychiatrist nominated by the state.' " *Id.* at 466 n.10 (quoting Smith v. Estelle, 602 F.2d 694, 707 (5th Cir. 1979)). And, finally, in another footnote, the majority indicated that it was not holding that the Fifth Amendment would apply to "all types of interviews and examinations that might be ordered or relied upon to inform a sentencing determination." *Id.* at 469 n.13.

64. *Id.* at 466–67.

65. *See* 384 U.S. at 467: "[W]ithout proper safeguards the process of in-custody interrogation of persons suspected or accused of crime contains inherently compelling pressures which work to undermine the individual's will to resist and to compel him to speak where he would not otherwise do so freely."

66. *See, e.g.*, Aronson, *Should the Privilege Against Self-Incrimination Apply to Compelled Psychiatric Examinations?*, 26 STAN. L. REV. 55, 65–66 (1973). Professor Aronson argued that the atmosphere at a psychiatric examination is no less coercive than that at a police interrogation. He noted that psychiatrists are trained to elicit material subjects seek to hide and sometimes are not averse to using tricks and compulsion to achieve this end. Moreover, he pointed out that a defendant subjected to a psychiatric examination will generally be isolated from family, friends, and attorney, and that the psychiatrist may use a series of interviews in order to break down the defendant's resistance to questioning. For other articles considering the application of the Fifth Amendment privilege to psychiatric exams, *see* Danforth, *Death Knell for Pre-Trial Mental Examination? Privilege Against Self-incrimination*, 19 RUTGERS L. REV. 489 (1965); LeFelt, *Pre-trial Mental Examinations: Compelled Cooperation and the Fifth Amendment*, 10 AM. CRIM. L. REV. 431 (1972); Comment, *Compulsory Mental Examinations and the Privilege Against Self-incrimination*, 1964 WIS. L. REV. 671; Note, *Requiring a Criminal Defendant to Submit to a Government Psychiatric Examination: An Invasion of the Privilege against Self-Incrimination*, 83 HARV. L. REV. 648 (1970); Note, *Mental Examinations of Defendants Who Plead Insanity; Problems of Self-incrimination*, 40 TEMP. L.Q. 366 (1967).

67. *See supra* notes 9–10 and accompanying text.

68. 425 U.S. 564 (1976).

69. *Id.* at 578–80 (plurality opinion of Burger, C.J.). A unanimous Court held that the particular defendant in *Mandujano* was not entitled to relief in any event because that defendant was convicted of committing perjury before the grand jury, and the privilege against compelled self-incrimination does not sanction perjury. For a thorough analysis of the issues involved in *Mandujano, see* Stone, *supra* note 6, at 154–64.

70. 425 U.S. at 580.

71. *Id.*

72. The *Miranda* decision involved four separate cases. In each of them "law enforcement officials took the defendant into custody and interrogated him in a police station for the purpose of obtaining a confession. The police did not effectively advise him of his right to remain silent or of his right to consult with his attorney." 384 U.S. at 440.

73. 429 U.S. 492 (1977).

74. *See also* Beckwith v. United States, 425 U.S. 341 (1976) (holding that *Miranda* not applicable to situation where defendant questioned in a private home by IRS agents who were investigating defendant's possible involvement in criminal tax fraud).

75. 429 U.S. at 493.

76. *Id.*

77. *Id.*

78. 275 Or. 1, 5, 549 P.2d 673, 675 (1976), *rev'g* 22 Or. App. 494, 539 P.2d 1122 (1975).

79. The Court emphasized that the defendant "came voluntarily to the police station," that "he was immediately informed that he was not under arrest," and that after confessing, he "did in fact leave the police station without hindrance." 429 U.S. at 495. For a critical view of the Court's analysis of these facts, *see* Stone, *supra* note 6, at 153–54.

80. 429 U.S. at 495 (quoting 384 U.S. at 444).

81. For an analysis of this aspect of the Court's opinion, *see* Stone, *supra* note 6, at 154.

82. 429 U.S. at 495.

83. The point was raised, however, by Justice Rehnquist in his concurring opinion. 451 U.S. at 475 (Rehnquist, J., concurring).

84. *Id.* at 467.

85. *Id.*

86. By emphasizing the fact that defendant was in custody, *id.*, the Court indicated that *Smith*'s holding could be confined to that context and would not necessarily apply to a situation in which a defendant on bail was interviewed by a government agent.

87. *Id.*

88. *Smith*'s holding, of course, does not go this far. There is no reason to suppose that the defendant in *Smith* viewed the examining psychiatrist as anything other than a government psychiatrist. Thus, based on its holding, the Court's language pertaining to government agents could be read to include only people known by the defendant to be government agents. However, the majority provided no indication that its language should be read in this strained fashion.

89. POLICE INTERROGATION AND CONFESSIONS, *supra* note 6, at 188–201.

90. [E]ven though a person is in custody, "surreptitious interrogation" is insufficient to bring *Miranda* into play. For unless a person *realizes* he is dealing with the police, their efforts to elicit incriminating statements from him do not constitute "police interrogation" within the meaning of *Miranda*. . . . It is the impact on the suspect's mind of the *interplay* between police interrogation and police custody—each condition *reinforcing* the pressures and anxieties produced by the other—that, as the *Miranda* Court correctly discerned, makes "custodial police interrogation" so devastating. . . . In the "jail plant" or other "undercover" situations, however, there is no *integration* of "custody" and "interrogation," no *interplay* between the two, at least none where it counts—in the suspect's mind. *Id.* at 195–96.

91. Once the defendant is arraigned, his Sixth Amendment right to an attorney comes into effect. Brewer v. Williams, 430 U.S. 387, 398 (1977); Kirby v. Illinois, 406 U.S. 682, 688 (1972). The Court has held that once the Sixth Amendment right attaches, defendants in custody are protected from a jail plant's attempt to deliberately elicit incriminating statements. United States v. Henry, 447 U.S. 264 (1980); Beatty v. United States, 389 U.S. 45 (1967), *rev'g* 377 F.2d 181 (5th Cir. 1967).

92. In *Smith* the Court did not delineate the precise form of *Miranda* warn-

ings required. Based on the Court's analysis, at least one of the warnings would not be applicable in the context presented in *Smith*. The Court strongly intimated that the defendant would not have the right to have an attorney present during the psychiatric examination. 451 U.S. at 470 n.14. Therefore, the government would not have to warn the defendant of his right to have an attorney present during the government's examination.

93. 446 U.S. 291 (1980). *Miranda* only prohibits "custodial interrogation." 384 U.S. at 478–79. In Rhode Island v. Innis, the Court defined interrogation as including not only direct questioning but also tactics "that the police should know [are] . . . reasonably likely to evoke an incriminating response from a suspect." 446 U.S. at 301. Whether an undercover agent would be required to give a suspect *Miranda* warnings before engaging him in conversation would depend on whether the agent's conversation would constitute interrogation within the meaning of *Innis*. For a prediction about the probable meaning of the *Innis* test, *see* White, *supra* note 12, at 1224–36.

94. 451 U.S. at 468 (emphasis added).

95. *Id.* at 467.

96. Prior to the psychiatric exam, no warnings whatsoever were given to the defendant in *Smith*. Thus, the Court's holding that basic *Miranda* warnings were required (including the warning of the right to remain silent, *id.* at 467) was sufficient to dispose of the particular case before it.

97. Under the circumstances of Smith's case, Dr. Grigson's testimony was not admissible at the guilt stage of the proceedings, and Smith would have no reason to think otherwise. Therefore, in order to enlighten the defendant about the incriminatory potential of his disclosures to the psychiatrist, it would be necessary to explain the possible relationship between his disclosures and the issue at stake in the penalty proceeding. Obviously, the clearest means of explaining this would be to tell the defendant that statements made by him to Dr. Grigson could be used by the jury to decide whether to sentence him to death.

98. However, in view of the Court's analysis, it would be questionable whether the defendant could be adequately informed of the incriminatory potential of his statements unless he were made aware of the possible relationship between the statements and the imposition of the death penalty. *See infra* text accompanying notes 107–09.

99. *See supra* text accompanying notes 83–85.

100. *See supra* text accompanying notes 54–56.

101. 384 U.S. at 475.

102. 431 U.S. 181 (1977).

103. The issue before the Court in *Washington* was whether a grand jury witness who was viewed by the government as a potential defendant was entitled to a warning that his testimony could lead to an indictment. The essence of the defendant's argument was that in the absence of such a warning, any waiver of his Fifth Amendment privilege would be unintelligent because there would be no basis for a conclusion that he was aware of the potential consequences of such waiver, 431 U.S. at 188–89. However, the Court branded this argument "largely irrelevant," *id.* at 189, because the real question for Fifth Amendment purposes was whether the defendant was compelled to give testimony, and his ignorance

about whether he was a potential defendant could have no bearing on that issue. *Id.* at 189–90. Thus, in this context the Court appeared to disregard *Miranda*'s requirement that a defendant's waiver of his Fifth Amendment privilege be knowing and intelligent. For an analysis of the *Washington* case *see* Stone, *supra* note 6, at 164–66.

104. Nothing in *Smith* is inconsistent with the lower court decisions holding that the interrogating officer need not inform the suspect of the specific nature of noncapital charges involved in order to obtain a valid waiver. *See, e.g.*, United States v. Anderson, 533 F.2d 1210, 1212 n.3 (D.C. Cir. 1976); Collins v. Brierly, 492 F.2d 735 (3rd Cir.), *cert. denied*, 419 U.S. 877 (1974). In most noncapital cases, it is not unreasonable to assume that the circumstances of the defendant's arrest will provide him with notice as to at least the general nature of the adversary interests at stake. A different analysis has been applied by some lower courts when this is not the case. *See infra* cases cited in note 109.

105. *See supra* text accompanying notes 53–56.

106. More precisely, the Court referred to the fact that the defendant was "given no indication" that the statements made by him to the psychiatrist might be used to secure his execution. 451 U.S. at 467. While this language refers to some kind of a death penalty warning, it does not suggest that the warning must be given in any particular words. *Cf.* California v. Prysock, 453 U.S. 355 (1981) (holding content of *Miranda* warnings need not follow verbatim the statement of warnings contained in the *Miranda* opinion).

107. The constitutional requirements pertaining to capital punishment legislation have been adumbrated by the Court in a series of cases. *See, e.g.*, Lockett v. Ohio, 438 U.S. 586 (1978); Gregg v. Georgia, 428 U.S. 153 (1976); Woodson v. North Carolina, 428 U.S. 280 (1976). *See generally* Gillers, *Deciding Who Dies*, 129 U. PA. L. REV. 1 (1980); Liebman & Shepard, *Guiding Capital Sentencing Discretion Beyond the "Boiler Plate": Mental Disorder as a Mitigating Factor*, 66 GEO. L.J. 757 (1978).

108. For example, during the year 1980, 187 defendants were sentenced to death. U.S. DEP'T OF JUSTICE, BUR. OF PRISONS, CAPITAL PUNISHMENT 1980, at 1. While this figure is large in comparison to the number of people sentenced to death in previous recent years, it is obviously small when compared to the total number of defendants charged and convicted of murder in 1980.

109. *Cf.* United States v. McCrary, 643 F.2d 323 (5th Cir. 1981) (stating in dicta that a knowing, intelligent, and voluntary waiver is not possible where the suspect is ignorant of the nature of the offense about which he is being interrogated); Schenk v. Ellsworth, 293 F. Supp. 26 (D. Mont. 1968) (defendant's Sixth Amendment waiver held invalid on ground that he was not given sufficient information to indicate that he was suspected of murder); Commonwealth v. Dixon, 475 Pa. 17, 379 A.2d 553 (1977) (holding that a valid waiver of *Miranda* rights requires that the suspect have an awareness of the general nature of the transaction giving rise to the investigation; where interrogating officials did not affirmatively provide suspect with such information, the commonwealth was required to prove by a preponderance of the evidence that defendant knew of the occasion for the interrogation).

110. *See supra* text accompanying notes 94–95.

111. 447 U.S. 625 (1980).

112. *Id.* at 637–38.

113. In *Beck*, the Court held that a statutory procedure precluding jury consideration of a lesser-included noncapital offense in a capital case was constitutionally impermissible. Stressing the significant difference between the death penalty and all other punishments, the Court indicated that it was not deciding that due process would require jury charges on lesser-included offenses in noncapital cases. *Id.* at 638 n.14.

114. The purpose of the warning is to alert the capital defendant to the possibility that his words may be used against him to secure a death sentence. In capital cases where no death penalty is ultimately imposed, the defendant's words have not in fact been used against him for this purpose. Therefore, the admission of a statement obtained in the absence of a death penalty warning should constitute reversible error only in those cases in which the defendant is actually sentenced to death.

115. *See, e.g.*, United States v. Henry, 447 U.S. 264, 272–73 (1980); Rhode Island v. Innis, 446 U.S. 291, 300 n.4 (1980). *See generally* POLICE INTERROGATION AND CONFESSIONS, *supra* note 6, at 139–244.

116. In fact the defendant had already been indicted. 451 U.S. at 457.

117. *Id.* at 470.

118. *Id.* at 471.

119. *See, e.g.*, United States v. Wade, 388 U.S. 218, 236–37 (1967). However, in Escobedo v. Illinois, 378 U.S. 478, 491 (1964) the Court did specify that the defendant's Sixth Amendment right was violated because he was "denied an opportunity to consult with his lawyer." However, *Escobedo*'s Sixth Amendment analysis was soon obliterated by the Court's decision in *Miranda*. *See generally* POLICE INTERROGATION AND CONFESSIONS, *supra* note 6, at 162.

120. The Court also suggested that the defendant's attorney does not have the right to be present at the psychiatric examination itself. 451 U.S. at 470 n.14. This point could be significant in cases in which the defendant's attorney consents to the psychiatric examination with the understanding that the evidence derived will be used for a limited purpose. If the attorney is not allowed to be present at the examination, it will be difficult for defendant to litigate the question whether evidence subsequently offered by the prosecution was derived from the examination. To alleviate this problem, a possible approach might be either to allow the attorney to view the examination (without being allowed to participate) or to require the government to provide a tape-recording of it.

121. *Id.* at 471.

122. *See, e.g.*, United States v. Henry, 447 U.S. 264 (1980); Massiah v. United States, 377 U.S. 201 (1964).

123. At least two commentators have referred to this possibility. *See* Enker & Elsen, *Counsel for the Suspect*: Massiah v. United States *and* Escobedo v. Illinois, 49 MINN. L. REV. 47, 56–57 (1964) (observing that although the government impropriety would be the same whether counsel happened to be present or not, *Massiah*'s Sixth Amendment rationale obfuscates analysis of this situation). *Cf.* Weatherford v. Bursey, 429 U.S. 545, 554 (1977) (while holding that undercover agent's meeting with defendant and his attorney to discuss defendant's de-

fense to a criminal charge did not violate defendant's Sixth Amendment right, the Court noted that a stronger Sixth Amendment case would be presented if the undercover agent had testified at the trial).

124. 451 U.S. at 471 n.16.

125. The three justices who declined to join the Court's opinion joined the majority in specifying that the defendant's Sixth Amendment right was violated because the government failed to notify defendant's attorney before conducting the psychiatric exam. 451 U.S. at 474 (Stewart, J., concurring) (joined by Powell, J.); *id.* at 475–76 (Rehnquist, J., concurring).

126. The requirement that the police notify the defendant's attorney obviously means that the attorney is entitled to play a part in making the waiver decision. Otherwise, the notice requirement would be meaningless because its effect could be easily defeated by the government. An officer could notify the defendant's attorney of a proposed psychiatric exam one minute before a government psychiatrist, as a preliminary to conducting the exam, sought to obtain the defendant's personal waiver of his Fifth and Sixth Amendment rights. Therefore, the notification requirement clearly implies that before the government can seek a personal waiver from the defendant, it must either obtain a waiver from the defendant's attorney or allow the defendant to consult with the attorney. Barring extraordinary circumstances, no competent attorney would presume to waive the important constitutional rights involved without first consulting with his client.

127. 430 U.S. 387 (1977).

128. *Id.* at 406.

129. *Id.* at 405–06.

130. *Id.*

131. 430 U.S. at 433 (White, J., dissenting) (joined by Rehnquist, J., and Blackmun, J.); *id.* at 417 (Burger, C.J., dissenting).

132. *Id.* at 413 (Powell, J., concurring).

133. United States v. Henry, 447 U.S. 264, 275 n.14 (quoting ABA MODEL CODE OF PROFESSIONAL RESPONSIBILITY DR 7-104(A)(1) (1979), which prohibits a lawyer from "[c]ommunicat[ing] or caus[ing] another to communicate on the subject of the representation with a party he knows to be represented by a lawyer in that matter unless he has the prior consent of the lawyer representing such other party or is authorized by law to do so"). Although the Court stated that the rule did not "bear on the constitutional issue" involved in *Henry*, its quotation of the rule would appear to suggest that at least when the Sixth Amendment is applicable, the Court views actions of all government agents as equivalent to action by the prosecution (that is, the government attorney). Thus, if the disciplinary rule were to apply, the prohibition imposed by the rule on government attorneys would apply equally to the police.

134. In *Williams*, the defendant had attorneys in both Davenport, Iowa and Des Moines, Iowa. However, at the time the interrogation took place, the defendant was in a police car traveling between Davenport and Des Moines. The defendant's Davenport attorney had asked for and been refused permission to accompany the defendant on the trip to Des Moines. 430 U.S. at 392. *See generally* POLICE INTERROGATION AND CONFESSIONS, *supra* note 6, at 112–37.

135. In *Williams* the defendant disclosed incriminating information after an officer in the police car delivered what has come to be known as the "Christian burial speech." 430 U.S. at 392–93. The Court specifically characterized this police conduct as "interrogation," 430 U.S. at 399–401, even though that was apparently unnecessary to a finding of a Sixth Amendment violation. *See* United States v. Henry, 447 U.S. 264, 270 (1980) (defendant's Sixth Amendment right violated when the government "deliberately elicits" incriminating disclosures.) *See generally* POLICE INTERROGATION AND CONFESSIONS, *supra* note 6, at 175–78.

136. Williams was convicted of first-degree murder under IOWA CODE ANN. § 902.1 (West 1979), which mandated a sentence of life imprisonment.

137. *Williams* itself illustrates this point. If Detective Leaming had sought to interrogate Williams before leaving Davenport, or after reaching Des Moines, Williams could easily have been provided access to his attorney. Moreover, had Leaming complied with Williams's attorney's request to join them in the police car for the trip, no problem of access would have arisen. In *Williams*, it seems highly probable that the police chose to interrogate (or attempt to elicit incriminating disclosures from) the defendant when they did so precisely because they knew that no consultation between the defendant and his attorney could take place at that time.

138. If the concept of feasibility is to be viewed broadly so that the government's prior opportunities to seek incriminating disclosures from the defendant may be taken into account, courts will be placed in the unfortunate position of seeming to pass on the good faith of the government.

139. 451 U.S. at 471.

140. On the contrary, lower courts have generally taken the view that in the pretrial context, a defendant may waive his constitutional rights so long as he has a basic understanding of the right itself. While a full appreciation of the right might be necessary to an optimal decision, it is not indispensable to a valid waiver. *See, e.g.*, United States v. Dorsey, 591 F.2d 922, 932 (D.C. Cir. 1978); State v. McKnight, 52 N.J. 35, 47, 243 A.2d 240, 251 (1968).

141. That is, the rule will apply in all cases in which the defendant is charged with a capital offense. Since the rationale for the rule is that a defendant's knowledge that the death penalty is a possible consequence will distort his decision-making ability, *see infra* text accompanying note 148, a question could arise whether the rule should apply in capital cases in which the defendant did not receive notice that the death penalty was a possibility when the Sixth Amendment right was waived and no death penalty was ever in fact imposed. In these cases, it is arguable that the potential application of the death penalty was not likely to impair the defendant's decision making.

142. An additional justification for tightening the safeguards relating to waiver is that the Court has expressed a commitment to adopting particularly strict procedural safeguards for capital defendants. *See supra* note 54.

143. 372 U.S. 391 (1963).

144. *Id.* at 398–99.

145. *Id.* at 394, 440.

146. *Id.* at 396–97 n.3.

147. *Id.* at 397 n.3.

148. *Id.* at 440. The Court added that in Noia's case language used by the sentencing judge made the threat of the death penalty "unusually acute." *Id.*

149. *Id.* at 440.

150. The Court has adhered to this analysis in cases subsequent to *Noia*. In United States v. Jackson, 390 U.S. 570 (1968), the Court considered the constitutionality of the federal kidnapping statute. The statute was structured so that a defendant could receive a death penalty only if he was found guilty by a jury; he could avoid any possibility of the death penalty so long as he waived jury trial. The Court held that the death penalty provision of the statute was unconstitutional because it placed undue pressure on defendants to plead guilty or to waive jury trial. In Corbitt v. New Jersey, 439 U.S. 212 (1978), however, the Court upheld the constitutionality of a New Jersey statute that provided that defendants guilty of first-degree murder could possibly avert a sentence of life imprisonment by entering a plea of non vult or nolo contendere to the charge. The statute provided that while defendants convicted by a jury of first-degree murder would be sentenced to life, defendants allowed to enter a plea of non vult or nolo contendere to the charge would be sentenced to either life or a term of not more than thirty years. The Court distinguished *Jackson* primarily on the ground that the death penalty was involved in that case but not in *Corbitt. Id.* at 217. While admitting that the New Jersey statute placed some pressure on defendants to waive their right to jury trial, the Court concluded that the pressure was of a different magnitude than that involved in *Jackson, id.*, and therefore was insufficient to render the New Jersey statute unconstitutional. *Id.* at 226. Since these cases deal with the question of what conditions may be placed on the exercise of a constitutional right, *see generally* Coffee, *"Twisting Slowly in the Wind": A Search for Constitutional Limits on Coercion of the Criminal Defendant*, 1980 SUP. CT. REV. 211, they are not directly germane to the present issue. Nevertheless, they further illustrate the Court's view that injecting the death penalty into the defendant's decision-making process may have the effect of substantially impeding (or even destroying) the rationality of that process.

151. A defendant's overwhelming desire to avoid the death penalty might easily lead him to believe that he could best achieve this goal by placating the government's desire to obtain incriminating information against him.

152. An unaided defendant who waived his rights because of a conscious or unconscious desire to be executed could not ordinarily be considered a rational decision maker. Because there is a risk that such a defendant is essentially consenting to execution, issues relating to the defendant's competency are ineluctably raised. *See, e.g.*, Gilmore v. Utah, 429 U.S. 1012 (1976), in which a closely divided Court upheld a capital defendant's waiver of any and all federal rights but only on the premise "that the State's determinations of his competence to waive his rights knowingly and intelligently were firmly grounded." *Id.* at 1015 (Burger, C.J., concurring).

153. 447 U.S. 264 (1980).

154. In *Henry*, counsel was appointed for defendant on November 27, 1972, six days after the government's undercover agent embarked on his effort to elicit

incriminating statements from the defendant. *Id.* at 266. The Court attached no significance to this sequence of events.

155. 430 U.S. at 398.

156. *See generally* POLICE INTERROGATION AND CONFESSIONS, *supra* note 6, at 216–22. In Kirby v. Illinois, 406 U.S. 682 (1972), the Court not only explicitly stated that "the right [to counsel] attaches at the time of arraignment," *id.* at 688, but also went on to indicate that the right will attach "at or after the initiation of adversary judicial criminal proceedings—whether by way of formal charge, preliminary hearing, indictment, information, or arraignment." *Id.* at 689. *Kirby*'s language could be interpreted to mean that the government's ordering of a psychiatric exam will be sufficient in itself to activate the defendant's Sixth Amendment right. Since the ordering of any psychiatric exam denotes a judgment that if competent the defendant should face trial on the charges against him, this action should be viewed as triggering the commencement of adversary judicial proceedings against the defendant.

157. In dealing with the Fifth Amendment issue, the Court only indirectly indicated that its analysis may be shaped by the fact that the defendant's words were used to secure the death penalty. *See supra* text accompanying notes 52–54, 95. In dealing with the Sixth Amendment issue, the Court never appears to attach any significance to the fact that the issue is raised in the context of a capital case. *See* 451 U.S. at 469–73.

158. The Court could have decided the case on due process grounds, *see supra* note 46, ruling that the prosecution's failure to provide advance notice of Dr. Grigson's appearance as a witness reduced Smith's potential for effective cross-examination and thereby undermined the jury's ability to assess the reliability of the psychiatrist's prediction of dangerousness.

159. Some lower courts have expressly held that a stricter standard of waiver must be applied when the defendant's Sixth Amendment right is at stake. *See, e.g.*, United States v. Mohabir, 624 F.2d 1140, 1147 (2d Cir. 1980). *See generally* POLICE INTERROGATION AND CONFESSIONS, *supra* note 6, at 275 nn.139–40.

160. *See* United States v. Henry, 447 U.S. 264, 273 (1980); Rhode Island v. Innis, 446 U.S. 291, 300 n.4 (1980). *See generally* White, *supra* note 12; POLICE INTERROGATION AND CONFESSIONS, *supra* note 6, at 138–224.

161. Ordinarily the defendant's Sixth Amendment right will attach at or before the time of arraignment. *See supra* note 156.

162. *See* Gardner v. Florida, 430 U.S. 349, 357–58 (1977) (plurality opinion).

The Psychiatric Examination and the Fifth Amendment Privilege in Capital Cases

In determining which capital defendants shall be sentenced to death,[1] evidence relating to the defendant's mental abnormalities is of particular significance. The deeply aberrational nature of many capital crimes marks them simultaneously as those that will kindle society's strongest retributive impulses and those that may be the product of a personality so diseased or deranged that it should not be held to ordinary standards of accountability.[2] From the defendant's perspective, it may be essential to present expert testimony that will provide the trier of fact and/or the sentencing authority with some explanation for the defendant's aberrational behavior.[3] Whether or not such testimony is offered on behalf of the defense, the prosecution may wish to present expert testimony that will provide the government's view of the defendant's personality.[4] Very often, therefore, expert testimony from a psychiatrist will be material to the critical issues at stake in a capital trial.

Ordinarily, a psychiatrist will be in the best position to testify about a defendant's mental processes when she has personally conducted a psychiatric examination of him.[5] From one perspective, therefore, it would seem logical that in cases in which psychiatric testimony is potentially significant, both government and defense psychiatrists should be able to conduct psychiatric examinations of the defendant so that each can give the fact finder and/or sentencing authority the presentation most favorable to its position.

Of course, this perspective fails to take account of the defendant's Fifth Amendment privilege against self-incrimination. Invoking the privilege, the defendant may claim that he should not be forced to submit to a psychiatric examination that will enable a government psychiatrist to present incriminating evidence at his trial or penalty proceeding. In *Estelle v. Smith*,[6] the Supreme Court held that under the circumstances presented in that case, the Fifth Amendment privilege applied to preclude the state from admitting evidence obtained from a court-ordered psychiatric examination of the defendant at the penalty stage of his capital trial.[7] In many respects, the circumstances of the *Smith* case were unusual.[8] After defendant Ernest Smith was indicted in Texas for murder, the trial judge informally, and apparently without notice to the defense attorney,[9] ordered the prosecuting attorney to arrange a psychiatric examination of the defendant by Dr. James P. Grigson in order to determine Smith's competency to stand trial.[10] Prior to Smith's trial, Dr. Grigson already had achieved some notoriety. After listening to his testimony in numerous capital cases, Texas juries almost invariably voted for death sentences, thus earning him the nickname "Dr. Death."[11] In the *Smith* case, Dr. Grigson did nothing to impugn the accuracy of this nickname. Although his original examination of Smith had been solely for the purpose of determining competency,[12] he testified at the penalty trial that the defendant was an extreme sociopath who showed no remorse for the crime committed and who would be likely to kill again if given the opportunity.[13] After hearing Dr. Grigson's testimony, the jury imposed the death penalty.[14]

In holding that the Fifth Amendment required the exclusion of Dr. Grigson's testimony, the Court necessarily determined that defendant's Fifth Amendment privilege was applicable when he was subjected to Dr. Grigson's pretrial psychiatric examination.[15] Nevertheless, the majority expressly limited its Fifth Amendment holding to the situation presented in *Smith*. Chief Justice Burger stated that no Fifth Amendment issue would have arisen if Dr. Grigson's findings had merely been presented at a hearing on the issue of defendant's competency to stand trial.[16] Moreover, he expressly reserved judgment on whether the Fifth Amendment would apply to "a sanity examination occasioned by a defendant's plea of not guilty by reason of insanity at the time of his offense."[17] And, finally, footnote 13 of the opinion further limited the scope of the Court's Fifth Amendment holding by emphasizing that *Smith* does not "hold that the same Fifth Amendment concerns are necessarily presented by all types of interviews and examinations that might be ordered or relied upon to inform a sentencing determination."[18]

In light of the Court's analysis, then, *Smith*'s Fifth Amendment holding is limited. For example, future cases might be distinguished on the basis of either the status of the person supervising the examination[19] or the nature of the conduct evaluated during it.[20] Even more significantly, perhaps, the Court's explicit reservation of the question whether the Fifth Amendment would apply to "a sanity examination occasioned by a defendant's plea of not guilty by reason of insanity at the time of his offense"[21] raises the more general issue of what relationship, if any, a defendant's injection of an issue relating to his mental capacity should have on the application of his Fifth Amendment privilege to evidence obtained as a result of a psychiatric examination. More specifically, the question is whether a defendant who raises an issue related to mental capacity at the trial,[22] pretrial,[23] or penalty[24] stage of the proceedings, or who presents expert testimony based on a psychiatric examination at any stage of the proceedings, may be precluded from asserting Fifth Amendment objections to a government psychiatric examination or to particular questions asked during it.[25]

Obviously, if raising an issue and presenting expert psychiatric testimony in support of it will not result in a forfeiture of the defendant's Fifth Amendment privilege, then merely raising the issue without presenting expert psychiatric testimony will not do so. Thus, this article will be concerned primarily with the Fifth Amendment issues raised when a defendant presents expert psychiatric testimony in support of a defense at trial or pretrial or as a mitigating circumstance at the penalty hearing.[26] These issues are significant for a variety of reasons. Most immediately, there are a number of capital cases now pending in which defendants' death sentences are being challenged specifically on the ground that government psychiatric testimony was admitted in violation of the Fifth Amendment privilege.[27] For these defendants, determining the scope of the Fifth Amendment's application may quite literally be a matter of life or death. Perhaps even more significantly, determining the relationship between the Fifth Amendment privilege and the government's use of psychiatric testimony will have a dramatic impact on the extent to which such testimony will be presented in future capital trials. The scope of the Fifth Amendment's application to psychiatric examinations will significantly shape the nature and quality of expert psychiatric testimony presented on behalf of either the government or the defense[28] in both capital[29] and noncapital cases.[30] Moreover, the issues to be resolved in determining the relationship between the Fifth Amendment and the psychiatric examination have a significant bearing on the interrelationship between the defendant's Fifth Amendment privilege and his constitutional right to present testimony in his own defense.[31]

The issues reserved in *Smith* may arise in a great variety of contexts because the circumstances under which a defendant may seek to present psychiatric or nonpsychiatric testimony in support of an issue relating to his mental state are virtually unlimited. For example, at the pretrial stage, a defendant may present expert psychiatric testimony for the purpose of showing he is not mentally competent to stand trial;[32] at trial, a defendant charged with perjury may present expert psychiatric testimony in support of a claim that his mental condition rendered him incapable of realizing that he was testifying falsely under oath,[33] or a defendant may present psychiatric testimony in support of an insanity defense[34] or a claim of diminished capacity;[35] and at the penalty stage of a capital trial, a defendant may present psychiatric testimony either for the purpose of rebutting government evidence that an aggravating circumstance is present because "there is a probability that the defendant would commit criminal acts of violence that would constitute a continuing threat to society,"[36] or to show that at the time of the capital crime, the defendant

was suffering the type of mental or emotional distress that would constitute a statutorily recognized mitigating circumstance.[37]

In all of these cases, the prosecution may argue that because it has a
special need to obtain evidence to rebut the psychiatric testimony offered
on behalf of the defendant, the defendant who provides notice of an intent to present such testimony[38] must submit to a government psychiatric
examination so that the government psychiatrist will be able to make an
informed judgment of the defendant's mental state. Then, if the defendant presents expert psychiatric testimony in support of an issue at the
pretrial, trial, or penalty stage, the government will be permitted to present psychiatric testimony based on the government psychiatric examination. This doctrine may be characterized as the "waiver by offer of
psychiatric testimony" doctrine.[39] The second part of this essay, under
the heading "The 'Waiver by Offer of Psychiatric Evidence' Doctrine,"
provides a detailed analysis of the "waiver" doctrine. The discussion
seeks to place the doctrine in a proper constitutional perspective and
then deals with its application in the situation in which the defense is
seeking to introduce psychiatric testimony in support of an insanity defense. This part and the following part of the essay, headed "Application
of the 'Waiver' Doctrine When Defense Psychiatric Testimony Is Offered at the Penalty Stage of a Capital Trial," conclude with an attempt
to delineate the circumstances under which the waiver doctrine may be
constitutionally applied.

In such circumstances, a defendant may seek to present expert psychiatric testimony even though he has absolutely refused to submit to a
government psychiatric examination or refused to answer questions
posed during that examination. When this occurs, the court must define
the appropriate remedy for the defendant's failure to submit. In the
fourth part of the essay ("Appropriate Sanctions") this issue is considered in a context in which a defendant seeks to present psychiatric testimony in support of an insanity defense.

The essay concludes with some general observations about the implications that acceptance of the analysis presented in it might have for
the trial of capital cases.

The "Waiver by Offer of Psychiatric Evidence" Doctrine

Exploring the Implications of the Doctrine

In order to explore the implications of the "waiver by offer of psychiatric
evidence" doctrine, it is helpful to start with a paradigm case. A defendant is charged with capital murder. His defense is twofold: first, he

claims that the prosecution is unable to meet its burden of proving that he in fact killed the victim; second, he claims that if it is found that he did kill the victim, he should be acquitted by reason of insanity because he was mentally irresponsible at the time that the killing occurred.[40] Before trial, defendant provides notice of an intention to present expert psychiatric testimony in support of his possible insanity defense. At the prosecutor's request, the court orders defendant to submit to a government psychiatric examination so that the government will be able to present its own expert testimony on the insanity issue. The defendant invokes his Fifth Amendment privilege to refuse to answer questions or to provide other testimonial communications to the government psychiatrist.[41] Pursuant to the waiver doctrine, the court rules that the defendant may not invoke his privilege if he wishes to offer his own expert psychiatric testimony at trial.

On the surface, this application of the waiver doctrine appears to force the defendant to choose between two constitutional rights. *Chambers v. Mississippi*[42] holds that a defendant has a constitutional right to present reliable exculpatory evidence in his defense at trial,[43] and *Estelle v. Smith*[44] holds that a defendant also has a right to invoke his Fifth Amendment privilege in response to a government psychiatrist's questions when the results of the psychiatric examination are to be used as government evidence at the trial or penalty stage of the proceedings.[45] Under the waiver doctrine the defendant will lose one constitutional right[46] if he chooses to assert the other.

In a line of cases beginning with *Simmons v. United States*,[47] the Supreme Court has held that the government may not force a defendant to surrender his Fifth Amendment privilege "in order to assert another" constitutional right.[48] Although *Simmons*'s analysis has been criticized,[49] the principle articulated in that case—that the government should generally be precluded from imposing conditions that will make it impossible for a defendant to exercise a constitutional right—seems sound as a general proposition.[50] When a defendant is compelled to elect between two constitutional rights that may be asserted independently,[51] that principle is violated, because by its nature the compelled election makes it impossible for the defendant to exercise one of the two constitutional rights. Thus, the compelled choice imposes an unconstitutional condition on each of the constitutional rights.[52]

Nevertheless, as Professor Peter Westen's provocative critique of *Simmons*[53] suggests, because constitutional rights cannot generally be viewed as absolutes, *Simmons*'s focus on whether one right must be given up in order to assert another sometimes results in an overly simplistic analysis. In many situations, whether a constitutional right exists depends on the particular context in which it is being asserted. Thus, in some compelled election situations the government can properly maintain that the defendant is not really being forced to choose between constitutional rights, but rather that the rights involved are simply not applicable in the specific context in which the defendant is seeking to assert them.[54] The reason for this is that the government may properly make the relinquishment of another constitutional right a condition for the exercise of the right in question.[55]

Of course, this merely states the issue. The problem arises in determining the circumstances under which the government may properly make relinquishment of one right a condition for the exercise of another. In his analysis of the problem,[56] Professor Westen concludes that a balancing approach is appropriate. The validity of a compelled election can best be resolved by simply "balancing the state's interest in compelling the election against the individual's interest in being relieved of the election."[57]

The difficulty with this type of a balancing process is that it is too vague. The test provides little guidance because it does not inform a court how the competing interests should be assessed or weighed. Moreover, by permitting an ad hoc assessment of government and individual interests, it risks evisceration of constitutional rights.[58] To illustrate, suppose the government passes a law requiring criminal defendants to choose between testifying in their own defense and being represented by an attorney at trial. Under Westen's balancing approach, the government would be able to assert that the infringement imposed by this requirement is justified by substantial governmental interests. For example, the government might claim that the individual interests adversely affected by the compelled election are more than counterbalanced by the election's positive impact on the integrity of the fact-finding process. According to this argument, the integrity of the process would be enhanced because defense attorneys tend to obfuscate the truth in all cases, and particularly those in which defendants testify in their own defense. The fact that this kind of argument would have to be considered under Westen's balancing test is enough to expose the test's inadequacy. Obviously, if governmental interests relating to the elimination of defense trial attorneys are allowed to be balanced, then the government is allowed to provoke a reassessment of a constitutional judgment that has already been made.

Instead of balancing the competing interests, a more appropriate approach is to assess whether the two rights involved in the compelled election are incompatible in the sense that allowing the defendant to exercise both of them will have the effect of diminishing the scope that should be afforded at least one of the two rights.[59] Under this approach, the focus should be on whether the "incident" attached to the exercise of each constitutional right is one that merely has the effect of enhancing the basic fairness secured by the right itself. When this condition is met with respect to one of the two constitutional rights, the effect of the incident attached to the other must also be considered;[60] and if it appears that that incident does not substantially diminish the scope that should be afforded to that constitutional right, then the compelled election is constitutional.[61] Obviously, this approach does allow for a certain balancing of interests once the basic showing of incompatibility is made.[62] If this first condition is not met, however, *Simmons*'s principle should be applicable and the compelled election should be invalidated without regard to a balancing of interests.

The testimonial waiver doctrine under which a defendant who elects to testify in his own defense is required to relinquish his Fifth Amendment privilege with respect to certain questions put to him on cross-examination[63] provides a clear example of the way in which the incompatibility approach should be applied. In this situation a defendant is seemingly forced to choose between exercising his constitutional right to testify in his own defense[64] and his Fifth Amendment privilege to refuse to incriminate himself. This particular election may be justified, however, because a defendant's right to testify cannot be viewed as a constitutional absolute. The scope of the right to testify must be related to the underlying reasons that give rise to it. Because the right to testify is recognized only within the context of our adversary system, a defendant could not elect to present testimony from a place other than the witness stand, to present hearsay testimony, or to testify without making some kind of commitment to tell the truth. Similarly, because cross-examination is recognized as our most effective means of testing the reliability of trial testimony,[65] the demands of our adversary system dictate that a defendant's right to testify must be conditioned upon a willingness to submit to some degree of cross-examination. Accordingly, at a certain point the apparent compelled election involved in the testimonial waiver doctrine is permissible because at that point the defendant's right to testify in his own defense is incompatible with his Fifth Amendment privilege.

Significantly, however, the extent of the incident attached to the defendant's right to present testimony is limited. Under the more appropriate interpretation of the testimonial waiver doctrine,[66] the government's right to cross-examine is limited to matters that relate to the defendant's direct testimony.[67] The justification for this limitation is that so long as the government is able to examine the defendant from its own perspective with respect to the facts testified to on direct,[68] its interest in thwarting the presentation of a distorted or "garbled"[69] version of defendant's testimony will be adequately safeguarded.

Of course the government might argue that a broader scope of cross-examination would permit an even more accurate assessment of the defendant's trial testimony. Allowing the government to compel answers about subjects on which the defendant has not chosen to volunteer information seems only tangentially related to the governmental interest in assessing the accuracy of defendant's direct testimony, however.[70] Moreover, if the government is permitted to adduce this kind of testimony on cross-examination, it would potentially be in a position to obtain incriminating statements that have no particular connection with the defendant's direct testimony. Thus, imposing this broader incident on the defendant's right to testify would result in hardships that are neither closely related to nor necessitated by the government's interest in advancing the basic fairness of the defendant's constitutional right to present testimony. Accordingly, imposing the broader incident should be rejected on two grounds: first, it is not a necessary incident to the right to present testimony, in the sense that it is a built-in feature of that right; second, it would be especially unfair to defendants because the detriments imposed would not be only those that reasonably relate to advancing the fairness of the constitutional right exercised by them.[71]

To elaborate this second point, it might be said that in imposing an incident on the defendant's exercise of a constitutional right, the government should be limited to a tit-for-tat response. If the defendant exercises his constitutional right to present testimony, allowing cross-examination that is limited to the scope of defendant's direct testimony is justifiable, tit-for-tat, because in a sense the government is only trying to deal with evidence injected into the case by the defense. The defense has been allowed to present testimony from its perspective; now the government is granted an opportunity to examine the same testimony from its perspective. It is doing no more to the defense than the defense did to it.[72] On the other hand, if cross-examination goes beyond matters relating to the defendant's direct testimony, the government is allowed more than to give tit-for-tat; in addition to testing the credibility of the defendant's testimony, it gets an opportunity to obtain additional incriminating statements that may ease its burden of establishing the defendant's guilt in either the present case or a subsequent one. This kind of *disproportionate* penalty for the exercise of a defendant's constitutional right is an independent reason for determining that the incident imposed on that right is unconstitutional.[73]

The testimonial waiver doctrine is significant not only in defining a situation in which an apparent election between two constitutional rights has been upheld but also as a doctrine that deserves comparison to the one under scrutiny here. Invoking the testimonial waiver doctrine by way of analogy, the government might argue that a defendant does not have a constitutional right to present expert psychiatric testimony free from the "legitimate demands of the adversary process."[74] Under this view, the situation created by the waiver by offer of psychiatric evidence doctrine is distinguishable from the compelled election between constitutional rights involved in cases like *Simmons*[75] because of the close relationship between the two constitutional rights involved. As in the case of the testimonial waiver doctrine, the defendant's exercise of his right to present testimony gives rise to the government's need for the evidence the defendant seeks to withhold by exercising his Fifth Amendment privilege.[76] Moreover, as in testimonial waiver situations, the government may claim that the evidence the defendant seeks to withhold is precisely that which is needed to test the truthfulness of the defense testimony. And, finally, the government may assert that the evidence obtained will be used only to achieve this objective; that is, evidence made available to the government as a result of the defendant's compelled election will be used only for the limited purpose of rebutting comparable evidence offered on behalf of the defendant.

Based on this analysis, the waiver by offer of psychiatric testimony doctrine seems almost precisely analogous to the testimonial waiver doctrine. The incident attached to the defendant's constitutional right to present evidence is justified because it merely allows the government to present evidence that is calculated to lead to a more discriminating assessment of the evidence presented by the defendant. Moreover, because the incident is limited to achieving this objective, the government is exacting no more than tit-for-tat; the defendant will suffer no detriments other than those that inevitably flow from permitting another assessment of his psychiatric testimony. Under this view, then, forcing the defendant to elect between presenting psychiatric testimony and refusing to answer questions at a government examination is justified; like the election involved in the testimonial waiver doctrine, this forced choice will do nothing more than advance the basic fairness of the constitutional right to present defense testimony. In order to evaluate the accuracy of this analogy, however, it is necessary to explore the differences between the two waiver doctrines in greater detail.

The Two "Waiver" Doctrines Compared

Obviously, the two waiver doctrines do not operate in exactly the same way. Under the testimonial waiver doctrine, a defendant who testifies at trial is required to submit to cross-examination. Under the waiver by offer of psychiatric evidence doctrine, however, the government seeks more than the right to cross-examine the defense psychiatrist. Rather, the claim is that the proffer of this defense testimony should give the government the right to conduct a pretrial psychiatric examination of the defendant.

Because of this basic difference between the two doctrines, the defendant may claim that the waiver by offer of psychiatric evidence doctrine cannot be justified. As I have already stated,[77] if the Constitution were to provide expressly that a defendant has a right "to testify," that right would carry with it certain concomitant burdens, including the condition that the defendant be subjected to some form of cross-examination. Because cross-examination's utility as a truth-testing device is a principle that is deeply ingrained in our legal consciousness,[78] conditioning the defendant's right to testify upon submission to some form of cross-examination would almost certainly be viewed as necessary to a proper functioning of our adversary system.

A defendant could certainly argue that the waiver by offer of psychiatric evidence doctrine is distinguishable. If the Constitution expressly provided that defendants have a right to offer psychiatric evidence, no one could say that a recognized historical incident of that right is a requirement that the defendant submit to a pretrial government psychiatric examination. Moreover, imposing this incident on the defendant's exercise of his constitutional right seems to be less necessary than the incident imposed in the testimonial waiver situation. Arguably, this is not a situation in which the government is seeking to test the reliability of testimony by subjecting it to cross-examination. The government will obviously be permitted to cross-examine the defense psychiatrist, and it is doubtful whether the defendant's refusal to speak to the government psychiatrist deprives it of a means of conducting an effective cross-examination. In examining the defense psychiatrist, the government would ordinarily have access to material that would open up various avenues of inquiry. For example, under most jurisdictions' discovery rules, the prosecutor would be able to obtain hospital records relating to defendant's prior mental history,[79] the defense psychiatrist's report of her mental examination of the defendant,[80] and reports of at least some prior mental examinations performed by other psychiatrists on the defendant.[81] In some situations, the prosecutor could also inquire into the nature of the mental examination conducted by the defense psychiatrist, and, using any relevant information relating to the defendant,[82] seek to test the basis for her conclusions. In addition, the prosecutor could of course inquire into the psychiatrist's bias, including any predisposition she might have to present favorable testimony on behalf of defendants.[83]

Nevertheless, a government psychiatric examination would significantly enhance the government's ability to test the truthfulness of the defendant's psychiatric testimony.[84] Indeed, in many situations the examination could be viewed as equivalent to cross-examination, because the defense psychiatrist would in a sense be presenting the defendant's testimony. For example, if the defense psychiatrist testifies to the opinion that at the time of the killing the defendant suffered from an insane delusion that led him to believe that he was squeezing a grapefruit rather than strangling his victim, she is probably saying essentially that the defendant told her that he believed he was squeezing a grapefruit at the time of the killing and that she believes his story. If this is the case, then the testimonial waiver doctrine seems to be very nearly applicable.[85] The government can claim that at least in such a situation, cross-examining the defense psychiatrist is not sufficient because it is the defendant's story that is critical. Accordingly, because the government examination allows the government its only means of directly evaluating the defendant's credibility, attaching this incident to the defendant's exercise of his constitutional right to present psychiatric testimony seems justified by the needs of the adversary system.[86]

Nevertheless, as it is presently applied, the waiver by offer of psychiatric evidence doctrine differs from the testimonial waiver doctrine in both scope and timing. The first difference is particularly striking. A defendant who testifies in his own defense at trial will be subjected to cross-examination by the government, but will be protected by the rules of evidence and the presence of counsel. Thus, the questions permitted will ordinarily be limited to those that relate to the subject matter of defendant's direct testimony[87] and are otherwise proper.[88] In contrast, the scope of questions that may be put to a defendant during a government psychiatric examination is apparently limitless, and under current practices any limits that might be appropriate could not be enforced because the defendant is not represented by counsel at the examination.[89] Moreover, the available empirical data[90] show that the government psychiatric examination appears to more closely resemble an incommunicado police interrogation than the type of courtroom questioning that is ordinarily permitted on cross-examination. An account of a typical examination indicates that the psychiatrist must be prepared to use trickery to elicit material that subjects seek to hide and must be relentless in overcoming their resistance. Moreover, the psychiatric examination is likely to be more probing than either a courtroom cross-examination or a police interrogation because, as Meyers puts it, the goal of the examining psychiatrist is to get "a sounding of the depths of the patient's personality."[91] And, finally, the psychiatrist's skill and special training may enable her to use techniques that are completely beyond the reach of an examining attorney.[92]

The difference in the nature of the examinations conducted relates to the infringement on the defendant's Fifth Amendment privilege. The Supreme Court has recognized that the privilege is designed to protect a variety of interests, including not only the basic one of maintaining an accusatorial system[93] but also the less clearly defined concern for protecting individuals against the cruelty involved in government coercion that invades their mental privacy.[94] Because of the potential scope of the government psychiatric examination, the waiver by offer of psychiatric evidence doctrine clearly results in a greater infringement on the latter Fifth Amendment interest than the testimonial waiver doctrine does; that is, the psychiatric examination's greater potential intrusion on mental privacy creates a greater infringement on the defendant's Fifth Amendment privilege.[95]

Moreover, the psychiatric examination also differs from cross-examination of the defendant in that it is designed to take place before trial. In this particular context, the difference in timing is critical, because it creates the possibility that the two types of examinations will have a significantly different impact on the "fair state-individual balance" that is the essence of the accusatorial system.[96] The justification for the government examination is that it will provide the government with evidence that may enable it to rebut the defense psychiatric testimony.[97] The unrestricted pretrial psychiatric examination permitted by present procedures allows the government an opportunity to do much more than this, however. Because the issues of guilt and penalty are so inextricably related to the issue of sanity, it is virtually inevitable that even a moderately wide-ranging psychiatric examination will elicit material that is relevant to all three issues. If the psychiatrist or any other witness is permitted to use material gained from the examination for the purpose of enhancing the government's case on the issues of either guilt or penalty, then, clearly, the incident attached to the defendant's right to present psychiatric testimony constitutes something more than a tit-for-tat response. In other words, the condition attached to the defendant's exercise of his constitutional right would not be one that merely ensures the basic fairness of the right itself, but rather one that allows the government to secure advantages that have no relation to its interest in testing the credibility of the defense psychiatric testimony. If this is the case, then the compelled election permitted by the waiver by offer of psychiatric testimony doctrine should be unconstitutional.[98] Thus, in order to assess the constitutionality of this doctrine it is necessary to consider whether any safeguards currently imposed or potentially available are adequate to prevent the government from obtaining this type of advantage.

Safeguards to Limit the Effect of the "Waiver by Offer of
Psychiatric Testimony" Doctrine

In order to prevent the government from obtaining more than tit-for-tat
by giving a psychiatric examination, it is appropriate to impose a "use"
limitation on testimonial evidence derived from the examination. The
government should not be permitted to use the fruits of the examination
for any purpose other than presenting testimony relevant to the defendant's insanity defense.

The first step toward enforcing this use limitation is to prohibit the
examining psychiatrist from testifying for the government at the guilt[99]
or penalty stage of the proceedings. This limitation in itself would obviously not be sufficient, however, because it would not prevent the government from using statements obtained as a result of the examination to
lead to other evidence. For example, a defendant's account of what happened after the killing might enable the prosecutor to uncover incriminating tangible evidence;[100] his relation of prior criminal activity might
enable the prosecutor to find additional witnesses who could testify
against the defendant at the penalty stage;[101] more subtly, a defendant's
account of the killing itself might enhance the prosecutor's ability to
shape his trial strategy by providing him with a clearer understanding of
either the circumstances of the crime or the character of the
defendant.[102]

In *Kastigar v. United States*,[103] the Court upheld the constitutionality of a statute requiring a witness who invokes the Fifth Amendment
privilege to testify after a grant of use-immunity.[104] The Court indicated
that the grant of use-immunity will be coextensive with the witness's
Fifth Amendment privilege so long as the government is required to
prove that any evidence subsequently presented against the witness "is
derived from a legitimate source wholly independent of the compelled
testimony."[105] The issue in the present case is analogous to the one
presented in *Kastigar* because in both situations the government's use of
the individual's compelled testimony should be strictly limited to the
purpose for which it is authorized.[106] Thus, the government may argue
that in the present context, imposition of *Kastigar*'s use-derivative use
limitation will be sufficient to bring the incident imposed on defendant's
exercise of a constitutional right within the range of acceptability—that
is, to the point where the incident imposed merely advances the fairness
inherent in the right to present psychiatric testimony.[107]

Kastigar's analysis suggests that in the present context a properly
enforced use-derivative use limitation should be accepted as a proper
means of limiting the use of statements obtained during the government
examination to authorized purposes.[108] But merely imposing the *Kasti-*

gar rule would not in itself provide adequate protection against unauthorized use of statements made to the government psychiatrist, because it would not provide the defendant with safeguards comparable to those available to the defendant in *Kastigar*. Under current procedures, the defendant exposed to a government examination is not permitted to have an attorney or other outside observer present during the examination, and no record of the information obtained from the defendant during that examination is made. Therefore, the nature of the testimonial information disclosed during the examination will be fully known only to the government psychiatrist.[109] Without knowing the content of the testimonial evidence revealed during the psychiatric examination, the defense generally would not be in a good position to know whether evidence presented to establish guilt or penalty was derived from statements made during the psychiatric examination.[110] Thus, only the prosecutor's good faith could be relied on to enforce any limitation on the use of statements made by the defendant during the government psychiatric examination. As the Court intimated in *Kastigar*,[111] this safeguard is insufficient to ensure the effective implementation of a use restriction.[112] Accordingly, under current procedures, the psychiatric testimony waiver doctrine allows the government to exact more than tit-for-tat, because it does not foreclose the possibility that the government will be able to use evidence obtained as a result of the government psychiatric examination for other purposes than that of testing the credibility of the defense psychiatric testimony.

Moreover, the procedure employed at trial also may provide insufficient protection against impermissible use of defendant's statements to the government psychiatrist. In most jurisdictions, the issues of guilt and sanity are determined at a single proceeding.[113] Although the government psychiatrist will be required to confine his testimony to the issue of sanity,[114] in supporting his conclusion with respect to that issue he almost inevitably will testify to statements made by the defendant that relate to the issue of guilt.[115] Thus, the jury will hear government testimony that relates to both sanity and guilt, but that is inadmissible on the latter issue as a result of the defendant's Fifth Amendment privilege. In *Jackson v. Denno*[116] the Court concluded that evidence that is inadmissible as to the defendant's guilt because of the Fifth Amendment privilege may not be presented to the jury with a limiting instruction.[117] That ruling seems to be applicable in the present context. If the issues of guilt and sanity are being adjudicated in a single proceeding, the risk that the jury would disregard limiting instructions and consider defendant's incriminating statements on the issue of guilt would appear to be at least as great in this situation as it was in *Jackson*.[118]

Thus, under present procedures the "waiver by offer of psychiatric evidence" doctrine allows the prosecution an opportunity to do more than merely test the credibility of defense psychiatric testimony. In particular, there is a risk that evidence derived as a result of the government examination will be used to strengthen the prosecution's case with respect to issues on which the defense presented no psychiatric testimony.[119] And in some situations, there is an additional risk that the jury will not properly limit its consideration of government psychiatric testimony but will take that testimony into account with respect to issues on which it is not admissible. Accordingly, the waiver doctrine as it is presently administered should be unconstitutional because the incident attached to the defendant's constitutional right to present psychiatric testimony exceeds that which is necessary to advance the basic fairness of the constitutional right.

In order to determine whether the waiver doctrine could be constitutional, it is necessary to consider the safeguards that might be imposed to eliminate the unfair advantages that potentially accrue to the government under current procedures. Obviously, the problem of the jury's improperly using the government psychiatrist's testimony on the issue of guilt could be eliminated by providing for a bifurcated proceeding at which adjudication of the issue of sanity is deferred pending determination of the defendant's guilt. Although some jurisdictions already mandate this procedure whenever the defendant's sanity is at issue,[120] it might seem unduly cumbersome, especially since in capital cases it might create the necessity for three separate proceedings.[121] To minimize the strain on judicial resources, it might be appropriate to hold that the split verdict procedure must be employed only when requested by the defendant[122] and mandated by the interests of justice.[123]

The more difficult problem is to minimize the possibility that the prosecution will use evidence derived from the psychiatric examination for unauthorized purposes. Toward this end, several safeguards might be used: first, the defense could be provided with a full and accurate transcript of the government psychiatric examination; second, the defendant could be allowed to have counsel present at the psychiatric examination; third, the government psychiatrist could be prohibited from asking the defendant about the circumstances relating to the act he is charged with committing; and finally, the government psychiatric examination could be postponed until some later stage of the proceedings.[124] If any of these safeguards or some combination of them will be sufficient to prevent the prosecution from using the fruits of the government psychiatric examination for an unauthorized purpose, then, with that safeguard or safeguards, the waiver by offer of psychiatric evidence doctrine should be constitutional.[125] In that event, the safeguard or safeguards imposed should be those that will strike an optimal balance between protecting against infringements on the defendant's Fifth Amendment privilege and promoting the government's interest in a fair and expeditious procedure. Assuming that a variety of different procedures will adequately protect the defendant's rights, the government should probably be allowed to impose those that least interfere with its legitimate interests.[126] On the other hand, if no combination of safeguards will eliminate the potential for improper prosecutorial use of the fruits of the examination, then the waiver doctrine should be held unconstitutional on the ground that the incident attached to the defendant's exercise of a constitutional right amounts to an excessive penalty.[127] Accordingly, it is appropriate to evaluate some of the safeguards that might be used to limit the prosecutor's potential ability to use evidence obtained as a result of the government psychiatric examination.

Providing Defendant with an Attorney during the Examination or with a Transcript of the Completed Examination

Providing defendant with an attorney during the examination, or with a transcript of the completed examination, are safeguards designed to achieve essentially the same end. In theory, each will provide the defense with complete information about statements made by defendant to the psychiatrist during the government examination. If both in fact fulfill this objective, the procedure of recording the examination and supplying the defense with a transcript would seem preferable on grounds of administration and efficiency. Providing for the presence of a lawyer when a tape-recorder could do the job just as well is obviously an inefficient use of resources.[128] Moreover, a recording machine is less likely to inhibit the normal flow of a psychiatric examination.[129] Of course, the defense might object that the government psychiatrist could distort the record provided by turning off the machine at appropriate times. Assuming this is a real problem, the presence of a defense attorney would not be needed to counter it. In appropriate cases,[130] a neutral observer could be required to monitor the examination so as to ensure that all of it was accurately recorded and transcribed.

Pursuant to this safeguard, the defendant's knowledge of the content of his compelled testimony would be equivalent to that which a grand jury witness would have of grand jury testimony compelled by a grant of use-immunity. Accordingly, the government might argue that, given this safeguard, imposing *Kastigar*'s use-derivative use prohibition provides defendant with sufficient protection against unauthorized use of statements made to the government psychiatrist. There is one critical difference, however, between the present situation and the one presented in

Kastigar. In the latter situation, the prosecutor at the defendant's trial can be someone who had no involvement in the defendant's earlier grand jury testimony and has not examined that testimony.[131]   In the present situation, on the other hand, it is totally unrealistic to expect that the prosecutor will not be familiar with the content of statements made by the defendant to the government psychiatrist. Since the psychiatrist is likely to be an important government witness, the prosecutor will naturally engage in discussions with her as a necessary part of preparing his case. In the course of these discussions, he will inevitably learn the content of communications made by the defendant to the psychiatrist.

This difference is significant because once a prosecutor knows the content of a defendant's immunized statements, he is in a position to use that knowledge advantageously even though he does not exploit it to obtain additional evidence. As a leading case from the Eighth Circuit put it:

Such use could conceivably include assistance in focusing the investigation, . . . refusing to plea bargain, interpreting evidence, planning cross-examination, and otherwise generally planning trial strategy.[132]

In the present situation, the possibility that the prosecutor might be able to use the compelled testimony for the purpose of shaping his trial strategy with respect to the issue of guilt is particularly great[133] because, if the psychiatric examination is not limited in some way, statements made by the defendant to the government psychiatrist will almost inevitably relate to the central facts at issue in the case.[134]   Thus, the prosecutor's access to statements made during the examination will enable him to learn critical facts that are not likely to be accessible to him through any other source. In most situations, knowledge of such facts at the pretrial stage will help the prosecutor shape his trial strategy, because he will be in a position to anticipate the type of testimony that may be offered at trial by either the defendant or other defense witnesses.[135]   Since the government's potential advantage with respect to the issue of guilt is not minimal,[136] some additional safeguard should be required to prevent this impermissible use of defendant's compelled testimony. As in the situation involved in *Kastigar*, it is not sufficient to hold merely that the government will not be allowed to admit evidence derived from the compelled testimony.   Rather, on the issue of guilt the Court's language in *Kastigar* itself is pertinent: the compelled testimony should not be used "in *any* respect."[137]

If this analysis is accepted, then some additional safeguard is needed to prevent the government from obtaining an improper advantage as a result of the compelled psychiatric examination. Among the various approaches that might be taken, two seem especially promising: first, the scope of the psychiatric examination might be restricted so that the government psychiatrist would not be permitted to ask the defendant anything about the act he is charged with committing;[138] and, second, the examination might be postponed until after the defense completed its presentation on the issue of guilt.[139] The potential advantages and disadvantages of these safeguards deserve consideration, but of course in the final analysis the question is whether either of them will prevent the prosecutor from using statements made during the psychiatric examination to obtain a tangible advantage in the determination of guilt.

Restricting the Scope of the Examination

The value of restricting the scope of the examination so that it will not include inquiries into the circumstances of the alleged crime would be that it would significantly reduce the possibility that the prosecutor would have access to material that would assist him in mapping his trial strategy. If the examination were thus restricted, the prosecutor would still be able to learn something about the defendant's character[140] and thought processes.[141] Arguably, even this kind of information would assist him in the sense that it might make it easier for him to plan an effective cross-examination.[142] But at some point it seems appropriate to hold that such potential assistance becomes minimal.[143] Thus, if the government psychiatric examination is restricted so that the psychiatrist is not permitted to ask the defendant anything about the act he is charged with committing, the defendant would appear to be sufficiently protected against the unauthorized use of statements made during the government examination.[144]

The difficulty arises in applying and administering this test. For example, suppose that a defendant is charged with killing a bartender. Under the suggested approach, the government psychiatrist would be prohibited from asking the defendant about the circumstances of the alleged killing. But would she be permitted to ask the defendant whether he had previously threatened the bartender? Or whether he had any special hostility toward bartenders? Obviously, under this approach, the problem of drawing lines would be very difficult.

The problem of administering the rule might be even greater. How could the psychiatrist be prevented from asking improper questions? What remedy would be appropriate if such questions were asked? And how should the court deal with a situation in which the defendant makes significant incriminating admissions that are not responsive to any question asked by the psychiatrist? Although these problems are severe, they do not appear to me to be insurmountable. In general, lines defining the areas of prohibited inquiry could be drawn[145] and sensible approaches to enforcing them effectively could be used.[146] If this is correct, then combining this safeguard with one of the two already discussed would be sufficient to save the constitutionality of the waiver by offer of psychiatric evidence doctrine.

Postponing the Psychiatric Examination

In some ways postponing the government psychiatric examination until after the defendant has completed his case on the issue of guilt[147] would seem to be an even more effective safeguard. Obviously, this delay would prevent the prosecutor from planning his cross-examination of defense witnesses on the basis of statements made by the defendant during the psychiatric examination.[148] This remedy would also be superior to the previous one in that it would not be difficult to administer. The government psychiatrist would be free to conduct a normal psychiatric examination.

The disadvantage of this safeguard, however, is that it would result in an actual disruption of the defendant's trial. A government psychiatrist would generally not be able to complete an effective examination in less than a few hours.[149] Defendant's absence from the courtroom during the time of the examination would mean that the trial would have to be halted. Moreover, there might be a substantial additional delay after the examination while the psychiatrist evaluated the data collected in order to prepare her testimony and the prosecuting attorney consulted with her. This delay would have a serious impact on legitimate government interests. First, it would obviously increase the strain on scarce judicial resources.[150] Even more significantly, perhaps, it would be likely to impair accurate fact finding, because the jury's memory of critical testimony presented before the delay would be likely to be weakened.[151] Because of these considerations alone,[152] it seems appropriate to hold that this safeguard should be used only if no other combination of procedures will protect the defendant against unauthorized use of statements made during the psychiatric examination. Accordingly, the safeguard of restricting the scope of the psychiatric examination should be viewed as preferable. If that approach appears ineffective, then postponing the examination should be considered.

Application of the "Waiver" Doctrine When Defense Psychiatric Testimony Is Offered at the Penalty Stage of a Capital Trial

As has been noted,[153] defense psychiatric testimony may be offered in support of various issues and in a wide variety of contexts. In most of these contexts, the conclusions reached in the second part of this essay provide a proper framework for analysis. If the defense wishes to offer psychiatric testimony in support of an issue that relates to guilt[154] or in support of a claim that the defendant is not mentally competent to stand trial,[155] the analysis of the paradigm case presented there should be applicable.[156] In these situations, the government psychiatrist should be allowed to question the defendant at a psychiatric examination so long as adequate safeguards are imposed. As in the paradigm case, the safeguards generally should be (1) providing the defense with a full and accurate record of statements made by defendant to the government psychiatrist, and (2) restricting the scope of the psychiatric examination so that the defendant is not asked about anything that relates to the act he is charged with committing.[157]

When the defendant offers to present psychiatric testimony at the penalty stage of a capital trial,[158] however, additional considerations are pertinent. First, because of the breadth of the issues involved in a penalty trial, the safeguards proposed for preventing impermissible prosecutorial use of statements made during the government psychiatric examination are less likely to be effective. To illustrate, suppose that defense seeks to present psychiatric testimony to establish the mitigating circumstance that "defendant was under the influence of extreme mental or emotional disturbance."[159] Restricting the government's psychiatric examination to matters that do not relate to the alleged criminal act might not be a sufficient safeguard because, even with this limitation, the psychiatrist would still be likely to learn about matters relating to the defendant's prior criminal history, his propensity to commit future criminal acts, and his general background and character. Since all these might be at issue in the penalty trial,[160] the prosecutor's access to statements made during the government examination would be likely to assist him in planning his strategy for examining witnesses at that proceeding.

Of course, these same concerns would be present whenever a capital defendant offers psychiatric testimony on any issue. The government psychiatric examination would include material that would be likely to assist the prosecutor if the case reaches the penalty stage.[161] Thus, it might seem logically consistent to hold either that the waiver doctrine should not be applied at all in capital cases, or that in those cases the safeguards required should be the same whether defense psychiatric testimony is offered during the trial or at the penalty stage.

My position, however, is that it is appropriate to apply different rules in the two situations. Thus, when defense psychiatric testimony is offered during a capital trial, so long as the appropriate safeguards are in effect,[162] the waiver doctrine may be properly applied; on the other hand, it should not be applied if the defendant merely seeks to offer psychiatric testimony at the penalty stage. In that situation the defendant should be allowed to present psychiatric testimony without being required to submit to questioning at a government psychiatric examination. My reasons for making this distinction are twofold: the first relates to a pragmatic balancing of the interests involved in the two situations, and the second pertains to the special concern for imposing procedural safeguards when a defendant's life is at stake.

The import of the analysis in this essay has been that as an approach to situations in which there is an apparent compelled election between constitutional rights, a general balancing test should be eschewed.[163] Rather, the focus here has been on whether the two rights involved are incompatible, and where they are, on whether the compelled election imposes an impermissible burden on one of the two rights.[164] Nevertheless, in cases in which the rights are incompatible and the only question is whether the condition attached to the exercise of one of them exacts too great a price, some balancing seems inevitable. The extent to which we will tolerate an onerous condition will to some degree depend on the gains yielded by that condition. Thus, in the present situation the extent to which we will tolerate a risk that the prosecution will use statements made during a psychiatric examination for improper purposes must depend in some measure on the extent to which the examination promotes legitimate government interests.

When a defense psychiatrist testifies on the issue of sanity, the government's legitimate need for evidence derived from a psychiatric examination is very significant. As the Supreme Court suggested in *Smith*,[165] evidence derived from this source may be the government's only means of effectively rebutting persuasive evidence presented on the sanity issue by the defendant. Moreover, if the government is unable to rebut evidence of the defendant's insanity, in most jurisdictions[166] it will lose the case: the defendant will be acquitted by reason of insanity. Thus, the government psychiatric examination directly promotes the government's important interest in obtaining an accurate verdict in criminal cases.

In contrast, the government's failure to rebut defense psychiatric testimony offered at the penalty trial will not have the same potential impact on the jury's determination. Even if the jury believes that the "defendant was under the influence of extreme mental or emotional disturbance," this will not necessarily lead them to reject the death penalty. At most,[167] they will treat that factor as a mitigating circumstance to be weighed with the other aggravating and mitigating circumstances involved in the case.[168] Thus, although a government psychiatric examination would promote the government's legitimate interest in obtaining an accurate death penalty determination, it is highly uncertain how *much* it would actually do so. Because the extent to which the government interest would be advanced is so questionable, the potential risks[169] of the examination necessarily loom larger.[170]

Furthermore, since holding in *Gregg v. Georgia*[171] that a system of capital punishment is not necessarily in violation of the Eighth Amendment, the Court has evinced an increasing concern[172] for protecting the procedural rights of capital defendants. In particular, the Court has been adamant in insisting that fair and fair-seeming procedures be applied at the penalty stage of a capital trial. Thus, in *Gardner v. Florida*[173] the Court broke with past precedent to hold that a judge could not impose a death sentence on the basis of a confidential presentence report unless the contents of the report were first disclosed to the defense.[174] In reaching this result, the Court emphasized that "[i]t is of vital importance to the defendant and to the community that any decision to impose the death sentence be, and appear to be, based on reason rather than caprice or emotion."[175] Moreover, in *Estelle v. Smith*[176] the Court not only held that the procedural protections of the Fifth Amendment privilege are fully applicable at the penalty stage[177] but also intimated that the Fifth Amendment protection provided at that stage will be greater than that provided to a defendant at trial.[178] These decisions[179] suggest that when a government psychiatric examination relates only to the question whether the death penalty will be imposed, the degree to which we should tolerate the risk that the prosecutor will use the fruits of the examination for impermissible purposes must be less. If this is true, then in the present situation, given the slight extent to which the examination advances legitimate government interests, the risk that the prosecutor may use the fruits of that examination for impermissible purposes is too high.

Appropriate Sanctions

If the waiver by offer of psychiatric evidence doctrine may be properly applied in certain situations, what sanction should be imposed when the defendant refuses to cooperate with the government psychiatrist? Suppose that a defendant gives notice of his intent to present expert psychiatric testimony in support of an insanity defense. Pursuant to a state statute, the trial judge appoints two psychiatrists to examine him. When they attempt to interview him, however, he answers only some of their questions, refusing to answer others, despite the fact that he has no legitimate basis for such refusal.[180] At trial, defendant seeks to offer expert psychiatric testimony. May the court properly exclude this testimony? If not, what remedy should be imposed?

From one perspective, the sanction of exclusion may appear appropriate. After all, if the defendant may be forced to elect between presenting expert psychiatric testimony and invoking his Fifth Amendment privilege during a government psychiatric examination, then it logically follows that a defendant's assertion of his Fifth Amendment privilege should cause him to lose the right to present expert psychiatric testimony. In upholding the exclusion sanction, a number of lower courts have implicitly accepted this rationale.[181]

One problem with this line of analysis is that the exclusion sanction raises serious problems under the Sixth Amendment right to compulsory process. *Washington v. Texas*[182] holds that the compulsory process clause guarantees a defendant the right not only to subpoena defense witnesses but also to present evidence relevant to a material issue.[183] The defendant may argue that a rule that rigidly applies the exclusion of psychiatric testimony sanction whenever the defendant refuses to answer the government psychiatrist's questions is no less arbitrary than the state rule of incompetency that was condemned by the Supreme Court in *Washington*.[184]

To date, the Court has considered only one case in which the constitutionality of an exclusion sanction was directly at issue. In *United States v. Nobles*[185] two eyewitnesses to a bank robbery testified that defendant was the robber.[186] Defense counsel sought to impeach their credibility by showing they had made prior inconsistent statements to a defense investigator who had interviewed both of them and preserved the essence of their remarks in a written report.[187] When the witnesses either denied making the alleged inconsistent statements or stated that they could not remember them, the defense investigator was called to testify about the statements made.[188] In response to the prosecutor's request, the trial judge ruled that a properly edited copy of the investigator's report should be submitted to the prosecutor at the completion of the investigator's impeachment testimony.[189] When defense counsel stated that he did not intend to produce the report, the trial judge ruled that the investigator would not be allowed to testify about the statements made to him by the witnesses.[190]

The Supreme Court held that this ruling was proper. After determining that the trial judge could properly require defense counsel to disclose the relevant portions of the investigator's report,[191] the Court determined that the "preclusion sanction was an entirely proper method of assuring compliance with its order."[192] Defendant's Sixth Amendment compulsory process claim was rejected because, as the Court put it, "[t]he Sixth Amendment does not confer the right to present testimony free from the legitimate demands of the adversarial system . . . ."[193] The Court suggested that unless the investigator's report were produced to provide a check on the truth of the investigator's testimony, that testimony itself would be of much less value.[194] The Court also stated that once the trial judge decided that the jury should hear "the full testimony of the investigator" rather than a truncated portion of it, the judge should not be deprived "of the power to effectuate that judgment."[195]

Nobles's analysis suggests that in assessing the validity of an exclusion sanction, two concerns are particularly germane. The first relates to the evidentiary value of the testimony to be excluded. *Nobles*'s result may be justified on the ground that given the defendant's failure to disclose the investigator's report, the investigator's testimony was of such dubious value that a court could properly rule it inadmissible. The point is not that this evidence would necessarily fail to meet minimum standards of reliability; rather, on the particular point at issue, the Court's concern is with requiring production of the most reliable evidence available.[196]

Of course, a second concern is also intertwined. *Nobles*'s analysis clearly suggests that the exclusion sanction will be appropriate if it is a necessary means of enforcing a proper evidentiary ruling. Thus, the trial judge in *Nobles* might properly have found that excluding the investigator's testimony was a necessary means of forcing the defendant to present the more reliable evidence of the investigator's testimony—the report. If this were the case, the exclusion sanction would seem appropriate not only to ensure presentation of the most reliable form of evidence to the fact finder but also to prevent unfairness to the government. The investigator's testimony without the report is not only less reliable than the testimony with the report; it is also likely to be more favorable to the defendant. Thus, if the defendant is able to present this testimony, because of the defense's purposeful refusal to comply with the trial court's proper order the government will be placed in a less favorable position than it would have been had the judge's evidentiary ruling been complied with. The exclusion sanction would then be justified as a necessary means of preventing the defendant from obtaining this type of unfair advantage.

While *Nobles* does not discuss constitutional limitations on use of the exclusion sanction, the Court's compulsory process decisions[197] make clear that the government's right to exclude reliable material evidence offered by the defense must be narrowly confined. As Professor Westen has demonstrated, "[t]he prevailing standard . . . derives from *Washington*: The state may not use disqualification to further its independent interests if less drastic means are available."[198] Thus, in order to justify the exclusion sanction in the present situation the government should be required to show that there are no less drastic means of enforcing its legitimate interests.

Determining whether the exclusion sanction is the least drastic means of enforcing the government's legitimate interests depends on precise definition of those interests. If, pursuant to the waiver doctrine, the court properly rules that defendant must answer questions posed during a government psychiatric examination, the government has an interest in obtaining reliable evidence, as the government examination is needed to help the jury make an accurate assessment of the defense psychiatric testimony.[199] Moreover, based on *Nobles*'s analysis,[200] the court has an independent interest in enforcing its evidentiary ruling.

The government may argue that in this situation as in *Nobles*, less reliable evidence, in the form of the defense psychiatric testimony, should be excluded because by refusing to answer proper questions posed during the government examination the defense prevented production of more reliable evidence. It impermissibly prevented the government from fully presenting its perspective on the issue in question to the jury. In support of this position, the government may rely not only on *Nobles* but also on lower court cases dealing with the appropriate sanction to be applied when a defendant who testifies as a witness refuses to answer questions properly asked on cross-examination. Although authority dealing with this issue is sparse,[201] the prevailing view appears to be that if the defendant refuses to answer questions that relate to the core of his testimony, as opposed to those that pertain to merely collateral matters,[202] the trial judge has discretion to impose the sanction of striking his entire testimony.[203] Given that in some situations the defense psychiatrist may be viewed as presenting the defendant's testimony,[204] the government may argue that the remedy imposed in cases involving a violation of the testimonial waiver doctrine should be appropriate in the psychiatric testimony context as well.

There are significant differences between the two situations, however. First, it should be emphasized that defense psychiatric testimony can never be treated as the precise equivalent of a defendant's testimony. Even if the defense psychiatrist's testimony is based on what the defendant told her, her evaluation of his credibility is a filter through which his story must pass. Her testimony will never simply repeat the defendant's story; it will present his story as evaluated by her. And, since the psychiatrist will be subject to cross-examination, the prosecution may independently test the credibility of the defendant's story by examining the defense psychiatrist's evaluation of it.[205] A government psychiatrist's testimony, based on her own examination of the defendant, may provide an additional opportunity to evaluate the credibility of the story defendant told the defense psychiatrist, but loss of such testimony will never impair the government's interest in obtaining an accurate assessment of defense testimony as much as failure to cross-examine a defendant-witness impairs its interest in obtaining an accurate assessment of his testimony.[206]

Moreover, in most cases a defendant's failure to answer a proper question or questions posed by a government psychiatrist will be likely to have less impact than a refusal to respond to proper cross-examination at trial. Obviously, a refusal to respond to a government psychiatrist will not cause an actual disruption of trial, because it will occur at a pretrial proceeding. And such a refusal cannot be generally viewed as an affront to the judge's authority, because, at least if the defendant submits to the examination and answers certain questions, he will probably not have clear notice that he is legally required to answer the question posed.[207] Even more significantly, perhaps, a defendant's refusal to answer particular questions is far less likely to impede successful completion of a psychiatric examination than it is to stymie a trial prosecutor's effort to conduct an effective cross-examination. Because the psychiatrist will base her evaluation on all data collected,[208] it is unlikely that a defendant's refusal to respond to a particular line of inquiry will severely impair her ability to reach a conclusion. Indeed, the psychiatrist may be able to draw certain inferences from his refusal to answer, and thus his refusal to respond to a particular line of inquiry is not likely to be critical.[209]

Accordingly, the testimonial waiver remedy cases should not be viewed as closely analogous to the present situation. They may be helpful, however, in defining an appropriate limit on the use of the exclusion sanction in the present context. Drawing on Wigmore's analysis,[210] lower courts have stated that when a defendant or other witness improperly refuses to respond to cross-examination that relates to a collateral issue, a motion to strike that witness's trial testimony should be denied.[211] Although the definition of a collateral issue is murky,[212] in the present context it should be defined as one that is not of central importance to the examination. In the context of a psychiatric examination, however, a defendant's refusal to answer questions will not be of central importance unless the refusal impairs the psychiatrist's ability to reach a conclusion about his sanity. Accordingly, if the defendant submits to a government psychiatric examination and answers enough questions to allow the psychiatrist to reach such a conclusion, the exclusion sanction should not be appropriate. In testifying to her conclusion about the defendant's sanity, the government psychiatrist will of course be allowed to testify about the defendant's refusal to answer certain questions. In most cases, this alone should be sufficient remedy for the defendant's refusal to answer proper questions.[213]

Even when the defendant's refusal to cooperate is so pervasive that the psychiatrist is unable to form an opinion on the issue of sanity, the remedy of excluding defense psychiatric testimony is not necessarily appropriate. At the least, the trial judge should be required to find specifically that only the excluding sanction will adequately serve the legitimate government interests at stake.[214] In most situations, the government's related interests in promoting a reliable assessment of defense testimony and preventing the defendant from obtaining an unfair advantage may be safeguarded by less drastic alternatives. First, the government psychiatrist should be permitted to tell the jury that the defendant refused to answer her questions.[215] Moreover, the court should be permitted to comment on the defendant's refusal to speak to the government psychiatrist,[216] perhaps instructing the jurors that they may properly take his refusal into account in weighing the credibility of his statements to his own psychiatrist. As a supplemental remedy, in appropriate cases the defendant's refusal to cooperate with the government psychiatrist might be weighed against the defendant when the question to be determined is whether the government has presented sufficient evidence to require the issue of sanity to be submitted to the jury.[217]

These remedies will certainly promote the government's interest in obtaining a reliable evaluation of the defense psychiatric testimony. They should also be sufficient to prevent the defendant from obtaining an unfair advantage as a result of his refusal to cooperate. While a judicial comment on that refusal is not the equivalent of a government psychiatrist's testimony, it would be a rare case in which a defendant or defense counsel would be likely to conclude that receiving an adverse judicial comment instead of possibly adverse government psychiatric testimony would be to his tactical advantage.[218] Thus, the proposed remedies would deter the defense from refusing to answer proper questions in order to gain an advantage; and in most cases they would place the government in at least as strong a position as it would have had if the defendant had fully cooperated with the government psychiatrist.[219] Under the circumstances, that should be sufficient to protect the government's legitimate interests.

Conclusion

In light of the Court's holding in *Estelle v. Smith*, the waiver by offer of psychiatric evidence doctrine is of particular interest, because when that doctrine is applied a defendant is seemingly forced to elect between the constitutional right to present expert psychiatric testimony and the constitutional right to invoke his Fifth Amendment privilege during a government psychiatric examination. In exploring the ramifications of the waiver doctrine, I have first attempted to develop the approach to be used when a defendant is apparently compelled to elect between two constitutional rights and then have applied that approach to the specific situation involved in the waiver doctrine.

Focusing on the situation in which the defendant offers expert psychiatric testimony in support of an insanity defense, I conclude that the waiver by offer of psychiatric testimony doctrine is theoretically defensible. Given that the defendant's right to present psychiatric testimony may be tempered by the legitimate needs of the adversary system, the compelled psychiatric examination provides an appropriate means of allowing the government to test the credibility of the defense psychiatric testimony. The government's right to impose conditions on the defendant's constitutional right to present psychiatric testimony must be limited, however, by its legitimate interest in ensuring fairness in the exercise of that constitutional right. Thus, I conclude that the waiver doctrine will be constitutional if, but only if, the government is effectively prevented from using the fruits of the compelled psychiatric examination for any purpose other than the legitimate one of obtaining evidence for use on the issue of the defendant's sanity.

As it is currently applied, the waiver doctrine does not effectively prevent the government from using the fruits of the compelled psychiatric examination to strengthen its case on the issues of guilt or penalty. Unless safeguards adequate to prevent such use are imposed, the doctrine should be unconstitutional. After evaluating various alternatives, I conclude that the minimum safeguards required are as follows: first, the defense should be provided with a complete and accurate transcript of the government psychiatric examination; second, the government psychiatrist should be prohibited from questioning the defendant about any circumstances related to the act he is charged with committing; and finally, in appropriate cases the issues of guilt and sanity should be bifurcated so that in determining the defendant's guilt, the jury will be prevented from improperly considering government psychiatric testimony that is admissible only on the issue of sanity.

Although the case in which defendant offers psychiatric testimony on the issue of sanity provides a framework of analysis that applies to most other situations, the case in which the defense presents expert psychiatric testimony at the penalty stage of a capital trial is one that must be treated differently. Based partly on a pragmatic balancing of the interests involved and partly on a concern for affording stricter procedural safeguards when a defendant's life is directly at stake, I conclude that in this situation the defendant should be allowed to present expert psychiatric testimony without being required to submit to any government psychiatric examination.

If this analysis is accepted, the defense will be confronted with a difficult tactical choice. When favorable expert psychiatric testimony is available, they will need to decide whether to offer it in support of an insanity defense and thus subject the defendant to an examination that may result in government psychiatric testimony's being offered to rebut that insanity defense, or to preserve the testimony so that if the defendant is convicted of the capital offense it may be presented at the penalty trial without fear of rebuttal. Since the insanity defense is seldom accepted and many capital defendants are primarily concerned with avoiding the possibility of the death penalty,[220] a significant number of capital defendants probably will choose to present their expert psychiatric testimony only at the penalty stage. In some respects, this result may be beneficial. The empirical data suggests that in many cases the jury or judge[221] will be interested in evaluating expert psychiatric testimony only for the purpose of determining whether or not the defendant should be executed. If this is so, it seems appropriate that defense psychiatric testimony should be introduced only for that purpose; that is, as a means of showing that the defendant should not be sentenced to death.

From one perspective, the consequences of this analysis may seem anomalous. A capital defendant may not present expert psychiatric testimony in support of an insanity defense unless he is willing to submit to a psychiatric examination that may lead to expert testimony that will be used by the government to rebut that defense. On the other hand, once convicted of the capital offense, the defendant may submit exactly the same psychiatric testimony at the penalty hearing without fear that he will be required to submit to a government examination. Nevertheless, this result appears designed to accommodate the competing interests in a reasonably equitable fashion. Moreover, whether or not one accepts the analysis of the psychiatric testimony/examination election presented in this essay, it is undeniable that the forced election will present special difficulties for a defendant whose life is directly at stake. In certain cases at least, expert psychiatric testimony clearly may be the most vital form of mitigating evidence that can be presented. *Lockett v. Ohio* and its progeny indicate that the defendant has a constitutional right to present this evidence at the penalty trial.[222] This right should not be conditioned on the defendant's submitting to a psychiatric examination at which he knows that communications made by him to the psychiatrist can be used to result in his execution. Such a result would appear to be contrary to the Court's articulated goal of providing fair and fair-seeming procedures at the penalty stage of a capital trial.

NOTES

I am particularly indebted to Albert W. Alschuler for his helpful criticism of an earlier draft of this essay. While he cannot be held responsible for my analysis, his comments greatly deepened my understanding of the issues addressed in the essay. I would also like to thank Peter Arenella, John Attanasio, Tom Gerety, and Mark Nordenberg for their helpful comments on earlier drafts, and Mary Beth Taylor for her invaluable research assistance.

1. Based upon the Supreme Court's latest decisions, the Constitution does not prohibit the death penalty. *See* Gregg v. Georgia, 428 U.S. 153, 187 (1976) (plurality opinion). The Court has indicated, however, that with one possible narrow exception mandatory capital punishment will be unconstitutional. *See* Woodson v. North Carolina, 428 U.S. 280 (1976) (holding mandatory sentence of death upon conviction of first-degree murder unconstitutional); Roberts v. Louisiana (Roberts II), 431 U.S. 633 (1977) (per curiam) (invalidating statute requiring death penalty for intentional killing of firefighter or peace officer engaged in performance of lawful duties), *id.* at 637 n.5 (reserving the question "whether or in what circumstances mandatory death sentences may be constitutionally applied to prisoners serving life sentences"). Thus, in death penalty cases, the jury must first determine whether the defendant is guilty of the capital offense, and then, if a capital verdict is rendered, the jury or other sentencer must decide whether the defendant shall be sentenced to death. For an illuminating treatment of some of the procedures used for deciding which capital defendants shall be sentenced to death, *see generally* Gillers, *Deciding Who Dies*, 129 U. PA. L. REV. 1 (1980).

2. For an excellent discussion of the problems involved in determining the issue of sanity in capital cases, *see* C. BLACK, CAPITAL PUNISHMENT: THE INEVITABILITY OF CAPRICE AND MISTAKE, 52–55 (1974). With vivid examples, Professor Black demonstrates that although "[w]e are committed, as a society, not to execute people whose action is attributable to what we call 'insanity,' " nevertheless, "where the crime exhibits a total wild departure from normality, we come exactly to the point where consideration of the insanity problem is at once most necessary and most difficult." *Id.* at 52–54.

3. In an interview with the author conducted on June 28, 1982, John L. Carroll, an Alabama attorney who had tried dozens of capital cases, noted that a sentencing jury is much more likely to be merciful if it is provided with some explanation for why the convicted capital defendant acted as he did. Moreover, in a recent decision the Supreme Court emphasized that in certain circumstances evidence "of severe emotional disturbance is particularly relevant" mitigating evidence. Eddings v. Oklahoma, 455 U.S. 104, 115 (1982). *Eddings* vacated an Oklahoma death penalty on the ground that the trial judge failed to consider the sixteen-year-old defendant's turbulent family history, which included beatings by a harsh father, as well as severe emotional problems. *See also* Bonnie, *Psychiatry and the Death Penalty: Emerging Problems in Virginia*, 66 VA. L. REV. 167,

181 (1980) (commenting on "[t]he indispensability of psychiatric testimony in capital cases").

4. *See, e.g.*, Estelle v. Smith, 451 U.S. 454 (1981) (discussed *infra* in text at notes 6–18).

5. A psychiatrist who has not personally examined the defendant will generally be permitted to testify so long as she has some other basis for reaching a conclusion on the issue in question. *See, e.g.*, People v. Smith, 93 Ill. App. 3d 26, 416 N.E.2d 814 (1981) (psychiatrist testifying at trial need never have interviewed the defendant in order to develop an opinion about the defendant's sanity at the time of the crime); Commonwealth v. Scarborough, 491 Pa. 300, 421 A.2d 147 (1980) (proper for a qualified medical expert to offer an opinion on a person's mental condition based solely on a hypothetical question, interviews with people connected with the defendant, and an analysis of tests conducted on the defendant).

While admissible, the extent of the psychiatrist's knowledge goes to the weight of her testimony; thus a psychiatrist who testifies after merely observing the defendant and evaluating records will obviously be susceptible to cross-examination impeaching the basis of her conclusions. For an example of a case in which this type of cross-examination was apparently successful, *see* United States v. Hiss, 88 F. Supp. 559 (S.D.N.Y. 1950). On the basis of courtroom observation only, a defense psychiatrist characterized the government's star witness as a psychopath. On cross-examination, the prosecutor forced the psychiatrist to acknowledge that the personality traits on which he based his conclusion were shared by well-known and highly respected people, including the psychiatrist himself. *See* Slovenko, *Witnesses, Psychiatry and the Credibility of Testimony*, 19 U. FLA. L. REV. 1, 11 (1966). *See also* R. TRAVER, ANATOMY OF A MURDER 376–82 (1958) (describing effective cross-examination of a government psychiatrist whose testimony that defendant was sane at the time of the killing was based only on personal observation of the defendant during trial).

6. 451 U.S. 454 (1981).

7. *Id*. at 468. As an alternative ground for its decision, the Court held that the government's failure to notify defendant's attorney of the scope of the psychiatric examination violated defendant's Sixth Amendment right to counsel. *Id*. at 471. For a discussion of the implications of this aspect of the Court's holding, *see generally* White, *Waiver and the Death Penalty: The Implications of* Estelle v. Smith, 72 J. CRIM. LAW & CRIMINOLOGY 1522, 1539–47 (1981).

8. For a fuller discussion of the record in *Smith, see* White, *supra* note 7, at 1524–26.

9. 451 U.S. at 458 n.5.

10. *Id*. at 457.

11. *See* TIME, June 1, 1981, at 64.

12. 451 U.S. at 465.

13. *Id*. at 459–60.

14. *Id*. at 460. For an analysis of the type of testimony offered by Dr. Grigson, *see generally* Dix, *Expert Prediction Testimony in Capital Sentencing: Evidentiary and Constitutional Considerations*, 19 AM. CRIM. L. REV. 1 (1981).

15. The Court concluded that the defendant's Fifth Amendment privilege

was violated "because the State used as evidence against [him] the substance of his disclosures during the pretrial psychiatric examination." 451 U.S. at 465. This conclusion was necessarily premised on a finding that at least if the results of the examination were to be used against him at trial or penalty, the defendant had a Fifth Amendment privilege to decline to answer questions during the psychiatric examination conducted by Dr. Grigson. *See id.* at 466.

16. *Id.* at 465.

17. *Id.*

18. *Id.* at 469 n.13.

19. *See, e.g.*, Vanderbilt v. State, 629 S.W.2d 709 (Tex. 1981) (unnecessary to decide whether *Smith* applied to a psychological exam in which a psychologist gave the defendant a battery of psychological tests).

20. In limiting its Fifth Amendment holding, the Court declined to decide to what extent the Fifth Amendment would preclude the psychiatrist from testifying about the defendant's conduct, as opposed to his statements. 451 U.S. at 464–65. In United States v. Gholson, 675 F.2d 734 (5th Cir. 1982), a case decided after *Smith*, the Fifth Circuit held that *Smith* applied to preclude the government psychiatrist from testifying at the penalty trial that the defendant's refusal to answer his questions evidenced a lack of remorse. *Id.* at 741. Since *Smith*'s underlying premise is that a defendant has a constitutional right to refuse to answer the government psychiatrist's questions, 451 U.S. at 465, *Gholson*'s holding appears to be entirely consistent with *Smith*'s rationale. *Smith* essentially holds that for Fifth Amendment purposes a government psychiatric examination must be treated as equivalent to a custodial interrogation. In *Miranda* the Court made it clear that "it is impermissible to penalize an individual for exercising his Fifth Amendment privilege when he is under police custodial interrogation. The prosecution may not, therefore, use at trial the fact that he stood mute or claimed his privilege in the face of accusation." 384 U.S. at 468 n.37. Under *Smith*, the same result should apply to prohibit the government from using the defendant's exercise of his privilege to show lack of remorse at the penalty hearing.

Moreover, since the government psychiatric examination is essentially calculated to probe the defendant's mental processes, *see infra* notes 90–91, it would appear that, based on the Court's analysis in Schmerber v. California, 384 U.S. 757, 764 (1966), almost any psychiatric testimony derived from the examination would be within the protection of the Fifth Amendment privilege. For an analysis of this issue, *see* Wesson, *The Privilege Against Self-Incrimination in Civil Commitment Proceedings*, 1980 Wis. L. Rev. 697, 703–18. *See generally* C. Mc-Cormick, Law of Evidence 287 (2d ed. 1972); Arenella, Schmerber *and the Privilege Against Self-incrimination: A Reappraisal*, 20 Am. Crim. L. Rev. 31, 36–42 (1982).

21. 451 U.S. at 465.

22. Among the issues relating to mental capacity that might be raised at trial are the defenses of insanity, diminished capacity, and automatism.

23. Prior to trial, the defendant might raise the issue of his competency to stand trial. In *Smith* the Court ruled that whether or not the defendant raises this issue, the government is entitled to a mental examination specifically di-

rected to the issue of competency, provided that the government psychiatrist will be allowed to use the testimonial communications made during the competency examination solely for the purpose of testifying on that issue. *See* 451 U.S. at 465.

An extra dimension may be added to the pretrial election dilemma when the capital defendant is indigent and the jurisdiction will not provide funds that will allow the defense to obtain an independent psychiatrist. In order to explore the possibility of presenting expert psychiatric testimony in support of a defense at trial or as a mitigating circumstance at penalty, such a defendant may find it necessary to submit to a court-ordered examination conducted by a government psychiatrist. If the government psychiatrist is then permitted to testify for the government about incriminating statements made by the defendant, the defendant's Fifth Amendment privilege to remain silent (at the examination) comes into direct conflict with his Sixth Amendment right to explore available defenses. Recognizing this conflict, the Fourth Circuit in Gibson v. Zahradnick, 581 F.2d 75 (4th Cir. 1978), held that the government psychiatrist would not be permitted to testify on the issue of guilt because "[e]xercise of [a defendant's] right to a competency determination to prove that he was insane at the time of the act cannot be conditioned upon a waiver of his constitutional privilege against self-incrimination." *Id.* at 80. Perhaps an even more appropriate way of resolving this dilemma would be to hold that an indigent capital defendant who shows signs of mental disturbance should be allowed sufficient expenses to retain a defense psychiatrist who will render an independent examination of the defendant's mental state.

24. At the penalty hearing, defendant might raise myriad mitigating circumstances relating to his mental or emotional condition. For example, he might claim that his crime was the product of a severe mental or emotional disturbance; alternatively, he might assert that in view of his good mental condition he is extremely unlikely to present a future danger to society.

25. The Fifth Amendment privilege recognized in *Smith* relates only to a right not to answer questions posed during the government psychiatric examination. If, as I have suggested, the privilege extends to all testimonial evidence *see supra* note 20, however, then, a defendant whose Fifth Amendment privilege is applicable should not be forced to submit to a psychiatric examination, because such an examination is designed to delve into the defendant's mental state.

26. The question whether a defendant may be forced to elect between raising an insanity defense and asserting Fifth Amendment objections during the government psychiatric examination is addressed in a footnote, however. *See infra* note 86.

27. *See, e.g.*, State v. Smith, 131 Ariz. 29, 638 P.2d 696 (1982) (psychiatrist appointed by the court at defendant's request testified for the government on the issue of defendant's sanity); Booker v. State, 397 So. 2d 910 (Fla. 1981) *application for stay of execution denied*, 413 So. 2d 756 (Fla. 1982) (defendant claimed that government cross-examination of defendant who testified to loss of memory at penalty phase was predicated upon psychiatric reports stemming from defendant's pretrial mental examination). Vanderbilt v. State, 629 S.W.2d 709 (Tex. 1981), *cert. denied*, 456 U.S. 910 (1982) (psychologist who premised his conclu-

sions in part upon psychological tests administered by his assistant testified for the government at sentencing).

28. Of course, it is impossible to predict exactly what impact a particular ruling on the Fifth Amendment issue will have on the quality of the expert psychiatric examination presented either in any particular case or in all cases. A ruling that a defendant who presents expert psychiatric testimony will not be permitted to interpose Fifth Amendment objections to a psychiatric examination designed to enable the government to present its own expert psychiatric testimony for a limited purpose (or for any purpose) may result in a situation in which both the government and the defendant will present expert psychiatric testimony of a high quality. On the other hand, the defense may conclude that not presenting psychiatric testimony is preferable to having the defendant subjected to a psychiatric examination that will enable a government psychiatrist to present testimony that relates to a material issue in the case. In that situation, the result of the rule restricting the defendant's Fifth Amendment privilege may be to eliminate all expert psychiatric testimony.

29. The limited empirical evidence suggests that expert psychiatric testimony is most likely to play an important role in capital cases. For example, in their classic study of jury behavior, Kalven and Zeisel found that "[t]he defense is raised in only 2 percent of all the cases and three quarters of these are homicide cases." H. KALVEN & H. ZEISEL, THE AMERICAN JURY 330 (1966). *See generally* S. KADISH & M. PAULSEN, CRIMINAL LAW AND ITS PROCESSES 583–84 (2d ed. 1969).

30. For a significant noncapital case applying a variation of the waiver doctrine, *see* United States v. Hinckley, 525 F. Supp. 1342, 1350 (D.D.C. 1981) (so long as defendant's counsel intended to offer evidence of insanity at trial, suppression of evidence from compelled psychiatric examination was not required to protect privilege against self-incrimination).

31. *See infra* text at notes 47–62.

32. *See, e.g.*, Drope v. Missouri, 420 U.S. 162 (1974); Pate v. Robinson, 383 U.S. 375 (1966).

33. *See* People v. Segal, 54 N.Y.2d 58, 429 N.E.2d 107, 444 N.Y.S.2d 588 (1981).

34. *See, e.g., Hinckley*; United States v. Cohen, 530 F.2d 43 (5th Cir. 1976).

35. *See, e.g.*, People v. Cruz, 26 Cal. 3d 233, 605 P.2d 830, 162 Cal. Rptr. 1 (1980).

36. TEX. CRIM. PROC. CODE ANN. § 37.071(b)(2) (Vernon 1981). Two other state death penalty statutes provide for this type of aggravating circumstance. *See* VA. CODE § 19.264.2 (Cum. Supp. 1981); IDAHO CODE § 19-2515(f)(8) (1979). A third state recently repealed a similar death penalty statute and replaced it with one providing capital punishment for aggravated first-degree murder. Under this statute, future dangerousness is a factor the jury may consider in deciding whether leniency is merited. *See* WASH. REV. CODE ANN. § 10.95.070(8) (Supp. 1982).

37. This type of mitigating circumstance is recognized under many states' capital punishment statutes. *See, e.g.*, COLO. REV. STAT. § 16-11-103(5)(b) (1978), § (S.1)(a) (Cum. Supp. 1981); CONN. GEN. STAT. ANN. § 56a-46a(f)(2)

(West Supp. 1982); FLA. STAT. ANN. § 921.141(b)(6) (West Supp. 1982); 42 PA. CONS. STAT. ANN. § 9711(e)(2) (Purdon Supp. 1981); WASH. REV. CODE ANN. § 10.95.070(2) (Supp. 1982). Moreover, under Lockett v. Ohio, 438 U.S. 586 (1978), the defendant has a constitutional right to proffer this type of evidence to the capital sentencer as independent mitigating evidence, whether or not it fits within a statutorily recognized category of mitigating evidence. *See infra* note 158.

38. In most jurisdictions, defendants are required to provide notice of an intention to present psychiatric testimony that bears on the issue of sanity. *See, e.g.*, PA. R. CRIM. P. 305C(1)(b).

39. In a context in which the insanity defense is at issue, some courts have explicitly stated that the defendant's offer of expert psychiatric testimony constitutes a waiver of the Fifth Amendment privilege. *See, e.g.*, Battie v. Estelle, 655 F.2d 692, 701 (5th Cir. 1981) (dictum); United States v. Albright, 388 F.2d 719, 726–27 (4th Cir. 1968) (holding). *See generally* Note, *Requiring a Criminal Defendant to Submit to a Government Psychiatric Examination: An Invasion of the Privilege Against Self-Incrimination*, 83 HARV. L. REV. 648, 667 (1970). As other courts have recognized, this doctrine of waiver cannot be justified on the ground that the defendant's act of presenting expert psychiatric testimony constitutes a voluntary and intelligent relinquishment of his Fifth Amendment privilege. *See, e.g.*, Commonwealth v. Pomponi, 447 Pa. 154, 160, 284 A.2d 708, 711 (1971). Rather, the waiver doctrine represents a conclusion that for reasons of policy the defendant's act of presenting expert psychiatric testimony should result in a forfeiture of his Fifth Amendment protection. *See* United States v. Cohen, 530 F.2d 43, 47–48 (1976).

40. In most jurisdictions it is perfectly proper for a defendant to assert an insanity defense without conceding that he committed the act that constitutes the alleged criminal offense. *See, e.g.*, United States v. Clark, 617 F.2d 180, 186 n.12 (9th Cir. 1980); Mason v. State, 49 Ala. App. 545, 274 So. 2d 100 (1973). *See also* CAL. REV. CODE § 1016. For an exposition of this statute, *see* D. LOUISELL & G. HAZARD, INSANITY AS A DEFENSE: THE BIFURCATED TRIAL, 805 (1961).

41. Even if his Fifth Amendment privilege is applicable, the defendant may be required to submit to a government psychiatric examination in some circumstances. *See Smith*, 451 U.S. at 465. Unless the waiver doctrine applies, however, it seems clear under *Smith* that absent a showing that the defendant intelligently waived his Fifth Amendment rights before making any statements to the government psychiatrist, the government will not be permitted to present psychiatric testimony based on the defendant's statements at either the guilt or penalty phase of the trial. *See id.* at 466–69.

42. 410 U.S. 284 (1973).

43. In *Chambers* a defendant charged with the murder of a police officer called as a witness one McDonald, who on three prior occasions had orally admitted the killing and had made but later repudiated a written confession. The Mississippi courts ruled that the defense was not permitted to cross-examine McDonald as an adverse witness since under Mississippi's "voucher" rule a party could not impeach his own witness. It also held that the testimony of the three persons to whom McDonald confessed was inadmissible hearsay. The Supreme

Court concluded, however, "that the exclusion of this critical evidence, coupled with the state's refusal to permit [the defendant] to cross-examine McDonald, denied him a trial in accord with traditional and fundamental standards of due process." *Id.* at 302. For an incisive analysis of the *Chambers* case, *see* Westen, *The Compulsory Process Clause*, 73 MICH. L. REV. 71, 151–56 (1974).

44. 451 U.S. 454 (1981).

45. See *supra* text at notes 15–18. Based on *Smith*'s limited holding, the Court could hold that when a defendant presents psychiatric testimony, the Fifth Amendment right recognized in *Smith* is simply not present. As a matter of Fifth Amendment jurisprudence, however, it seems preferable to begin with the premise that the defendant will be permitted to invoke the Fifth Amendment privilege in situations that are functionally similar to that presented in *Smith*. Then the question whether the defendant's presentation of expert psychiatric testimony should cause him to lose the privilege may be directly considered.

46. Most jurisdictions now recognize that expert psychiatric testimony relating to a specific mental state of the defendant is competent evidence. *See, e.g.*, Commonwealth v. McCusker, 448 Pa. 382, 292 A.2d 286 (1972) (expert psychiatric testimony admissible on issue whether defendant acted in heat of passion held competent); People v. Sanchez, 112 M.2d 1005, 446 N.Y.S.2d 164 (1982) (psychiatric testimony concerning defendant's IQ held competent for defense of duress); People v. Parks, 195 Colo. 344, 579 P.2d 76 (1978) (expert psychiatric testimony regarding defendant's mental ability to make free and intelligent decisions at time of arrest held relevant).

47. 390 U.S. 377 (1968).

48. For cases applying the *Simmons* principle, *see* Lefkowitz v. Cunningham, 431 U.S. 801, 807–08 (1977) (person cannot be forced to choose between his First Amendment right of association and his Fifth Amendment privilege against self-incrimination); Brooks v. Tennessee, 406 U.S. 605, 612 (1972) (defendant cannot be forced to either testify at the beginning of his defense or not at all). *See generally* Westen, *Incredible Dilemmas: Conditioning One Constitutional Right on the Forfeiture of Another*, 66 IOWA L. REV. 741, 744 n.10 (1981); Note, *Resolving Tensions Between Constitutional Rights: Use Immunity in Concurrent or Related Proceedings*, 76 COLUM. L. REV. 674 (1974).

49. In Crampton v. Ohio, a companion case to McGautha v. California, 402 U.S. 183 (1971) Justice Harlan qualified the analysis presented in *Simmons*, concluding that when the government compels the defendant to elect between two constitutional rights, while the defendant "may have a right, even of constitutional dimensions, to follow which-ever course he chooses, the Constitution does not by that token always forbid requiring him to choose." 402 U.S. at 212–13. *See generally* Westen, *supra* note 48, at 743–44 n.10. As Westen indicates, *id.* at 744 n.10, despite Justice Harlan's recantation, the Court has applied the *Simmons* principle in post-*Crampton* cases. *See supra* note 48.

50. The *Simmons* approach may be justified on both historical and policy grounds. As the Court recognized in Portash v. New Jersey, 440 U.S. 450, 459 (1979), a primary purpose of the Fifth Amendment privilege is to prohibit certain types of government-imposed choices absolutely. In today's society, perhaps the paradigm example of a prohibited choice is one in which the defendant is faced

with the cruel trilemma under which he is forced to choose among incriminating himself, committing perjury, or suffering the penalty of contempt. *See generally* M. BERGER, TAKING THE FIFTH 209–19 (1980); L. LEVY, ORIGINS OF THE FIFTH AMENDMENT 266–332 (1968); Friendly, *The Fifth Amendment Tomorrow: The Case for Constitutional Change*, 37 U. CIN. L. REV. 671, 694–95 (1968). As Justice Harlan's analysis in *Simmons* implicitly recognizes, when the defendant is forced to choose between exercising the privilege and asserting some other constitutional right, the choice presented can be viewed as analogous to that involved in the cruel trilemma described above because in both cases the defendant will be forced to suffer a clearly identifiable and obviously significant penalty if he attempts to exercise his privilege to remain silent. Thus, there are at least prima facie grounds for concluding that this type of choice should be absolutely prohibited.

51. As Westen points out, *"Simmons* has nothing to say about constitutional entitlements that are the logical converse of one another, because, by definition, they cannot by their nature be given simultaneous effect." Westen, *supra* note 49, at 743 n.7. For example, a criminal defendant may not simultaneously exercise his constitutional right to testify at trial and his constitutional right not to testify at trial. *Id*.

52. For discussions of the problem of unconstitutional conditions, *see, e.g.*, Westen, *supra* note 48, at 753–58; Van Alstyne, *The Demise of the Right-Privilege Distinction in Constitutional Law*, 81 HARV. L. REV. 1439 (1968); Comment, *Another Look at Unconstitutional Conditions*, 117 U. PA. L. REV. 144 (1968); Note, *Unconstitutional Conditions*, 73 HARV. L. REV. 1595 (1960).

53. Westen, *supra* note 48.

54. One of several examples discussed by Westen relates to the scope of a defendant's right under the double jeopardy clause not to be subjected to retrial following certain types of mistrial. The reason the defendant can be compelled to elect between his constitutional right not to be retried following a mistrial and his (presumed) constitutional right to move for mistrial is that "the defendant's right to have the need for a mistrial measured by the strict 'manifest necessity' standard . . . does not exist if the mistrial was granted at the defendant's request." Jeffers v. United States, 432 U.S. 137, 152 (1977) (plurality opinion). *See* Westen, *supra* note 48, at 752.

55. *See id*. at 749.

56. *Id*. at 753–58.

57. *Id*. at 757. Westen also quotes with approval some of Justice Harlan's language in *Crampton*: The "question is whether compelling the election impairs to an appreciable extent any of the policies behind the rights involved." *Id*. at 755, quoting 402 U.S. at 213. There would appear to be a distinct difference between these two tests, however, because the quoted test focuses directly on the election's effect on the constitutional rights at stake rather than allowing for an ad hoc balancing of government and individual interests. It is not clear that Justice Harlan intended his statement in *Crampton* to have this meaning, however, because a fuller quote of his statement is: "[t]he *threshold* question is whether compelling the election impairs to an appreciable extent any of the policies behind the rights involved." 402 U.S. at 213 (emphasis added). Thus, Jus-

tice Harlan may have intended his statement to articulate merely the first prong of his balancing test. For Fifth Amendment cases in which Justice Harlan set out a more detailed balancing test, *see, e.g.*, California v. Byers, 402 U.S. 424, 439–53 (1971) (Harlan, J., concurring); Garrity v. New Jersey, 385 U.S. 493, 506–08 (1967) (Harlan, J., dissenting). Spevack v. Klein, 385 U.S. 511, 522–23 (1967) (Harlan, J., dissenting). *See generally* Arenella, *supra* note 20, at 52–53.

58. In other contexts, the dangers of an unstructured balancing test have frequently been commented on. *See, e.g.*, Frantz, *The First Amendment in the Balance*, 71 Yale L.J. 1424, 1440–48 (1962).

59. Thus, in the case of the law requiring criminal defendants to choose between testifying in their own defense and being represented by an attorney, the two constitutional rights involved are not incompatible. The government cannot plausibly argue either that making the relinquishment of the right to a trial attorney a condition of the defendant's right to testify promotes the fairness of the right to testify or that conditioning a defendant's right to be represented by a trial attorney on his not testifying at trial enhances the fairness of the right to a trial attorney. On the other hand, when the government compels the defendant to elect between his right not to be tried again following certain types of mistrials and his right to move for a mistrial, *see supra* note 54, the two rights involved are incompatible. The government can properly claim that allowing the defendant's double jeopardy protection to extend to most situations in which defendant requests a mistrial would disserve important government interests that should be considered in determining the scope of the defendant's double jeopardy protection. *See, e.g.*, United States v. Tateo, 377 U.S. 463, 466 (1964).

60. As Westen points out, whenever the defendant is compelled to elect between two constitutional rights, the burden imposed on each of them must be considered. *See* Westen, *supra* note 48, at 757. However, this should not mean, as Westen suggests, that the burden attached to each constitutional right should be weighed independently. Rather, since the compelled choice must be justified, if at all, on the basis of the interrelationship between the two rights, the burden imposed on each must be considered in conjunction with the burden imposed upon the other one.

61. If the scope afforded the second constitutional right is substantially diminished, then the compelled choice should be unconstitutional on the ground that an unconstitutional condition is attached to one of the two constitutional rights involved. This point is more fully developed *infra* in notes 62 and 71.

62. Thus, the determination of whether the scope of constitutional right is substantially diminished cannot be made in isolation; the relationship between the gains achieved by the incident attached to the first constitutional right and the costs incurred as a result of the incident attached to the second constitutional right must be taken into account. Accordingly, the extent to which the incident attached to one constitutional right is a necessary means of advancing the basic fairness inherent in that right is a factor that should be considered in determining whether the incident attached to the second constitutional right imposes an impermissible burden on the exercise of that right.

63. *See* Jenkins v. Anderson, 447 U.S. 231, 238 (1980) (dictum); Brown v. United States, 356 U.S. 148 (1958) (holding). *See generally* McCormick, *supra*

note 20, at 278–82; Note, *Testimonial Waiver of the Privilege Against Self-Incrimination*, 92 HARV. L. REV. 1752 (1979); Comment, *Testimonial Waiver of the Privilege Against Self-Incrimination and* Brown v. United States, 48 CAL. L. REV. 123 (1960).

64. *See* Faretta v. California, 422 U.S. 806, 819 n.15 (1975) (dicta). *See generally* Westen, *Order of Proof: An Accused's Right to Control the Timing and Sequence of Evidence in His Defense*, 66 CAL. L. REV. 935, 964–74 (1978).

65. *See, e.g.*, 5 J. WIGMORE, WIGMORE ON EVIDENCE § 1367 (Chadbourn rev. 1974): "[N]o safeguard for testing the value of human statements is comparable to that furnished by cross-examination and . . . no statement . . . should be used as testimony until it has been probed and sublimated by that test . . ."; C. McCORMICK, *supra* note 20, at 43: ". . . [T]he opportunity of cross-examination [is] an essential safeguard of the accuracy and completeness of testimony."

66. *See, e.g.*, United States v. Lamb, 575 F.2d 1310 (10th Cir. 1978); United States v. Dillon, 436 F.2d 1093 (5th Cir. 1971). *See generally* C. McCORMICK, *supra* note 20, at 280; Westen, *supra* note 48, at 750–51; *Testimonial Waiver of the Privilege Against Self-Incrimination and* Brown v. United States, 48 CAL. L. REV. 123, 131 (1960).

67. Some commentators suggest that the test should be framed even more narrowly. Thus, McCormick advocates a rule under which "an accused who testifies forfeits his privilege only insofar as forfeiture is necessary to enable the prosecution reasonably to subject his testimony on direct examination to scrutiny regarding its truth." C. McCORMICK, *supra* note 20, at 281.

68. Such examination could naturally include some inquiry into defendant's credibility but could not delve into collateral issues. Under any test, determining the precise limit on the scope of defendant's cross-examination will be difficult. For a discussion of lower court cases, *see Testimonial Waiver*, 48 CAL. L. REV. at 126–28 (1960).

69. *See* United States v. St. Pierre, 132 F.2d 837, 840 (2d Cir. 1942) (opinion of Judge Learned Hand stating that the purpose of the testimonial waiver doctrine is to prevent the defendant from presenting a "garbled" version of the critical facts).

70. As Westen puts it, "his testimony creates in the state no greater interest in now examining him about the matter than the state possessed before he ever testified because his testimony has no bearing on the matter on which the state now wishes to interrogate him." Westen, *supra* note 48, at 750.

71. To put this point within the framework of my previous analysis, *see supra* text at notes 59–62, it could be said that in a compelled election situation, the burden imposed on a defendant's exercise of one constitutional right (in this case, his privilege not to testify at trial) will be more likely to result in a substantial diminution of that right if the burden bears relatively little relationship to the goal of advancing the fairness that is inherent in the exercise of the other constitutional right (in this case the defendant's constitutional right to present testimony in his own defense).

72. This is not meant to suggest that the government should always be permitted to do to the defendant whatever the defendant does to it. Rather, in the present context, the point is that the permissible infringement on the defendant's

Fifth Amendment privilege should be no more than that which allows the government to test the credibility of the psychiatric testimony injected into the case by the defendant. For an elaboration of this point, *see infra* note 98.

73. The incident imposed in this particular situation should also be unconstitutional under *Simmons* because given that requiring the defendant to forfeit his Fifth Amendment privilege on questions that do not relate to the subject matter of his direct testimony will not advance the fairness secured by his right to testify, the two constitutional rights are not incompatible and no compelled election should be permitted. The point to be made, however, is that even if the cross-examination at issue were to be viewed as promoting the fairness inherent in the right to present testimony, it should be unconstitutional because the government would be allowed to exact too great a price in exchange for advancing its legitimate interests created by the defendant's exercise of his right to testify.

74. United States v. Nobles, 422 U.S. 225, 241 (1975). The *Nobles* case is discussed *infra* in text at notes 185–96.

75. *Simmons* held that a defendant cannot be forced to choose between his right to testify in support of a Fourth Amendment claim and his Fifth Amendment privilege against being compelled to present incriminating testimony at a pretrial suppression hearing. For a more detailed discussion of *Simmons*, holding, *see* Westen, *supra* note 48, at 741–42.

76. In contrast, when a defendant confronted with the *Simmons* election testifies in support of a Fourth Amendment claim, the government is presented with a kind of evidentiary windfall if it is allowed to use this evidence to establish the defendant's guilt at trial. Since the government's use of the evidence is quite unrelated to the defendant's Fourth Amendment testimony, the government is in a much better position with respect to the determination of guilt than it would have been had the defendant not elected to pursue his Fourth Amendment claim.

77. *See supra* text at notes 64–65.

78. *See supra* note 65.

79. *See, e.g.,* FED. R. CRIM. P. 16(b)(1)(B); PA. R. CRIM. PROC. 305(c)(2)(a), COLO. R. CRIM. PROC. 16(II)(b) (1977).

80. *Id.*

81. *Id.* Reports prepared by defense psychiatrists not called as defense witnesses at trial would probably not be subject to discovery. *See generally* Saltzburg, *Privileges and Professionals: Lawyers and Psychiatrists*, 66 VA. L. REV. 597, 625–30 (1980). Thus, discoverable reports would probably only include those prepared by psychiatrists not associated with the defense. If the defendant has had a significant prior history of mental problems, such reports are likely to exist.

82. In addition to information relating to the prior mental history of the defendant, *see supra* text at notes 79–81, the prosecutor could make use of any relevant information relating to the circumstances of the crime itself.

83. *See generally* C. MCCORMICK, *supra* note 20, § 40, at 78–81.

84. Without a government psychiatric examination, the government would sometimes be unable to obtain an independent expert opinion on the issue in question. As Professor Robert Aronson says, "Cross-examination would be

greatly hampered without some independent or contradictory explanation by another expert." Aronson, *Should the Privilege Against Self-incrimination Apply to Compelled Psychiatric Examinations?*, 26 STAN. L. REV. 55, 72 (1973).

85. Of course, the doctrine is not precisely applicable, because before being presented in court the defendant's story must first be believed by the defense psychiatrist. This point is elaborated *infra* in text at notes 205–06.

86. For the expression of a similar view, *see* Aronson, *supra* note 84, at 71–72.

Based on this analysis, it seems clear that a defendant's mere raising of an insanity defense should not be sufficient grounds for compelling him to answer questions posed in a psychiatric examination. Since raising the defense does not in itself produce evidence that needs to be subjected to the safeguards of the adversary system, the two constitutional rights involved (i.e., to plead a recognized insanity defense and to invoke a Fifth Amendment privilege during a psychiatric examination) cannot properly be viewed as incompatible. For a recent case rejecting the waiver by plea of insanity doctrine, *see* Battie v. Estelle, 655 F.2d 692, 702 (5th Cir. 1981) (mere submission to a psychiatric examination does not itself constitute a waiver; thus a defendant can invoke his privilege when he does not introduce mental health expert testimony). For pre-*Smith* cases applying the waiver by plea of insanity doctrine, *see, e.g.*, Lee v. County Court of Erie County, 27 N.Y.2d 432, 267 N.E.2d 452, 318 N.Y.S.2d 705, *cert. denied*, 404 U.S. 832 (1971) (holding that the privilege against self-incrimination is waived when a defendant interposes his insanity defense); United States v. Cohen, 530 F.2d 43, 47–48 (5th Cir.), *cert. denied*, 429 U.S. 885 (1976) (dicta) (compelled psychiatric examinations are permitted when a defendant has raised an insanity defense, since the government will seldom have a satisfactory method of meeting defendant's proof on the issue of sanity except by the testimony of a psychiatrist it selects).

87. *See supra* note 66 and accompanying text.

88. For some of the myriad objections that might be raised to questions asked on cross-examination, *see, e.g.*, C. MCCORMICK, *supra* note 20, at 11 (argumentative, misleading, or indefinite questions all improper).

89. At present, government psychiatric examinations are invariably conducted without the presence of defendant's counsel or any other outside observers. *See generally* Wesson, *supra* note 20, at 701. In *Smith* the Court cited with seeming approval the Fifth Circuit's observation that "an attorney present during the psychiatric interview could contribute little and might seriously disrupt the examination." 451 U.S. at 470 n.14, quoting Estelle v. Smith, 602 F.2d 694, 708 (5th Cir. 1979). *See* C. MCCORMICK, *supra* note 20, at 47, 54. For some of the numerous lower court cases holding that the presence of counsel is not constitutionally required at the examination, *see, e.g.*, United States v. Cohen, 530 F.2d 43, 48 (5th Cir. 1976); United States v. Bohle, 445 F.2d 54, 67 (7th Cir. 1971); United States v. Baird, 414 F.2d 700, 711 (2d Cir. 1969), *cert. denied*, 396 U.S. 1005 (1970); United States v. Albright, 388 F.2d 719, 726–27 (4th Cir. 1968).

90. *See, e.g.*, H. DAVIDSON, FORENSIC PSYCHIATRY 23–29 (2d ed. 1965); A. FREEDMAN, H. KAPLAN, & B. SADOCK, 2 MODERN SYPNOSIS OF COMPREHENSIVE TEXTBOOK OF PSYCHIATRY 343–53 (1961); Gerand, "Psychiatric Evalua-

tion," in A. BROOKS, LAW, PSYCHIATRY AND THE MENTAL HEALTH SYSTEM 21–26 (1967). Meyers, *The Psychiatric Examination*, 54 J. CRIM. L., CRIM. & POLICE SCIENCE 431 (1963). *See generally* Wesson, *supra* note 20, at 715–16; Aronson, *supra* note 84, at 65–66.

91. Meyers, *supra* note 90, at 442.

92. *See, e.g.*, Packer, *Use of Hypnotic Techniques in the Evaluation of Criminal Defendants*, 9 J. PSYCHIATRY L. 313 (1981) (discussing the use of hypnosis and hypnotic drugs as an aid to evaluating criminal defendants). For an early illustration of the range of examining techniques available to psychiatrists, *see* Leyra v. Denno, 347 U.S. 556 (1954) (police psychiatrist used deception and something akin to hypnosis to induce defendant to confess to murder).

93. *See In re* Gault, 387 U.S. 1, 47 (1967) ("[t]he privilege reflects the limits of the individual's attornment to the state and in a philosophical sense insists upon the equality of the individual and the state"); Murphy v. Waterfront Commission, 378 U.S. 52, 55 (1964) (one interest protected by privilege is that of maintaining a "fair state-individual balance"); Culombe v. Connecticut, 367 U.S. 568, 581–82 (1961) (plurality opinion of Frankfurter, J.) (elaborating "the basic notion that the terrible engine of the criminal law is not to be used to overreach individuals who stand helpless against it"). *See generally* 8 J. WIGMORE, WIGMORE ON EVIDENCE 317 (McNaughton rev. 1961); Friendly, *supra* note 50, at 694–95.

94. *See* Couch v. United States, 409 U.S. 322, 327 (1973) (privilege protects "a private inner sanctum of individual feeling and thought and proscribes state intrusion to extract self-condemnation"); Murphy v. Waterfront Commission, 378 U.S. 52, 55 (1964) (interests protected by the privilege include protecting the individual against the "inhumane treatment and abuses" involved in the coercion of testimonial information and reserving for the individual "a private enclosure where he may lead a private life"). At least two commentators have stated that it is "not easy to square the privacy interest as a prime purpose of the privilege with immunity statutes that require surrender of privacy." McKay, *Self-Incrimination and the New Privacy*, 1967 SUP. CT. REV. 193, 230. *See also* Friendly, *supra* note 50, at 689. One response to this point, however, is that the different policies protected by the privilege must be considered in conjunction with each other. Thus, as Professor Arenella points out,

> any attempt to explain the privilege's proper scope which relies exclusively on substantive values such as privacy or moral autonomy is bound to fail. Similarly, a proceduralist view of the privilege cannot offer an intelligible explanation of the privilege's scope without reference to normative values to explain what constitutes a fair state-individual balance of advantage in an accusatorial system.

Arenella, *supra* note 20, at 40 n.58.

95. In view of *Smith*'s dicta to the effect that the government psychiatric examination conducted in that case would have been permissible if the government psychiatrist had merely testified on the issue of the defendant's competency to stand trial, *see supra* text at note 16, it is doubtful whether the Court would be willing to hold the government psychiatric examination unconstitutional merely because of its potential for invading mental privacy. Nevertheless, the examina-

tion's significant potential infringement of this interest is a factor that should be considered in shaping an appropriate constitutional rule.

96. *See supra* note 93.

97. *See supra* text following note 76.

98. The government might argue that so long as the waiver doctrine is a necessary means of promoting its legitimate interest in obtaining evidence that will enable it to test the credibility of the defense psychiatric testimony, the fact that the doctrine allows it to gain additional benefits unrelated to this legitimate interest should not render the doctrine unconstitutional. In support of this position, the government might assert that in fulfilling its legitimate interest, its sole responsibility is to minimize the harmful consequences to the defendant. Thus, the argument would be that if its interest in obtaining reliable psychiatric testimony on the issue of sanity cannot be achieved by any less burdensome alternative than one that allows the government to obtain evidence that incriminates the defendant on the issues of guilt and/or penalty, the alternative that permits these harmful consequences to the defendant should be recognized as legitimate.

Of course, acceptance of this argument would mean that so long as the waiver doctrine (or any other doctrine) is necessary to promote a legitimate government interest, that doctrine must be recognized as constitutional regardless of the burdens it imposes on the defendant's Fifth Amendment privilege. The problem with this position is that it fundamentally misconceives the nature of the relationship between the government and the individual under our constitutional system. Because the constitutional protections recognized by the Bill of Rights belong to the individual and not the government, it is improper to allow them to be eviscerated merely because doing so will promote a substantial governmental interest. As I have previously stated, *see supra* text at notes 59–62, when dealing with a situation in which the exercise of some other constitutional right is incompatible with a full recognition of the Fifth Amendment privilege, a defendant may be compelled to elect between the two constitutional rights if the resulting infringement on the interests protected by the Fifth Amendment privilege are not substantial. In this particular context, the resulting infringement on the defendant's Fifth Amendment privilege will be substantial unless it is essentially limited to providing the government with the evidence it needs to test the credibility of the defense psychiatric testimony. To put it another way, the government's legitimate interest should allow it to give tit-for-tat—in this case, to obtain government psychiatric testimony that may be used to rebut the defense psychiatric testimony offered on the issue of sanity. If the government is also allowed to strengthen its case on the issues of guilt and/or penalty, however, then instead of giving merely tit-for-tat, it is allowed to give something more like kapowie-for-tat. In this situation, because the burden imposed on the defendant's Fifth Amendment privilege is excessive, the compelled election imposed by the government should be unconstitutional regardless of the legitimate interests it may serve. Compare *supra* text at notes 70–73.

99. In most jurisdictions it is expressly provided by rule or statute that in this situation the government psychiatrist will not be permitted to testify on the issue of guilt. *See, e.g.,* Fed. R. Crim. P. 12.2(c); Ill. Ann. Stat. §§ 115–16 (Smith-Hurd 1981).

100. For instance, the defendant might tell the government psychiatrist the location of the gun he used to shoot the victim, thus enabling the prosecution to recover the gun and use it in evidence against him.

101. For example, the defendant might tell the government psychiatrist about his participation in previous robberies, disclosing their times and places. This would enable the prosecutor to interview victims of unsolved robberies with a view toward obtaining their testimony against defendant at the penalty trial.

102. For example, if defendant told the psychiatrist that the killing occurred in self-defense after the victim threatened to use a weapon on him, the prosecutor could prepare his case with an eye toward rebutting that particular defense. Moreover, if during the examination the defendant showed a propensity to lose his temper when pressed by the psychiatrist, that information might prove invaluable if the defendant afforded the prosecutor an opportunity to cross-examine him at trial.

103. 406 U.S. 441 (1971).

104. *Id.* at 442.

105. *Id.* at 460.

106. Under *Kastigar*, the witness's testimony must be used only to provide information to the grand jury before whom he is testifying. In the present situation, defendant's statements to the psychiatrist must be used only to provide the government with psychiatric testimony that relates to the issue of sanity. *See supra* note 98 and accompanying text.

107. *See supra* note 98 and accompanying text.

108. That is, the *Kastigar* dissent's argument that imposing a use-derivative use prohibition on a defendant's compelled testimony can never be the functional equivalent of allowing a defendant to invoke his Fifth Amendment privilege, *see* 406 U.S. at 468–69 (dissenting opinion of Marshall, J.), must be rejected on the basis of *Kastigar*'s holding. For an elaboration of the problems involved in effectively enforcing a use-derivative use limitation, *see generally* Strachan, *Self-incrimination, Immunity and Watergate*, 56 Tex. L. Rev. 791 (1978).

109. Under the circumstances, it seems most unlikely that a defendant who is being examined because he possibly suffers from serious mental problems will have sufficient acuity to remember what information he divulged to the government psychiatrist. *Cf.* United States v. Wade, 388 U.S. 218, 230–31 (1967) (emphasizing that an unaided defendant will not be able to recreate the prejudicial aspects of a pretrial confrontation).

110. *Cf.* Alderman v. United States, 394 U.S. 165, 183 (1969) (holding that defendants seeking to establish that evidence derived from illegal wiretaps is being used against them are entitled to examine records of the illegally tapped conversations). Justice White's language in *Alderman* seems directly applicable to the present situation: "[I]f the hearings are to be more than a formality and [defendants] not left entirely to reliance on government testimony, there should be turned over to them the records of those overheard conversations which the government was not entitled to use in building its case against them." *Id.*

111. In responding to the objection that the use and use-derivative prohibition could not be adequately enforced, the Court emphasized that a person afforded this form of immunity "is not dependent for the preservation of his rights

upon the integrity and good faith of the prosecuting authorities." 406 U.S. at 460.

112. In contrast, when a witness testifies before a grand jury in response to a grant of immunity, a court reporter will make a complete transcript of his testimony. If that witness is subsequently prosecuted by the government, the witness-defendant will be allowed to examine his grand jury testimony in order to determine whether evidence offered by the prosecution is derived from his immunized testimony. *See, e.g., In re* Minkoff, 349 F. Supp. 154 (D.R.I. 1972).

113. *See generally* Louisell & Hazard, *supra* note 40, at 824.

114. *See supra* note 99.

115. It would be theoretically possible to provide that the government psychiatrist would be permitted to testify only about his conclusion on the issue of the defendant's sanity and not about any inculpatory statements the defendant made to him. This alternative would be unsatisfactory, however, because, as one state court put it, "[t]he opinion of an expert witness is of little value to anyone in a court proceeding when it is separated from the facts on which it is based." State *ex rel*. Johnson v. Woolrich, 279 Or. 31, 36, 566 P.2d 859, 861 (1977).

116. 378 U.S. 368 (1964).

117. In *Jackson* the Court invalidated the procedure under which defendants' confessions were admitted to the jury together with instructions that they should be considered on the issue of guilt only if the jury first determined them to be voluntary. The Court concluded that the risk that the jury would disregard the instructions was so substantial that the procedure violated due process. *Id*. at 389.

118. Professor Wesson suggests that the risk that the instructions would prove ineffective is greater in the present situation than in *Jackson* because the instructions "would ask jurors to make intrinsically complex and difficult judgments in identifying the circumstances under which they may consider a defendant's statements." Wesson, *supra* note 20, at 713-14. Nevertheless, the present Court may not be inclined to extend the principle recognized in *Jackson* to new situations. In Parker v. Randolph, 442 U.S. 62 (1979), a case that limited *Bruton's* holding that cautionary instructions will not be sufficient to protect a defendant's Sixth Amendment right to confrontation when a codefendant's statement that incriminates the defendant is admitted at their joint trial, *see* Bruton v. United States, 391 U.S. 123 (1968), a plurality of the Court emphasized that juries will not generally be viewed as unable to follow cautionary instructions. Rather, "[t]he 'rule'—indeed, the premise upon which the system of jury trials functions under the American judicial system—is that juries can be trusted to follow the trial court's instructions." 442 U.S. at 74 n.7 (plurality opinion of Rehnquist, J.).

119. Thus, in the present case there is a risk that evidence derived from the examination will be used to strengthen the prosecution's case on guilt and/or penalty.

120. *See, e.g.*, People v. Daugherty, 40 Cal. 2d 876, 256 P.2d 911, *cert. denied*, 346 U.S. 827 (1953). *See generally* Note, *Pre-Trial Mental Examination and Commitment: Some Procedural Problems in the District of Columbia*, 51 GEO. L.J. 143, 155 (1962).

121. The Court has strongly intimated that death penalties may only be constitutionally imposed pursuant to a bifurcated procedure under which the issues of guilt and penalty are separately determined. *See* Gregg v. Georgia, 428 U.S. 153, 190–92 (1976) (plurality opinion). Obviously, if a bifurcated procedure is required in both capital cases and those in which a defendant's guilt and sanity are each at issue, then a trifurcated procedure under which the issues of guilt, sanity, and penalty are all separately considered will become necessary in capital cases in which the defendant chooses to contest the issue of guilt and raise an insanity defense.

122. The bifurcated procedure creates some disadvantages for defendants. *See, e.g.*, Louisell & Hazard, *supra* note 40, at 808, 815, 823 (suggesting that a bifurcated trial may inhibit appeals for sympathy at the guilt stage and the prior finding of guilt may prejudice the jury at the sanity stage); 40 FORDHAM L. REV. 827, 849–55 (1972). Thus, at least in cases in which the defense is not seriously contesting the issue of factual guilt, defendants would likely prefer to have the issues of guilt and sanity determined in a single proceeding.

123. In determining whether this test is met, the judge would have to focus on the potential risk that trying the issues of guilt and sanity would prejudice the defendant because the jury trying the case would improperly consider government psychiatric testimony on the issue of guilt. Of course, determining this kind of issue prior to trial is extremely difficult.

124. For example, if a bifurcated procedure is used, it might be appropriate to postpone the government psychiatric examination until after the conclusion of the guilt stage. Then, if the defendant were found not guilty, no examination would be required. For further discussion of this remedy, *see infra* text at notes 147–52.

125. That is, in the present situation the defendant may be properly compelled to elect between presenting defense psychiatric testimony on the issue of sanity and invoking his Fifth Amendment privilege on questions asked during the government psychiatric examination.

126. On the other hand, defendants may argue that among the feasible safeguards, the government should be required to employ those that will reduce infringements on the Fifth Amendment privilege to the lowest possible level. Pursuant to the analysis I have delineated, however, the government should be required to do no more than prevent infringements on the privilege that do not reasonably relate to promoting the fairness inherent in the defendant's right to present psychiatric testimony.

127. *See supra* note 98 and accompanying text.

128. Since the examination is likely to consume at least several hours, *see supra* authorities cited at note 90, requiring the presence of attorneys at the government examination would undoubtedly consume a great deal of lawyers' time.

129. The attorney's potential for inhibiting the flow of the examination was noted by the Court in *Smith. See supra* note 89. If an attorney's presence at the examination were constitutionally required, it is of course not clear to what extent the attorney would be permitted to participate in any way in the examination.

130. These might include all those in which the defense specifically chooses

to raise this issue. Any more restrictive rule, such as requiring the defendant to show a basis for believing that the government psychiatrist could not be relied on to keep the machine on at appropriate times, would be virtually impossible to administer.

131. In formulating procedures designed to effectuate *Kastigar*'s use-derivative use prohibition, one commentator proposes that "the prosecutor in a trial of a witness who has previously testified under a grant of immunities [should be required to] swear that he has not had access to the privileged testimony or to any information derived from it." Note, *Standards for Exclusion in Immunity Cases After* Kastigar *and* Zicarelli, 82 YALE L.J. 171, 186 (1972).

132. United States v. McDaniel, 482 F.2d 305, 311 (8th Cir. 1973). In *McDaniel* a defendant testified under a grant of transactional immunity in a state court. A federal prosecutor read the immunized testimony without being aware that it was given under a grant of immunity. Later, the defendant was indicted on a federal charge. For other cases applying *McDaniel*'s principle, *see, e.g.*, United States v. Rice, 421 F. Supp. 871 (E.D. Ill. 1976); United States v. Darnau, 359 F. Supp. 684 (S.D.N.Y. 1973). *See generally* Strachan, *supra* note 108, at 110–14.

133. The present case is distinguishable from *McDaniel* in that the defendant has already been indicted at the time the immunized statements to the psychiatrist are made. Thus, there is less likelihood that the statements could be used to focus the investigation or to channel charging discretion. On the other hand, there is some possibility that his knowledge of the defendant's statements might cause the prosecutor to refuse to plea bargain.

134. Many cases that have distinguished *McDaniel* have done so on the ground that the defendant's immunized testimony was only tangentially related to the issues involved in the subsequent prosecution or did not give the prosecution anything new. *See, e.g.*, United States v. Pantone, 634 F.2d 716, 721 (3d Cir. 1980) (*McDaniel* distinguished because defendant's grand jury testimony "concerned matters different from . . . the arrangement on which the trial here focused . . . . [C]areful scrutiny of the record here reveals that defendant's claim of a relationship between his immunized testimony and retrial is tenuous at best"); United States v. Catalano, 491 F.2d 268 (2d Cir. 1974) (*McDaniel* distinguished on ground that whereas there a large body of incriminating testimony was read by the prosecutor, in the present case defendant's testimony before the grand jury was given cautiously and only in response to leading questions).

135. For example, a defendant's statement to the psychiatrist that the killing occurred in self-defense may not only assist the prosecutor in preparing to cross-examine the defendant but also enable him to better plan his interviews or examination of possible eyewitnesses.

136. In distinguishing *McDaniel*, at least one court has suggested that when the prosecutor's access to immunized testimony will result in only a minimal advantage, this is not enough to violate the requirements of *Kastigar*. *See Pantone*, 634 F.2d at 722.

137. 406 U.S. at 433 (emphasis in original).

138. Recognizing the efficacy of this safeguard, the New Jersey Supreme Court in State v. Whitlow, 45 N.J. 3, 210 A.2d 763 (1965), directed that the gov-

ernment psychiatrist should not inquire into the circumstances of the alleged offense unless such inquiry is necessary to the formation of an opinion on the issue of sanity. *See id.* at 10, 210 A.2d at 775.

139. Another possibility would be to provide that the defendant should only be required to submit to a court-ordered psychiatric examination and that the psychiatrist conducting the examination should testify as a court witness, subject to cross-examination by both parties in court but restricted from disclosing the results of the examination to the prosecutor prior to trial. If rigidly enforced, it is questionable whether this procedure would assist the prosecutor in evaluating the credibility of the defense psychiatric testimony. Because of the complexities involved in evaluating psychiatric testimony, it is likely that prior access to a psychiatrist's testimony would often be indispensable to the effective use of it. Moreover, since court psychiatrists would be likely to have a close relationship to the prosecutor, the safeguard might prove to be unenforceable in any event.

140. For example, he might learn that the defendant loses his temper easily. *See supra* note 102.

141. He might learn that the defendant is slow in responding to questions or that he does not seem to be able to reason in a logical fashion.

142. Or, as the Third Circuit said in *Pantone*, 634 F.2d at 722, it could provide the prosecutor with "a degree of psychological confidence he might otherwise lack."

143. *See supra* note 136.

144. Obviously, this rule would make it more difficult for the government to obtain reliable psychiatric evidence that might be used to rebut the defense psychiatric testimony. Nevertheless, the government's task would not be impossible. Since the psychiatric examination is calculated to "plumb the depths" of the patient's personality, *see supra* note 91, the patient's account of a particular incident would constitute only one small part of the total examination. Moreover, if the psychiatrist believed that she needed some understanding of the facts of the case in order to form an opinion on the issue of the defendant's sanity, reports containing at least the prosecution's version of those facts would probably be available to her. Thus, in most cases restricting the examination in this way would probably not prevent the government psychiatrist from forming an opinion on the issue of sanity and would not significantly impair the prosecutor's ability to test the credibility of the defense psychiatric testimony.

145. As a first step toward drawing such a line, I would suggest that the government psychiatrist be barred from seeking to elicit information about the particular criminal transaction that forms the basis for the charges against defendant. In defining the exact boundaries of a criminal transaction, cases interpreting the phrase "same act or transaction" in rules such as FED. R. CRIM. P. 8(a) should prove helpful. *See also* Ashe v. Swenson, 397 U.S. 436, 454 n.8 (1970) (Brennan, J., concurring). Thus, in the hypothetical involving the killing of a bartender, the psychiatrist should be barred from asking the defendant about the killing itself or the events leading up to it, but not about his general feelings toward bartenders.

146. Pursuant to the safeguards I have suggested, the psychiatrist could not

be prevented from asking improper questions. Nevertheless, in most cases, preexamination instructions to both the defendant and the psychiatrist would probably be effective. Thus, in ordering the examination the Court should direct the psychiatrist not to ask (or seek to elicit information) about the particular criminal transaction at issue and defense counsel should instruct defendant to say nothing about that transaction.

If defense counsel believed that the psychiatrist violated the terms of the court order, this claim could be presented to the appropriate judge. If the judge found that the psychiatrist improperly elicited statements relating to the criminal transaction, fashioning an appropriate remedy would be very difficult. One approach would be to treat the psychiatrist as a tainted witness. To guard against impermissible use of the wrongfully obtained statements, the psychiatrist could be barred from testifying and directed not to speak to anyone about statements made to her during the examination. If the psychiatrist had already consulted with the trial prosecutor, the judge would have to remove that prosecutor from the case and direct the new prosecutor to refrain from any activity that might enable him to learn the contents of the statements made during the examination. In some cases this remedy might not be sufficient, and more extreme ones, including even dismissal of the charges against the defendant, might have to be considered.

The case in which the defendant volunteers incriminating statements concerning the charge against him poses a special problem. The reason for limiting the scope of the psychiatric examination is to prevent excessive infringements on defendant's Fifth Amendment privilege. When the defendant volunteers incriminating information despite the fact that it has not been elicited by the government, however, no infringement on his privilege has occurred. *See* Rhode Island v. Innis, 446 U.S. 291, 300 (1980); Miranda v. Arizona, 384 U.S. 436, 478 (1966). Therefore, even though the use-derivative use limitation should apply to these statements (since, though unsolicited, they are made in response to a quasi grant of use-immunity), allowing the prosecution access to such incriminating statements does not appear to create a constitutional problem.

This result may seem slightly troubling because a mentally unstable defendant's anxiety about the pending charges might often provoke him to disclose incriminating information relating to the charge against him in the course of any discussions with the psychiatrist. Therefore, in the interest of fairness the psychiatrist might be required to warn the defendant not to say anything concerning the charges against him or even to stop him if he begins to discuss that transaction.

147. This remedy would be feasible even if the issues of guilt and sanity were determined in a single proceeding. The government psychiatrist would ordinarily be called to testify as a rebuttal witness, after defense testimony on the issues of guilt and sanity was completed.

148. Defense testimony would be complete before the examination. *See supra* text at note 139.

149. *See supra* authorities cited at note 90.

150. Thus, the delay would place additional burdens on witnesses and jurors, and probably also on the attorneys involved in the case and the judge.

151. *See* E. LOFTUS, EYEWITNESS TESTIMONY 53 (1979) (noting that numerous experiments establish that one's memory of events decreases over time).

152. Postponing the examination until after the defendant's case on the issue of guilt would result in additional disadvantages. First, any possibility that a pretrial examination could lead to an expeditious conclusion of the case (as would be likely to occur if, for example, the government psychiatrist agreed that the defendant was insane at the time the alleged crime was committed) would be lost. Even more importantly, perhaps, postponing the examination would have deleterious psychological effects that would be likely to reduce its efficacy. Conducting a psychiatric examination would not be easy under the best of circumstances, and conducting it in the middle of a criminal trial would obviously increase the difficulties. The defendant's heightened concern about the outcome of the trial would be likely to inhibit the type of free discourse that might be essential to an effective examination, and the psychiatrist's enhanced awareness of her role as an agent for the government might diminish her ability to evaluate the data gleaned from the examination in an objective fashion.

153. *See supra* text at notes 32–37.

154. *See, e.g.*, People v. Segal, 54 N.Y.2d 58, 429 N.E.2d 107, 444 N.Y.S.2d 588 (1981) (psychiatric evidence offered in a perjury prosecution to show that defendant's mental condition rendered him incapable of realizing that he was testifying falsely under oath); People v. Newton, 8 Cal. App. 3d 359, 87 Cal. Rptr. 394 (1970) (psychiatric evidence offered in a murder prosecution to show that defendant was unconscious at the time he fired the fatal shot).

155. *See supra* note 32.

156. When defense psychiatric testimony is offered on an issue that relates to guilt, it may seem that restricting the scope of the government examination so that it cannot inquire into the question of factual guilt will render it futile. In fact, however, this safeguard should generally have no more effect on the efficacy of the examination in this case than it does in one in which the defendant's sanity is at issue. In both cases, the issue to be determined by the psychiatric testimony is not whether the defendant committed the act charged, but rather whether his mental state at the time of the alleged act was such that it diminished or eliminated his culpability. Thus, my prior explanation of why a government psychiatrist should be able to reach a conclusion about the defendant's sanity without examining him on the circumstances of the alleged criminal act, *see supra* note 144, should be applicable to this situation also.

157. *See supra* text at notes 128–46.

158. Under Lockett v. Ohio, 438 U.S. 586 (1978), a defendant has a constitutional right to present evidence that relates to a mitigating circumstance at the penalty stage of a capital trial. In *Lockett* the Court held that Ohio's death penalty statute was unconstitutional. The statute provided that upon a conviction for specified categories of murder, the penalty of death was mandatory unless the sentencer determined that one of three narrowly drawn mitigating circumstances was present. 438 U.S. at 607. The pivotal plurality opinion concluded that this sentencing scheme was unconstitutional because

the Eighth and Fourteenth Amendments require that the sentencer, in all but the rarest kind of capital case, not be precluded from considering *as a*

mitigating factor, any aspect of defendant's character or record and any circumstances of the offense that the defendant proffers as a basis for a sentence less than death.
438 U.S. at 604 (plurality opinion of Burger, C.J.) (footnotes omitted). For an analysis of the implications of *Lockett, see* Hertz & Weisberg, *In Mitigation of the Penalty of Death:* Lockett v. Ohio *and the Capital Defendant's Right to Consideration of Mitigating Circumstances*, 69 CAL. L. REV. 317 (1981).

159. 42 PA. CONS. STAT. ANN. § 9711(e)(2) (Purdon Supp. 1981). For statutes in other jurisdictions containing similar provisions, *see supra* note 37.

160. The defendant's prior criminal history will be material to a specific aggravating circumstance in most jurisdictions, *see, e.g.*, 42 PA. CONS. STAT. ANN. § 9711(e)(d) (Purdon Supp. 1981) (aggravating circumstance present if "defendant has a significant history of felony convictions involving the use or threat of violence to the person"); the defendant's propensity to commit future criminal acts will be relevant to an aggravating circumstance in a handful of jurisdictions, *see supra* note 36; and, of course, the defendant's general background and character will necessarily be relevant to potential mitigating circumstances in all jurisdictions, *see supra* note 150.

161. Of course, the case will reach the penalty trial only if the defendant is convicted of the capital charge and the prosecutor proceeds to seek the death penalty.

162. *See supra* text at 149.

163. *See supra* text at notes 58–59.

164. *See supra* text at notes 59–62.

165. *See* 451 U.S. at 465: "When a defendant asserts the insanity defense and introduces supporting psychiatric testimony, his silence may deprive the state of the only effective means it has of controverting his proof on an issue that he interjected into the case."

166. Although the Court has held that a jurisdiction may impose the burden of proving an insanity defense upon the defendant, *see* Rivera v. Delaware, 422 U.S. 877 (1976) (per curiam); Leland v. Oregon, 343 U.S. 790 (1952), only a few jurisdictions have shifted the normal burden of proof with respect to this issue. *See, e.g.*, People v. Lee, 92 Cal. App. 3d 707, 155 Cal. Rptr. 128 (1979); Trace v. State, 231 Ga. 113, 200 S.E.2d 248 (1973). *See generally* Annot., 17 A.L.R.3d 146 (1976).

167. *Lockett* directs only that the sentencer "not be precluded from considering as a mitigating factor" evidence proffered by the defendant. *See supra* note 150. Thus, with respect to a death penalty statute that does not recognize "extreme mental or emotional disturbance" as a mitigating factor, the jury would be perfectly free to reject defendant's claim that this kind of evidence should be considered mitigating. For a contrary view on this point, *see* Liebman & Shephard, *Guiding Capital Sentencing Discretion Beyond the "Boiler Plate": Mental Disorder as a Mitigating Factor*, 66 GEO. L.J. 757 (1978) (arguing that a state is constitutionally required to recognize some form of emotional disturbance as a mitigating circumstance).

168. Apparently no jurisdiction now holds that establishing a particular mitigating circumstance will preclude imposition of the death penalty. Under

the modern statutes, the jury is required to weigh any mitigating circumstances against such aggravating circumstances as may be present. *See, e.g.*, GA. CODE ANN. § 27-2538 (Supp. 1981).

169. *See supra* text at notes 158–60.

170. In addition, the government psychiatric examination takes on a somewhat macabre aspect when it is conducted essentially for the purpose of obtaining evidence that will lead to a sentence of death. A defendant's awareness of this fact would be likely to cause considerable anxiety as well as decreasing the probable efficacy of the examination. These are additional factors to be weighed in the balance.

171. 428 U.S. 153 (1976).

172. Even before *Gregg*, the Court had expressed a commitment to the principle that increased procedural safeguards are appropriate when a defendant's life is at stake. For a classic explanation of the Court's differing approach to capital and noncapital cases, *see* Stein v. New York, 346 U.S. 156, 196 (1953): "When the penalty is death, we, like state court judges, are tempted to strain the evidence and even, in close cases, the law in order to give a doubtfully condemned man another chance." *See also* Reid v. Covert, 354 U.S. 1, 77 (1957) (Harlan, J., concurring). *Cf.* Corbitt v. New Jersey, 439 U.S. 212, 217 (1978) (distinguishing New Jersey's non vult statute from the statute involved in Jackson v. United States, 390 U.S. 570 (1968), principally on the ground that the death penalty was not involved).

173. 430 U.S. 349 (1977).

174. The Court overruled Williams v. New York, 337 U.S. 241 (1949), stating that *Williams*'s rationale should no longer be controlling because the "Court has acknowledged its obligation to re-examine capital-sentencing procedures against evolving standards of procedural fairness in a civilized society." 430 U.S. at 357 (plurality opinion of Stevens, J.) (footnote omitted).

175. *Id*. at 358.

176. 451 U.S. 454 (1981).

177. 451 U.S. at 463: "Given the gravity of the decision to be made at the penalty phase, the state is not relieved of the obligation to observe fundamental constitutional guarantees."

178. In particular, the Court intimated that statements made by defendant to a government psychiatrist could not be used by the prosecution at the penalty trial unless the defendant was informed "that the compulsory examination would be used to gather evidence necessary to decide whether, if convicted, he should be sentenced to death." *Id*. at 467. For a discussion of this aspect of the Court's opinion, *see* White, *supra* note 7, at 1534–38.

179. For additional authorities expressing the same principle, *see generally* Winick, *Prosecutorial Peremptory Challenge Practices in Capital Cases: An Empirical Study and a Constitutional Analysis*, 81 MICH. L. REV. 1, 20 nn.68–69 (1982).

180. If the defendant claims a legitimate basis for refusing to answer some questions, then presumably the examination could be halted until the judge rules on the validity of the defendant's objections.

181. *See, e.g.*, United States v. Handy, 454 F.2d 885, 888–89 (9th Cir. 1971)

(dicta); United States v. Baird, 414 F.2d 700, 708 (2d Cir. 1969) (dicta); People v. Segal, 54 N.Y.2d 58, 444, 429 N.E.2d 107, N.Y.S.2d 588 (1981); Blaisdell v. Commonwealth, 372 Mass. 753, 364 N.E.2d 191, 202 (1977) (dicta); Lee v. County Court of Erie County, 27, N.Y.2d 432, 267 N.E.2d 452, 457–58, 318 N.Y.S.2d 705 (1971); Parkin v. State, 238 So. 2d 817, 822 (Fla. 1970); State v. Whitlow, 45 N.J. 3, 10–11, 210 A.2d 763, 774–75 (1965).

182. 388 U.S. 14 (1967).

183. 388 U.S. at 23.

184. For helpful discussions of the constitutional issues raised by the exclusion sanction, *see* Westen, *supra* note 43 at 108–17; Note, *The Preclusion Sanction: A Violation of the Constitutional Right to Present a Defense*, 81 YALE L.J. 1342, 1343–52 (1972).

185. 422 U.S. 225 (1975).

186. 422 U.S. at 227.

187. *Id.*

188. *Id.* at 228–29.

189. *Id.* at 229.

190. *Id.*

191. *Id.* at 233–40.

192. *Id.* at 241.

193. *Id.*

194. "The investigator's contemporaneous report might provide critical insight into the issues of credibility. [On one hand], the jury might disregard the investigator's version altogether. On the other hand, [the report might] strongly . . . corroborate the investigator's version and . . . diminish substantially the reliability of that witness' identification." *Id.* at 232.

195. *Id.* at 241.

196. The rule applied by the Court bears a close relationship to the best evidence rule, a doctrine that provides that a party who desires to introduce a writing into evidence will ordinarily be required to introduce the original writing unless he can establish that the original is not available. *See generally* C. Mc-CORMICK, *supra* note 20, at § 230. The best evidence rule, which has deep historical roots, is undoubtedly premised on the notion that a party's failure to produce an available primary source necessarily renders suspect the secondary source that is in fact produced.

197. *See, e.g.*, Washington v. Texas, 388 U.S. 14 (1967). *See generally* Westen, *supra* note 43.

198. Westen, *supra* note 43, at 137.

199. *See supra* text at notes 84–86.

200. 422 U.S. at 234–36.

201. Many cases have dealt with the problem of defining the appropriate sanction when a witness improperly refuses to answer questions on cross-examination. *See generally* 5 J. WIGMORE, EVIDENCE *supra* note 65, § 1391, at 137.

202. According to Wigmore, this distinction should be controlling whenever a witness refuses to answer questions on cross-examination. *See id.*

203. *See* United States v. Panza, 612 F.2d 432 (9th Cir. 1980); People v. McGowan, 80 Colo. 293, 251 P. 643 (1926).

204. *See supra* text at notes 79–83.

205. In evaluating a defendant's mental state, a psychiatrist will not ordinarily expect a defendant to be completely truthful, and in some cases she may find his lies to be more revealing than his accurate statements.

206. *See supra* text at notes 79–83.

207. Based on the analysis presented in this article, defendant ordinarily will have a right not to answer questions that relate to the criminal transaction that forms the basis for the charges against him. Thus, determining whether a particular answer is required will sometimes be very difficult. *See supra* text at notes 144–46.

208. *See, e.g.*, Meyers, *supra* note 90, at 434.

209. In contrast, a defendant's refusal to answer a single question on cross-examination may have a critical impact on the prosecutor's ability to test his truthfulness. For example, in the *McGowan* case, a defendant testified that he was not at the scene of the crime but was with a young lady at the time the crime was committed. On cross-examination, he refused to give the name of the young lady he was with. As the court pointed out, this refusal prevented the prosecution from subpoenaing her in order to test the truthfulness of the defendant's story. 80 Colo. at 253, 251 P., at 645.

210. *See supra* note 195.

211. *See, e.g.*, United States v. Panza, 612 F.2d 432, 439 (9th Cir. 1980) (dicta); United States v. Cardillo, 316 F.2d 606, 611 (2d Cir. 1963) (holding).

212. *See generally* C. McCormick, *supra* note 20, at 98–100.

213. In many cases, a jury would be likely to perceive a defendant's refusal to answer the government psychiatrist's proper questions as evidence that he has something to hide, and therefore that his insanity (or other defense) may be somewhat disingenuous.

214. *Cf. Panza*, 612 F.2d at 443 (dissenting opinion of Sneed, J.) (asserting that sanction of striking defendant's trial testimony should not be used unless the trial judge specifically determines that that remedy is necessary to serve the ends of justice).

215. *See, e.g.*, Karstetter v. Cardwell, 526 F.2d 1144 (9th Cir. 1975).

216. *See, e.g.*, Lee v. County Court of Erie County, 27 N.Y.2d 432, 267 N.E.2d 452, 458, 318 N.Y.S.2d 705 (1971).

217. As a practical matter, it is a very rare case in which the defendant's evidence of insanity is so compelling as to raise the possibility of a directed verdict of not guilty by reason of insanity. *See generally* Annot., 17 A.L.R.3d 146 (1976). Thus, this remedy would not be used very often.

218. In many situations, there might be a real possibility that the government psychiatric testimony would be favorable, thus strengthening the defendant's insanity defense.

219. By pointing up the difference between the defendant's conduct toward his own psychiatrist and the government psychiatrist, the judicial comment might suggest that the defendant was seeking to hide evidence from the government and the jury. This could prove extremely damaging to the defendant's case. *Cf.* Griffin v. California, 380 U.S. 609, 614 (1965) (discussing the potential impact of a trial judge's comment on a defendant's failure to testify).

220. Interview conducted by the author with John L. Carroll on June 28, 1982.

221. In several jurisdictions the determination whether a capital sentence shall be imposed is made by the judge. *See, e.g.*, FLA. STAT. ANN. § 921.141(1) (West Supp. 1980); ALA. CODE 13, §§ 11-1-11-9 (1977). *See generally* Gillers, *supra* note 1, at 14, nn.51–52.

222. It might even be argued that unlike the constitutional right to present psychiatric testimony at trial, the right to present psychiatric testimony at the penalty stage is not incompatible with defendant's Fifth Amendment privilege. The former constitutional right, though first recognized in *Lockett*, is at least partially derived from the historically recognized right to allocution. *See* McGautha v. California, 402 U.S. 183, 217 (1971). Because a capital defendant's right to allocution was absolute, *see* Barrett, *Allocution*, 9 MO. L. REV. 115, 117–21 (1944), it is at least arguable that the government has less right to impose conditions on a defendant's constitutional right to present psychiatric testimony at the penalty stage than it does to impose them on his right to present similar testimony at trial.